DATE DUE

The Nature of the Beast

Other Books by Milton Mayer

Anatomy of Anti-Communism (with others; 1969)

Speak Truth to Power (with others; 1955)

Steps in the Dark (with John P. Howe; 1931)

The Revolution in Education (with Mortimer J. Adler; 1958)

Young Man in a Hurry: William Rainey Harper (1957)

They Thought They Were Free: The Germans, 1933-45 (1955)

The Tradition of Freedom (ed.; 1957)

Humanistic Education and Western Civilization (with others; 1964)

What Can a Man Do? (1964)

If Men Were Angels (1972)

Man v. *the State* (1969)

The Art of the Impossible: A Study of the Czech Resistance (1969)

The Nature of the Beast

Milton Mayer

Edited by W. Eric Gustafson

University of Massachusetts Press   Amherst, 1975

All new material copyright (c) 1975 by
The University of Massachusetts Press
All rights reserved
Library of Congress Catalog Card Number 74-21243
ISBN 0-87023-176-6
Printed in the United States of America

Library of Congress Cataloging in Publication Data

Mayer, Milton Sanford, 1908-
    The nature of the beast.

    Essays and speeches.
    I. Title.
AC8.M4126   081   74-21243
ISBN 0-87023-176-6

To the memory of
E.A. ("Red") Schaal
Clarence E. Pickett
Henry J. Cadbury
of the American Friends Service Committee

The harvest truly is plenteous, but
the laborers are few. Pray ye therefore
the Lord of the Harvest, that he will
send forth laborers into his harvest.

Contents

The Nature of the Beast

Introduction: The Remote Possibility of Communication

The eminence you have just laid upon me is something less than I was led to expect. My expectation was grounded on a promise made twenty-five years ago by the then President of this University. He told me that he had confirmed my claim to having been the only undergraduate ever placed on permanent probation, in token of which distinction he proposed to grant me the honorary degree of P.P. I am not so gauche as to say that the honor I have here tonight is a poor substitute. But I cannot refrain from observing that it is a substitute.

In anticipation of the solid specie into which I expect to convert the fame and the plaque given to me this evening, I shall favor you with a recitation of my triumphs in the field of communication. This recitation will serve two purposes. First, it will demonstrate the wisdom of the selection committee for this year's award; and second, it will instruct my fellow alumni in the art in which, I think I may say in all modesty, I am recognized as a grand master.

I was a slow starter. When I was two years old, my mother told Dr. Isaac Abt that she was worried because I didn't talk. He said she would be more worried when I did. But my first really spectacular communication was not until the Christmas issue of the *Daily Maroon* in 1927, which carried a full-page spread in the form of Christmas greetings to sundry personages. My co-author was Al Widdifield—God rest him—but the spread was not signed. When the Dean discovered the authorship, he had us up for blasphemy, stripped us of our by-lines, shaved our heads, and instituted a censorship which marked the beginning of the decline of the *Maroon* to its present vacuous estate.

It was only a few years later—I was still a mere boy—that I scored my second sensation, this one in the sports pages of the *Chicago Evening Post*, where I depicted Knute Rockne as an illiterate herring-choker and the Fighting Irish as Poles and Italians. This communication precipitated a visit to the paper's publisher by the Notre Dame Club of Chicago, followed by a general boycott by the Irish, the Poles, the Italians, and the Norwegians. Within six months the *Post* folded,

Text of address accepting the Communicator of the Year Award of the University of Chicago, 8 June 1967. (c) *University of Chicago Magazine*, November 1967.

and two or three hundred communicators, I among them, undertook to communicate to their fellow-Chicagoans the advisability of eating apples—or at least buying them.

In due season, the memory of my Fighting Irish communication having faded, I became a reporter for the then *Chicago Evening American*. Here I registered a truly memorable communication: my report, over the phone, of the accidental death of a florist on the Near North Side. His name was Dion O'Bannion. Three inveterate sportsmen had entered his flower shop and began cleaning their sawed-off shotguns in preparation for a hunting trip. As so often happened in the wilds in those primeval days, the guns went off. I communicated this report by telephone to Billy McCloud, our man at the Chicago Avenue police station, saying that Mr. O'Bannion had fallen dead among his chrysanthemums. Billy asked me to spell chrysanthemums. I had a go at it, but Billy could not, for the life of him, get it straight. After a while he said, "Hell, let's make it roses," but a communicator has first of all to be a stickler for the facts. I stickled for chrysanthemums, but there was no dictionary in the Chicago Avenue police station, and by the time Billy and I reached agreement on the spelling we had missed the deadline—and the *Daily News* had hit the street ahead of us and sold 50,000 extra copies. It was not long thereafter that the owner of the *American* unloaded it on the *Tribune*.

I was now ready, and my employer agreed, to move my communications facilities to new fields, one of which was Higher Learning, an enterprise just getting started in America. It was getting started, as you all know, right here on the Midway, which hadn't seen anything like it since Little Egypt. I went to the President of the University of Chicago and told him that I wanted to be saved from William Randolph Hearst. "How much is Mr. Hearst paying you?" said the President. "Ninety a week," I said. "I'll give you forty-five," said the President. "I can't live on that," I said. "You didn't say you wanted to live," he said, "you said you wanted to be saved. You cannot be saved any cheaper."

As a result of this triumphant communication I found myself occupying the position of Toady to the President.

Now up until that moment, the President had had an excellent image. It suddenly began to disintegrate. He alienated the alumni and the students by abolishing football; the faculty by depreciating the departments; the scientists by praising philosophy; the philosophers by praising Aquinas; the donors by coddling Communists; and the entire human race by opposing war. Of course it was I who had thought up all these operations, but I thought it advisable, in the interest of communication, not to put my signature to them. Instead

I communicated them under the pseudonym of Robert Mayer
Hutchins.

Within a few years after my takeover, the University was on the
ropes. The Protestants had been outraged by the communications of
Mortimer Adler, and the Catholics by G.A. Borgese. What was wanted was a communicator to outrage the Jews, and I leaped into the
breach.

My felicitous communication appeared in the *Saturday Evening
Post* and produced a reaction which devastated both the Curtis Publishing Company and the University (amid whose ruins we gather
tonight). It was assumed in some circles that I wrote all the President's articles and that he wrote mine. It was necessary to get rid of
us both. The Ford family met the University's need—as it has so often
since—and took the President off the University's hands. As for me,
it was back to the merits of the rosy red apple.

I may interpolate here that there is nothing so important to the
communicator's effectiveness as the title of his communication. Take,
for example, the communication which disgraced my wonderful
mother. I called it, "Grandma Ought to Have Her Head Examined."
So, too, the title of the historic *Post* article. My thesis was the well-
worn platitude that the Gentiles are no good and that nobody should
imitate them. I was, in a word, making out the case for the Jew. The
title I used was, "The Case against the Jew."

This masterpiece of communication moves me to tell a tale out of
school. Twenty years afterward a benefactor of the University, who
had withdrawn his beneficence on that occasion, found himself next
to the former President at a dinner. Their relations had not been
warm since the benefactor had pulled the Persian rug out from under
the President, but they were still on a first-name basis, as all communicators are. "Bob," said the ex-benefactor, "do you remember
an article by a fellow named Mayer in the *Saturday Evening Post*?"
"Vaguely," said the ex-President, whom we shall call Bob. "Well,"
said the ex-benefactor, "a fellow got me to read it the other day,
and, you know, the article itself was all right. But the title was mis-
leading." The ex-President is reported to have lost his powers of
communication at that point.

But the memory of man is short—a point the communicator must
always consider—and within a few years of my triumph in the *Saturday Evening Post* I was climbing to new peaks. I achieved my Matter-
horn in Syracuse, New York, where I was arguing that the psychological cost of world government would be intolerable to loyal Americans. I was asked what I meant by psychological cost and responded
by bellowing a quotation from a newspaper columnist who said that

the advocates of world government would hand down the American flag, trample on it, and spit on it. I had neglected to put quotation marks around the quotation, and the next morning's paper carried a headline at the top of page one: "Chicago Prof. Says Spit on Flag."

As a result of the investigation that followed this interesting communication, the D.A. of Onondaga County, N.Y., exculpated me by finding that what I had *really* said was that the advocates of world government wanted to desecrate the flag. This communication, in turn, wrecked the World Government movement and, as a consequence, the world. The words I had used without quotation marks were subsequently inserted in the Congressional Record, whence, with immunity, they winged—and, twenty years later, continue to wing—their way from chapter to chapter of an organization of patriotic ladies united by the sentiment that one American Revolution was enough.

The years were passing, and still untouched by my practice of the art of communication were the professors who had been nearest and dearest to me in my undergraduate days—Philip Schuyler Allen, Percy Holmes Boynton, and Robert Morss Lovett. I was writing an article about Robert Lovett, and Phil Allen said I should go to Puerto Rico and talk to Ferdie Schevill about him. "If you handle Ferdie right," said Phil, "he'll do all your work for you." I wrote Prof. Schevill saying that Phil Allen had said that if I handled him right he'd do all my work for me. Prof. Schevill, upon receiving this communication, announced that he was not a man to be handled and would not consent to a meeting with the impudent pup who had written that letter. Percy Boynton—who was also in Puerto Rico—joined Robert Lovett and Phil Allen in attempting to mollify Ferdie Schevill. The end of their efforts was the estrangement of these four lifelong friends, each from the other. When my article about Robert Lovett appeared under the title, "Portrait of a Dangerous Man," the author of *The Red Network* pointed to the title as proof, from the pen of his own admirer, that Robert Morss Lovett was a communist.

For several years thereafter, I achieved no new heights in my chosen field, and I supposed that there were none to be achieved. In spite of the general affluence of those middle years, and in spite of my triumphs, my fortunes languished. Nobody bought apples any more; everybody was buying pomegranates. I had to turn to the lecture platform in order to support my little ones in the manner to which I had taught them to intend to be accustomed.

My platform appearances—I have already spoken of Syracuse, N.Y. —have been one *succès d'estime* after another, right up to my latest performance, a couple of weeks ago at the University of Wisconsin, where I was retained to engage the First Secretary of the Soviet Embassy in a colloquy. Since I believe in making love, not war, and a communicator does not care what, but only how, he communicates, I delivered myself of a eulogy of the Soviet Union as the Workers' and Peasants' Paradise. In passing I suggested, but only suggested, that there were still to be found there one or two insignificant and vestigial remnants of the corrupt bourgeois life of the West—but these, I said, were being speedily eradicated and within sixty days at the most the Union of Soviet Socialist Republics would be the first absolutely perfect society in history. I sat down bowing in homage to the First Secretary of the Embassy of the first absolutely perfect society. He rose and, pointing to me, said to the audience, "This man is an ideological enemy of peaceful coexistence," and left the platform. The Middle East crisis followed almost immediately.

There, my friends, you have a succinct and greatly abbreviated account of a communicator's most unforgettable (would they were otherwise) communications. You have learned how—if I may borrow an expression from another great communicator—I brought home the coonskin on the wall. You have heard how this little life of mine has flown away. But it has its lessons for the communicator, and I share them with you. I have learned that there are dreadful obstacles to communication.

One of them is the communicator's conviction that he is funny. He *may* be—as I certainly was when I wrote Ferdie Schevill—but the communicatee may not think so.

Another obstacle is his insistence on communicating when he has nothing to communicate. I once advised a great man of your acquaintance to take a year off, and when he asked what for, I said, "To think," and he said, "I have not thought since I discovered that I could get a degree from Yale without thinking, and I am too old to start now." And he hurried off to deliver the keynote address to the American Council of Learned Societies.

Still another obstacle is the unwillingness of people to be communicated with. Only consider: Christ tried to communicate three things: There shall be neither friend nor enemy (that is, no war); neither Greek nor Jew (no racism); neither bond nor free (no exploitation of man by man). It would be supererogatory of me to point out what little success the communicator of *all* the years has had in communicating even with those who think they adore Him.

But these obstacles are as nothing. As everything is the necessity that people be in a humor to receive your communication. You cannot put them in that humor by assuming that their motives are worse than your own, or that they don't understand anything but force, or that the world is divided into good and wicked people and that hanging Kaiser Bill will save you from the peacetime conscription which Woodrow Wilson called the root evil of Prussianism.

This greatest of all theological errors, with its pernicious train of personal and political consequences, is itself the consequence of the communicator's unwillingness to receive communications from those who disagree with him. So endemic and epidemic is this unwillingness that tautologies like "intercommunication" have had to be concocted to make the point.

Unlike the snake charmer, the communicator learns, not by doing, but by learning. My only complaint is that my clamorous career has left me no leisure to learn. It has been a hard living, being a communicator, or attention-getting device. I yield to no man in my attachment to Alma Mater, but I would not have to be peddling plaques today if I had gone to a good trade school instead of learning to let communication grow from more to more, that the human din may be increased.

Part One

Education: We Are

Amputated Greeks

To Know and To Do

The Renaissance seems to have ended at Verdun, at least for the Europeans; and there are signs, only fifty years afterward, that the Americans are beginning to read the lesson that Europe learned on Mort Homme Hill: Man is not going to be an unqualified success. Progress is no longer axiomatic. Pessimism (or apathy, which is predigested pessimism) is becoming pervasive. Even the Communists' "new man" is nothing more than a ceremonial expression nowadays. This is the age—whatever else it is—of waning confidence.

As the age of confidence the Renaissance was more of a birth than a rebirth: Bacon's assertion that knowledge is power would have astounded all the men who had gone before him—the fallen Oedipus no less than the fallen Adam. They had been taught to expect Verdun. So had the prophet who said of the great nations of old, "They are wise to do evil, but to do good they have no knowledge."

Bacon was nonetheless right and the Renaissance nonetheless real. Knowledge *was* power. Man powered with knowledge was, and is, as a god. But the power is proving to be independent of its generator. Like the Sorcerer's Apprentice, it needs no command to fetch water faster and faster. The water rises, and knowledge is a consternation: Rare indeed the commencement orator who does not wag his head over the discrepancy between man's moral and intellectual progress.

But what if morality is not progressive? And what if there is no necessary, or even probable, connection between morality and knowledge? What if (*horrible dictu*) the human crisis is first and last and always a moral crisis and not an intellectual crisis in the least?

When the late President Kennedy said that "science has no conscience of its own," he was doing more than quoting Rabelais; he was saying something revolutionary about education. He was saying (if science includes the highest sciences) that education is of conditional service to man, and if the condition is not met it is of no service at all.

Look at the general disorder of our time. When most men have less than a hundred dollars a year and the per capita expenditure on war in "peacetime" is fifty, what is there that intelligence can tell us?

Reprinted from *Saturday Review*, 15 February 1964. Based on an essay in *Humanistic Education and Western Civilization* (New York: Holt, Rinehart, and Winston, 1964).

When the most knowledgeable (and therefore the richest) societies, with the longest history of civilized institutions, lead the world in suicide, insanity, alcoholism, divorce, crime, and delinquency, what critical need have they (or, for that matter, the least knowledgeable societies) of knowledge? What is it the Communist needs to *know* who wants free elections in Mississippi but not in Germany, or the anti-Communist who wants bases ninety kilometers from Russia but not ninety miles from Florida?

The sovereign faith in education is everywhere in the world established now. What for Jefferson was the keystone of the democratic arch has become the keystone of the democratic and the nondemocratic arches. If we can find a way to make use of universal education in the universal crisis, it would seem that we should do so. We would not make any such demand of bingo or tap dancing or swinging on the old front gate; we may make it of education because education is everywhere the great public enterprise.

We pedagogues have been willing to exploit the enterprise without examining its premise that the more of it there is the better off we shall be. Our trade secret consists in our being supposed to have a secret when we haven't. What we have is a skeleton in the multi-purpose closet in the form of the unexamined premise.

The public pressure that fills the schools with junk is irresistible because we have nothing to resist it with. Why shouldn't driver training be compulsory? Driving is a moral problem, which the public thinks, mistakenly, can be solved by teaching. So, too, when the Russians launched their *Sputnik*: Out went the new humanities, in went the new technologies, and up went the preprofessional preparation of technicians. Why not? Had the schools been doing anything whose high purpose would justify their going on doing it? The Russians presented a moral problem—the *evil* of Communist success—and the American people wanted it solved. The schools stood ready to hand.

In the theocratic centuries the asserted object of teaching was morality as a means to salvation. The object continued to be asserted long after the age of the priests. Yale undertook to transmit not only *Veritas* but *Lux*; Oberlin was consecrated by its charter to "the total abolition of all forms of sin"; and the Haverford catalogue maintains the primacy of the moral capacity to use the skills of learning for worthwhile ends. Such private institutions have no legal impediment to their transcendent aims; they are over the wall of separation upon which the safety and security of the secular state rest like Humpty Dumpty. But public education, at all levels, is forbidden by the First

Amendment to abolish sin, tamper with moral capacity, or ask which
ends are worthwhile.

What ever made us suppose that it could do these things even if the
law allowed? What evidence is there, now or ever, that even under the
most sacred auspices education could produce morality? In its sacer-
dotal prime it made men good churchmen. Had the churchmen been
especially good men, Dante would have had to do without the first
two parts of his three-part comedy and Luther without all ninety-five
of his Ninety-Five Theses.

The truly parochial schools still try to improve the adolescent soul
that will be known by its fruits. They make no bones about meaning
to make men good. And their alumni are all of them fine fellows. But
I do not know that they are finer than the alumni of Yale, Oberlin, or
Haverford—or of City College. And they should be, if morality can be
taught. Indeed, a weighted analysis should show that college graduates
are better behaved in later life than non-college graduates and the top
of the class than the bottom; and the Doctors than the Masters. *Hélas!*
as Sarah Bernhardt used to say.

Morality is action, and we know that action and knowledge are
wholly separable in, for instance, mathematics. But the separability
appears in the practitioners of all the other disciplines besides—in the
logician whose personal life is eccentric, in the gluttonous physiolo-
gist, in the physicist who rounds a sharp curve at 80 m.p.h. One of
the great political scientists of our time dismisses civil disobedience
as anarchy because law is the indispensable condition of community—
and asks a friend to slip a Swiss watch in through Customs. "We
imagined," said G.A. Borgese of Italian Fascism, "that the universities would be the last to surrender. They were the first."

But mankind requires a moral purpose (or the color of one) in the
institutions it supports, including war. There are no honest apostles
of wickedness. Men want to be good and to live among good men,
and if they have not found it feasible to be good themselves they
want their children to be good. Al Capone, protesting that "Insull's
doing it, everybody's doing it," was appealing his conduct to the
moral standard of the community. For goodness alone is the bond of
men, and unless knowledge can be shown to have a causal (or at least
predisponent) connection with it, the best education is only an
amenity.

Our search for the connection takes us at once to the epistemo-
logical commonplace that descriptive knowledge accumulates and
normative knowledge does not. Twentieth Century man does not
have to learn that the seat of fever is the blood—or that the world is
flat—before he can learn that it isn't. He starts with the latest break-

through. But there are no breakthroughs in the moral realm: Relativity is new, but moral relativism is as old as Thrasymachus. The *Odyssey* takes us the long, long way home of the tired businessman who *really* loves his wife; the *Apology* assembles the Un-Athenian Activities Committee; and Sophocles owes his big Broadway hit to his study of Freud. Man the ingenious has no ethical or political ingenuity.

Why not? Why isn't moral advance as ineluctable as scientific, and moral fact as persuasive? Why isn't "righteousness by the Law"? The schoolmen thought that reason rules the intellect despotically but the appetite constitutionally; the appetite ("which moves the other powers to act") vetoes reason when reason threatens its closest interests. It is about *me* that I can't "think" straight—about me and my family and my friends, my race and my religion, my party and my country and my age. I am the victim of what elementary psychology calls reflexivity, in which the subject and object of inquiry are one.

Whoever deals with himself deals unscientifically—including that hero of the endless serial, the Man in White. Not, of course, when we see him in Surgery. There he is working on an external organism. We stay the knife in his hand and ask him if this *man*—this Haman, this Hitler—ought to live or die. He says it is none of his business, and we ask him whose it is. He doesn't know; he suggests that we try the psychiatrist down the hall.

The psychiatrist down the hall replies by reading from his *New Introductory Lectures*: The physician "has no need to consider whether the patient is a good man, a suicide, or a criminal. . . . It is not the business of the analyst to decide between parties." What is the business of the analyst? "To send them away"—he is still reading— "as healthy and efficient as possible." "But this is Haman! This is Hitler." The psychiatrist— τῆς ψυχῆς ιατρός , or doctor of the soul— shrugs and says, "Keep going down the hall."

Down the hall the judge is instructing the jury in that which is instructable: the law. But in that which is not—the good and evil of men that brings them into court—the jury is the judge. Twelve ordinary men whose only competence is their relative freedom from reflexivity. The petit juror, not the judge, is the judge of morals, just as the petit voter, and not the political scientist, is the judge of politics. What moral knowledge seems to want is the scientist's dispassion without the scientist's science.

With the Renaissance impact of secularism, pluralism, and science, moral doctrine lost the unity (and therefore the authority) with which it was so long advanced as the index, if not the compulsion, to action. Nowadays we have surveys of moral doctrines. The survey, or

peep-show, has much to be said for it. It steers clear of the preroga-
tive (no longer claimed by the church) to tell the child what is right
and wrong. It avoids the parental storm that engulfs the teacher who
presumes to teach (or even to have) a doctrine. And it keeps the
moral philosopher out of the moral hole. The student in fourth (or
fourteenth) grade who asks, "Why should I be honest?" or "Where
do we go when we die?" can be sent down the long, long hall.

Natural science, unlike moral science, never did claim to be able to
make men good. (To be sure, its practice fortifies such virtues as
patience, initiative, and open-mindedness, but so do burglary, baby-
sitting, and philosophy.) It teaches what it knows can be taught and
delivers the goods—the goods that enable us in peace to live longer
and less laboriously and in war to fight longer and more effectively.
It doesn't try to tell us what to live or fight for, or whether labor is
bad for us or longevity good. These are the "insoluble" problems
that have to be taken to the man still further down the ever-lengthen-
ing hall.

Some of the designers of the atomic bomb pleaded secretly with
Mr. Truman that it not be used. Some of them entrenched themselves
behind the admirable scientific attitude of suspended judgment, and
one of them, a Nobel laureate, piously passed the buck: "If anybody
should feel guilty," he said, "it is God, who put the facts there." (Mr.
Truman, who had a sign on his desk reading, "The buck stops here,"
may have envied them their pleas in avoidance).

Apparently a scientific lifetime does not help a man decide
whether or not to explode an atomic bomb. And in the summer of
1963 the nation's lawyers decided to straddle the civil rights issue as
the only possible compromise between the Northern and Southern
delegates to the American Bar Association. How learned must I be—
and in what?—in order to know what to do about the atomic bomb
and civil rights?

I am told that the modern world, with all its complexity, requires
more learning of me than my forebears had. Not in my case; I recall
none of the crises of my life (there have been more than six) that I
might have met better had I known more. But a little of my great-
grandfather's incorruptibility might have come in handy. I have lied
as a matter of course and cheated and stolen when I "had to." I have
jettisoned principle when the wind howled and thanked God that I
am as other men are. And on the occasions of unavoidable moral
choice I have mobilized my good reasons for doing bad things and
emerged as a trimmer whose object all sublime is to get on in the
modern world of A.D. or B.C. 1964.

I am told that the fortunate form of government under which I

live requires a great deal of knowledge of me as a citizen. I have to
understand public finance—which the public financiers, who don't
have to understand anything else, dispute. I have to know whether
Cambodia is east or west of North or South Vietnam and why we are
fighting *there*. I have to have a judicious opinion on Guinea, Guiana,
and Ghana. I am, in a word, producing more history than I can possibly consume. Without a righteous specialist in all these matters—or
with an unrighteous one—I am lost.

Morality aside, I am told that I have to have more technological
knowledge than my father, who didn't have an automatic transmission.
Why isn't just the opposite true? The neighborhood crawls with automatic transmission men. And the work I am likely to get (if I am
looking for work) requires me only to press the button every time
the bell rings—a procedure which Pavlov's dog discovered long since
is easier learned on the job than from books. When Herbert Hoover
was asked about Telstar, he said, "I belong to a generation that just
doesn't grasp all that." Don't we all? And what difference does it
make?

True, the conversion of knowledge to precept and precept to
action is said to take prudence, and a man wants some sort of head
for it; but as an excuse for helplessness it is one with the suspended
judgment of the scientist who devises the bomb. A man lies bleeding
by the road. Shall I use my automatic transmission to stop my car?
The priest and the Levite were graduates of the Harvard Medical
School, as the Samaritan was not. He misplaced the tourniquet. Too
bad; but he was the only hope of him who had fallen among thieves.

We are asked if we mean to dispense with natural science. We reply:
only with as much of it as we absolutely have to. It is nice to know
that the earth goes round the sun, that man and a candle flame both
metabolize, and that the angle of reflection is equal to the angle of
incidence. It is nicer to know these things than to have to depend
upon those who do. But the competence I want *and for which I can
not depend upon another* is moral competence, and I can not get it
from science.

But the experimental method of science is a peculiar contribution
to the intellectual enterprise. Can we find a moral use for it? Perhaps,
in its distinction from the nonexperimental method of the humanities
and the social sciences, yes. If our student learns both procedures
(along with the principles that underlie them), we may hope that he
will never confuse the two and try to investigate essentially human
materials scientifically (as the Nazi physicians did) or essentially
scientific materials humanistically (as the party out of power does).
The conditions under which we study men—including ourselves—are

not controlled conditions. We may shoot a cabbage full of enzymes and see what happens, but not a man. *Human* life is not an experiment—at least not our experiment.

Shall we then put a little more of our student's time into, say, esthetics? Music is said to have an inordinate power to soothe the savage breast—which comes closer to the moral crisis than all your metabolism. But we must aim at appreciation, not at theory: It is not musicology that soothes the savage breast. The trouble with the arts—music no less than medicine—is that a man may be both an artist and a swine. And this is true of the liberal artist too. Why, then, shouldn't we exhaust the possibilities of teaching decency (or at least exhaust ourselves looking for them) before we do our student the dubious favor of putting tools, even the finest tools, in his hand?

Watch out with your liberal arts, your arts of reasoning, or you will have equipped a grammatical, rhetorical, and logical monster to rationalize his monstrosities. You will have beefed up a part of a man—the part unique to men and to angels, and to fallen angels. Dewey may have been wrong in many things, wrongest of all to proclaim a science of pedagogy (as if a man could be *taught* to be a Dewey); but he was righter than he was wrong. He was right to insist, with Carlyle, that the end of man is an action and not a thought, however noble, and righter still to resist the compartmentalization to which the liberal, no less than the servile, arts are susceptible.

The child comes to school—as the man to life—with his sneezes, his lusts, his dreams, and his grandfather's grandfather all in one bundle; and on them his docility, or teachability, depends.

Is there anything clearly teachable (as Dewey's techniques were not) that may serve us? What of the study of man as a moral—and therefore immoral—being? We have argued against the moral utility of the teachable, and here we have the teachable again. But morality, which can not be taught, can be taught *about*. Is there a way or ways in which human action may (*may* is as much as we ask for) be influenced by the knowledge of human action? That it need not be, we know; we know that the humanists are not necessarily good men or any better than the biologist or the janitor who empties the biologist's wastebasket. And the supposition that social scientists are politically liberal rests upon the susceptibility of their field to controversy, not upon them. There are social—unlike humanistic or natural scientific—doctrines that the public does not want mentioned unless they are mentioned pejoratively. And there are social scientists, and not a few, who will mention them pejoratively, and not a few more who will mention them not at all. It takes more than science to make a man good.

The disciplines that deal with man as man: ethics, politics, psychology, sociology, social anthropology, history, natural theology, and the principles of metaphysics, jurisprudence, and economics. These are the disciplines, and they alone, that speak to the human crisis. What makes us think that they will be heard? The answer is that our parlous case mut be made on the precarious faith that there may be a kind of postnasal drip by means of which some of what goes into the head will find its way to the heart.

In this precarious faith a studied acquaintance with man's moral struggle may commend itself to our crisis curriculum in several ways. It may urge sensitivity upon our student and intensify such sensitivity as he already has. It may sharpen his ability (though he may not be any the better for it himself) to tell a good man from a bad one. It may somehow, as Plato suggested, "anchor" the good man's goodness. Finally, his intercourse with the goodness and badness of men living and dead may—only may—exemplarily endear the one and dishearten the other to him.

The ancients had too few books. We have too many. But good books are better than bad books, and great books are great even though the two words are capitalized. Some of our texts may be remote in time or place, but so is progress; and their very remotion (so Alec Meiklejohn found at Amherst) may help our student escape the *Teufelskreis* of reflexivity. They will be masterpieces of the liberal arts, those tools of the verbal trade whose mastery constitutes a kind of graduate literacy. Why not teach the arts exemplarily too and use morality (the way the *Dialogues* do) as the material of their instruction? Some of our texts will be in foreign languages, which we can use to read them and to communicate with our fellow men confronted around the world with the common human crisis.

The ancients took a cyclical view of the human condition. Men, even gods, soared and plummeted in a lifetime, in a single day, and "those cities which once were great are now nothing, while those that are great were once nothing." With the Renaissance behind us, the invalidity of the cyclical view is still to be demonstrated. It will not be demonstrated by new methods—not even when they are called methodologies—for teaching the irrelevant or by the construction of more stately mansions for our cyclotrons.

We are not visionary these days, no more so (if no less) than our fathers who stoned the prophets. And our children, unless they are black, reject neither the image we present nor our preoccupation with images. There must be reality somewhere—the reality of what we are and where we are (and how we got there); and of what, if anything, can be done about it.

But the faith of the more recent fathers that education would disclose that reality turns out to be sterile. And its sterility illuminates our situation.

We are amputated Greeks. We have been cut off—we have cut ourselves off—from the mysticism that threaded Greek rationalism. An Italian in Thirteenth Century Paris, Aquinas by name, was the liveliest of all the Greeks; he undertook to prove the existence of God by reason alone. We dying Greeks undertake to prove we-care-not-what by reason alone and we wind up in the thrall of Emerson's Things and *their* meaningless mystique.

We know what goodness is, and we always have; Machiavelli knew, and Moses. But we do not know how to make men good. It is going on two-and-a-half millennia since the first discussion of education opened with the question, "Can you tell me, Socrates, whether virtue is acquired by teaching or by practice . . . or in some other way?" Perhaps the question is not be answered; in which case we may concentrate on a succession (better yet, a continuum) of gaieties in contented conscience. But perhaps another two-and-a-half millennia of unrelenting inquiry will produce the answer; all the more reason for getting started at once.

ROTC: The Lower Learning

It was quiz night in Sophomore English. My moppets had their little beaks in the *Iliad*, and the classroom was quiet. I sat there scratching my sores and tutelarily wondering if college students still wondered what they were supposed to "get" out of five hundred pages of barbarous battle cries, hideous war whoops, and rebel yells. The silence was suddenly rent (as Homer would say) by barbarous battle cries, hideous war whoops, and rebel yells from somewhere inside the building; and just as suddenly restored. It was as if we had touched down on the plain of Troy and then taken off again.

The next morning I received a call from Major Veepings of the Reserve Officers' Training Corps, who asked if he might speak with me. I told him that I was at his armed service, and he said: "Professor Mayer, I want to apologize on behalf of the ROTC for the disturbance in the building last night, and to ask if it would be possible for you to find another building for your evening class. You see, sir, we have a Counterinsurgency course on Tuesday evenings, and Colonel Murgatroyd is afraid that some of your students might misunderstand what is going on." ("You mean," I said to myself, "understand.")

I told the Major that I would withdraw my forces, thanked him for the use of the barracks, and decided to do something I had not done for going on fifty years, namely, think about ROTC (or Rot-cee, as the kids call it).

What I had thought about Rot-cee going on fifty years ago wasn't flattering. Unpossessed of the martial virtues, I reprehended them. Besides, the country I grew up in was not a martial country. In those days, the statutory quota of 100,000 was the large standing army which President Washington had opposed as "dangerous to our liberties." But the recruiters on Skid Row could not find anything like 100,000 end-of-the-line derelicts to fill the quota. In the Preparedness campaign of 1916 the Secretary of what was then called War had to appeal to restaurants to remove their No Soldiers Admitted signs.

After the defeat of Kaiser Bill the citizen army (average schooling: four years) was demobilized. But the dying echoes persisted into the

Reprinted from the *Progressive*, December 1968.

early 1920s. When I reached high school in 1921 the ROTC was attracting the filling-station set of the future; a few years later, not even them. When I entered the University of Chicago in 1925 everybody who was anybody was kicking it. (Chicago had never let it in.) The immigrant hatred of "European" militarism seemed to have survived the raptures of the Great War.

World War II was strictly business. By 1943 the colleges and universities were wholly converted to war training, war research, and war production. Kill-or-die for real put the kibosh on Rot-cee. But in 1948 the United States of America adopted peacetime conscription (which Woodrow Wilson had called "the root evil of Prussianism"). ROTC immediately revived, with an instant correlation between enrollment and the Berlin airlift, Korea, and the Cuban missile crisis. Vietnam sent it soaring. "Increasing draft calls motivate additional men to apply to ROTC," says the commandant at Berkeley, where enrollment leapt from 253 to 795 during the great escalation of 1965-66. Last spring, with graduate students callable under the new draft regulations, many units reported a 100 percent increase in applications.

If, in the 1950s, you did not especially want to canoe the Yalu River or, in the 1960s, explore the Mekong Delta, and you could not pass a science course, you enrolled in Military Science and got a guaranteed deferment. It was axiomatic (as it still is) that you could not flunk Military Science; an axiom supported by the Army's own advertisement that its six-week summer training camp "takes the place of the two-year ROTC Basic Course." If you hup-hup for two years more of five fifty-minute periods a week, you can hardly miss an ROTC Scholarship which pays your tuition, books, and laboratory expenses, and $50 a month besides.

This doesn't mean that your mother raised her boy to be a soldier; on the contrary, it means a fighting chance of not fighting. In 1962, the compulsory ROTC programs (which 40 percent of the students always found one way or another of ducking) had a 70 percent dropout after the required two years. Not now; four years of being fired at with blanks by college chums has a certain contemporary charm. Draft-age patriots would rather be red, white, or blue than dead.

The once high hope of getting rid of Rot-cee has gone glimmering. As a better 'ole than Vietnam it is cemented into the campuses of 250 colleges and universities across the country. It has, of course, no more to do with the higher learning than it ever had. It has to do with marching up the hill, and, if you haven't had your head shot off at the top, down again.

It does not produce good officers, because virtue is not absorbed through the soles of the feet. The only way the Army—any Army—can get good men to be trained as officers is to dragoon them. And this it can't do on the campus. Beginning in 1923 (when the University of Wisconsin threw it out) compulsory ROTC faded from all of the better (and most of the worse) institutions at the rate of twelve units a year. It faded fighting, though, until, the attrition unabating, the Army finally "approved of" voluntary programs in spite of the fact that the changeover means an instantaneous drop of never less than 80 percent of the enrollment. Two years before the compulsory program was dropped by the University of Massachusetts in 1962, it was opposed in a student survey by 75 percent of the males *and by 90 percent of the conscript cadets*. In wartime 1942, 80 percent of the draftees selected for Officer Candidate School were college graduates; less than 6 percent of them were Rot-cee products.

Sixty-one of the ROTC units—the big ones—are in the land-grant colleges, established by the Morrill Act with Federal funds derived from the sale of the Western lands. The wholesome purpose was instruction in the agricultural and mechanical arts. But there was a war on at the time—the time was 1862—and the new cow colleges were required to offer a course in "military science and tactics." It was under this requirement that Rot-cee was born in 1916.

In time many of the land-grant schools became state universities. Most of them (and all of the best of them) no longer require ROTC. But there is no getting rid of it altogether; under the land-grant act they have to offer it. And such anguish as they may harbor is assuaged by the money that's in it. The ROTC Vitalization Act of 1964 *doubled* the scholarship funds of one state university. The money would seem to be wasted, at least in peacetime; of 2,000 lieutenants commissioned at the University of California in Los Angeles, only 200 have chosen a military career. Only in total war, when the Army Reserve is sent into combat, is there a possible payoff; but the total wars have to be no more than ten years apart or the boys who won their spurs in Rot-cee will be as archaic as the spurs.

For the students, the come-on, aside from postponement of that trip to the no longer Mysterious East, is the counting of ROTC credits toward graduation. Faculties generally despise the program, except for the A.&M.-phys-ed-campus-police amalgam and an occasional Army man in the natural sciences. Where academic bodies have the opportunity (as they did at Boston University), they strip it of its credits, reducing its positive student appeal to the money they get if they stick it out. Occasional professors of engineering, looking for scholarships for their fledglings, fancy the Army's magnanimous grants for advanced training, but the Engineering Council for Professional Development strenuously opposes Rot-cee credits toward an engineering degree.

What's money, when the safety of the nation is at stake and sound bodies in a sound skin are wanted? There is no stopping the American Army these days—at least not by Americans. And Rot-cee's piddling eighty-one million dollars a year is bargain-basement public relations. (President Johnson recently upped that figure by at least one hundred million by extending the program to 12,000 high schools.) Land-grant school administrators, necessarily preoccupied with "image," for which read "money," do what they can to appease the faculty opposition, which invariably includes the most articulate men on the campus. Many administrators have resisted such Washington "suggestions" as sending freshmen a canned letter plugging the program. But Chancellor Roger W. Heyns of the University of California, with Reagan & Co. breathing down his neck, recommends that "every entering male student, who has not made other arrangements to serve his military obligation, seriously consider joining one of the Reserve Officer Training Programs offered at Berkeley. . . . All of the programs are an intergral part of the university curriculum, provide for Selective Service deferment, and include attractive pay provisions." If you suppose that it is a scandal for a university chancellor to urge one part of the curriculum rather than another, and to use its noneducational merits as an enticement, you have another supposition coming.

President Asa S. Knowles of Northeastern University, a private institution in Massachusetts, is ROTC's academic showpiece. Addressing a recent meeting of newly appointed Rot-cee instructors, he said, "You must be prepared to face intellectual hostility. The war in Vietnam is not a popular war. There are many Americans who oppose our involvement in it. Many of these people may be found on the college campus. Whether they speak out of ignorance, sincere disagreement, or are merely parroting the ideas of others, the fact remains that they have a right to speak. The college campus is no military reservation. . . . You must expect to have to defend your beliefs in the face of learned opponents. . . . The recitation of pat answers will fall on deaf ears. Appeals to patriotism are virtually meaningless. I do not mean to suggest that I condone this situation. I merely wish to inform you that it exists."

What President Knowles failed to account for was the intellectual hostility of these unpatriotic parrots *before* Vietnam—a hostility greatly exacerbated, but only exacerbated, by the war. Rot-cee may not be the only nonintellectual program on the campus, but it is the only one that is, by universal and traditional definition, anti-intellecual.

Last year a subcommittee appointed to investigate ROTC reported
to the Faculty Senate of one land-grant institution that "the law and
political realities preclude a decision that ROTC has no place on the
campus." Members of the Senate's Academic Matters Committee
"generally sensed that somehow the military was different, not a part
of the academic family," and the subcommittee expressed its "doubts
concerning the quality of the program, quality of instruction, and
quality of educational material."

War, though it may not be a liberal art, is an art, and like all arts is
acquired on the job. The place to learn soldiering is the Army. Rot-cee
is a pale imitation of the Army, and a still paler imitation of the job
on the battlefield. If, however, the essence of soldiering is drill, drill,
and more drill, Rot-cee has its use, all the way from about-face to
Operation of Telephones and Switchboards. In Military Science I, the
Leadership Laboratory Program includes Squad Drill, Platoon Drill,
Company Drill, Mass Drill, Review of Drill, Manual of Arms, Practice
for Fall and Spring Review, and Fall and Spring Review; all told,
fourteen hours out of thirty. In MS II, Leadership Laboratory includes all the drill all over again, plus Saber Manual and Command
Voice. (Obey Voice does not appear in the curriculum.)

The Counterinsurgency course, given in MS II and again in MS III,
was the one that broke up my sophomore English class by providing
a sound track for the *Iliad*. Its objectives include "[the familiarization]
of the student with the nature and causes of insurgency." No small
objective, this, it is attained in five hours with the help of one of
many manuals that serve as Rot-cee textbooks. (They are all prepared
by the Department of the Army.) *Selected Readings in Guerrilla and
Counterguerrilla Operations*, published in August 1966, and still in
use in 1967-68, informs the rising military scientist that "in South
Vietnam today we have over 10,000 Army officers and men advising
the Vietnamese forces. The nature of their duties is such that soldiers
in Vietnam are being shot at by the Vietcong and are sustaining some
casualties." (There are other minor anachronisms, e.g., "[It is] the
opinion of many ARVN commanders and their U.S. advisers that in-
discriminate, saturation-type aerial or artillery bombardments are
detrimental to the winning of the counterinsurgency war. One does
not influence people to 'join the cause' when his [sic] family, home,
and friends are subjected to bombs in the front yard. [It is] better to
use 'friendly persuasion' and secure a citizen, than to drive people
into the Vietcong camp. When in doubt of [sic] whether a group
[village] is 'friendly' or 'enemy' use 'psywar.' ")

In the unlikely event that psywar is not 100 percent effective, there has to be an antiguerrilla force, "a hunter-killer outfit capable of beating the guerrillas at their own game. . . . The problem of creating the ideal soldier for the hunter-killer units is the most difficult part. " He must engage in friendly persuasion and (among other things) Armed Propaganda. Armed Propaganda "is the tactic of intimidating, kidnapping, or assassinating carefully selected members of the opposition in a manner that will reap the maximum possible psychological benefit." I have not been able to find out exactly how the five-hour course in counterinsurgency teaches the American college boy to intimidate, kidnap, or assassinate carefully selected members of the opposition. The syllabus of the Special Forces course, though it includes Escape and Evasion, Jungle and Arctic Survival, and St. Patrick's Day Parade, does not list kidnapping or assassination as such.

Rot-cee is not content to teach young men how to crack other young men's heads. They have to crack their own in the program's "academic" courses—those for which the Army is most insistent that the college or university give credit toward graduation. These courses are preeminently three in number, American Military History, The United States Army and National Security, and The Role of the United States in World Affairs. (The last in particular drives historians and political scientists up the wall.)

The competence of the men who teach these "academic" subjects is determined by the Army, not by the college or the university (which may reject an Army appointee, but almost never does in practice; and in any case finally has to accept one). If he is the commandant of the unit, the Army contract requires the institution to give him a full professorship.

His fellow professors have him cornered on the campus, and he can't get at them. What he can get at is the cadet who doesn't have the Rot-cee spirit. A major at Berkeley is telling his charges about SLAM, a Mach 3 missile with a cruising altitude of 50-100 feet. "Even if it misses its target," he says, "the sonic boom it creates will kill enough people to make it worth while." Some of his students are looking at him hard-eyed—or he thinks they are. "The Air Force," he goes on, "has broken the sound barrier and the heat barrier and is tackling the speed of light." More gaslight glares. "In spite of Einstein and his theories our boys are working out ways to fly twice, three times the speed of sound." Audible snickers now. "Go ahead and laugh, but those that do will some day be marching to the goose-step and tune of the hammer and sickle."

But the student who really wants to take Rot-cee is not generally of the snickering sort. "We don't have radicals in the ROTC," says a major on one of the country's more radical campuses, Wisconsin.

"There are obnoxious elements here."—For the past ten years the Anti-Military Ball at Madison has been outdrawing the Military Ball on the same night.—"They laugh at the flag-wavers, but what we need is more flag-waving." The future flag-wavers (with, in the event, at least one obnoxious element in their midst) enter a classroom and are told not to take notes and not to tell anyone what they are about to see. What they are about to see—this at the University of Washington —is a series of three slide pictures. The first is a map of the U.S. West Coast with red dots marking the major cities and towns; the second an identification of the red dots as chapter headquarters of the Student Non-violent Coordinating Committee (SNCC), Students for a Democratic Society (SDS), the Du Bois Clubs, and other "Communist dominated, Communist influenced, and Communist oriented" student groups; the third a procession of three ducks with this legend below it: "If it walks like a duck, talks like a duck, and lays eggs like a duck, then it's a duck."

After the showing the commandant requests that the cadets prepare files on fellow students involved in these organizations. Three trusted Rot-cees are assigned to correlate the information. When the story of this educational operation broke last year, Washington's president sent an outraged letter to the Commanding General of the U.S. Sixth Army. The Army confirmed the report that it was furnishing this "guidance program" material to the ROTC and volunteered the information that the program was being offered in ROTC units at twenty-six colleges in eight Western states.

Three-fourths of the Berkeley student body had voted against compulsory ROTC in 1940; the California regents, pushed by Chancellor Clark Kerr, abolished it in 1962, twenty-two years later. Down the years the Berkeley anti-Rot-cee campaign mounted, and in 1960 a student group announced that it was going to picket. "If I or any of my staff find anyone picketing in uniform," said the campus commandant, "that student may find it very difficult to pass the course." An honor student who had got an A in Rot-cee at mid-term found it not difficult, but impossible. When the National Student Association and other organizations protested the F that followed, the commandant said that the offender ought to have been expelled and arrested, and the NSA was informed by the Executive Office of the Army Reserve and ROTC Affairs that the action was appropriate reprisal for advocacy of a voluntary program.

Such modest restraint as the "academic" manuals display is not likely to weigh heavily against the officers' lectures, orders, warnings, "guidance kits," and slide shows. The restraint of the ROTC manuals

themselves is minimal. Their assumptions are neither arcane nor
exotic. The first is that the blessings of life and liberty are won and
preserved by war and preparation for war; and the history of the
United States is adduced to prove the point. The second is that
"world Communism" is the implacable and insatiable enemy of mankind represented by the United States ("and our allies," presently
unspecified); that there might be any other enemy or, indeed, any
other evil abroad or at home is excluded. The third is that human
wickedness (from which the Free World is happily exempt) is the
cause of Communism; and the best that can be said for those who
think otherwise is that they are "a motley of blind idealists, political opportunists, regenerate [sic] criminals, and misled individuals."

Given the military status of the cadet, the military status of the
teacher, and the authority of the U.S. Government as the publisher
of the "academic" texts, these two to four years of incessant thunder
on the right ought to have a fair chance of transforming (or forming)
the susceptible young man into a reflexive defender of a world that
never was.

Unless he is a history major, he will never know why, or what,
Nazism and Fascism were or, indeed, that there ever were such things;
much less, that soldiers were hanged at Nuremberg *because* they
obeyed their superior officers' orders. None of these things will he
know after reading *The Role of the United States in World Affairs*;
or why the free election in Vietnam required by the Geneva Agreement was never held, or how the government of Guatemala was overthrown, or what put an end to the U-2 flights over Russia. What he
will know, reading *American Military History*, is that President
Truman "relieved General MacArthur of command in the Far East
in one of the most controversial episodes of the [Korean] conflict,"
but he will never know why (or even why it was controversial). But
he will have read the sixty-eight-page oversized brochure in techni-
color, *Your Career as an Army Officer*, with the following words of
General MacArthur centered in headline type on page 1: "Yours is
the profession of arms . . . the will to win . . . the sure knowledge that
in war there is no substitute for victory, that if you lose the nation
will be destroyed, that the very obsession of your public service must
be duty, honor, country." No one will ever tell him (not even, come
to think of it, if he is a history major) about faith, hope, love.

But he is not likely to be a history major if he's in Rot-cee.

His heroes will all be American generals like General MacArthur,
whether they won, lost, or drew. And he will learn that when they
lost or drew it was still a great day for the Americans: "Although
Pershing failed to capture Villa, the activities of American troops in

Mexico and along the border were not wasted effort. . . . Many defects in the Military Establishment, especially in the National Guard, were uncovered in time to correct them before the Army was thrown into the cauldron of war in Europe. One other result that can be attributed to the experiences of the Army on the border, in part at least, was the passage of much-needed legislation affecting national defense."

His heroes will not include civilians *or* admirals—not in *Army* ROTC: "Few Americans at the outset [of the war with Spain] had any notion that the limited campaign envisioned in Cuba and Caribbean waters would almost immediately be expanded by an aggressive Navy to include operations on the other side of the world"; but fortunately "the American soldier and his immediate superiors took the bungling in high places in stride and demonstrated an aptitude for improvisation equal to the highest traditions of the Army."

When it comes to developing *leaders*, the Army does not concede that anything surpasses Rot-cee, and "in the process it also develops the kind of junior executive or manager needed in every field of civilian endeavor." Another of its star-spangled plugs, this one entitled, *Where the Leaders Are*, addresses itself to "the young man who wants to be 'where the leaders are' on his college campus and in a military or civilian career after college," and it warns him that "many college men, if they do not take ROTC, miss this instruction in developing self-discipline, physical stamina, and bearing because comparable leadership training and experience are not normally provided in the academic courses required for a college degree. . . . No course outside of the ROTC offers this kind of leadership training."

I recently called on the commandant of a large land-grant college unit. "May I make a suggestion, sir?" said the commandant, a chicken colonel. "You may, sir," I said. "We have," said the colonel, "just received a copy of a new documentary for use in the high schools. Propaganda, you know. In color." "I know," I said (omitting the "sir" because he did). "I haven't seen it myself yet, and I have a man ready to run it. Would you like to see it?" "Yes," I said, adding the "sir" this time on my own initiative. "The man" was a sergeant-major, who leapt to attention as we entered the projection room. "Run it when ready, sergeant-major (whose name, sewn on his jacket, was not Gridley).

The title of the documentary was *Those Who Lead*; the subtitle, *Follow the Leaders to ROTC*. The next frame said, "*A Report by Chet Huntley*." "I'll bet they didn't get *him* cheap," said the colonel. "No, sir," I said, wondering who the devil the colonel thought "they" were. "There are two kinds of people," Chet Huntley began, "those who lead and those who follow. Those who take ROTC are those who want to lead." I thought of the 97 percent of the male students who do not take ROTC, and I shuddered for my country.

It went on like that, for twenty-six minutes, complete with brilliant young officer-scientists in the laboratory ("I am not at liberty to reveal the exact nature of my research") and gala young officer-husbands leaping into their sports cars after kissing their lovely young wives good-bye at the doors of their new suburban homes ("Social life centers around the Officers' Club"). "These young Americans know where they're going.—The Army pays the bill.—The Army pays all the bills.—'When my tour of duty is over I plan to go to law school on the G.I. `Bill.'—Balancing the officer's responsibilities are higher pay and the privileges of rank.—'I'll be able to go with him, as an officer's wife, to many interesting places in this country and abroad. My husband and I both think it's a good deal.'—An officer's pay and allowances look pretty good after less than two years out of college.—'We hire reserve officers whenever we can.'—There always will be those who lead and those who follow." Good night, Chet.

The raw sell for the high school kids, without any disquieting reference to doing and dying in one of those interesting places abroad. But in the unlikely case that any of the kids are unpersuaded by the carrot, Chet lets them have a quick glimpse of the stick: "When you go on active duty, as you have to in any case . . ." You're darned right that these young Americans know where they're going, and if they don't go quietly with Chet they'll be turned over to the secular arm for trial by fire in one of those interesting places abroad.

"Let's look closer now at today's Army officer. Who is he . . . what are his duties? His primary duty is leadership." *Well, sir, if you say so, sir, if it's my DUTY . . . but do you think I'm cut out for it, sir?* We'll cut you out for it: "There is no such thing as a born leader. The ability to lead and to inspire others to follow is learned." *Where, sir?* "The Army Reserve Officers' Training Corps exists to develop these abilities." *In ME, sir?* Yes, even in you; you belong to "an elite group of young men, who have qualified for college." *But I qualified for college by being white and making it through high school, sir. But I wouldn't mind getting to the top, if it isn't too hard. Is it hard, sir?* "While it is not always easy to become a leader, it is well worth the effort. It is one sure way of getting to the top."

Now it's great to be a leader, whether you get there via the Marlboro, Mustang, or Military Science route. But what Rot-cee does is

make followers of men who are already disposed to be followers.
The second lieutenant follows the first lieutenant (who follows the
captain), and the five-star general follows Harry Truman or loses the
Far Eastern command. None of them leads anybody. All of them
command or obey.

However handsomely the cadet has done in that branch of Leadership Laboratory described as Command Voice, the Voice will never
be heard in the presence of a statutory superior. The self-discipline
that Rot-cee advertises consists of his doing whatever a statutory
superior orders him to do . The first thing the prospective doughface
is told is that he salutes the uniform, not the man. But leadership is
the leadership of men and of statutory equals.

The reason why "no course outside of the ROTC offers this kind of
leadership training" is that a college or a university that is any good
at all does not offer what neither it nor anyone else can deliver. To
the extent that a college tells its students that this course or that (or
all of them together) "will contribute to success in any career you
may follow after graduation," it is a bad college; and to the extent
that a university does it, it is not a university at all.

The college or university that maintained that leadership can be
taught—much less trained—would be running a confidence game.
But at one point in the game, Rot-cee makes a much less pretentious
claim. One of the objects of Leadership Laboratory is "to convince
the individual that it is both desirable and possible for him to be an
effective leader." *That* the con man can do, given the convincible
individual. No fewer than fourteen courses in the Berkeley ROTC
program are intended "to give the student a sense of mission." But
education does not try to convince or give a sense of mission; it tries
to teach. ROTC has no resemblance to education. What it is may be
a great thing in itself and a great asset to the national life. *Where* it is
is wrong.

It may be able to liberate nations. It can not liberate men, because
men are liberated by reason, and it is not the soldier's (including the
five-star soldier) to reason why. It can not liberate men, because
reasonable men are free to choose for themselves. The Army's characteristic treatment of choice is found in another four-color flier
called, *Your Son and the ROTC*. Your son's alternatives "in the
barest terms" are two, and two only: ROTC or induction into "active service."

The alternatives are alternative ways of going into the Army. The
alternative of not going into the Army (an alternative provided by
Congress and specified by the Selective Service Act) is not mentioned
anywhere in the "literature" of the ROTC, and young men who have

heard of conscientious objection have heard of it from sources other than the institution which claims to be "a process of education which trains a man's attitudes and teaches him to respond to the correct and ethical way of doing his duty. It teaches honesty."

If Rot-cee were to turn honest, it might teach honesty by its example. Even then it would not be an educational process. For the end of education is an informed and insistent intellect, and the end of intellection is choice. No free choice—no free men. No free men— no free world.

The Life of Professor Riley

Back in the thirties Julius ("The Just") Heil got himself elected Governor of Wisconsin by running against the University (like Ronald Reagan in the sixties). As soon as he took office he summoned the University's President and asked him how much work his professors did. The President said that the teaching load averaged twelve hours. "Well," said the Governor, "that's a long day—but it's light work."

I teach six hours—a week—myself.

Now there are some services (like the bull's and the ICBM's) that are not to be calculated by the hour, but mine are not among them. I regard my $14,400 salary as a considerable head of lettuce, and most of my full professorial peers across the country have it even better in the seller's market. The institution I adorn has just hired a mathematics professor at $30,000. But what I teach is more important than mathematics: What I teach is that mathematics doesn't tell you whether or not to drop its end product on the Vietnamese. Why shouldn't I get $35,000? Or $50,000?

Other great (and not so great) universities are paying best-selling professors up to $100,000, which is what the President of General Motors was getting a little while back. In those days I used to meet Professor William E. Dodd going downtown on the streetcar to pick up an extra $300 a year for night work—he that had been the American Ambassador to Berlin and did not own a second car or, indeed, a first. The professor's used to be a life of service and sacrifice.

"Junior staff's" still is, in a poor (but not necessarily bad) university where the lower ranks teach twelve, even fourteen, hours, with as many as one hundred fifty students and three or four separate preparations three times a week. But I am senior staff, in a rich (but not necessarily bad) university whose average pay for full professors has gone up from $10,387 to $17,306 in the past five years.

At $14,400 I am just about low man on the ivy. My colleagues used to tell me that I ought to demand a great deal more money. When I told them that I did not need a great deal more money—I was already living like God in France, as the Germans say—they told me that there is no such thing as not needing a gread deal more money. So now I tell them that the reason I lie low is that I do not want to draw the Administration's attention to my sinecure.

I made that mistake once. Bob Hutchins had his feet on the President's desk at the University of Chicago when I went in one day, twenty years ago, and told him that I had an offer elsewhere. He asked me why I was telling him about it, and I said that I thought I might be able to use it as a lever on him to get a raise. "You will be hoist," he said, "by your own lever. You are not worth what you are getting now. You are growing old without growing wise—that's from Sophocles—and you have more money now than any but a wise man can bear and carry—that's from Plato. Stop bothering me, and get wise."

I got wised up, instead, and learned to row, row, row my boat gently up the ladder, achieving rank and, at last, tenure by avoiding low company and offering my body to be consumed by committee meetings. Now I cannot be dislodged for anything short of genocide, and I am able to rig my teaching schedule so that I can say Thank God It's Wednesday and turn my attention to my lawn, my car, my pool, and my research.

My research project is "The Absence of Bohemian Glassblowers among the Basques from 1406 to 1414," and there is not much that I can do about it around here. Come the end of May I hop the first rattler for Biarritz (the nearest livable place to the Basques) on my three-month vacation with pay. Besides my three months, I have ten days in the spring and two weeks at Christmas, plus Paul Revere Day, Veterans' (formerly Armistice) Day, and Aaron Burr's Birthday. Fringe benefits (in addition to my half-pay sabbatical, my pension, and my Blue Cross) include office supplies from the departmental closet and a library of "examination copies" of books which I have told the publishers I am considering for use in my courses.

I have, to be sure, to publish or perish; but it doesn't much matter what. A flawless compilation of the irregular endings in the aorist optative middle in the *Iliad* will, and usually does, do. I tell you no lies: There are now federal grants in, *mirabile dictu*, the humanities for research projects specifically requiring the use of computers. It is possible to publish *and* perish.

Of course I put in more than six hours a week. I have to seem to have read papers—"Keep them short"—"Awkward sentence structure. You can do better than this"—and advise my advisees to work harder, take it easy, and not worry about grades. Then there are ever longer meetings of ever larger committees in the ever greater democracy of the higher learning. It all comes to, not six, but forty-six or eighty-six hours a week.

But is it work? I am paid for reading (or for once having read) the best books ever written or (as it appears) ever likely to be, and for shooting my cuffs in front of row upon row of contemptuous kittens and cowboys whom I will send to Vietnam (or, worse yet, home) if they betray their contempt. I have worked in my time—between professorships—and I know what work is. Work is having to get something salable on a blank sheet of paper before the day (or the night) is done. But reading good books? Making syntactical chin-music? Punishing the young for their youth?—Why should a man be paid for doing the things that rejoice him?

The professor is one of the few men alive who enjoy doing what they are doing and—who knows?—doing something useful. If he brings a fitful five-minute light into the eyes of his every fiftieth student, he may have done more for the race than the packager or the premier. And to this satisfaction he adds his inhabitance of pleasant places. He alone sees the grass of a weekday. He alone walks the woods without truancy. He alone finds a place to park his car. Heaven—and all this too.

He undergoes no surveillance, submits no sales reports, and does nothing more for the War Effort than assert that he is what the country is fighting for. You would suppose, and so would I, that a man so unsupervised and unanswerable, so overpaid and underworked, would be a guiltless gilt-edged goldbricker. Not the professor. His liberty in a lockstep world condemns him to a self-sentence of life at compulsive labor. Ichabod Crane in his tatters never knew the guilt of the American professor with his two-car garage and his two-chicken pot.

Having drained himself dry in those six to twelve hours a week of minnesinging to unrapt sex bombs (and bombers), he totters off to a colleague's party on Saturday night and stands up talking shop—his varicosity, his head, and his feet killing him. Sunday morning, when he ought to be asleep, or in church, or both, he is grading papers against the dreadful dark of Sunday night, when he has to go over his aged and undecipherable lecture notes for Monday.

He is always worried and always tired. His sex life is a laugh and his wife's a good long cry. He is too brought down even to get to the free movies on campus—*but not to attend all the lectures the county round*. I put it to you: Why would a lecturer ever be a lecturee, except he be pursued by the Furies?

So flies his little life away, without prospect of expiation until, his course and his courses run, he achieves the instant oblivion of the grave and his first untroubled night's sleep (if God is dead) in a flagelliform lifetime.

But who feels for the guilt-ridden rich, or ever has? The professor
used to be a put-upon man, at least as much to be pitied as scorned
(unless his research produced a sure cure at home or a sure kill abroad).
He had a collar-turning slattern of a wife who despised his pretensions,
a litter of kids with prematurely weak eyes, and a thin gray line of
credit at the shoe store and the grog shop. The reason he wore shaggy
tweeds with elbow patches, and sucked on a pipe, was that tweeds
were durable, his elbows were out, and Granger Rough Cut was a
nickel a shtickle; and it was cheaper to suck the pipe than to light it.
These interesting appurtenances have long since become appurtenant
to Madison and other Avenues, even unto the nonmalignant pipe, and
they no more reflect a condition of life on the campus than they do
in the countinghouse.

The Children's Crusade

The nice thing about being two-headed is that you can be of two minds without being schizophrenic. I am of two minds about this country's present convulsions. My heart is in the highlands with the hellers. But my head—. It's an old head, mine, without much wool on the top of it in the place where the wool ought to grow. Let me tell you what it is like to be old in the United States of America in 1969.

My generation accepted the precepts of its parents, and they were the same precepts our parents had accepted from theirs. We violated the precepts, naturally; but we accepted them. Your generation rejects them. We were wrong, and you are right. The precepts were good precepts, but still you are right. You are right because precep‧torial is as preceptorial does. We were—and, of course, are—pious frauds. You are impious Abélards.

That's the one big change. The other one is this: The America of my youth is vanished without much more than a trace. It was an unjust and an uncouth America, but a generous and a visionary one. Its golden door was open and the lamp was bright beside it. Its very existence was a terror to tyranny everywhere, lest its spirit be infectious. In its perfectly splendid isolation it cultivated the techniques, if not the arts, of peace. In the first eight years of my life in Chicago, I never once saw a soldier. America was still, as it was intended to be, a refuge from chauvinist horrors. If someone had told my father—no one did—that he had to take a loyalty oath, he would have said, "What do you think this is—Russia?"

Gone; all gone now, to be replaced by the garrison state and the last best hope of preserving the status quo ante all over the world.

If, then, you can understand what it is to be old in this country in 1969, you will be able to understand why I am of two minds about the country's present convulsions: on balance, the changes I have seen in my time have been for the worse. I am afraid for my country.

But I am of one mind about certain aspects of its convulsions:

First: The revolution of the young blacks, formerly Negroes, is nothing but the Jim Crow branch of the American children's crusade.

Address delivered as Regents' Lecturer at the University of California at Santa Barbara, 5 May 1969. Reprinted from the *Gadfly*, Fall 1969. (c) Great Books Foundation, 1969.

What the American Negro is saying to the American white is what the American young are saying to the American old: "I don't dig you. I don't love you. I don't honor you. I don't obey you." Whether it's Vietnam and "Hell, no, we won't go," or the ghetto and "Hell, no, we won't stay," the message is the same. The parochial concern of the Negro should not obscure the common cause against an America that was promises made with its fingers crossed.

Second: The revolution of the young Americans, white, black, red, or pink, is nothing but the American branch of the world revolution of the rising generation—and the American branch is behind the times. The French branch has pulled down de Gaulle. The Spanish and Japanese branches have driven Franco and Sato up the wall. The Italian branch has made it impossible to govern Italy. The German branch has paralyzed Prussianism, and the Czech branch has immobilized Communism. In our characteristic American provincialism we suppose that we have something special going here. The only thing that is special, indeed, unique, is your elders' effort to persuade you to call yourselves kids in the hope that you won't take yourselves seriously.

Third: The revolution is overdue—the revolution which Jefferson and Jeremiah invoked when they said that God's justice would not sleep forever. The evils that were containable under kings are no longer containable under politicians. A world that spends more on war than it does on health and education combined is not susceptible of reform. It calls for revolution. But revolution is not the same thing as rebellion. The aftermath of the Russian Revolution instructs you that revolution is not a matter of systems but of men; as the men are so will the revolution be.

John Locke never heard of law and order, but he had heard of divine right. "When men are miserable enough," said Locke, "they will rebel, cry up divine right how you will." I think he should have said "desperate enough" instead of "miserable enough." The difference between submissive misery and desperate rebellion is hope. And the difference between rebellion and revolution is intelligence. The young everywhere, black, white, poor, rich, have the desperate certitude of hope along with the adolescent possibility of intelligence.

We who are old, hopeless, and like the Bourbons before us, so irremediably unintelligent that we can not distinguish rebellion from revolution, will escape the denouement if we are thoughtful enough to shoot ourselves immediately. You who are young will wage the contest and win it. You don't need God or the big battalions on your side. All you need is the actuarial table, and you've got it. My object here is to persuade you to win a revolution instead of a rebellion—to make your victory stick. The reason my head tells me no-no though there's yes-yes in my heart is that the only way to make a revolution stick is to wage it in a way that revolution has never been waged before. No revolution—not the French, not the American, and not the Russian—has ever stuck.

What is wanted is intelligence. That the status quo is unintelligent is superbly self-evident. But the revolution against it is not ipso facto intelligent. If it strikes with the wrong weapons at the wrong people for the wrong reasons, it will prove to have been unintelligent. If it assumes that there is nothing wrong with power and that a transfer or redistribution of power will improve the human condition, it will prove to have been unintelligent. He who says, "This ruler is a fool, but when I am a ruler I will not be a fool," is already a fool. It is not power that corrupts, but the unintelligent belief that power is not necessarily corrosive.

The revolution has got to be intelligent, and the Negro revolutionary has got to be especially intelligent, first, because he is its natural leader and, second, because he is fighting in an exposed position. If he rebels unintelligently, he will go down faster than the white rebel whose pallor restrains (though it does not disable) the counterrevolution. In the counterrevolutionary society it is a solemn duty to clob-, ber the white revolutionary, but a positive pleasure to clobber the black one.

To ask the Negro to be more intelligent than the white is not to ask very much. It is only to ask him to use the intelligence he already has, acquired in the only way intelligence is ever acquired: through suffering. If all he has learned through suffering is how to burn, baby, burn, he hasn't learned anything more than the white man, whose technological triumph consists of burning babies. If blackie is no more intelligent than whitey, it seems hardly worth his while to have spent three centuries in faithful attendance at the school of suffering.

If the Negro does not use his superior intelligence, he is lost. He is lost because an ignorant little man can not beat an ignorant big one. He can not fight whitey's way and win because whitey has the wherewithal. Whitey has overkill; blackie has underkill. The inference is inescapable. Along toward the end of 1941—but prior to December 7 of that year—Prof. Morris Cohen listened while a Jewish colleague said, "I just want to bash in a few Nazi heads before I die." Somebody turned to Cohen and said, "And what do you think?" "I think," said Cohen, "that bashing in heads is for the 96 percent—not for the 4 percent."

Even the 96 percent can not win that way now. It took the winners of the First World War fifteen years to realize that they had lost it. It took the winners of the Second World War only five. What keeps the

winners of the Third World War from launching it is the suspicion that
they have lost it in advance of its launching. They can't bash in a few
Russian or American heads without being bashed back. Their unintelligent alternative, as every schoolboy knows, is a balance of
terror which is ruinous in any terms and in its own terms unreliable.
Their only hope is to save their faces: It is an open secret that the
Americans will agree to surrender to the Viet Cong if the Viet Cong
will agree to proclaim an American victory. Old Whitey seems to be
at the end of the road. The inventor of the lynching-bee at Calvary,
the auction-block at Charleston, and the shoot-out at Verdun, he
seems to have no more inventions.

You who are young—above all, you who are non-Caucasian and
therefore preconditioned to intelligence—are called upon to go out
and turn the world upside down, like the Apostles before you. Like
them, you do not need any baggage. You do not need black studies,
because intelligence is not absorbed through the epidermis. You do
not need black dormitories, because intelligence is not contracted by
sleeping with people. You do not need black awareness, because intelligence is aware of itself and everything else. You need the intelligence you acquired in the course of your suffering; nothing more.

It is not enough to do your thing; the thing has got to be the sensible thing to do. The sensible thing to do is not to demand the debasement of education on the ground that a debased education is what
you are fit for, but to demand the improvement of an already debased education and the compensatory qualifications of which you
have been deprived. You do not want a bad education. You want a
good education, and the intelligence you acquired at the school of
suffering tells you what a good education is not.

A good education is not vocational training, because training is
not education. Animals and slaves are trained. Men are educated. The
purpose of education is not a job; that's the purpose of apprenticeship.
The purpose of education is human freedom. You don't want Dow
Chemical or ROTC off the campus; you want everything off the
campus that has nothing to do with education for human freedom.
That takes care of the organizations just mentioned. It takes care of
the placement office, and it takes care of home economics and physical education and business administration and journalism and speech
and three miles of beach and four years of fraternities and all the
other goodies with which your elders have tricked out the higher
learning in the hope that they could keep you quiet in a rest home
for rich adolescents. You don't want war research thrown off the
campus; you want everything thrown off the campus that has nothing

to do with education for human freedom—including war research and industrial and commercial and labor research. You don't want the applied sciences of law and medicine and engineering and theology off the campus, but across the street where they can take advantage of pure research without diverting it from its purity.

Your motto has got to be the motto of my alma mater, and it has got to be properly parsed. The motto of my alma mater is, "Let knowledge grow from more to more, that human life may be enriched." My alma mater abandoned the enrichment for the knowledge, the end for the means, and achieved the first self-sustaining nuclear chain reaction, whose enrichment of human life in Hiroshima may be known to you.

There is nothing you can do to disrupt the American campus that hasn't been done by your elders. Don't connive with your elders in its disruption. Revolutionize it. Revolutionize it intelligently on the intelligent ground that is has forfeited its legitimacy and prostituted its independence. A university 50 percent of whose budget is provided by the producers of overkill is monopolized by them and every one of its procedures tainted. The Supreme Court once held that control of 6 percent of the market for automobile magnetos was enough to constitute a monopoly in the industry.

Some of you are challenging the adequacy, even the relevancy, of education, even of the best education, to the enrichment of human life—a challenge your elders have ducked ever since education became the national religion. Many of you have raised a still sharper issue: Education has always presupposed authority—the rightful authority, in respect of teaching, of those who know over those who don't. Its business has always been supposed to be the transmission of knowledge by those who already had some. It has lost its authority. It has lost its authority because its practitioners have lent themselves, on campus and off, to the production and perpetuation of deadly error. Authority stripped of its rightfulness is authoritarianism. You are right to repudiate authoritarianism without authority. But you are mortally wrong if you think that you will improve your situation by replacing your elders' authoritarianism with your own.

Your intelligence, as it rejects authoritarianism, rejects the struggle for Negro rights as such and for student rights as such. Such struggle is self-interested and is therefore no different in principle from the self-interest that disgraces your elders. There is no such category as Negro rights or student rights because there is no such category as Negro or student. Either there are human rights or there are none. Either you are first of all men, and only then black men or white men, or you are nothing. Because you are men, you are not be depreciated or badgered. Because you are men, you are not to be manipulated. Because you are men, you are not to be conscripted or enslaved. When the Negro was a slave, and the white man called him a black, he said, "I'm a man."

The Negro does not have to be superhuman or saintly. He has only to be intelligent. What was good about Martin King was his intelligence. He apprehended that his salvation lay in man's. He would not lift a finger to save one man or one country. His race was the one race, man, without regard to the amount of melanin in his skin. He knew the perdurable agony of man in his own person. Persecution was his teacher, and he learned from his teacher how to speak for man.

Who else will speak for man? Not whitey. Whitey has his advantage to lose if he does. He has battened on partiality—on racism, on nationalism, on the exploitation of his brother black and white. Whoever fights for partiality is playing whitey's game and playing into whitey's hands, perpetuating the intolerable separation of man into species. Separatism is for the birds; there is only one surviving species of the class *Homo*, and that is *Homo sapiens*, intelligent man. Whoever speaks for man must refuse to let any man be segregated by anybody—even by himself.

Just as there must be one world or none, so there must be one culture or none. That culture is Man's. Asian and African and European studies in America are justified only by the American's ignorance of Asia, Africa, and Europe; that is, they are not justified at all. The black culture of the African-descended American, like the Irish culture of the Irish-descended American, is an atavism that denies the primacy of manhood and asserts the nonexistent racial purity of the tribe which, wherever it has been found in anything like pure isolation, has invariably been found to be culturally backward. If I can not understand the writings of Eldridge Cleaver because of my skin color, then Eldridge Cleaver can not understand the writings of Shakespeare because of his. Everybody, and not just the Nazis, will burn the books.

What is wanted here is unanswerable intelligence. Attack education for its present debasement, and you are unanswerable. Challenge it as authoritarian, and you are unanswerable. Assert your right to live without killing, and you are unanswerable. Demand justice and not advantage, and you are unanswerable. Call upon the church, not for $500,000,000 in special reparations for the Negro but for $500,-000,000 in general justice for the poor, and you are unanswerable.

But call policemen "pigs" and you are answerable by those who remember the Nazis calling the Jews *Schweinehunde*. Call public officials "fascists" and you are answerable by those who remember fascism. Call for power and you are answerable by those who remember the Caesars and the Hapsburgs and the Romanovs. Call for black faculties and black curricula and you are answerable by those who call for humanistic faculties and humane curricula. Call for separatism and you will have on your side—though they kill you—the supremacists who have the necessary overkill to maintain the separatism you call for. Do you want separate but equal opportunity? You will get the separate opportunity and suffer, as you always have, the inequality that follows ineluctably from the separation of the minority from the majority.

The Negro racist, like the white racist, bases his racism on dignity. But men can not shoot or burn or brawl their way to dignity; if they could, the American white man would be the most dignified man on earth. Does it make you feel good to occupy an administration building and horrify the straights and terrify the timid and license the governor to turn on the tear gas? Do you want to feel good or to be intelligent? Do you want a rebellion or a revolution? Dignity is not a matter of feeling good—of the mumbo-jumbo of "black is beautiful" or "America the beautiful." America is no more beautiful than Africa and black is no more beautiful than blue. Malcolm X Day is about as meaningful to its celebrants as the Fourth of July is to its.

I wish that you could make your demands negotiable, but I don't see how you can if you make them intelligent. I don't see how a little more or less overkill can be negotiated. I don't see how a little more or less ghetto or a little more or less nerve-gas research or a little more or less CIA can be negotiated. But you can not achieve your properly nonnegotiable objectives by throwing a rock through the window on the ground that the owner of the window understands nothing but force. He understands force, all right, and he has it. You have got to try to raise the level of his intelligence to the point where he can comprehend that the travesty of the campus and the ghetto and the battlefield is finished.

A generation which elects a Lyndon Johnson or a Richard Nixon has no visible intention to negotiate. It will pay lip service to negotiation, providing that the shape of the table is right and as long as it doesn't have to stop doing the only thing it knows how to do. Harvard University had three hundred years to clean house on the basis of negotiable demands. The people who rightfully deplore your claim to amnesty have amnestied themselves since the world began. You man recall Cain's general demurrer to the complaint that he had failed to discharge his responsibility to his brother.

Old Whitey may be unintelligent and out of steam, but he still has his pristine cunning. If he is persistently, but subserviently, pushed, he will propose gradualism, by which he means gradually wearing you down. He isn't wicked. He is unconcerned. His unconcern is not immoral. It is unintelligent. By power posessed, he can not understand what the Apostle meant by saying that we are all members one of another. He can not understand what the Savior meant by saying that he who takes the sword will perish by it. He can not understand what the prophet meant by proclaiming the greater damnation of those who devour widows' houses and make long prayers for a pretense. He didn't mean to be like this, any more than you do. Power benighted him, and he walks in the noonday as in the night. If I may paraphrase an eminent Harvard alumnus—a hundred generations of people like your elders is enough. If you turn out to be the hundred-and-first, you are lost.

Your elders have torn down Vietnam and kept the ghettos in their place, and now they say that you want to tear things down without having anything to put in their place. Don't let them get you into that bag. You don't have to have anything to put in the place of the present shambles. The Lord God Jehovah did not tell your ancestors and mine what to put in the place of Sidon and Tyre. He told them, "You shall walk in my path *and I will show you my way*." It is easy to think up the right thing. What is hard is to stop doing the wrong one. The Lord didn't tell your ancestors and mine to do good. He told them, "Cease to do evil—*learn to do good*." You need only to be intelligent.

If you are intelligent, the totalitarian spirit—which unintelligently obeys all laws—will call you anarchists. Be ye not dismayed. True, anarchy is the second worst condition of human society. The worst is tyranny. If you will not have tyranny, then you, like the intelligent founders of this republic, must take your chances on anarchy. The Nuremberg decision of the International Military Tribunal in 1946 *requires* anarchy of the soldier who is ordered to perform inhuman acts. Disorder is no worse than injustice, which is the institutionalization of disorder. When the laws are rooted in violence and maintained by violence, they must not be obeyed. Socrates was right, not wrong, when he said, "Men of Athens, I love you, but I shall obey God rather than you." John Brown was right. Mohandas Gandhi was right. Martin King was right. And Thomas Aquinas was right seven and a half centuries ago when he said that an unjust law is no law and does not bind a man in conscience.

There is a higher law. The higher law does not have to be very high to be higher than the Selective Service Act or the Internal Revenue Act; only more intelligent. You must study the German experience of the 1930s, when the most literate nation on earth, mistaking literacy for intelligence, elevated ignorance to power and cut its own head off. You must study the German experience and learn that neither the government nor the majority is by definition a good judge of justice. Civil disobedience may be treasonable. Be ye not dismayed: It is not necessarily unpatriotic. A patriot will set his country right if he can, but in no case contribute to its continued delinquency.

I am one of the elders of whom I speak. You terrify me. You terrify me because I have got mine, which I got by the exercise of the good precepts I got from my parents, plus being white and landing on my feet every time I fell on my face. You do not terrify me with your popguns; I have ten machine guns for every one of your popguns. You terrify me because you show some small sign of social maturity, of civic responsibility and human concern. Your elders, like me, are nice people, but they did not mature. You have seen them playing cop-and-robber at home and overkill in their worldwide playpen. Television reveals the infantilism of their attention span. They can not talk; they can sit mesmerized, or they can shout or mumble. They made you mumble, "one nation, indivisible," and after you had mumbled it a few thousand times, some subversive told you that 5 percent of the American people have 20 percent of the nation's income and 20 percent have 5 percent of it, and you began to become what your elders call cynical, that is, intelligent. The day you complete the process your elders will fall off the stage of history; you won't even have to push them.

The President of Notre Dame says that "we need a rebirth of academic, civic, and political leadership—a sharing of those yourhful ideals and dreams, whether they are impossible or not." The President of Notre Dame is right. But whose fault is it that we need such a rebirth? How did we come to be so needy, with so rich a heritage and so profligate a land? How are we to be reborn? What does "a sharing of those youthful ideals and dreams" mean? What have your elders got to offer as their share? Not youth or ideals or dreams.

Their ideals are money, fame, and power, and they dream of bigger and better sugar plums. They are old: they have run out of time to choose: They no longer have the choice to free the Negroes or fight a civil war to enslave them. All they can do now is cry up the divine right of law and order and shudder for themselves as they see it in action and observe the lawlessness and disorder it brings in its train. Our black brethren are freeing themselves impatiently. For three centuries they waited patiently—so patiently that Whitey, who takes impatience for manliness, took them for sheep who look up to be fed and look down when they aren't. They waited at the end of the line, and no matter how short the line got they were still waiting. They waited at the back of the bus, and no matter how empty the bus was they were still at the back. Their patience is beginning to be exhausted.

Whitey had no intention of living up to his profession that all men are created equal, and you know it and I know it and he knows it. As sovereign citizen—holding the country's only permanent political office—he was its ruler. He could not pass the buck for his derelictions. What the country was was his doing; was, and is. Too late, too late—he can not exit now. He has boxed himself in.

His tragic flaw was his possession by power and the consequent corruption of his intelligence. He did not understand that no man can free another because no man can enslave another. Whitey wanted blackie to act like a freedman. But blackie isn't a freedman; no man is. He is a free man, and a free man because he's a man. Therein lies his dignity—not in the grace of his master—and he loses it not by being in chains but by chaining himself to the humiliating values of his master. Whoever would want to be and do and have what the American white man is and does and has is not a man but a slave and, like the American white man, an unhappy slave at that.

You are the young. Your elders' only hope is your intelligence. Your intelligence may be undeveloped, but it is not yet corrupted. I hear that you are hopheads, and I regret to hear it: I'm a wino, myself. Hopheads you may be, but you are not yet fatheads. You are still young. You have been forced by the American educational process to undertake your own education. You are not be put down or put off, because you have been set to wondering. What set you to wondering was, I suppose, the two victorious world wars your elders waged and lost in the process of winning them. Coming in the wake of these wingless victories, you would have had to be catatonic epileptics not to have wondered. Wonder is the beginning of wisdom. You are wising up. All you have to do is be wise and keep the pressure on. All you have not to do is what e. e. cummings called up-grow and down-forget.

Your intelligence tells you that in this mongrel society—we are every last one of us mongrels—the only solution to the race problem is miscegenation. There was a time when an Irishman could not be elected President. There was a time when a Catholic could not be elected President. There was even a time when a fighting Quaker could not be elected President. The change in our national attitude was the result of what we Dixiecrats call "mixing." Hybrid corn and hybrid pigs are of higher quality than the original stocks, and there is no evidence whatever that hybrid man is not. Since 70 percent of all the American "blacks" are part-"white," and millions of American "blacks" have passed unknowingly into the white race so-called,

the racist who says he wouldn't want his daughter to marry a Negro—
or a white man—has no way of knowing whether she does or she
doesn't and neither has she or her fiancé. As long as pigmentation
provides our mongrel society with the one discernible other, and as
long as whitey is ineducable by anthropology, psychology, and theology, the only solution is to make indiscernible others of us all.

Five hundred years would do it. But, then, five hundred years of
education for freedom would make intelligent human beings of us
and it wouldn't matter any more what color we were. But we have
run out of time. It isn't the future that's dark—it's the present. If you
in your generation do not bring light to the world, if you spurn a
little suffering undergone for the sake of intelligence, the wave of the
present will roll over you and, like your elders, you will be heard of
no more. *Après vous, le déluge.*

The Whelps

I hope I am recovering from what I hope is the last speech I ever hope to try to deliver on a college campus. Just before the student strike last month, I highballed it out to San Fernando Valley State College in California to participate, I was told, in a forum with Tom Hayden of the Chicago Seven. I couldn't resist the invitation. First, there was the money—and, as Robert M. Hutchins said long ago, a businessman may have ideals, but a university professor will do anything for money. Second, there was Tom Hayden, to whom I'm attached. And third, there was the vestigial hope of enlightening the young or (who knows?) being enlightened by them.

The young were there, in quantity. They were spread all over the grass—and you could smell the grass. A rock and roll band polluted the air. Squad cars of Governor Reagon's macemen rolled around the campus, and my hosts pointed out to me the genteel sprinkling of plainclothes dicks who, in California, are actually planted as students.

The first speaker was a middle-aged honky who was running a worthy project in Watts. He tried to persuade what he mistakenly thought was his audience to join his ghetto crusade. They jeered and cursed him down—calling him their four-letter names and a liar besides—and I learned later that part of the wrecker technique is to interrupt the speaker with false accusations, rattle him, and break up the meeting.

The wreckers were a minority—but not a minuscule minority. They were perhaps a hundred out of a thousand. And the nine hundred, as everywhere, didn't know what to do and did nothing. It was a disheartening spectacle of the lights going out in America (where they never were very bright). Maybe the most disheartening part of it was my own sinuous suspicion that if I were a young Californian I would be one of the wreckers.

In my time I've been heckled by little old ladies in tennis shoes—but these were bare-chested brawlers with no shoes at all. And unlike the little old ladies, they ought to have been on my side, and I knew they weren't. I began to be worried. I'm an old straight with an old straight doctrine to peddle—stolen from Thomas Aquinas and

Reprinted from the *Progressive*, June 1970.

Thomas Jefferson—and I was afraid they'd tear me to pieces. I knew that they wouldn't listen to me; and if they tore me to pieces I'd never get my money.

My hope lay in the next speaker. He had been inserted into the program at the insistence of the campus conservatives (*ahem*) and he was crazy enough to make the scene. Or not so crazy. He was a darling of the Birchers and was running for Congress. This was his chance, and his only chance, at an audience of a thousand people, and if he goaded them to riot against him and activate the police, he might, like Reagan, be elected.

Before he had an opportunity to open his mouth in behalf of our totally victorious President's total victory policy in Vietnam, the crowd (by this time I was thinking of it as a mob) was calling him everything it could think of—which wasn't much, but wasn't polite. The kindest thing they called him was killer.

I was now terrified in spades. These prisoners of American sybaritism were at war, and the Amazonians of the species were especially bellicose. The worst of it was that they didn't seem to be enjoying their own high jinks (certainly nobody else was). They were miserable. Miserable young Americans, loaded to the gills with hatred and equipped with a set of expletives designed to prevent communication.

The Birchite speaker "blew his cool," of course, and the blood lust of the wreckers was intensified accordingly. But he brazened it out until, in sudden short order, he finished and ducked; and now it was my turn.

I wished I were home in western—not eastern—Massachusetts where nothing is heard but the song of the bird, and the skies are not cloudy all day.

I thought I might save my skin and my money by proclaiming myself a friend of Tom Hayden. I thought I might save myself by using the argot of the young. (But the honky from Watts had tried that line disastrously.) I thought I might save myself by commending my gray hairs to the commiseration of the barn-burners. I even thought I might save myself by telling them that my very own little boy was the manager of a San Francisco acid rock band called the Grateful Dead.

But I thought that none of these credentials would save me from what the French call the *enragés*, and I might as well go down with my flag flying. All at once I was tired of trying to figure out gimmicks to save my skin from people who wanted my skin no matter what I said and did. So I hauled myself to the platform and got wired for sound—an infernal machine that would make a wrecker out of a white mouse—and said it straight. I said that what the young needed

was intelligence to save themselves from the pit into which their unintelligent elders had fallen.

And lo!—they stood still for me. They stood still, and shushed
each other, and cheered me, and when I finished shooting my cuffs
they grabbed my hand and some of them hugged me and some of the
most Amazonian of the Amazonians insisted on kissing my weathered
old cheek.

It really happened, and it really happened the way I have said, and
neither modesty nor immodesty helps me understand it.

I don't want to do it again. It's too hard on an old man who ought
to be spending his deliquescence at home trying to learn how to
write. And I might not get off so happily next time. But I'm glad I
did it this time, and I think I learned something which I want (as we
stuffed shirts say) to share with you.

They listened reverently to Tom Hayden—I forgot to say that he
spoke before me—because they took him for one of their own, and
they will revere no one else. They may not have noticed that Tom
eschews obscenity and abuse and urges them to act intelligently.
They would not, and will not, stand still for do-gooders like the
middle-aged honky working in Watts—because they smell the Establishment repairman in him. Of course they wouldn't stand still
for the Birchite candidate for Congress any more than they would
stand still any more—hear this now—for Eugene McCarthy or Bobby
Kennedy. They're past all that.

Why did they stand still for me? I think that they stood still for
me because I didn't try to tell them that they were good or bad boys
and girls. (They know whether they're good or bad boys and girls.)
I think they stood still for me because I told them, and meant it,
that a world as badly shot as this one is not susceptible to reform
but has to be revolutionized. I think they stood still for me because I told them that it was I who made that world the way it is
and got fat in it as an always constructive critic. I think they stood
still for me because, contrary to their expectation, I talked to them
as if they were educable (not educated) persons whose distress, however deplorable its vocalization, was justified.

They are not to be bought off with a twenty-four-billion-dollar
flagpole on the moon. They are not to be bought off with tricks
designed to give them still more goodies and keep them quiet in the
world the way it is. They don't like the world the way it is—though
they have no inhibition against living off it. And the fact that it's
always been that way does not divert them from the view that it
never should have been that way. They are not to be bought off with
the right of eighteen-year-olds to vote for Nixon or Humphrey. They

are not to be bought off or sold out, or crushed with truncheons or washed away in Governor Reagan's bloodbath.

They mean to be revolutionary, and they should be, and the hope of the world (and a very slim hope it is) is that the revolution, whose barkers they are, will be a revolution and not a rebellion; that is, that it will be intelligent. But intelligent or not, the revolution will be; even though they, too, will be its victims if, like their unintelligent elders, they put their faith in the American virtue of violence.

They are obnoxious to us, but we were obnoxious to them, to life itself, before they became obnoxious to us. Their unmannerly tribe increases, and they are not the black or the poor (or the stupid). I tell you, my friends, that God in his mysterious way may be (I say no more than may be) working his wonders through these implacable whelps in their à la mode rags and tatters. They are all dressed up and nowhere to go—but they are not, for the moment, disposed to follow you and me any further down the path to perdition.

Organizing the Ruins

I used to be a union man, and I am going to be a union man again, but this time around I know what I am going to be a union man for. I am going to be a union man for (1) wages, (2) hours, and (3) working conditions. The last time I was a newspaperman possessed of professional ideals. My professional ideals induced me to join a union of newspapermen. This time I am a professor in a university, possessed of what passes current for realism.

The university is being unionized, and only a nitpicker would insist on a distinction between union and unification or unification and unity. The success of the effort is assured. Its single remaining obstacle is the crumbling conviction of some professors that theirs is a profession and not a trade.

Thus the unity of the university, long ago shattered by secularization and specialization, is being restored, not, to be sure, in the interest of the intellectual love of God but in the interest of temporal security (and bodily security at that). The same interests that disunite society, namely, wages, hours, and working conditions, unite it when it is under perceptible attack by a common enemy. Survival—the precondition of any wages, hours, and working conditions at all—draws the warring members of the society together, however ephemerally, in the common defense of its members' Darwinian interest. That is what is happening in the academic grove this slow season.

The faculty of my university is "organizing" under the banner of a Society of Professors which is not a society but a trade union. As professors they once professed something beyond wages, hours, and working conditions. They professed the advancement of knowledge and its dissemination among young men and women who were determined to learn. As professors in a university they professed a *universum* whose last end (therefore its first principle) was peace. To achieve unity now, they have only to stop professing their profession, recognize the naked condition of their existence, and unite and fight. This they are in the process of doing. As tradesmen their transcendent (not their exclusive) interest is in bargaining with their bosses. Even pointy-heads know that the only way to bargain with—i.e., against—

Reprinted from the *Center Magazine*, May/June 1973.

the bosses is to do so collectively. The minuet settles nothing. The war settles everything.

So I go to war again as a union man. The last time (going on forty years ago) I was satisfied with my wages, hours, and working conditions, but my boss, one W.R. Hearst by name, acted as if my profession were a trade. It was on that Fourth-of-July issue that I joined the Newspaper Guild as a charter member. What persuaded me was not Heywood Broun's demand for better wages, hours, and working conditions; what persuaded me was Broun's demand that W.R. Hearst and his fellow tradesmen be persuaded to recognize that they and their hirelings were consecrated to the practice of a profession.

It did not take forty years, or even four, to strip me of my illusion and compel the confession that the Guild was an organization of semiskilled soft-hats consecrated to the same goodies that W.R. Hearst himself enjoyed. We were, and are, all very good fellows in the newspaper trade, but we know now that we are plying a trade. We do not mean to go to the stake or the cleaners when one of our illusioned brethren goes to jail for maintaining Heywood Broun's professional ideal of a free and responsible press. We know ourselves now for what we are, tradesmen in a shrinking market.

We professors are coming to know ourselves, too. What holds us back is our designation: we are professors. But the designation has long since lost its pristine character. It does not certify that we teach well or learn much of anything. It certifies that no ax can touch us. After six probationary years—in most places—we get lifetime tenure or we get fired. Our fellow professors decide. Since our fellow professors do not have to pay our wages and do not like to fire a fellow professor, most of us get tenure, from which we can not be dislodged unless we commit a capital crime at high noon in the presence of three unimpeachable witnesses. More than half of the country's college teachers have tenure, and the tribe increases, in every case committing the institution to a capital investment of a quarter or a half million dollars.

The asserted purpose of tenure is to protect our freedom to teach unpopular doctrines, study unpopular subjects, and circulate unpopular conclusions. It is a purpose which ought to be available to churchmen, newspapermen, and, come to think of it, absolutely everybody in a democracy; it is only an explication of the First Amendment. Most of us, like most churchmen and most newspapermen, do not avail ourselves of these pleasant prerogatives and never have. Most of us, like most of them, are hacks. Still, ours is a high-grade purpose, maintained by our insistence that we are practicing a profession and not plying a trade.

Tenure is now under furious fire. The ostensible reasons are the ossification of the higher learning in the mortmain of the higher age bracket; the rigidity imposed on changing conditions when, for example, there are ten tenured professors of Greek (ancient) and two students interested in Greek (modern); and the assumption undemonstrated (and undemonstrable) that once a professor gets tenure he lies down on the lifetime job. This last is a canard arising from a yahoo view of human nature; I do not know of a tenured colleague who does not work very hard, if for no loftier a goal than to excite his wife's admiration or at least her pity.

The real reason tenure is under fire is that in a period of tight money it costs a great deal of money.

The American university, like everything else in America, has fallen into the hands of the fixers, or administrators. Their low statutory function in the university is to minister to the professional needs of their professional betters, but this is not what they do. In the private schools they answer only to the tradesmen who constitute the board, in the public schools to the tradesmen who constitute the legislature. Both sets of tradesmen reprobate education as a profession and— observing the clamor of the professors—see it as a racket like their own whose practitioners are after as big a buck as they can get for making as little a bang as the law requires. Since education is nothing but a custodial scheme for the young who can not be absorbed by the labor market or the army, why shouldn't a professor work forty hours a week instead of four and keep sixty or a hundred students quiet instead of thirty or twenty or, good God, in the upper reaches of graduate work, one or two? Why should a flannelmouth who works four hours a week have four months' vacation?

When times were good a professor did not deign to answer such questions. Had he deigned, he would have said, "I am a professor." A Cambridge Latinist, when he was asked what he was doing for the British war effort in the 1940s, said, "I am what England is fighting for." He needed to say no more. But times are bad now and getting worse. If a professor should reply today by saying, "I am a professor," when a yahoo asked him why he should enjoy pleasant prerogatives, the yahoo would say, "So what? Every second bum on the block is a professor."

With the transmogrification of the college into a high school, the professoriat has lost caste. It has lost further caste by trying (in vain) to "get with it"—the antecedent of the "it" being the sartorial, tonsorial, and uproarial whimsies of students. And it has lost what little caste remained to it by forswearing the shreds and patches that bespoke its unworldly dignity. The tradesman does not want dignity.

He wants money and as much of it as he can get, and there isn't anywhere he won't go to get it, and there isn't anything, in a pinch, he won't do for it.

It is politically difficult to cut the heart out of elementary and secondary education—though for Mr. Nixon the difficult is not the impossible. It is politically easy to lay the ax to the higher learning, which is a work-free shelter for superannuated "kids" to begin with.

The taxpayers understand what the elementary school, even the high school, or at least the junior high school, is supposed to do: it is supposed to keep the kids quiet. If the college did not cost so much and would keep the kids quiet, they would put up with that, too. But it costs so much and does not keep the kids quiet. What the kids learn in college are four four-letter words, plus the fabrication of cannon-crackers, plus amnesty, abortion, and acid. And what the kids learn in college they learn from the professors. All this was all right as long as the children of the rich did it at the expense of the rich, but who needs it at the expense of the non-rich? The colleges are politically defenseless, the universities as research institutions defensible only to the extent that they produce utilitarian marvels like the atomic bomb.

The professors' wages during the shortage decade of the 1960s rose (at full professorial rank) by 83 percent. I am a full professor, and at twenty thousand dollars I am probably the lowest man of my rank on the local totem pole. I live like a king, and the corruption oozes from my every cholesterine pore. And I have tenure. My security blanket is impermeable as long as I restrain myself from committing a capital crime at high noon in the presence of three unimpeachable witnesses. If I should be dead drunk the rest of my life and never again meet a class, my tenure might be attacked. But I have never heard of a case in which that happened.

What the administrators are demanding now in behalf of the tradesmen is the abolition or constriction of tenure. In the Virginia, Maryland, New Jersey, California, and Massachusetts systems, and in private schools like Rochester, Stanford, and Cornell, the attack on tenure—to get rid of it altogether, or to freeze it, or to establish a quota for it—is in various stages of success, and in another hundred-or-so places it is well under way. To forestall the attack or mitigate its impact, individual institutions are putting the squeeze on the faculty, with the result, in a time of declining enrollment, that men and women who have had twenty or more years of schooling which, whatever it has prepared them for, has unprepared them to mine coal or sell haberdashery, are teaching in high schools or elementary schools or are on the dole.

Unionization is rolling across the campuses almost irresistibly. The competing unionizers are the National Education Association (unionizing me), the American Federation of Teachers (A.F.L.-C.I.O.), and the American Association of University Professors. The N.E.A. is running far ahead of the A.F.T. because the A.F.T. is an *ausgesprochene* organization of low-level bindle stiffs who go out on strike, and professors do not want to confront the ultimate logic of their unionization. The A.A.U.P. is trailing, since it is, or has been until now, an association of scholars and gentlemen which delivers gentlemanly rebukes, sometimes successfully, in generally isolated grievance cases.

Recently warning the California professors that the right to strike "cancels out civil service, tenure, and some of the other things which public employment provides," Governor Ronald Reagan insisted on reminding them that collective bargaining "eventually involves the right to strike . . . and you cannot strike against the people." Governor Coolidge of Massachusetts invoked this doctrine against the Boston police a half-century ago and rode it to the White House. Governor Reagan might not be able to turn the same trick in 1973, but by 1976 conditions might be more propitious for him.

The administrators, or fixers, mean business. One of them, Chancellor Maurice B. Mitchell of the University of Denver, is quoted in *U.S. News & World Report* as saying that "once an individual has tenure he cannot be penalized for holding or expressing unpopular views, for poor teaching, for failure to contribute to the intellectual life of the university, or even for an apparent lack of ordinary intelligence or moral responsibility that might be inferred from . . . views or actions." Now Mr. Mitchell comes (as he says) "out of the business world" and he may not be able to express himself clearly. If, however, he really means what he seems to say, it would appear that holding or expressing unpopular views should be equated with poor teaching and, like poor teaching, be penalized. It would seem further that somebody other than a professor's peers is competent to identify (and penalize) failure to contribute to the intellectual life of the university; that a merely apparent lack of ordinary intelligence or moral responsibility should be penalized; and that there is somebody up there somewhere ready and eager to define such commodities and to infer them in an instant case.

However the Mitchells of the academic world are parsed, they mean business. The colleges and universities were not much good before the business world moved in on them frontally. The reason that they were not much good is that they allowed the business world to buy and sell them in terms of its and not their own definition of ordinary intelligence and moral responsibility. Their disintegration in

terms of any higher standards has long been complete. Almost everywhere the curriculum, where it has been designed at all, has been
designed to keep the students and the Mitchells quiet. It has failed, as
it should have, on both counts.

Disintegration is an invitation to destruction. The universities per-
sist today by force of habit. The Mitchells seem to be bent on kicking
the habit in behalf of a society that would not like education if it
knew what it was and does not like what goes on in the schools
(which it mistakenly takes for education).

It is not clear to me that a ceasefire—in the form of unionization—
will solve any of the educational *or* academic problems that beset
us, such as academic freedom and mortmain. (Surely the contract,
like all union contracts, will protect job seniority at all costs.) It is
unclearer still that the determination of a professor's competence,
worthiness, or failure or success in realizing his youthful promise can
be made contractually. Pandering to the students (and ultimately in-
sulting them), the get-with-it college or university now asks them to
grade the professors, and, in the age of the clown, clowns like me
come up with the best report cards. What machinery will the union
contract substitute for the travesty that calls the educator to judge-
ment at the hands of the educatee? What machinery for the evalua-
tion of teaching and research will take the place of the infinitely
fallible, infinitely inequitable judgment of men and women who,
however dim their lights, profess a profession?

It is likely that the faculty of my university will be successfully
unionized within the year and go to war, in the first instance, against
the administration and ultimately against the governor and the legislature. One of my colleagues says, "better two packs of wolves than a
pack of wolves and a flock of sheep." So much for the consecrated
community. So much, too, for the public respect, and public restraint,
which consecration enjoins.

Like all universities, mine has long since fallen apart in spirit. It is
not a consecrated community. It is not any kind of community,
except in enormous facade. Now its very facade will come down in
the adversary relationship that in trade and government has brought
us where we are today. I suppose that the relationship might just as
well be open as covert and the undeclared war declared.

But I feel bad about it. I feel bad about it because I still find myself
saying "my" university. It isn't really mine. It isn't anybody's. It isn't
a question of low morale but of none at all. In the eight years I have
been there it has tripled in size. The campus, which eight years ago consisted of a capricious melange of red brick-and-acropolis, is now

covered over with upended and horizontal concrete. Students are nameless swarms in a turnstile, and faculty members who are un-aquainted no longer nod when they pass one another. I do not know half the members of "my" department and nobody ever sees a central administrator (or goes to a convocation, where one might be seen at a distance). I do not know a colleague who is not depressed or, beyond depression, calloused.

So I suppose we tradesmen might as well get on with it and proceed from the beguiling idiocies of relativism and relevance to the business of organizing what Dylan Thomas once called the university factory; and contribute our effete bit to the participatory anarchy into which the *universum* of the thirteenth century has fallen.

Part Two

Nice Guys Finish

M. Tepper's Manifest Destiny

He may have known—in 1941, when he was twenty-eight years old—that the Philippine Islands were in the Pacific Ocean. I don't believe he knew he had a Manifest Destiny in them. He probably didn't know where, or what, Guam was, and I am sure that he had never heard of Leyte. Who had?

He won Guam and Leyte for us, though. And there's a medal on his chest (I suppose it's still on his chest) that says so. He hasn't asked us why we sent him to do it, or what we wanted them for, or what we are going to do with them. And he isn't going to.

"I remember one time," one of his staff sergeants wrote, "it was shoot our way back or not at all, and the advance depended on our patrol getting back. Tepper spotted a slit in the circle and told us to follow him. We had to get up to follow him, and we didn't want to, and I guess he knew it. I know he knew it. So he got up and spit on his finger, like you do to tell the wind, and turned and said, 'Heck, fellows—them's only bullets.' That's not what they gave him the medal for. That's just the way he was."

That's just the way he was. Not ignorant. Not illiterate. He could have known all about Guam and Leyte in 1941. (He must have hit them—Guam, at least—in high school geography.) He could have known about his Manifest Destiny and the discovery by President William McKinley of our responsibility to raise up Our Little Brown Brothers wherever they happened to belong to somebody else far enough away. But that was Big Stuff, for Big Thinkers like you and me. M. Tepper took *our* word for the Big Stuff. His specialty was the Little Stuff—heck, fellows, them's only bullets—and in his specialty he excelled.

He was the fourth of Miss Julie's six children, four boys and two girls. Miss Julie was a Hagedorn and a Herzfeld, and she knew that Germans weren't Huns who amused themselves by cutting off the hands of Belgian babies. If she had been told that a Soviet Special Commission had discovered that Nazis used Polish children for target practice, she would have said she could not believe it. Not being able to believe announcements of this sort, in the first world war, she

Reprinted from *Common Sense*, May 1945.

found herself, at the end of it, with four rising sons and a pacifist turn of mind. She was just an American mother, who said she would rather be dead than see her sons soldiers. She lived to see her sons soldiers, and to die.

But she lived longer than she should have, angina being what it is. Maybe it was the intravenous morphine, twenty years of it. But one of her doctors thought it was something else entirely. He thought it was the specialist in Little Stuff, M. Tepper.

M. Tepper always bounced into her sickroom and bounced on her bed, and slapped her around, and hollered, "How ya doin', Julie, wanna fight?" And when somebody said to the doctor that Miss Julie shouldn't be subjected to such roughness, the doctor, who was an old-fashioned sort of fool, said that nobody knew, or at least *he* didn't know, what an angina patient should be subjected to. All he knew, he said, was that Miss Julie was better after a session of rough-house with her fourth-born, and maybe *that* was what kept her alive.

Did I say roughhouse? He was my own height, about six feet, and twice as heavy. When we saw each other, he picked me up, and I had to say pretty please, with cane sugar on it, before he threw me down. Once, when we were hunting together, I was just plain pooped and when he picked me up to carry me down the steepest damn ravine in all Alabama, I got good and mad and fought like hell and said I would make it, and I did. Like the six fellows behind him on Leyte.

He liked to hunt, and fish, and drink, and have a time for himself (and everyone else), and let the Big Thinkers like you and me worry about Guam, and Leyte, and Manifest Destiny, and Our Little Brown Brothers. He didn't want to go to college. He wanted to hunt, and fish, and roughhouse with Miss Julie and with his own Miss Sophie, and do just enough work to stay alive. Since he worked in his family's store, and since storekeeping at Tepper Brothers, as at Macy's and Field's, is still a matter of whether you like the storekeeper, he flourished. Since storekeeping was a gyp, and since M. Tepper would tell you, "My friend, these genuine guaranteed domestic imported root-de-toot patent-leather-paper-all-the-way-through shoes will last you two weeks or your money back," why not trade at Tepper's?

That's enough about M. Tepper, the man who said, "Heck, fellows —them's only bullets." That's enough about him except about how funny he was. (Don't tell us, Mayer, *please* don't tell us, how funny he was.) You haven't heard, for instance, how he and his three brothers, all of them state championship high school basketball players, organized Tepper Brothers Basketball Team with a fifth man for a ringer. M. Tepper ordered up the uniforms, and by way of designation he had them inscribed TEPPER BROTHERS, and by way of number he had them inscribed 59¢, 49¢, 39¢, 29¢, and 19¢.

Manifest Destiny is Big Stuff, out of M. Tepper's line. And it's too late now to explain it to him. It is too late now because M. Tepper knows every yard of Guam and Leyte, and eighteen square feet of them in particular. It is too late this time around, because M. Tepper has his medal on him, if they bury them with medals. It is too late now because M. Tepper, the specialist in Little Stuff, took and kept his platoon out in front with him and handled the patrols because he knew how to hunt; and didn't ask, "Just exactly *whose* is this Manifest Destiny?"

Well, hell, we all die. And well, hell, M. Tepper, late lieutenant of infantry, U.S. Army, lived out thirty-two years of life and lived them right up to here. So he, though I loved him, is only one of a million, maybe one of two million, G.I. Josephs whom I shall not see again. Well. Hell.

Well, hell, M. Tepper, *I* will live on, and *I* will look placidly and uncomprehendingly at the newspaper maps that show Leyte as a dot in an ocean, and *I* will crusade for the Four Freedoms and draw my 2¼ percent interest. And if *I* do not sleep, *you* sleep on Leyte, where you met your Manifest Destiny without 2¼ percent interest. And if *I* do not crusade, *you* crusade, in the Philippines, which are far away from the steepest ravine in Alabama. And if *I* do not let *my* blood cry out against what Mr. Roosevelt called in his last written document "this *impractical, unrealistic* settlement of the differences between governments by the mass killing of people," then let *your* blood cry out from the ground.

May His Tribe Decrease

Kind of choking and welling, I read the words of William Randolph Hearst, Jr., on the front page of his unraveling string of newspapers: "It is fifteen years ago this date that Pop left us, and even now I can not think about him very long or talk reminiscently about him without kind of choking up and hot tears welling up in my eyes."

Me, or mine, too.

We were colleagues and co-workers, William Randolph Hearst, Sr., and I. We never actually met, because his beat was the Hearst Castle at San Simeon and mine was the Wabash Avenue police station in Chicago. The only contact we ever had was a teletype message from San Simeon to Chicago beginning, as usual, "Chief says," and signed, as usual, "Willicombe," Willicombe being the Chief's panjandrum.

What the Chief said, on that occasion, was that I was to be fired from the *Chicago Evening American*. He had received a complaint about me from General Charles Gates Dawes, Calvin Coolidge's Vice-President. I had interviewed the General at lunch, and when the General reached for the check I said, "No, sir—you can't buy me with the blue-plate special." I hadn't said a word about the time the General and Blond Billy Lorimer shuttled the assets between their banks to fox the inspectors, but the General took umbrage anyway.

Still and all, I was once a Hearst man, and I think I may say that all that I am today I owe to William Randolph Hearst, Sr.

The Hearst papers were the stuff that nightmares were made on. You couldn't even believe the weather report. But we were all getting rich, from the Chief at the top to me at the bottom, and that was all any of us cared about.

Then the bottom, with me on it, dropped out. The store replevined the electric toaster I was buying on the installment plan. The Chief had been buying up continents. The store moved in on him, and the Hearst empire wound up a baker's half-dozen of rags.

But the mere passing of the Chief, fifteen years ago this date, raised the level of American journalism. You are hard put today to think of a newspaper as bad as Hearst's were. But under Young Bill, now Old Bill, you sometimes catch a clumsy glimpse of the days of unblessed memory.

Reprinted from the *Progressive*, October 1966.

While Young Bill, now Old Bill, choked and welled the other day, his *San Francisco Examiner* ran a four-column thirty-six-point headline: "UC PROF DODGES SUBPOENA, SKIPS U.S. FOR MOSCOW," with a three-line subhead: "Stephen Smale, Supporter of VDC-FSM." In three one-sentence paragraphs, Ed Montgomery, *Examiner* Staff Writer, told the story:

Dr. Stephen Smale, University of California professor and backer of the Vietnam Day Committee and the old Free Speech Movement, is either on his way or is in Moscow, the *Examiner* learned today.

In leaving the country, he has dodged a subpoena directing him to appear before the House Committee on Un-American Activities in Washington.

One of a number of subpoenaed Berkeley anti-war activists, Dr. Smale took a leave of absence from UC and leased his home there before his trip abroad.

The next day, under a two-column, eighteen-point headline, "MOSCOW-BOUND UC PROF NOT AVOIDING SUBPOENA," without a by-line, the *Examiner* reported that Dr. Smale had gone to Moscow to receive the Field Medal at the International Congress of Mathematicians, and that his UC leave had been granted last January. The story ended, "A headline in yesterday's *Examiner* about Dr. Smale and the House Un-American Activities Committee was open to an incorrect inference that he had gone to Moscow to avoid the subpoena issued by the Committee."

It was fifteen years ago this date that Pop left us. But he didn't leave us empty-handed. He left us Young Bill. And Ed Montgomery, *Examiner* Staff Writer. Young Bill and I have never met, but I know Ed Montgomery like the back of my own hand. Yea, knowing the back of my own hand, I know him.

Jeb Magruder

Before the Watergate testimony of Jeb Magruder is forgotten, Friends may want to ponder the young man's justification of the Nixon campaign criminality by the antiwar criminality of William Sloane Coffin—and William Coffin's rejoinder.

None of the seven senators who heard Jeb Magruder's testimony thought to ask him if he really thought he could equate civil disobedience with the behavior of burglars, perjurers, and conspirators to obstruct justice. If, as William Coffin said, his former ethics student appears to have failed the ethics course, the seven senators may be said to have failed the logic course.

But William Coffin says further that the student's failure was the teacher's: "As his ethics teacher, I wish now I had stressed the errors and illusions that stem from the fear of being a loser. . . . I wish I had pointed out the paradox of winners being losers. . . . I wish I had stressed the importance of solitude. I wish I had emphasized that it is the individual consciences of history which, as opposed to the mass mind, best represent the universal conscience of mankind. . . . Maybe these emphases would have helped Jeb to develop individual convictions."

William Coffin fails the pedagogy course.

Like so many others at the national wailing wall these days he blames the schoolboy's derelictions on the schooling. But Jeb Magruder had the best schooling that money can buy and, in William Coffin, the best teacher that a schoolboy can have. The teacher fails the pedagogy course because he thinks that schooling can do what it can't.

He might have passed the course had he remembered Plato's dictum that the city educates the man—the city, not the schoolhouse. He fails it because he confused the intellectual with the moral and theological virtues—a confusion the late Cardinal Barberini pointed out to Galileo: "It is your business to show men how the heavens go, ours to show them how to go to heaven."

The cardinal was wrong, too. In a sense unavailable to mere teachers, cardinals can "show" men the way to heaven, but they can not

Reprinted from *Friends Journal*, 1 September 1973.

make them take it. The rich young ruler turned sorrowfully away when, in answer to his question, Christ told him to sell what he had and give it to the poor and take up his cross. It takes more than a cardinal or a Christ—and how much more than a teacher—to "show" a man.

As a teacher "of" ethics, William Coffin could, and doubtless did, teach his student everything that can be taught about right and wrong. What he couldn't do—and what he mistakenly thinks he could have done, had he been a better teacher—was to teach his student to do the right and eschew the wrong. To know is not to do; there is no evidence that it even conduces to doing. All that the teacher of ethics can do is teach *about* ethics—and luxuriate in the undemonstrated and indemonstrable hypothesis that the student will be moved to learn for himself what can not be taught by somebody else.

The city educates the man. Jeb Magruder did not, and could not, get his ethical education from William Sloane Coffin. Like the rest of us, he brought some of it to college with him and got some of it in the course of his extracurricular hours. The only thing that distinguishes him from the rest of us was his opportunity to do his graduate work at the White House.

Down to Terre Haute

Went down to Terre Haute the other day to see Gene Debs. It was his hundredth birthday and I figured there'd be quite a turnout. But the street was quiet and the home place was quiet —needed a coat of paint bad, but, then, it always did—and Gene was sitting in his rocker on the porch. The day was unseasonably warm and sunny, but the old fellow was bundled up pretty tight. Not much flesh and blood on him, but come to think of it, there never was.

Doesn't smoke any more, but he still chews that long cheroot, and he hasn't a tooth in his head. Never took care of his teeth. Still wearing his silver-rimmed specs, and his eyes are as bright as ever, but I don't believe he sees very much any more, or maybe he doesn't try. I guess when you get to be a hundred, things are a lot of work.

Otherwise he hadn't changed, hardly, but those long bony fellows never do. He was pretty bent, but he was that as far back as I could remember him. He tried to get up, and I took his hand and pushed him back. His first words, then, were "Who d'you think you are, son, George M. Pullman?" Frisky old dog. "Nope," I said, "Justice Oliver Wendell Holmes." He grinned up at me wickedly. "You know," he said, "I'd forgotten all about the 'great dissenter.' Didn't dissent about me, though," and he cackled and went on. "Yes, sir, I was a clear and present danger. Obstructing the war. Never did get it obstructed, though," and he cackled again. "That's what I should've told 'em in Cleveland. 'Gentlemen, you have convicted me of obstructing the war. That's what I was trying to do, but I didn't know I had succeeded.' " We both cackled, and then I sat down.

I handed him a box of cheroots and said, "Happy birthday, Gene." "Happy birthday?" he said, "Why, I'd clean forgotten this was the day. I shouldn't have, either. I've been hearing from a lot of people."

"Socialists?" I said.

"Yep, socialists," he said. "Asian and African socialists."

"And American?" I said.

Gene seemed to peer at me the way a foreigner does who isn't sure he understands you. Then he said, "Are there any American socialists?"

Reprinted from the *Progressive*, November 1955.

"Lots," I said. "Young people"—"I reckon they think I'm dead," said Gene, "it's been so long since they've heard a peep out of me" —"and," I went on, "a few old socialists, too." "'Old socialists,'" said Gene, with some spirit, "that's what I'd like to see, *old* socialists. Seems to be easy when you're young; natural, like. Harder when you're old and dreaming of death instead of life."

"Gene," I said, "what happened to socialism in America?"

He sighed a long sigh and said, "Well, the old socialists died, the old Germans and Irish and Swedes—."

"And new ones were born," I said.

"No," said Gene. "that's where you're wrong. Socialists stopped being born and that's what happened to socialism. Socialists are born, not made, and when Socialists stopped being born, there were no more socialists."

"There's one," I said.

"More than one," said Gene.

" 'There are today,' " I said, ' "upwards of sixty million socialists, loyal, devoted adherents to this cause, regardless of nationality, race, creed, color, or sex. They are waiting, watching, working through all the weary hours of the day and night. They feel—they know, indeed —that the time is coming—.' "

I stopped. His head was bent, and a tear had fallen on his hand in his lap. "I'm sorry," I said.

"Oh," he said, looking up and blinking and forcing a smile, "that's all right. I'm just thinking of the day I said those words."

"There were twelve in the crowd," I said, "and there wasn't a socialist among them." Gene cackled, softly. "Twelve honest American farmers," he said, "good men, good men. I watched them while they were being impaneled. Good men, good men. But they could no more help convicting me than I could help 'obstructing' the war."

"Were Wilson and Holmes good men, too?" I said.

"History says so," said Gene, closing his eyes, "and I guess I agree with history. I scared 'em, I guess. They didn't believe in revolution. I do." I noticed the difference of tenses.

"Still?" I said.

"Still," said Gene. "After Russia and Italy and Germany, I still believe in revolution. While you're quoting what I said in court, you ought to remember what I said in Canton three months before. I said, 'The I.W.W. in its career has never committed as much violence against the ruling class as the ruling class has committed against the people.' That's the statement that the District Attorney told the Attorney General was 'the kind of criticism of the government of the United States which I believe Congress intended to forbid by its enactment

of the Espionage Act.' That's what they really indicted me on—
though they never said so in court—and that's what really convicted
me.''

"Why that," I said, "when you said in court, 'I have been accused
of having obstructed the war. I admit it. Gentlemen, I abhor war. I
would oppose the war if I stood alone.' That, my friend, is what I
should suppose convicted you. It was wartime, and you stood in a
United States courtroom and said, 'war is the trade of savages and
barbarians.' Isn't that what convicted you?''

"No," said Gene, "I think not. I think that every man in that courtroom, including the prosecutor, the judge, and the jury, agreed with
me. They wouldn't say it themselves, of course, but they wouldn't
convict another man for saying what they all knew was true, and
what every man knows is true. No, it was what I said in praise of the
Bolsheviki—even though I added that they might fail in the end—and
the I.W.W. It wasn't war or peace that worried them, it was revolution.
And it wasn't their lives that they thought they might lose, but their
money that they knew they would lose. The I.W.W. was as red a flag
in 1918 as Communism is in 1955—and, in America, as much of a
straw man.''

"So you're not an anti-Communist, even now?" I said.

"Even now," said Gene. "I leave anti-Communism to my successors
in the 'Socialist movement,' formerly the Socialist Party. Anti-Communism means exactly what anti-I.W.W.-ism meant. It means an excuse
for conscripting half the world's workers to kill the other half. I
know you've got to be anti-Communist to be effective in politics,
but I'm not a politician and the Socialist Party wasn't a political
party back in those days.''

"You did pretty well in the 1920 campaign," I said. "You got a
million votes"—"Nine hundred fifteen thousand, three hundred and
two, to be exact," said Gene, smiling—"and that's an awful lot more
than any of your 'effective' predecessors or successors ever got.''

"That," added Gene, and his wrinkled old eyes were flashing behind his specs, "was because we stood somewhere.''

"You stood in Atlanta Penitentiary," I said.

"That helped, too," said Gene. "The fact that I was in prison when
even the *New York Times*—even A. Mitchell Palmer—decided I wasn't
a criminal meant that we stood somewhere. We weren't 'constructive
critics.' We weren't popular-fronters, recruiting young idealists for the
wars of the New Freedom or the New Deal or the New Look. We said
'No'—in those days—and a million people wanted somebody to say
'No.' A hundred million, maybe, but only a million were up to going
all the way.''

"Times have changed," I said.

"Yes," said Gene.

"What changed them?" I said.

"The Russian revolution," said Gene. "It doesn't matter how it came out; what matters is that it happened. It proved that the revolution *could* happen. It was the death-knell of capitalism. In its death-throes capitalism will electrocute anybody who gives away the secret of the atomic bomb, because the atomic bomb is (or was) the only secret capitalism has left. Now the revolution is everywhere; misguided, perverted, yes, but everywhere, and you're either a revolutionary, whether or not you know it, or a counterrevolutionary, and the counterrevolutionaries include all—well, almost all—the 'socialists' and all of the 'former socialists.' They're the best advertisement the counterrevolution has,"

"And the pacifists?" I said.

"I don't know," said Gene, and he seemed to be thinking hard. Leastwise all the heat went out of his voice all at once, and when the heat goes out of Gene Debs' voice, even on his hundredth birthday, you know he's thinking hard. "I don't know," he repeated.

"But you're a pacifist," I said. "Always were."

"I don't know," said Gene. "You know," he raised his head, "I'm darned if I'm *good* enough to be a pacifist."

"Neither am I," I said.

"But you are one," said Gene.

"I didn't say I wasn't one," I said, "only that I'm darned if I'm *good* enough to be one."

Gene really laughed hearty at that one. "I guess," he said, "that that's about the size of it, as far as I'm concerned. Whatever they did to me, they couldn't make me mad. So they thought I was a pacifist. But, comrade, when I saw what they were doing to other people, the state militia murdering women and children in the Colorado mines —I remember saying, that time, that 'every district of the miners' union should purchase and equip and man enough Gatling and machine guns to match the equipment of Rockefeller's private army of assassins.' You wouldn't call that pacifism, would you?" And all the dried-prune wrinkles of his face grinned at once.

"Sometimes," said Gene, taking the cheroot out of his mouth, and turning it around in his fingers, as he always did, "I wish I'd had a chance to get an education. There are things I don't understand. I don't understand about God and immortality. Always believed in 'em. Still do," and he cackled again and said, "I still believe in everything I always believed in. There's a fool for you, comrade."

"You mean," I said, "that you 'stood somewhere.' "

He looked at me quizzically. "Yep," he said, "I guess that's it, all right. I'm a standpatter. Some of these other fellows, they learn something new and they switch around. They don't hardly any of them say what they said twenty, thirty years ago. Most of 'em say the opposite, when you boil 'em down. They must have learned a lot. I never had time to. Work, work, work. And now I'm too old to learn."

"You always were," I said.

"What's that?" said Gene, pretending that he hadn't heard me.

" 'Socialists are born, not made,' " I said.

Gene cackled, very softly. Then he turned his long skull up to the sun, and the sun flashed on his specs and glittered on that great bald dome. His eyes closed, and he began to breathe heavily. His mouth opened, and I got quietly up and took the half-chewed cheroot out of his mouth and put it into the battered old one-cigar case that lay on the floor beside him. I stood there a while. He was sleeping. A flight of jet planes went screaming by. He didn't wake up, but I thought he smiled a little. But it's hard to tell when a very old man is smiling.

I tiptoed down the stairs. They creaked, but Gene slept on. I started down the street, and, to my surprise, I found myself whistling "The St. James Infirmary." I stopped, and wondered why, of all things, "The St. James Infirmary." And then I started whistling it again and let the words go through my head as I whistled. When I got to the last two lines, I knew why:

Put a twenty-dollar gold-piece on my watch-chain
So the boys will know I died standing pat.

Then I stopped and said out loud:

While there is a lower class, I am it;
while there is a criminal element, I am of it;
while there is a soul in prison, I am not free.

Then I cackled and said, "That must have gone over big with those twelve farmers."

Then I said out loud:

I have no country to fight for; my country is the earth, and
I am a citizen of the world.

And I said, "Holmes delivered the unanimous opinion of the Court and said, 'We are of the opinion that the verdict on the fourth count, for obstructing and attempting to obstruct the recruiting service of the United States, must be sustained.' Wilson said, 'I will never consent to the pardon of this man. This man was a traitor to his country.' Harding ordered him—still a prisoner—to come to the White House from Atlanta, alone, and the warden drove him to the train in his car and Gene got on the train and went into the diner and ordered fried chicken. And Harding held out his hand and said, 'Mr. Debs . . . ' and released him from prison. But he never was pardoned and he never had his citizenship restored, and now he's a hundred years old."

Then I went on down the street and met James Whitcomb Riley. "Where you been?" said Riley. "Down to see Gene Debs," I said. "Where *you* been?" "Up to see God," said Riley, "and we was reminiscing, and I asked Him how He come to make Gene Debs, and He says, 'Let Me see, that was just a hundred years ago today. I remember I was feeling mighty good, and I didn't have anything else to do all day.' "

Massa's in de Groun'

Death must have been a terrible blow to Colonel McCormick. He had seen men die, and he knew that death cuts men down to a handful of dust. He could not have believed that death, which took dispensable men every day, would take him too, or would even try. For he was indispensable. Without him the Republic would be lost, and God would not allow the Republic to be lost.

But God understood the Republic better than Colonel McCormick did. What the Colonel did not understand is that God invented the Republic precisely to keep men like McCormick, indispensable men, from living forever. The Colonel was an absolute ruler; it took an absolutely absolute Ruler to cut him down to size.

I suppose the Colonel was one of the strongest men of our pusillanimous age. This is not to say that he was a good man. I think he wasn't. I'm pretty sure he wasn't. But I don't know. I know that he did great evil. The picture he ran in the *Chicago Tribune* of the "dog tag" which every American would have to wear under social security —that was great evil. And it was small compared with a thousand or ten thousand other evils he did. But I don't know that he was evil, or good. I just know what he did.

Why should we speak only good of the dead? I can see why we should speak only good of all men, lest in judging, we be judged. But the evil that men do lives after them. And so, while the elegies still perfume the air, I speak of the evil of Colonel McCormick, lest my countrymen mistake elegy for truth and, as a consequence, evil for good.

The elegies, which the Colonel's staff drummed up to fill the *Tribune* after his death, were of three kinds. The first went down the line; these were McCarthy's, Jenner's, Dirksen's, et al. The second, like Eisenhower's, pleaded *nolo contendere* and spoke of the freedom of the press and the like. The third, mostly from European papers , took the line that whether the Colonel was right or wrong, you had to admit that he stood firm and fearless for what he thought right.

But what if what he thought right was wrong? If that were the

Reprinted from the *Progressive*, May 1955.

case—and I think it was—it would have been better if he had stood
infirm and fearful. If a man is a fighting fool, the fact that he is a fool
is important, too.

The Colonel was a fighting fool. He fought—and successfully—the
establishment of a graduated income tax as the basis of Illinois taxation in the Twentieth Century and said that it meant "tampering
with the State Constitution." (The last time the revenue section of
the State Constitution was tampered with was in 1837.) He fought
WPA leaf-raking because he believed that men who couldn't find
work should not eat, and he is quoted, and I think correctly, as saying
when he looked down from his Tribune Tower office at an unemployment march, "They ought to be shot." He fought—and won—the
exposure of the true story of the killing of his gangster crime reporter, Jake Lingle, and, having placed the *Tribune's* own lawyer in the
State's Attorney's office, framed a St. Louis pistol, or professional
murderer, to take an easy rap and bury the truth forever. Even the
Tribune never called this pistol anything worse than a "hired killer,"
and the Colonel was able to suppress the question, "Who hired the
hired killer?"

That was the Colonel, a strong, wrong man. Don't say that it's easy
to be strong when you have a couple of hundred million dollars in
your gloves, because history is against you there. Princes are as likely
to be weak as paupers. The Colonel was strong, and his strength was
in him, not in his roll. He was a fighting fool. But what made the
Colonel fight?

I think it's a pattern. The Colonel was the grandson of strong men
—McCormick, the harvester man, and Medill, the publisher man—and
the son of weak men. His father and mother were weak because *their*
fathers were just too strong. Their weakness was their rebellion, as
the Colonel's strength was his. And it seems to me that this genealogy
is common in the descendants of great men, and maybe that's what
made the Colonel fight all the time. He had to be strong. He didn't
have the guts to be weak.

In his strength and his folly he did good things as well as evil.
Always standing alone—because he could not bear company—he destroyed Mayor Big Bill Thompson and Governor Len Small, who were
eating up Chicago and Illinois respectively. The fact that they were
Republicans and so was he meant nothing to the Colonel. Standing
alone as Freedom of the Press incarnate, he beat the Minnesota "gag
law" in the Supreme Court and saved the principle of press freedom,
even though his own paper was, and continued to be, the unfreest in
America. For bad reasons—because he hated foreigners and Roosevelt,

in reverse order—he tried to keep his country out of war in 1917 and in 1941. Standing far from alone, but always out in front of the pack, he fought Franklin Roosevelt, and no American President, good or bad, ever needed fighting as badly as the Court-packing reformer.

It wasn't a couple of hundred million dollars that enabled the Colonel to stand alone—but a couple of hundred million, when you're in the mood to stand, comes in handy. It's easier for a publisher to take a tough line with a politician than to take a tough line with an advertiser. Few—almost none—ever do. What the editor of a country weekly thinks of the gas company doesn't matter; what matters is the weekly ad from the gas company, because without it he'd have no country weekly. City dailies are just about the same—except the *Tribune*.

Now that the Colonel's gone, the *Tribune* will be a little rounder of heel. This, too, is the fault of the fighting fool, because the people he hired were weak and he hired them because they were weak. Like every satrap, he didn't want his satrapy to be a debating society, and it wasn't. The *Tribune*—and maybe America—will not see the Colonel's likes again when it comes to fighting the advertisers, and, believe me, friend, advertiser control is no better than the independent fighting fool's.

Dear to my heart, and to every other reporter's who was ever told by the city editor that falling elevators aren't news, is the night, maybe fifteen, twenty years ago, when the advertising manager of the *Tribune*'s biggest department-store account called up the paper to speak of a story already on the street in the bulldog edition. The story was about the divorce of the owner of the store, and the advertising manager of the store just wondered, timidly, if the *Tribune* would tone it down a little in the later editions. Not kill it, mind you; just tone it down.

Now on this sort of deal the Colonel, by his own edict, had to be called in his fortress in Wheaton, whatever the hour. When he was given the pitch, he said, "Keep the story and throw out their advertising." When he was told that the paper would have to be torn up to do that, he said, "Tear it up." When he was told that the store had an advertising contract with the *Tribune*, he said, "Tear up the contract." And that's what happened. And a week later the department store came to the *Tribune* on its hands and knees to plead to be let back in. The country weekly can't do that, and neither, because their owners are not fighting fools, can the rest of the city dailies.

My old man, who believed in the *Tribune*, used to say, when I was a boy, that the Colonel was independent as a hog on ice, and I used to say, "But who wants to be a hog, Pop?" My old man thought I was crazy, but I wasn't. Who wants to be a hog?

The Colonel was sincere. But who isn't? He sincerely pursued
ignoble ends which to him, in his ignorance, appeared so noble that
they ennobled the use of the most ignoble means. He believed, in
his ignorance, and in his blasphemy, that he was ordained by God to
save the Republic from the Reds and the lunatics.

In the pursuit of the end ordained him he dedicated himself self-
lessly to the destruction of any institution, including the independent
universities and the foundations, and of any man, including any
scholar or statesman, who saw anything less than consummate evil
in social reform. It was under his short-lived aegis as owner that the
Washington Times-Herald gang faked the picture of Senator Tydings
and Earl Browder—and that was peanuts when it came to the Colonel's
fakes. I once found one hundred misstatements of fact in *one* front-
page story in the *Tribune*. I took a few months off to make sure that
they were misstatements of fact and, sure enough, they were.

I am sure that the Colonel was sincere, but who would want to be
the Colonel? As election day, November 2, approached in 1940, the
Tribune cried out, each day, "Only ten days"—nine days, eight days—
"left to save the Republic." He was sincere, but, as Roosevelt might
have said, look who's loony. The afternoon of election day the
Chicago Sun-Times ran the most inspired front-page streamer in
history: "Only 52 Days Left Until Xmas." Who would want to be
Colonel McCormick?

"Is the great king happy?" says Aristotle. Aristotle thinks not. Was
the great satrap happy? I think not. As far as I was ever able to learn,
he had no friends. Not one. They say he wanted none, but, if that is
so, who wants to be Colonel McCormick? He had sycophants. One of
them was Sanitary Ed Kelly, the corruptionist who succeeded Big
Bill Thompson and Ten Percent Tony Cermak as presiding officer at
the altar on which my city, Chicago, was sacrificed for a hundred
years. The Colonel had, in his youth, been president of the Chicago
Sanitary District, where he was honest, of course, and ignorant. He
had picked up a lad there, Ed Kelly, and pushed him along, and Ed
had flattered the Colonel, who would one day run the *Tribune*. When
Ed, who didn't know a drainage ditch from a hole in the ground,
became chief engineer of the Sanitary District, he borrowed enough
of the public's money to build a great cinder road leading nowhere
and called it McCormick Road.

McCormick Road—that poor, stolen accolade was all it took to
buy up the Colonel for life. Sanitary Ed became the boss of the corrupt New Deal machine in Chicago, and the Colonel hated the devil

less than he hated the New Deal. But Ed Kelly never came into the Colonel's line of fire. When Ed was revealed, by the Bureau of Internal Revenue, as having saved so much on a city salary that he owed $400,000 taxes on three years' income, the *Tribune* went down the line for Ed. You will say that it couldn't be done. But the Colonel did it.

The sycophants delivered the paper he wanted, every day, magnificently edited and printed, if you attach no morality to magnificence; the most readable newspaper in America, if you attach no morality to readability. And the Colonel took care of them with the world's highest pension system, with bonuses distributed from the satrap's Christmas largess, with wedding presents for their wives and weeds for their widows. He took care of them in such splendor that men whose wives needed wedding presents, or whose widows needed weeds, quit respectable papers to work for the *Tribune*. One of these men, who has risen from rags to a country estate, put it more or less succinctly when he said, in private: "Morality comes too high, what the hell."

In private, yes, but in public the sycophants knew they must never tell the emperor, when he asked them how they liked his new clothes, that he was naked. Once the Colonel got mad at Rhode Island and had one star taken out of the *Tribune*'s American flag. I'm not kidding. Somebody—I think it was the building manager—didn't know who had taken the star out and he rushed up to the roof and had it restored. That finished the building manager. When the Colonel wanted Rhode Island out of the Union, out it went. And nobody told the emperor that he was naked.

The *Tribune*'s own story of his funeral lists the following persons— and no others—who were present when the body of Colonel McCormick was taken from the library of his Wheaton fortress for military burial in the fortress grounds which, the Colonel's will provided, would forever after be maintained as a shrine with a $1,000,000 endowment:

> His batman from the Mexican war, as old as he but burying him. Soldiers who had served under him in 1918 in the 1st Division, so dear to his heart. The gardener who so long ago had selected with him the honeysuckle, lilacs, and Norway maples which now encircled his burial place.
>
> His Japanese valet, the weeping maids from his household staff, his pilots, the chauffeur who knew him so well. The executives of the far-flung publishing empire he had established.
>
> All stood quiet on the terraced slopes . . .

They had all stood quiet all their lives while he took them down the richly terraced slopes of public betrayal. They had all worked under him. They were his friends. I have never heard that he had another.

"Colonel McCormick," said Senator Joe McCarthy in his elegy, "will emerge as one of the great figures of the age. His enemies were the enemies of America; his supporters were those who want to keep America great and free. There is none to replace this brave soldier and great patriot." Aren't you glad? I am.

I am not glad that he is dead. I am not glad that any man is dead. I am glad he died peacefully. I wish all men would die peacefully. I thank God for whatever happiness the Colonel had in his lifetime. I thank God for whatever happiness there is. But I would not like to be, or to have been, the Colonel. "I dread to think," said Senator Jenner, who dreads to think, "what might have been the fate of our country in the post-Yalta era of co-existence, if the courageous voice of Colonel McCormick had not been lifted." But the Colonel himself could not co-exist; how could he suppose the country could? His Republic was himself.

His city was himself. But his paper was published in my city, and, along with Big Bill Thompson it was, I think, the worst thing that ever happened to Chicago; maybe worse than Big Bill, for Big Bill was accountable to an electorate, even to an electorate debased by a newspaper, while the Colonel, with his absolutely free and absolutely irresponsible press, was accountable only to God. A rich, independent newspaper can make or break a city; the *Tribune*, which exposed the Colonel's enemies and covered up for the city's, did more than Al Capone to break Chicago.

The Colonel died with one of his realities imperiled. In recent years, and especially since the *Tribune* has attacked Eisenhower as a dangerous radical, the *Tribune* has been slipping, and its slip is showing in its circulation, down from its New Deal peak of more than a million to its present 850,000. That's still the biggest standard-sized circulation in America, just as the *New York Daily News* (which the Colonel owned) has the biggest any-sized circulation in America. But there is something sick at the *Tribune*, and the Colonel knew it. And he knew —I imagine—that the sycophants to whom the princeless emperor left the management of the empire will go on being sycophants without the satrap's magic touch. He knew—I imagine—that unless the paper changes it will weaken, and he dreaded either prospect.

The Colonel is gone to his fathers (to his grandfathers, rather), and I wish him well there. But when you consider the unfortunate environment in which four million Chicagoans grew (an environment which the *Chicago Tribune* in part created), you will wish them well right here.

Sitting Shivah at Lutece

I'm in great shape," I said. "Absolutely," said my friend, R.C. McNamara, Jr., "only don't shake your head; it might fall off." I was observing my fifty-ninth birthday by burying my oldest friend, John Patrick Howe, sixty-two.

1. *Death is the opposite of the weather: Everybody does something about it, but nobody talks about it.*

2. *At the services I commended John Patrick Howe to the Lord (as I had so often commended the Lord to him).*

As the barely survivors left the church, I fell in with Bill Benton. He used to be William Burnett Benton, just as I used to be Milton Sanford Mayer. When he changed his name to William B. Benton, I changed mine to Milton S. Mayer, and when he changed his name to William Benton I changed mine to Milton Mayer.

"Consider," said Bill, "how often a man signs his name in this life and how much time you'll save." I asked him what I would do with the time I'd save. He said I would live and learn.

I can't say that I lived any better or learned any more than if I'd stayed just plain Milton Sanford Mayer. Whan I began changing my name I was shooting my frayed cuffs in the *Progressive*, and I still am, while Bill has accumulated a string of corporations, colleges, and orphan asylums.

3. *It would seem that you have to do more than change your name to make it.*

I asked Bill how he was.

"I'm in great shape," he said. I said, "Absolutely."

He thought we ought to commemorate John Patrick Howe by having dinner together. We ate at a beanery called Lutece. It was OK. After dinner Bill said we had just eaten at the most expensive restaurant in New York. I shook my head. It fell off.

The evening passed in recollection of John Patrick Howe, resting now (as when hadn't he?) in peace. With a bit of keening it might have been a wake, or, with a bit of wailing, what the Jews call sitting *shivah*. I recalled a song that John Patrick Howe and I used to sing in the days when death was something that happened to other people:

Reprinted from the *Progressive*, November 1967.

Oh, the night that Paddy Murphy died
   I never shall forget.
The whole damn bunch got
Stinking drunk
   And some ain't sober yet.
But there's one thing that occurred that night
   That filled my heart with fear:
They took the ice right off the corpse
   And put it on the beer.

(Chorus)

That's how they showed their respect for Paddy Murphy,
   That's how they showed
   Their respect when Paddy died.
That's how they showed their respect for Paddy Murphy,
   That's how they showed their honor
     And their Irish pride.

Bill and I recalled the blowing away of our friends as the leaves
blow away (more each day) in November. He recalled Adlai Stevenson
and "Harry" Luce. We both recalled Carl Sandburg. When we parted,
in the lobby of the Waldorf, which was like a tomb, our eyes were
filled with Lutece's champagne.

I hurried to the opposite coast to see who had been blown off the
Western Slope recently. Bob Hutchins was hanging on—as usual, without trying—at sixty-eight. "What is it like, O Cephalus," I said, "to
be old?" "The same," he said, "as it is to be young: not good." "And
what is the object of life?" I said. "To live through it," he said.

I observed that he was careful not to shake his head.

The Western Slope, or End of the Trail, is full of Convalescent
Homes, where the young have stashed the old to get them out of
sight, out of mind. All my old friends were in them, convalescing
from life. The cells are all sanitary and sunny. All any of these solitar-
ies wanted was to die among their loved ones at home. Where's home?

I concluded the celebration of my fifty-ninth birthday by medi-
tating the mutability of human affairs, and I remembered my arrival
at the home of John Patrick Howe on his sixtieth birthday. "Made it,"
he said when he greeted me.

Where did the time go that I saved by changing my name from
Milton Sanford to Milton S. and then to Milton? How did I improve
each shining hour? How much better is the crowd for my having
swelled it?

For all the good I've done myself or anyone else, I might as well have lived decently and died with a decent prospect.

4. *Gabriel gives Green Stamps too.*

Byanby

George Bye died last month, and I may die next month, so I'd better tell you about him this month.

George was a literary representative, or, as they call themselves when they can afford to say it straight, a writer's agent. George could afford to say it straight; he was the biggest man in the business. His clients included, over the last twenty, thirty years, Pershing, Lindbergh, Mrs. Roosevelt, Al Smith, and (this will kill you, as it almost killed George) M. Mayer.

First I will tell you how I happened to be George's client, and then I will tell you how it almost killed him.

In, maybe, 1939, young Bill Benton, who had made a million in the advertising business, got tired of the advertising business and told his old Yale classmate Bob Hutchins about it. Bob told Bill—as he told everybody—that Bill's trouble was that he had gone to Yale and was therefore uneducated. "I will pay you to get an education," said Bob to Bill, and he hired him as vice president of the University of Chicago.

A couple of years before, Bob had hired me away from Hearst's *Chicago American*.

"How much are getting at the *American*?" he said.

"Ninety."

"*Dollars?*"

"A week, and a hundred if I stay. And Mr. McCarthy says I'll be another Pegler."

"Who the hell is Mr. McCarthy?"

"The boss of the *American*."

"Well, I'm the boss of the University of Chicago, which is bigger and richer than the *American* and will soon be better, and I'll give you forty—"

"Dollars?"

"—a week, and forty if you stay. And you'll be another Homer."

"Homer who?" I said.

"Young man," said Hutchins, "your trouble—or, at least, the only trouble you have that I can cure—is that you are ignorant. I have never before encountered such ignorance except at Yale University,

Reprinted from the *Progressive*, February 1958.

and only among the faculty there. I can make you intelligent by paying you to read the Great Books. That is what I am paying myself to do. But you would have to be intelligent already, like me, to want to read them even for pay. You are a desperate case, but a red-hot brand from the burning. Forty a week."

"Make it forty-five," I said. "I have a wife and child."

"I have a wife and two children," said Bob, "and their tastes are a hundred times more expensive than yours and I am not paying myself a hundred times as much as I am offering you. Forty. And," he went on, "with every probability of a wage cut. When we cut wages around here, we cut administrative wages. We can not cut faculty wages because the faculty loves money. The administrators are idealists. You will be an administrator."

"But," I said, "forty dollars a week isn't enough to live on. A man has to live."

"Not necessarily," said Bob. "But only consider the perquisites. You will get ideas for magazine articles from the Great Books, and because no editor has ever read a Great Book the editors will think your ideas are original and will buy your articles.

"I will not try," he went on, "to persuade you of the worth of intelligence *in se*, because you are too ignorant to apprehend it. But you will be able to use expressions like *in se*, which my associate, Mr. Mortimer Adler, taught me." He kicked my feet off the desk. "Forty a week," he said. "Think it over. You have only the chains of ignorance to lose, and a world of goodies to win. Stick with me, kid, and you'll have money, fame, and power. What else is there? Don't be a chump."

My duties were to read the Great Books and assist Mr. John P. Howe. Mr. Howe's duty was to assist Mr. William V. Morgenstern. Mr. Morgenstern's duty (until Bill Benton arrived) was to keep the public from knowing that the university was there. Mr. Morgenstern, the public relations director, was under the illusion that a university was an institution of learning. He had put Zone of Quiet signs all around the place.

Bill took one look at the tennis courts and said, "This is a greater university than Harvard, and nobody has heard of it." Bob had told him always to say, "Greater than Harvard," never "Greater than Yale."

Bill also noticed that the university had been turned upside down, and when he asked who had done it everyone gnashed his teeth and said, "Hutchins." Bill decided that Bob should tell the world, in a *Saturday Evening Post* series, how he did it. This would put the university on the map, and, since the university needed money, Bill thought that there should be something on the map that the donors could point to.

So Bill took the train—I mean the Century—to New York and made a memorandum, en route, to have the physics department figure out a faster way to get to New York, maybe by rocket and call it *Sputnik*. In New York he asked who the three biggest agents were. He was told (if I remember rightly) that they were Brandt, Ober, and Bye. He asked which was the biggest of these, and he was told Bye.

So he went to George T. Bye & Company, at 535 Fifth Avenue, and walked into an unattended little anteroom with cracked and bleeding imitation leather upholstery. Off the anteroom opened two cubicles. One was empty. The other contained Mr. Jasper Spock, in a green eye-shade and a pair of black satin sleeves from his elbows to his wrists. "Who are you?" said Bill.

"I am & Company," said Jasper, who was.

"Where is Mr. Bye?" said Bill.

"He sometimes comes in on Wednesdays," said Jasper.

Bill turned to leave. On his way out he tripped in a hole in the rug and, as he picked himself up, saw the pictures of Lindbergh, Pershing, Roosevelt, Smith, et al., on the wall. They were all autographed the same way: "Baby, I love you."

"Who's baby?" said Bill.

"Mr. Bye," said Jasper.

George, when Bill found him, was, and remained, a small rosy man with a mustache. He looked like Santa Claus. He was Santa Claus. "Mr. Hutchins does not want money for these articles," said Bill, primly.

"I can not violate the canons of my art," said George, just as prim-ly. "We will charge the *Post* a few thousand dollars for these articles."

"Mr. Hutchins will just turn it over to the university," said Bill, "where it will be wasted."

"Not all of it," said George, "only 90 percent."

Bob then met George, and they adored each other. They were both zanies in sordid jobs that required straight faces. Bob said that there was only one hitch: "If you take me, you have to take my dog."

"Can he talk?" said George.

"He can't keep quiet," said Bob.

"What's his name?" said George.

"Mayer," said Bob.

"Can he write?" asked George.

"He can't even read," said Bob.

That is how the name of Mayer was added to that of Lindbergh, Roosevelt, Pershing, Smith, et al.

Within a couple of years I was rich. If I wrote anything down—a grocery list, for instance—I had to be careful to destroy it or it might fall into George's hands and appear in a magazine. The money was, while it and I lasted, astounding; usually fifteen hundred a crack. To-day, with inflation, that would be worth three thousand; in those days, without inflation, it was worth ten thousand.

Of course I paid a price, besides George's 10 percent. I had sold myself for money, and with money I got intergrity, popularity, and peace of mind. But I never got to read a Great Book, although I memorized all the titles and condensed a few of the books for, of course, the *Reader's Digest*. Bob and Bill were so disappointed in me that they both quit academic life and entered monasteries, the one in New York, the other in Washington.

I was a ruddy imitation of Bob, and that was enough for George. George was a lover of wild men, and that was enough for me. His clients included Westbrook Pegler, known to those who admired him as Old Beady-Eye; Heywood Broun, known to those who admired him as Old Red-Eye; and Alec Woollcott, known to those he admired. Pegler hated Broun, Broun despised Pegler, and Woollcott regretted both of them. George organized a softball team around New Canaan, Conn., where they all lived, with both Broun and Pegler on it. The team was called the Nine Old Men. Woollcott was umpire.

George's house at New Canaan was called Ten-Per-Cent Hollow. George's middle name was Thurman, but everybody assumed it was Ten-Per-Cent. George was as antipretentious as his office indicated, and, with no trouble at all, he was rich. He brought a modest lunch and a modest drink. He didn't have to entertain his clients; he let the publishers do that. He didn't have to entertain the editors; he let the publishers do that. It was impossible to say when George retired from business—there were so many Wednesdays when he didn't come in anyway—but in 1954 he sold *The Spirit of St. Louis* to the movies for a million dollars.

There was a legend that he never read anything; just sold it. And another that he studied every manuscript very carefully, with his genius for figuring out just which magazine it was best suited to, and then sent it to the *Reader's Digest*, where he got the most money. The relation of an agent to an editor, like that of an editor to an owner, is said to be sycophantic. Not George's. The editors came to see him, not he them, and not just on business, but on their day off. Theirs were friendships, and, since the success of a publication has nothing to do with what it publishes, his friends bought his client's stuff from him, including mine.

He didn't get rich off me. A couple of those fifteen-hundred-dollar deals a year took me a long way, and then I would write articles for the *Progressive*, and other little rags, where you say what you want to say and nobody eats. When I sold a piece to the *Progressive* for $25, I would send George a check for $2.50, and he would send me a $3 necktie. I was not only his most obscure client; I was his *only* obscure client. But he never neglected me for the others; he was fond of me; I guess he was one of the few men in or anywhere near the publishing business who could afford to be fond of anybody.

It was a case of symbiosis rather than organically grown intimacy between us; we knew each other instantly rather than well. I don't suppose I saw him twenty-five times in all. He wouldn't leave New York unless he had to, and he never had to except to go to the White House, where he had a couple of busy clients, and I wouldn't go to New York unless I had to, and I managed not to have to often. If he had anything important to communicate—anything, that is, about money—he telegraphed. His cable address was *Byanby*.

But my collection of George Bye letters, scattered through my files, is sizable, and I hope that Arlene Bye will gather and publish them. Somebody has to. They were all unset jewels, loving little masterpieces of irrelevance like, "I've been thinking of you, dear. If you've been thinking of me, we've been thinking of each other. Sincerely yours," Sometimes they reported on his teeth, with which he had trouble, sometimes on the Roosevelts, with whom he didn't. Pegler's agent and FDR got along handsomely.

In February of 1942 I finished an assignment for the *Saturday Evening Post*. It was the story of the typical small college, Muskingum, in New Concord, Ohio, "The College on the Hill." It was a good story. The *Post* accepted it and said, in writing, that it was peachy. They sent the final manuscript back for me to do a little cutting for space, and I did the cutting and sent it back. They were raising me to $2,000.

But on March my article, "The Case against the Jew," appeared in the *Post*, the title on the cover. I had tried to sell it, unsuccessfully, first to the *Nation* and then to *Harper's*. Then I gave it—I should have known better—to George to read. He sold it immediately to the *Reader's Digest*. The *Digest* wanted me to tone it down and I wouldn't. I bought it back from them. But on its way back George intercepted it and sold it to the *Post*.

It was the only important thing I ever wrote. And it was true. But March of 1942 was no time to tell the Jews of America (who were suffering vicariously for the Jews of Europe) that there was a case against the Jew. The case consisted of their being no better than the Gentiles, but they didn't read the case. The title was enough.

George and I—and the *Post*—were caught unawares. The morning the
magazine appeared with me all over the cover, George wired, "We're
wonderful." By afternoon we—and the *Post*—were mud.

In the ensuing pogrom of me by my fellow Jews, the *Post* retreated
in shameful disorder to a series of unprepared positions. It fired its
editor, reversed its editorial policy, reconstructed its format (and
doubled its price), spent a fortune running big ads in newspapers all
over the country explaining Just How It All Happened, and looked
for a prominent Jew to answer me in the new *Post*. The only one it
could find was Wendell Wilkie, who wrote an article saying that the
Jews were as wonderful as the Gentiles, which I hadn't said they
weren't. A few years later I met Wilkie and he said, "You know,
Mayer, *I* couldn't find anything wrong with that article of yours. It
must have been the title."

The Curtis Publishing Company was terrified. They knew there
was nothing wrong with the article, but they couldn't get Jews to
read it—not, that is, the Jews who matter. Orthodox Jews couldn't
see anything wrong with it, but Orthodox Jews don't advertise.
Independence Square rocked like a drunkard, and some of the people
in Independence Square went out and got drunk so as to rock with
the Square. A few days after the storm had broken—George is dead
now, and nobody else matters—George called me from New York
and said:

"Mildew, you know and I know that the *Post* accepted the
Muskingum article before the one on the Jews hit the stands. But
you're getting it back in this morning's mail with a form rejection
slip signed, 'The Editors.' There is no use trying to communicate with
them. They don't dare talk to you. They are scared to death. But I
am authorized to tell you that if you will submit an expense account
for $2,000 on that assignment, it will be honored."

"But," I said, "my expenses to New Concord, Ohio, were $37.58."

"I know it," said George. "So do they."

"But," I said "that is a dishonorable proposal."

"I know it," said George.

"I don't mind making dishonorable proposals—"

"I know it," said George.

"—but I don't like to receive them. And to accept this one would
be to contribute to the delinquency of a major. What would Benjamin
Franklin say?"

"He would say," said George, "that the *Saturday Evening Post*
prefers dishonor to death."

"I would like to get them off the hook," I said, "but I am too old to start faking expense accounts. I don't know how to do it."

"That's what I told them, Mildew," said George, "but that is their ultimatum."

"Then," I said, sententiously, "I can not get them off the hook, and that is my ultimatum."

"I'll deliver it," said George, and he did, and the *Saturday Evening Post* is still on the hook.

It was long afterward that I learned that George, too, had been threatened, like the Curtis Publishing Company, with the loss of his business if he didn't disown me. All he'd have had to do would be to take me off his list of clients. He wouldn't and he didn't.

I had never been worth much to him. Now I was a liability. For a few years at least—until the hysteria blew over—I would be out of the slicks. The editors all sent word to me that *they* knew the article was all right, but please don't come to see them. But I remained George's client, no longer obscure, only costly.

I don't mean that he was a hero. Standing up to the kind of pressure that was put on George would be nothing for anyone whose business it is to stand up. But George was an agent—the biggest in the business—and the business is not meant to be stood up in. He was just doing what, when it came unexpectedly to him, came naturally.

There are those of whom we say, when they die, that we shall not look upon their likes again. This is not what bothers me about George. What bothers me about George is that I shall not look upon *him* again until I find him taking 10 percent as agent for Holy Writ and turning over the rest to the Author.

Westbrook-the-Ripper

I knew him well enough to call him "Peg." (He called me "you.") Like every other kid in the business, I wanted to write like him and like nobody else. But my morbid interest in books carried me off prematurely, and, as I went, I heard my city editor sigh and say, "He might have become another Pegler." After that, no metal, in the form of slings and arrows, could touch me. *Another Pegler*.

Somebody ought to do an autopsy on Peg—not just cut his heart out—while he is still alive. I could do it, partly because I might have become another Pegler myself, and partly because I am for anybody who has the pack on him. The autopsy—any odds you want—would disclose that his heart is elephantine and his brain the size of a chicken's.

In my day he wrote—or, rather, spoofed—sports for the *Chicago Tribune*. Now sports is a simple business, peopled, on both sides of the cage, by simpletons. It is the crudest and most brutish of human indulgences—and none the less enjoyable for that—and Peg had a field day growling at the gorillas.

It never occurred to him that he knew anything about anything else—and he was right. He could tell you what time Washington made across the Delaware, but if you asked him *why* he crossed it, he would tell you to try the Reference Room down the hall.

It was rich meat on which our Westbrook fed, but it didn't matter as long as he hung around the cage. But Colonel McCormick, who knew a switchblade when he saw one, set him to slashing at the Roosevelts in the *Chicago Tribune*. Then Hearst bought him. A quarter century later Hearst tied the can to him. His act was stale—life was serious now—and (worse yet) unprofitable.

So now he ends his days stabbing away at the shade of Eleanor Roosevelt in a little extremist rag, and I could weep for Peg.

I could weep for him because I might have been another Pegler myself. And I could weep for him because he was (like everyone else) only partly wrong; 80 percent, if you like, or 90. Mrs. Roosevelt was a remarkable human being; but she was a human being. Peg couldn't bear her beatification—or any other human being's—and he was right.

Reprinted from the *Progressive*, April 1963.

Men may not be gorillas, but they aren't as good, least of all in politics, as they say they are when they deliver the elegy over a Party-Liner.

Adlai Stevenson said that Mrs. R. was a great democrat—and a great Democrat. You can't be both. There never was, and never will be, any Party Line down which any man or woman of consuming integrity can go—as who knows better than the American Ambassador who told the UN that his country was innocent of the Cuban invasion attempt and then went on to oppose Communist China's recognition?

As a great Democrat, Mrs. Roosevelt went down the Line every time. If you'd heard her, at the end of her career, seconding Stevenson's nomination at the 1960 Convention, you'd have predicted her hara-kiri at Kennedy's victory. But it didn't faze her. She was a Regular, but she always made a moral issue of it, and that's what Peg could not abide.

He was ignorant, intemperate, and intolerant; none of which made any difference in the muscle racket. But pretension in politics—and especially humanitarian pretension—drove him perpetually wild, He couldn't understand goodness, and when he saw it serving as a cover for interest he positively hated it.

He was hell with his portable, and they should have kept him working over the gorillas. He could understand them.

Part Three
Over the Falls

The American Spirit

We were once said (by the elder Holmes) to threaten every government in Europe *by our very existence*. This ascription of moral power would hardly be made nowadays. If we threaten any government nowadays, we threaten it by military power. We may be fearful to our enemies. We are no longer wonderful, not even to our friends; nor to ourselves.

We may say we have come of age, but what do we mean? What (as the children say) were we going to be when we grew up? Were we cradled to be what we are? Are we what we would like to be? What of the young Jeffersonian dream?

Parlous questions, these. Certainly a pattern of brutal expediency has begun to appear in our national behavior; is this what we would call maturity? Shameful act of state piles upon shameful act. Our defense of these acts is juvenile: We say that other people are even more shameful than we are or that others' shamelessness compels us to be just as shameful as they are (and strategically sooner, if possible). And for all of our expediency, we still seem unable to manage effectively.

A couple of random examples may be taken in point. When we landed troops in Lebanon, the Swedish chief of the UN observation team there said, dryly, that now that law had been replaced by force no further purpose could be served by the team. Again, at the last session of the UN political committee we succeeded, by the smallest majority yet, in *preventing discussion* of the recognition of Communist China, and our majority depended upon a dwindling cluster of satellite satraps who had shot themselves into power. We were isolated, with our fetid friends, by the reprobation of the people we call mature.

Are we mature when we say that it is not we, the American people, who do these things, but our rulers; as if we were children or subjects and not free adult citizens whose officials are their mere ministers? If our representatives misrepresented us, we would at least protest. But we don't. We take the shameful act of state indifferently; or even at the value our representatives put upon it, as a national triumph. All is won save honor.

Reprinted from the *Progressive*, January 1959.

Each such historical incident is only an incident and only historical, subject, like all incidents and all history, to aberration and contingency. But the past several years have yielded an habitual succession of such incidents, beginning no later, certainly, than August 6, 1945, when, like Hermann Goering after the shameful raid on Coventry, we justified what we did by saying that we did it to shorten the war. Shamefulness grown customary transcends historical niggling and carries us into the realm of principles. What do we *really* believe in?

To illuminate this question there must be laid alongside it another: What are we really *supposed* to believe in? From 1942 to 1945, while we passed the ammunition, we sang "Praise the Lord and Pass the Ammunition." But Mr. Roosevelt suggested, in a grisly contest to "name" the war, that we call it the War for Survival; and survival depends upon passing the ammunition, not upon praising the Lord (as witness the fate of the prophets. Of course we went right on printing "In God We Trust" on our currency). And for the past ten years we have done everything we have done on the ground that we do *not* believe in communism; no hope there, or in songs or mottoes or names of wars, of determining what we are supposed to believe in. We shall have to go back a bit.

This new nation was (1) conceived in liberty and (2) dedicated to the proposition that all men are created equal. The question at the time was whether any nation so conceived and so dedicated could long endure. It is 150 years since Jefferson, and the question is just as insistent as it was when the British government dismissed the "self-evident truths" of the Declaration as self-evident nonsense. The demoralization of our national practice calls for a reappraisal of our national precept. It is a hundred years since Lincoln. If what we are supposed to believe in is *wrong*, it is high time we found out.

Can a nation be *both* conceived in liberty *and* dedicated to the proposition that all men are created equal? Is America possible, or are we, like France, going to come a cataclysmic cropper, this century or next, no matter how effective or ineffective our callous behavior?

Reappraisal of this sort is bound to be what Mr. John Foster Dulles would have called agonizing. Perhaps that is why we don't undertake it. But it is fifty years since LaFollette, who like Lincoln, accepted the Jeffersonian faith implicitly; an appropriate occasion, in the light of those fifty years, to ask whether we bit off more than we could chew, and whether Holmes was premature.

The only instructive war in our history ended on July 4, 1826, in a draw. On that famous day Adams and Jefferson both died, and the

war between them was over. Wiser than any of us are likely to be,
they fought a fifty-year war of the intellect. Older than any of us are
likely to live to be, they went on fighting as patiently and persistently
as only good friends can fight, until they could fight no more; Jefferson crying up equality and Adams crying it down.

Of course neither one of them believed in democracy. Neither of
them believed that democracy would ever achieve liberty or preserve
it. Both believed in government by an aristocracy of the wisest and
most virtuous. But Jefferson believed that the people could be educated to choose such an aristocracy to govern them. Adams did not.
Adams believed that the people would always be the dupes—and, in
their folly, the willing dupes—of the rich, the cunning, and the cruel,
and would choose no others.

Jefferson had lived through the French Revolution and had seen
it miscarry. So he hedged; the true aristocracy of the best and ablest
men would be recognized and elevated to rule by an egalitarian electorate sobered by the diffuse possession of property, by the privilege
of participation in local government, and by three years of voluntary
(not compulsory) schooling available to every child at public expense.
This was the democratic gimmick. Its optimistic author hoped that
it would save liberty from equality; he knew that the first did not
necessarily follow from the second, however lightly he may have let
the Declaration imply that it did.

Jefferson's hedges against totalitarian democracy have grown higher
than even Jefferson dreamed. But the aristocracy he dreamed of has
not materialized. The good are spurned as do-gooders, the wise as eggheads, and the rulers, so far from being, as Adams predicted, the rich,
the cunning, and the cruel, are the spittin' images of the people.

One man, one vote; here we have the state, alone among all human
institutions, assigning no character to merit, counting men instead of
weighing them. The traitor to totalitarian democracy is the man who
suggests that anybody is abler than anybody else. Lincoln thought
that free Negroes shouldn't vote because they were not then competent; apparently, in his time, and to him, white skin was a guarantee
of competence; in ours, and to us, skin is.

Instead of the noble leadership which Jefferson hoped for or the
ignoble leadership which Adams feared, we have no leadership at all.
If we will have a tyranny, we ourselves will be the tyrant; we will
have no tyrant other. We will have state and national legislatures
unanimous on all mortal issues of liberty (on which we ourselves are
unanimous), interchangeable swarms of interchangeable bureaucrats

doing the actual governing, and as chief executive (the dreadful despot of yore!) an amiable fellow like ourselves who prefers articles to books, digests to articles, bridge to digests, and golf to bridge.

There is no use arguing with Euclid; two things equal to a third are equal to each other. What is there about Harry and Ike that looks alike? Their epitomic resemblance to us all. They don't represent us; they reflect us. When we smile, they smile. When we scowl, they scowl. When we take snuff, they sneeze. We like Ike (or Harry) because we are narcissists. We don't admire them, nor are we afraid of them. No danger of *their* being dictators over *us*. The founding fathers, obsessed with monarchial absolutists, may rest in peace.

"The Communists can arouse the hatred in people's hearts," Ike departs from his text to tell a cheering throng of 85,000, "but they are unable to satisfy the hunger in people's stomachs." The statement (intended to arouse the hatred in people's hearts) may be false, but its banality cheers the throng. The throng across the street is cheering itself in front of Harry. Harry sticks to his text, which he has written himself. "Dictators never settle down," says Harry, "they always want more. . . . Communist China must first abandon her ways of conquest," that is, settle down and never want more. The statement may be a non sequitur, but the cheered throng cheers its banality to the echo.

The cocky Harry and the pontifical Ike are each of them in each of us. In the inequalitarian society the little man says what the big man says; in the equalitarian society the big man says what the little man says. Harry and Ike take the words right out of our mouths.

A tyranny without a tyrant; a happy tyranny, where the tyrant and the tyrannized are one. In the totalitarian democracy the tyrant is all, or almost all. It can enact and repeal every imaginable and unimaginable amendment to the Constitution—including the first ten —but it does not need to. Its mere weight in every issue and in every locality is sufficient to suppress every deviation and smother every unpopular liberty that comes to its attention.

How close to this condition are we? Forget the radicals (try and find them, thirty-eight years after Debs in prison got near a million votes for President!) and everybody is a Republican or a Democrat; and a Republican or a Democrat is anything, except for the Democratic tenet that the Republicans are pacifists who will not spend enough money on guns and bombs. If the Negroes and the Communists would go away, the tyranny of almost all would be the tyranny of all. But the Communists were never here, and the Negroes want the right to be exactly like everybody else.

In the tyranny of all will there be a few men left who, in the words of the late Ralph Ingersoll, "pluck at our sleeve while we take aim at our enemies"? What will their fate be? We have already seen what the tyranny of almost all has been able to do in the past ten years of hot peace. Through our representatives—a few of whom have said publicly, and many privately, that they are afraid to defy us—we have circumscribed the right to radical dissent, the right to associate with circumscribed people, the right to get or keep a job on the basis of competence, and the right to travel. We have emasculated the American's right not to incriminate himself and, in addition, we have incriminated him not just for what he does and says but for what he thinks. And these circumstances, emasculations, and incriminations have all been upheld (however regretfully) by the Nine Young Men.

But a people bent upon the destruction of their own liberties do not need laws to help them achieve it. They have only to lower the big wet blanket of social pressure over the errant spark of individuality and put it out. The two most illiberal statutes we have do not require due process of law to be effective. Under the old Comstock Act, which makes it a crime to read any book the postmaster doesn't read, one man in the Port of New York decides what foreign films Americans may see. But Americans don't want to see foreign films unless they have naked women in them. So he lets them all in (unless they have naked women in them), no matter how subversive they are, because Americans can not be got interested in subversion.

The censoring is done at the box office. Understandable; the censor is the whole American people. So, too, with the Humphrey-Dies Act, which makes it a crime to think any thought that the two Hoovers don't think. Once a man is exposed thinking any such thought, the whole American people will starve him to death instantly.

After Alger Hiss was convicted on the testimony of a self-confessed sinner whose confession exhausted the entire calendar of sins except perjury in Baltimore, it wasn't necessary to suppress the new evidence of the Woodstock typewriter and the FBI's finagling therewith. The reason is that nobody cared. The American press, which is so venal that it will print anything anybody wants to read, didn't print the evidence about the typewriter because nobody wanted to read it. So, too, when the Rosenbergs were executed on testimony like that of Chambers; the Pope and some other cranks protested, but the American people weren't interested.

So, too, when Morton Sobell was called upon by strangers in his apartment in Mexico City, accused of being a man named Jones who had robbed a bank in Acapulco, and, as he reached for his identity

papers, was slugged and kidnapped and delivered to FBI agents waiting for him at the border 600 miles away. Mr. Huggins, the American immigration inspector on duty, with an FBI man at his elbow
made the notation, "Deported from Mexico," on his manifest. But
the Mexican government says that it did not deport him or send
Mexican officers to see him, slug him, kidnap him, or deliver him
to the FBI. Who did? Nobody knows. Nobody cares. Sobell hadn't
been accused of anything; he was *going to be* accused of something
a few months later, and that was enough for the whole American
people; they let one more of their liberties go by the boards because it was a liberty that didn't interest them.

The Supreme Court can equalize liberties, but it can not rescue
them from their destruction by the whole American people. The only
thing the lawyers can do is look up the law. Since the law does not
say anything about the way an American outside the country can be
brought into its criminal jurisdiction, there was nothing that the
lawyers could do about the liberty we lost with Sobell. Under the
emergency powers of our unrepealed Constitution the Supreme Court
could not protect the Nisei from us in 1942, any more than the German Court could protect the victims of the Nuremberg Laws in 1935
under the emergency powers of the unrepealed Weimar Constitution.

The only thing that can save liberty is the love of liberty. Liberties
that are popular need no saving; only those that are unpopular. The
acid test of liberty in the United States today is the liberty of its
most unpopular citizens to be what makes them unpopular. That
means the Communists. But the Communists are over the fence.

We like to think that the Army saved us from Senator McCarthy.
We don't like to think that in doing so it confronted us with the
choice between a Hitler and a Hindenburg and extended the military
domination of the civil power. Still less do we like to think that we
have not been saved from McCarthy at all, that McCarthy, though
he killed himself winning, won. But for the first time since the Alien
and Sedition Acts of 1798 a whole class of Americans are without
effective American rights. Adlai Stevenson would not be likely today
to maintain the right of Communists to be teachers, but Robert Taft
maintained it in McCarthy's heyday. It was Fair Deal Harry who said,
"I put my Communists in jail," and the most generally enlightened
state in the Union that replaced Bob La Follette, one of the best
Senators in our history, with Joe McCarthy. Do we suppose that the
next McCarthyism will be milder than the last?

Where everybody is free and equal, and nobody wants to be anything but equal, the destruction of liberty, not by invasion or subversion, but by deliquescence, is a breeze. The Danes surrendered to the

invaders in 1940 without firing a shot, but they declined to deliquesce; they kept their liberties on ice, and when they were liberated, five years later, their liberties were found to be perfectly preserved. We, who liberated them with plenty of shooting, somehow lost some of our liberties in the process. Jesus was taunted on the Cross with being able to save others' lives but not his own; but we know that he wasn't trying to save his own life. Maybe we aren't trying to save our own liberties.

We are certainly trying to save our lives—an effort that is not peculiarly American, or peculiarly human, or peculiarly herioc in a people who like to say that they would rather die on their feet than live, like the Danes for a while, on their knees. In the name of security—the summum bonum of rabbits and turnips—we have embraced the militarism which Adams and Jefferson dreaded and from which so many of our ancestors fled Europe in despair of the past and hope of the future. It was once an American axiom, spelled out in the Virginia and Vermont constitutions and elsewhere, that a great militarized nation was a totalitarian nation and that militarism was, by definition, immediately inimical to liberty and, ultimately, even to equality.

Militarism equalizes men by giving them each and all a tangible stake in its conformity. If you are under twenty-six and will get into line full-time for two years, and stay there part-time for seven, you get a GI home loan with no down payment. Will you want to argue with the Pentagon in the meantime? Visiting Moscow, Walter Lippmann reported with dismay "the universal dogma that profits are the compelling motive in American armament." The *New York Times* reports that the prices paid by the Pentagon have risen 3 to 5 percent every year. "When reporters asked the Pentagon officials whether they had appealed to the businessmen to try to pare their prices on military goods, Assistant Defense Secretary McNeil laughed. 'We hinted a bit,' he said."

We are all merchants of death now, under twenty-six or over. The value of my house has doubled in the past ten years. So has yours if you're lucky enough to be near a new military post or Defense Department contractor. Jefferson thought that a free press was integral to the preservation of our liberties, but our press, apart from its other interesting characteristics, is as freely and unanimously in favor of militarism as you and I are. In the profit system profit is the compelling motive, they say in Moscow. We're all making a profit on guns and deploring juvenile delinquency.

Fifty years ago in America a soldier was not to be seen, except in the Skid Row recruiting stations. The scandalous un-Americanism of the Grand Army of the Republic was so long remembered that until

President Wilson made his Preparedness appeal in their behalf, men in uniform were not admitted to respectable public places. And when this same President Wilson, preparing for peace three years later, proclaimed peacetime conscription to be the root evil of Prussianism, nobody outside the American Legion said him nay. In forty years we have deracinated the Prussian evil twice—in Prussia—and now we have peacetime conscription here.

The foundation of civil liberty is the devotion to civil society. We are fully militarized now—ready, willing, and in some quarters eager to defend or attack the world. We are the "garrison state" we shuddered at twenty years ago. And the preponderance of what we have done to ourselves is yet to be felt; the American generation which has been taught liberty by drill sergeants is only now beginning to assert itself. The military caste, implacable enemy of both liberty and equality, is just barely discernible in its beginnings.

The militarization of our country, itself a temporary equalizer, is one of the three great changes since La Follette. The other two are the equalization of economic and of racial opportunity. Neither Jefferson, nor Lincoln, nor even the La Follette of 1909 imagined the true magnificence of these two achievements in fifty years. The first began with the federal income tax—that Bolshevik institution—in 1914 and ended, I *hope*, with the bill I got from my plumber last month for 2 hrs. lbr. @ $30. My plumber is now equaler than I am.

Our advance against racial inequality has been still more phenomenal, coming to a spectacular, and certainly only temporary, culmination on May 17, 1954. Some of our Southern brethren are less passionate for equality than the rest of us would like them to be, but, with some slight nudging, they are eliminating the crime of segregation at least as fast as the rest of us are eliminating the sin of discrimination. Who can any longer doubt that fifty years from now new generations will no more hanker after overt racism than the present generation hankers after overt slavery?

But if I am a fool, and in my folly abdicate my liberty, and my plumber and my Negro get to be like me, just what will we be besides equal fools? Totalitarian democracy, the ineluctable consequence of equal foolishness, will, instead of being rampant and dominant, be absolute. The remaining cracks and crevices in its structure, such as the already narrowed right of conscientious objection, will be filled. The monologue will be monolithic.

And so we approach the point where, to our great astonishment, equality, the proposition to which we are dedicated, is the enemy of the liberty in which we are conceived, and the answer to our first

question—Can any nation so conceived and dedicated long endure?—
turns out to be: Maybe, and maybe not. Adams and Jefferson would
be just as astonished as we are.

Where, with all their wisdom and foresight, did they go wrong? If
they were misled at all in their surmises, it may have been by their
preoccupation with the single form of tyranny they knew so well—
the tyranny of an absolutist government over the people. We know
how the "strong government" Constitution barely squeaked through
—a Constitution so weak (Jefferson thought it too strong) that it
could not hold our people together for a century. Liberty, to our
first American ancestors, seemed to consist in the individual's freedom from oppression by the king. All of our subsequent immigration fortified this single focus; nearly all of our people came from
societies ruled by such tyrants.

Up to Jefferson's time men had not thought seriously of society
itself as the tyrant, if for no other reason than that they had thought
of social change as circular, with democracy as both successor and
precursor of tyranny. But the rising tide of equality, engendered by
the romantic and antiecclesiastical faith in the perfectibility of man,
beginning in Jefferson's time swept every objection before it. The
answer to oppression was democracy.

Jefferson had this faith, in restrained measure, as Adams and all of
the older Christian and pre-Christian philosophers had not. But within a decade after his death a young French aristocrat, freshly seeing
America, and accepting democracy as the most *just* form of government, thought he detected a fatal flaw in the democratic dream:
"Democratic communities"—this is de Tocqueville, *De la démocratie
en Amerique*—"have a natural taste for freedom. . . . But for equality,
their passion is ardent, insatiable, and invincible; they call for equality in freedom, and, if they cannot obtain that, they still call for
equality in slavery." (This same de Tocqueville wrote, a century and
a quarter ago, about America and Russia: "Their starting-point is
different, their ways are diverse, yet each of them seems called by
the secret design of Providence to control, some day, the destinies of
half the world.")

He found equality "the fundamental fact about America from
which all others seem to be derived. . . . All men and all powers seek-
ing to cope with this irresistible passion will be overthrown and destroyed by it." Including the free individual? "As the conditions of
men become equal amongst a people, individuals seem of less, and
society of greater, importance; or, rather, every citizen, being assimi-
lated to all the rest, is lost in the crowd, and nothing stands conspic-
uous but the great and imposing image of the people at large. This

naturally gives the men of democratic periods a lofty opinion of the
privileges of society and a very humble notion of the rights of individuals; they are ready to admit that the interests of the former are
everything, and those of the latter nothing."

How far had this "passion" affected the individualistic spirit of
America in 1835?—"I know of no country in which there is so little
independence of mind and real freedom of discussion as in America.
In any constitutional state in Europe, every sort of religious and
political theory may be freely preached and disseminated. . . . But in
. . . the United States there is but one authority, one element of
strength and success, with nothing beyond it . . . the omnipotence of
the majority."

This, then, was America, where, de Tocqueville said, everyone talked
and almost no one conversed, where equality produced conformity
and conformity identity; less than a decade after Jefferson was in his
grave. And what would happen to this America in another century?
In another century the industrial revolution would have matured.
"What can be expected," said de Tocqueville, "of a man who has
spent twenty years of his life in making heads for pins?" The century
passed. "The American voter," said James Reston in the *New York
Times*, Nov. 9, 1958, "is immune to ideological talk about everything except communism," with "a tendency to prefer personality"—
Jefferson would have said "demagoguery"—"to anything else."

All unsuspected by Jefferson or Adams, the real villains of the egalitarian piece are Euclid, Galileo, Newton, Faraday, and their hand-
maidens, Watt, Whitney, Stephenson (George, not Robert Louis or
Adlai), Bell. These are the scamps who opened the floodgates of
progress and inundated the Rousseauian woods forever, in India and
China and Russia no less (if a little later) than in America. These are
the unintending authors of the characteristic process of our time—
the liberation of peoples and the enslavement of persons.

This handful of conspirators have enabled us to get together whether or not we have anything to do, to talk to each other whether or
not we have anything to say, and to act in effective concord whether
or not we should act at all. They have enabled us, like our present
model, the Russians, to construct things that are so amazing that we
forget to wonder whether they should be constructed. In their innocence they have created all the Golems that rule us all equally. If to
talk like this is to be blackly pessimistic or, still worse, anti-intellectual,
we may ponder the warning of Rabelais, long ago, that science without
conscience is the ruin of the soul.

The flood of technological progress ensued almost immediately after Jefferson and Adams. They had both pointed with horror at what they both called the *canaille* of the cities of Europe—the millions of uneducated and unpropertied men pressed so close together as to be a homogeneous mob, a monstrous body wanting only a head. In Jefferson's time, as in Aeneas's, a Stentor could reach only a few thousand people with his voice, and a man with a missive or a missile could travel only a few miles a day. A hundred years later the villains, their villainy mass-produced, have made a contiguous and contented *canaille* of us all. We are one great city of 170,000,000, governed by those equalizers known as mass media of communication and mass means of transportation. The transportation has enabled us all to huddle together for a weekday in town or a Sunday in the country. The communication is one-way communication. (An American, said de Tocqueville, if he is addressing you alone is liable to begin by saying, "Gentlemen.") Big Brother, in all his guises of print, picture, and voice, does not have to watch us, any more than the snake charmer has to watch the snake; he has only to keep us watching him. All of us together.

The tempo of technology, besides equalizing our intelligences at the NBC-CBS level, equalized our hearts by spreading before us an ever-increasing abundance of goods within (or just beyond) the reach of all of us. We became the first people in modern history among whom poverty was only marginal, and the first society whose producers of luxury articles could own the articles they produced. The traitors to the new American spirit came to include those party-poops who held that human happiness was still possible to a one-car family.

It was not alone that we got rich; it was the way we got rich that prevented the rise of Jefferson's aristocracy of virtue and wisdom. Our folk heroes were Rockefeller, Carnegie, and Ford, none of whom was preeminently virtuous; still less so, wise. If Henry Ford could get a billion dollars together and still maintain that history is bunk, why should anyone else who wanted a billion dollars study history? From being nonphilosophical—like any raw people confronted with practical obstacles and practical opportunities—we proceeded aggressively and defensively to being antiphilosophical.

But the defense of liberty, not of one's own but of one's Communist neighbor's, is a matter of principle. It is impossible to defend liberty concretely without being abstract about it and seeing that it is applicable everywhere or nowhere. But abstraction is philosophy, and we are an antiphilosophical people.

We are not becoming more philosophical. The puny effort to introduce philosophy into our equalized educational system has been wiped out overnight by the Russian *Sputniks*. We have discovered that liberty does not produce technological superiority. Since what we want is technological superiority, liberty becomes superfluous, or a positive hindrance to be relegated from desuetude to destruction.

Is it possible that Adams and Jefferson overestimated our love of liberty in the first place? We cried liberty in 1776 while we maintained a slave society, and the offenses charged against George III in the Declaration make him sound, by comparison with the tyrants we have heard of since, like Peck's Bad Boy. We called for a "separate and equal station" among the powers of the earth; perhaps we were thinking about national independence when we talked about liberty. If the one is the same as the other, then the loss of the first means the loss of the second. This is the way the Hungarians and others, who never had liberty, seem to feel. It is not the way the Danes felt in 1940. Have we so little confidence in our love of liberty that we must sacrifice liberty to security lest, once we have chains, we will come to love them?

The "peculiar institution" of chattel slavery may have contributed, too, to a conception of liberty as corporeal. Even the Pilgrimage from Leyden was a matter of moving, and we have been moving around ever since. There are men still living who remember free land. The Americans who did not like a town or an occupation went somewhere else or got another. There were never enough men for jobs except in depressions. And even then a man *knew* he'd get a job soon. And if he turned out to be wrong—even if he died jobless—his hope was undimmed.

We were a new kind of people, hopeful and bold. In Europe, Asia, Africa, it was different and always had been. If a man lost a job he might never find another. So he was mighty careful not to lose a job, and to do and say whatever was required of him to find or hold one. Economic liberty should have nourished political liberty here.

We Americans could afford to be free. Liberty is a luxury of the rich, and that is why our talk of liberty in the world today falls upon deaf ears, on the ears of those who, if they ever dream of liberty, always struggle for bread. How can we imagine what it is to be hungry, to have had parents and grandparents who were hungry, and to know that unless we do something revolutionary, *anything* revolutionary, our children and our grandchildren will be hungry?

We could afford to be generous, and we meant to be. Our situation had made of us the most open-hearted people the world had ever seen. But we could not imagine the need. We can not still. A month after we and the Chinese between us had burned down 65 percent of the habitations of South Korea we were moved greatly to help; but five years afterward the need had barely been touched and we had forgotten Korea. Nor have we any idea how rich we are; two years ago we thought we had opened our hearts and our homes to the Hungarian refugees, but in the end we accepted the fewest (in terms both of our population and our national income) of any receiving country. (Switzerland, which did not exploit them for anti-Communism, accepted the most.)

We know we are gorged after Sunday dinner, but how gorged we are we can not imagine. The last time I heard about our surplus food commodities—they have since increased—they were costing us almost one million dollars a day for *storage*. We can not eat them, we can not give them away without wrecking the world market, by which we mean the "free" or capitalist market. Is it any wonder that the hungry do not hate Communist dictatorship any more than they hate capitalist democracy?

While our illimitable surpluses eat up our moral status abroad, our unlimited commitment to violence eats up our moral intentions at home. Our Secretary of Commerce tells us (not knowing that he is quoting Rudolf Hess verbatim) that we must have more guns and less butter. And if we, then certainly those we would like to feed. More than 90 percent of all our foreign aid is military, "extended indiscriminately," says Senator Fulbright, "to governments which serve the needs of the people and alike to those which do not." The hungry cry out for bread, and we give them iron; provided, of course, that their rulers chant the anti-Communist catechism. Is this maturity?

Why, alone among the Wester Nations, and the strongest and richest and most remote of them all, have we let liberty go for security and forged upon ourselves the shackles of fear represented by our unique pursuit of un-Americanism? Ours is not the soil in which revolution grows. What are we afraid of? We used to say that the difference between us and Nazi Germany was that here a knock on the door at dawn meant the milkman; are we less afraid now that we have our own secret police who take men from their beds? Would we be unafraid if the Soviet Union did not exist in a hungry world? If Communist China did not exist? Or if only our own kind of people, the rich, existed?

Neither the poor nor the rich necessarily dream of liberty. Incapable as we are of even imagining what it is like to be poor, we can only hazard a guess that when such people dream, they dream, not of liberty, but of bread. And what do the rich dream of? They are said to dream bad dreams of losing their riches; they have heard tell that nobody loves the rich.

If we, equal and equally rich, do not love liberty so much that we will sacrifice our riches to it and go for broke to keep it, and if we have never thought much about liberty anyway, it would be no wonder that we didn't see our liberties being lost. Neither, when they were rich and equal enough, did the Romans, and they were learned in liberty. When Christians were deprived of their liberties in Rome, the Romans saw no loss of liberty, since there were only a handful of Christians, who, in the Roman view, were all traitors anyway. When Communists are deprived of their liberties in America, the rest of us do not see that we are losing ours, because there are only a handful of Communists who, in our view, are all traitors anyway. We may prefer Christianity to communism, but the only way to be concrete is to be abstract.

Fear intensifies our equality, erasing from our faces all of our individuality and replacing it with the stricken visage of the girl on the colored cover of the paperback whodunits. The more bombs we have, the more frightened we are. What will set us free from the prison of fear to redress the imbalance between equality and liberty? There is no use talking about pacifism, because pacifism means saying no to the tyrannical many, not, as in colonial India, to the tyrannical one, and any independent people who would seriously thing of saying no would already be free.

Perfect love was once said to be capable of driving out fear. The same people who believed that the only good Negro was a lynched Negro—or that the only good Jew was a gassed Jew—used to believe that the only good Indian was a dead Indian. They acted accordingly, but their fear abided. "Let us then," said William Penn, "try what love will do, for if men see that we love them they will not wish to injure us." And in one American commonwealth, it worked as long as Penn and his followers governed. But is there any use talking about perfect love if we no longer believe *either* in the perfectibility of man *or* in the power of God? Jefferson believed in both.

Our achievements since Jefferson have been so remarkable that we are tempted to the worship of the work of our hands, like the Communists in Russia, and, like them, to the supposition that we can do anything. There *is* this side of the American spirit, classically represented by the story of Andrew Jackson's funeral. Like many generals, General Jackson turned religious after he was too old to fight, and after the preacher had preached his funeral sermon, one of the mourners turned to one of the general's slaves and asked him if he thought his master would go to heaven. "He will," said the slave, "if he wants to."

General Jackson was a do-it-yourself man. Ours is a do-it-yourself spirit. And unless everybody winds up doing the same thing himself, there is still there the vestigial sign of the love of liberty. But there are some things you can't do yourself. You can't drive out your own fear by getting there the fastest with the mostest. You can't get a man —or a world—with a gun. Mr. Dulles, who used to represent American Christendom in the World Council of Churches, told a Congressional committee, "The purpose of the State Department is to look out for the interests of the United States. Whether we make friends I do not care . . . I do not care whether they like us or hate us."

You can damn the torpedoes, but you can't damn mankind. Nor can you make yourself loved and trusted as long as you love only them which love you and put your trust in violence while you say you put your trust in God. This is phariseeism, and, like the Pharisees of old, who made long prayers for a pretense, ours will be the great-er damnation than theirs who do not pray at all. At least that's what they say in the World Council of Churches.

Nor will all they that shout, "Lord, Lord," enter the Kingdom. The massive mass society goes—as de Tocqueville observed—on one big kick after another. In our time there has been the Prohibition kick, and the automobile kick, and the stock-market kick, and the Roosevelt kick, and the liberation kick, and vitamin kick, and the psychiatry kick, and the un-American kick, and the tranquilizer kick. Now we have the Pentecostal kick, along with "Pray for Peace" on our postage cancellation machines. But God's justice sleeps, and the man who warned us that it would not sleep forever was not Billy Graham but Thomas Jefferson.

Columbus was stone sober when he said that he wanted to sail because the prophet Isaiah had promised a new heavens and a new earth. The *Mayflower*'s passengers were stone sober when they dedi-cated themselves and their adventure to the glory of God. When the three scientifically-minded authors of the Declaration sought a refuge for their heady doctrine of equality combined with liberty, they found it in the endowment by the Creator of all men. The American spirit is not only Jackson on his feet, but Lincoln on his knees.

Maybe, in order to escape worldly authoritarianism—of the one or the many—we have got to learn something that our silver-spooned experience has not taught us. The Greeks were fond of saying that man is schooled in suffering. Maybe we have got to suffer. It looks as if we might. We never have, and we won't like it. But Jefferson's God said, "I have refined thee, but not with silver; I have chosen thee in the furnace of affliction." Maybe we have got to get ourselves afflicted. It looks as if we are trying.

The Communists, too, pursue a durable balance between liberty and equality. But they believe that life and society are human experiments and that there is no God. But what if there is one? What if Jefferson was right? Then the revolution—at least the Communist revolution—will fail for want of the superhuman means proportionate to the superhuman end of conceiving a nation in liberty and dedicating it to the proposition that all men are created equal. The third author of the Declaration wrote an autobiography, and in it he speaks of his youth:

About this time, I conceived the bold and arduous project of arriving at moral perfection. I wished to live without committing any fault at any time: I would conquer all that either natural inclination, custom, or company might lead me into. As I knew, or thought I knew, what was right and wrong, I did not see why I might not always do the one and avoid the other. But I soon found that I had undertaken a task of more difficulty than I had imagined.

Ill Met by Moonlight

Twenty-four billion dollars later—at "only ten months' cost of the war in Vietnam"—we landed on the moon. "We landed on the moon." The term on which that statement turns is not "moon" or "landed" but "we." The "we" were three extraordinary (or extraordinarily skilled) men in a country of two hundred million; three men backed up by two or three hundred more who stood on the shoulders of forgotten mathematicians. (The thousands of mechanics and machinists might have been tooling up anything.) The rest of the two hundred million had another delirious go at the national pastime.

The national pastime is watching it happen—whatever it is. With the moon shot the spectator culture, in which all authority, all responsibility, all activity is transferred to the few, reached its zenith. The many are vicarious. They do nothing. They say nothing. They are nothing. They watch—in color.

This is nonparticipatory democracy.

This is what has turned off the young. This is what the rebels are all rebelling against, in America, in France, in Italy, Japan, Czechoslovakia. One out of ten young Germans conscripted for war refuses to go.

Nonparticipatory democracy is the ultimate American triumph. "We" landed on the moon.

It should have been one of the most marvelous events of all time. Out of context, it most certainly was. But in the context of the decade in which President Kennedy said "we" would do it, it was another disaster, another escape hatch, another bomb shelter, another retreat, another evasion, another confession of fabulous failure.

The American triumph was not the triumph of man, but the triumph of man's dehumanization by automatry and precision instrumentation; of the perverse application of science that poises man, in this generation, in this decade, and in this year, on the edge of annihilation. The astronaut's first words—he wouldn't know that the phrase was a variant of Mao's—were "a great leap for mankind." Into what? Into empty and still emptier space.

Emptiness.

Reprinted from the *Progressive*, September 1969.

The emptiness of a lost weekend.

It was millimicron perfect—except for one terrible miscalculation: It took Man along. Man the Meat-Grinder, at whose perfect touch everything turns to detritus. There in the skies was the surface of earth before Man the Builder built and Man the Wrecker wrecked. Pulverized rubble, like Dresden in May or Hiroshima in August a billion years later. Uninhabitable—like Stalingrad. Incapable of supporting life—like Warsaw. Contaminated? How could it be contaminated when the contaminator hadn't been there?

Man who made the earth what it is will make of the moon what he made of the earth and himself: ashes risen and fallen to ashes, dust risen and fallen to dust. Or won't he? And if he won't, why won't he? Were the cool, courageous, clean-cut young astronauts any different from the rest of us, any different when they came down from when they went up?

Heroes? Heroism, I suppose, is selfless audacity. Were our heroes more, or less, heroic than, say, those who, without benefit of an electronic armada, an avalanche of apotheosis, and a half million dollars from *Life* magazine, minister to the abandoned victims of contagious disease? Heroes? The astronauts were mighty daredevils on the highest-flying trapeze we've seen yet. But somewhere in Arkansas a mother watches her children chew their collard greens and drools in spite of herself; and somewhere the lame, the halt, and the blind stumble on without apotheosis; and somewhere—who knows? —a pretty girl still says no to the only pillow she'll get for her pretty head.

Heroes? There are all kinds of heroes, in the air, in the mines, out of prison and in, on the battlefield, at the burning building, along the riverside, and down the street. Some of them mute, inglorious, and *Helas!* unclean-cut. The cool, courageous, clean-cut young astronauts, most remarkably interchangeable with one another, are trained (more power to them and their training) to clean-cut young heroism by seasoned old trainers like Wernher von Braun, the genius of the Nazi V-2, whose heroism consisted of the surrender of his rocket brigade to the Americans instead of to the Russians in 1945.

Where were we going in such a hurry, and to do what? We were going to the moon to learn and to know. To learn what and to know what? Why, whatever there is to learn and to know. Man wants to know, to know all there is to know about "the world." Ah, yes, "the world." But the world was put into the hands of Man as its steward, and Man was not in the moon; Man was in Athens, where Socrates learned about Man without leaving Athens, and in Koenigsberg, where Kant learned about Man without leaving Koenigsberg. Horace did not have to go from Rome to the seacoast to learn what he learned; what he learned was that no ship (and no spaceship) ever sails leaving sorrow behind.

Sorrow, then, to the moon, man's import wherever he goes.

"But think of the fringe benefits, think of the unimagined and unimaginable dividends of it." Think of the fringe benefits of the sustained nuclear chain reaction, whose discoverers thought that it would be used not for power to explode whole cities but for power to meet the crying needs of human life. The benefits remain on the fringe a quarter century later, the power compounded remains in the Pentagon. Knowledge for its own sake turns out to be either an exercise in fatuity or an invitation to the waltz with Mephisto.

What did "we" expect to find there in the untroubled dust? What use could we put it to in our mortal need? Oh, joy, oh, excitement, oh, tension and terror and triumph—and tomorrow morning, despair again; bigotry, lovelessness, joylessness, loneliness, and war, war, war. Hunger, ill health, homelessness, joblessness, hopelessness. Walk the moon tonight ye dispossessed, and arise in the morning dispossessed: the moon is yours, but not the sixpence. "We" are rich—what of it if you are poor?

Inside the door the moon, in color. Outside the door, the ghetto in black and white. The moon in your living room, and the fire in the streets. The moon in an easy chair, and the murder in the Mekong Delta. The moon within touch, and the babies of Biafra too far away "to do anything about."

Was this trip necessary? We did it because we could do it: Invention is the mother of necessity. We didn't do it because we were challenged to do it; the Lord knows we have been challenged more sharply by the blacks and the tans and the poor and the young than we were by the mellifluous moon. We can't meet the tough challenges, but only the easy ones. And this one was the challenge the Russians were liable to meet first.

It was hard for the birdmen, to be sure, but it was insuperable for the balderdash bravoes, burning the midnight thesaurus to find hyperboles worthy of the customers' exaltation. They fell on their faces, as they were bound to in the transcendental nature of the case. Among the banality contestants Paul Goodman came off far from first with his proclamation that "it's good to 'waste' money on such a moral and esthetic venture. These are our cathedrals"—in which, of course, we shall worship Man. *Time* magazine walked off with an armful of For General Audiences Oscars with such entries as the announcement that Apollo was "a vindication of some traditional strengths and precepts in the American character and experience: perseverance, organizational skill, the willingness to respond to competition." (Do you remember Carl Sandburg's story of the cockroach that was blown off a window sill and landed in a heap of steaming rich manure and, when he appeared a few years later in gaiters, gloves, and spats, and was asked how he did it, replied: "Brains, gentlemen, brains and personality"?)

The American willingness to respond to competition—of "the Russians"—was what did it. But where is the American willingness to respond to the competition of the Norwegians in medical care, or of the French in race relations, or of the British in civil liberties, or of Switzerland in the war on poverty? Well, you know how it is: You can't expect us to compete with everybody in every event, and what are you, anyway, some kind of a Communist?

We beat the Russians, didn't we?

The real ecstasy of the occasion, the landfall of all landfalls, and the real thrill it occasioned in the hearts of marveling men the world over, was mortally tainted by its role as the culmination of a ten-year campaign in the Cold War. The Russians had seized the initiative with *Sputnik*. The struggle for the moon was the struggle for the world. The Cold Warriors all—Presidents Truman and Eisenhower, but especially Kennedy, Johnson, and Nixon—were eager and insistent to see our substance squandered to beat the Russians. We can't do anything that needs to be done, but that doesn't matter as long as we beat the Russians at what doesn't.

We beat the Russians, all right. And in beating them beat ourselves again, as usual. When the Russians launched *Sputnik*, the Cold Warriors of Washington informed President Eisenhower that we were technologically backward. So informed, President Eisenhower concluded that we had to pour out the public money, not for education, but for training. What was needed in a hurry was more technology and more technologists to catch up with the devilishly cunning Russian devils. Out the window went the modest recrudescence of the humanities which might have saved our colleges and universities. In the wide open door swept the human abaci—the automationists, the cyberneticists, and the computerists. The space program was the last nail in the coffin of the humanities and the social sciences, in a society that is dying for the want of them.

After watching *Sputnik* one evening in 1957 the two small sons of Steve Cary of Haverford College were in bed discussing the miracle. "I don't understan' how they do it," said the smaller. "How do they do it, anyway?" "Wubbuh bands," said his brother, "wubbuh bands."

We—if you want to know who "we" are—are the world's leading
manufacturer of wubbuh bands.

Now that we've got it, what will we use it for? A colony for the
riotous blacks? An Alcatraz for the criminals who have to get their
depletion allowance at gunpoint? A juvenile detention home for the
delinquents? A campus for the radicals? A compound for the peace-
niks? A campground for the poor? A graveyard for our beat-up cars?
A graveyeard for our shot-up sons? There must be a use for it. Or is
it use enough to use it for a twenty-four-billion-dollar flagpole?
The villains in the piece are the fliers of the plastic flag, and the
fliers of the plastic flag are not the engineers like von Braun—who,
like the admen of television, are born with a For Sale sign on them,
mere animated tools who do whatever they are told by whomever
they are told. The villains are the bloated chauvinists who pick up
the tools and use them to *their* purposes, the Congressmen who
decided, in their infantile birchism, that the UN flag was not to be
planted on the moon. What if Neil Armstrong had dissented then?
He would have changed, not the moon, but the world.
But he was only one of the precision instruments in the hands of
the Kennedys and the Johnsons and the Nixons and the Congressmen
—the makers of policy which ought to be made by the American
people and isn't. Why would an Armstrong dissent from the betrayal
of the last best hope of peace—the United Nations—when a Nixon
wouldn't and the cheerleaders and commentators wouldn't and the
Space Agency wouldn't and the Congressmen wouldn't? These are
free men, lacking only what Bismarck said the Germans lacked: civilian courage.
So the United Nations prepared a postcard, inscribed with the
preamble of the UN Charter promulgating peace through international law. Would the United States be so kind as to deliver this modest
representation to the moon? It would. But it did not. The reasons
given: Too late "for decontamination" and (I quote) "weight considerations"—of a postcard. And a few days later the rumors of U
Thant's resignation appeared again, the same U Thant who tried to
resign several years ago and yielded to American and Russian appeals
to stay on at the United Nations as the last best hope.

A twenty-four-billion-dollar bender, and all systems go for broke,
including the most intricate system of them all: Man. Man the Master,
who can do anything but live decently here where he is and with
what he has got, anything but use the knowledge he already possesses,
anything but do what he was told to do long ago: do justice, love

mercy, and walk humbly with his God. The astronauts' footsteps in the silent sands weren't humble. They were the dreadful footsteps of Man the Master, the Master of everything but Man.

American Man, who can do anything but live decently and can do it bigger and better than anybody else and live less decently. He's "done it again," just as he did it again at Hiroshima. (*Time* took the occasion to memorialize the "particularly American genius" of the Manhattan Project, which created the A-bomb—without bothering to inform its clear, concise, complete clientele that the particularly American genius of that splendid achievement was Einstein's, Franck's, Fermi's, and Szilard's, all of them Europeans.)

No question now whose show it is. It's "ours," "ours" who fly the flag to signify what "we" have done, enchanted to be Americans, that is, to have been born at a certain time in a certain place and then sat there. Show the flag to show your second-hand pride, and lock the door against the people across the tracks. The sentiment was genuine, and even the people across the tracks, gulled again, were transported by the Greatest Show off Earth—only to emerge from the tent into the flat reality of unconcern for their needs, hatred of their faces, and dread of their demands.

Conqueror of new worlds and despoiler of the old, American Man is the Alexander of the age, destined to hurry faster, and always faster, to Alexander's disconsolate end. But who is there, or ever was, to tell the Emperor that his space suit leaves him naked? Not the *New York Times*. In its invariable ineffability it reveals, through its man C.L. Sulzberger in Paris, "the renewal of faith in the United States by Europeans and the renewal of self-confidence by the Americans themselves. . . . America's evident bewilderment and increasingly masochistic insistence on self-denigration . . . has been swept away in one enormous rocket blast." The Easy American Way to instant faith and self-confidence: one enormous blast.

American Man has performed the neatest trick of any week to date. We are all tricky Dicks now. "The greatest week in the history of the world since creation," said the pious President Nixon (putting Holy Week in its place). It was a great week, all right. It began with Apollo 11 and ended with the pious President's state visits to the bloody tyrants who shore us up in Thailand, Indonesia, Pakistan, and South Vietnam, and on to Bucharest on the outside chance that we could buy our way into the anti-Soviet Communist tyranny there too. Do you blame the childish handful—I do—who refused even to watch it on television? Childish, yes; and the only form of protest given the few who see where we're headed (and it isn't for the moon).

The gloomy few, who would like to work for a world fit for men to live in right here and right now; it wasn't their night ball game. They were sour from the start. They sensed its real motivation—another aerial act. They foresaw its cost, least of all in money, most of all in the false faith in power that took the Roman and, more recently, the German technologists to the precipice and over it into ruin. The historians saw it for another swaggering adventure (and as a desperate bonus a diversion from the fatal adventure of Vietnam). The scientists (and not its applicators) saw it for the kind of engineering spectacular that reduces science to mythology. And the non-surfing segment of the young, implacably angered by what their elders have made of the earth, namely, green cheese, saw the whole thing as another bummer, an ego trip designed to tighten the stranglehold of the dead on the living. (And that's why "we" hate them.)

"The Greeks," said Stringfellow Barr, "could not broadcast *Oedipus Rex*—but they could write it." And Shakespeare could not bring man to the moon, but he could bring the moon to man in *A Midsummer Night's Dream*. It is further from here to the man who can compose the *Ode to a Nightingale* or the saraband of the *G Major French Suite* than it is from here to the moon. It is further from here to the man who shares his substance, knowing that it isn't his, than it is from here to the moon. It is further from here to the man who is satisfied with his work and his walk and his sunset and moonrise than it is from here to the moon. It is further from here, where we are, and where the black man and the yellow man and the brown man are with us, to an endurable life in a durable society than it is from here to the moon. Further, far.

November 22, 1963

*Neither [Kennedy nor Nixon] seems to be a man at whose funeral
strangers would cry.*
—Murray Kempton, *Progressive*, 1960

*When we saw him drinking the poison, we wept. "What is this strange
outcry?" he said.*
—Plato, *Phaedo*

The discussion had just resumed after lunch—this was
Eastern Standard Time—when a secretary came in and
put a note in front of the chairman, Professor Samuel
Cummings Carter. Carter looked at the note and said
to his eleven fellow philosophers around the table,
"President Kennedy has just been assassinated in Dallas," and went
on with the discussion.

"He should have adjourned the meeting then and there," said one
of the eleven philosophers a week later. The same group (plus a visitor)
were around the table. Carter was absent.

"But," said the visitor, "the discussion was important, wasn't it?"

"As important as the assassination of a President?" said another of
the philosophers.

"I should have supposed so," said the visitor, "to a company of
philosophers."

"Nonsense," said a third philosopher.

"His behavior was unspeakable," said a fourth.

"Did you all find it unspeakable?" said the visitor. (He knew that
three of the eleven had, because they had got up and walked out of
the room immediately after Carter's announcement, and one of them
had been crying before he reached the door.)

There was an unencouraging silence after the visitor's question,
and then one of the philosophers, a youngish man, said, "I suppose
he did the right thing. But it seemed somehow—incongruous. It still
does. Maybe it won't a year from now."

"So," said the visitor, "he was guilty of incongruity rather than
unspeakableness?" Silence, and the cross-grained visitor went on:

Reprinted from the *Progressive*, December 1964.

"You chide Carter for not having adjourned the meeting. Do you chide television for not having gone off the air?"

"Television's business is to inform," said another of the philosophers.

"And yours?" said the visitor. Silence again. "Why shouldn't you have stayed 'on the air'? And why shouldn't television have shut down like the department stores? Its business is no more to inform than theirs is to close. Its business is to make a profit. Isn't yours more important?"

The silence was angry now, and the visitor did not trust himself to go on.

One of the philosophers got up and studied his watch and said, "Back to work." Others got up, and the group dissolved. The visitor was left with an elderly philosopher, who had said nothing. The two were old friends. "It's the bathos," said the visitor, "everywhere. Even here."

"I know," said the elderly philosopher, "but you're in the wrong. So is Carter. You fellows think that ritual is infantile. You want society to be above it, to be 'adult.' But it isn't adult to be above ritual. It's angelic, but it isn't adult. Ritual and ritual alone holds society together."

"Primitive society," said the visitor.

"All societies are primitive," said the elderly philosopher.

I've run into individuals since who think that this detail or that was overwrought, but none who thinks (or in any case says) that the whole weekend of November 22-24, 1963, was a manifestation of the deepest social disorder. A minister finds the eternal flame at the grave "inappropriate." A commentator wonders why the widow had to have exactly ten Secret Service men to protect her for exactly two years. A town meeting in New England declines to erect a statue on the common. A geographer is worried about the precedent of changing ancient place names like Canaveral.

A detail here, a detail there. But no one seems to believe, now any more than then, that the whole thing was a manifestation of the deepest social disorder.

I'm not thinking of the Unseen Millions whose Giant Screen diet of mawk and mummery and mayhem (and assassination?) keeps them buying the cigaret than which no other brand has been proved to be less baneful. I am thinking of the hep—the non-bowlers and non-barbecuers and non-bucket-seaters. I am thinking of the philosophers, heirs of Socrates, who fell apart that weekend and were still fallen apart a week later. I am thinking of the theologian who wrote me, "I'm sick inside and drawn like a chicken over Kennedy's death.

But we pick up and start all over again."

Why should a man have been sick inside (or any sicker than he had been) or drawn like a chicken? What were we to pick up? What had we been carrying? Whither were we to start all over again? Where had we been going?

Of course we were shaken, every last one of us—and we should have been; but shaken like men and citizens, not drawn like chickens. Why in John F. Kennedy's fall fell we all? Who, and what, was he that his sudden death unstrung us as it did? Who and what were we that it touched off a riot of grief across the land?

(There was, to be sure, the classic catharsis of the true tragic spectacle, which always involves a ruler: if *he* is vulnerable, how vulnerable *we* must be; and the equally classic—and repressed—exultation: *He* is dead, and *I* am alive.) Mr. Kennedy (having closed the nonexistent missile gap) probably had more power to do violence than any man in history, and here he was powerless. He could deter the Russians but not the Americans. The Soviet tyrant goes through the streets of Moscow alone, and the American People's Choice is ineffectively surrounded by bodyguards. In the *Redbook* for November 1963, published before the assassination, European children were asked what Americans were like, and one of them said: "The average American is, of course, a Texan. . . . If he doesn't like who is his President, he usually shoots him."

Why? Who, and what, were we and are we, we shooters of Presidents, we freedom-lovers who indulge our freedom in 45,000 highway deaths every year and call for still more horsepower (and get it from freedom-loving free enterprisers)? Is there at the center of our freedom fixation a cataclysmic tension that provides the Oswalds to provide the cataclysm that releases the tension?

There has never been a people at once so fortunate and so unhappy. Witness Barry Goldwater, champion not of the dispossessed but of the possessed, of those who "never had it so good" and can't bear it. For the possessed are dispossessed of their confidence, and their anxiety drives them to refuge in a past that never was. Before Dallas we were (as of course we are again) pent up with no way to break, like a woman unable to expel at birth. Ours was, and is, the same hopelessness to cope that invites the relief of war in which, for four years (or three days) a people can smash the insolubles and let go, giving themselves over to whoop and holler and death and then tears.

We are a murderous people who love all kinds of freedom, and our disorder is deep. We are rich and fat and strong, and we will let no tyrant provide *us* with bread and circuses; we will each of us, in fine freedom, provide his own. In our singular historical and geographical accident, we are weaned on the inalienable right to euphoria, on the pursuit of kicks. We are the most lawless—and nonrevolutionary— people in the world. And becoming more so.

The Southwest was the ironical place for the author of the New Frontier to meet his end by the lynch law of the Old Frontier; ironical, too, that it provided the two slicked-up cowboys in ten-gallon hats, Johnson and Goldwater, to contest his succesion.

The Old Frontier, kept fresh, South, West, East, and North, by the free enterprise of the movies and television, is a crude (and, in happier times, comic) counterfeit of freedom. The shame and the shock and the hurt of last November 22—how could this happen here, in America the Beautiful?—has its instant parallel in the old aftermath sagas of the cattle-thief posses. But it happens here every day, in the streets, in the suburbs, even in the countryside, and in our shallow romanticism we work it out in a carnival of weeping and wailing and high resolve that, at its end, leaves us where we were, only a little worse disordered.

The loss of the President could not, in 1963, have been a national calamity, as, indeed, we have since seen that it wasn't. The very strength of our society is that the chief of state neither provides the society's strength nor takes it with him when, in a few years, he goes his way. The American Presidency is now a stupendous, self-sustaining apparatus, and on November 22, 1963, the office itself would be filled by a thoroughly knowledgeable and masterful *apparatchik*. That much we knew about Mr. Johnson.

And one of the weekend's infinite reruns on TV might have told us more: In 1960 the Democratic nominee for Vice-President was being interviewed by Walter Cronkite of CBS. "Of course, Senator Johnson," said Cronkite at one point, "you're first of all a Democrat," and the Senator said sharply, "Just a moment there. First of all I'm a free man—secondly an American, third a Senator, and fourth a Democrat."

"First of all I'm a free man, secondly an American"—hardly the words of a Texas pol *or* of a Massachusetts pol. But the country was overwhelmed, then and since, by the words of the fallen President, "Ask not what your country can do for you . . . ," words which could have been addressed just as appropriately by a Stalin to the Russians.

Three glassy-eyed days and nights we stared at a flag-covered coffin. Three days and nights we stared dewy-eyed at an heroically

demeanored widow denied a private occasion. Three days and nights
we conjured up a Euripidean voice that whispered, "What will become of you now? What will become of you now?"

A jag-prone people is fearsome to behold. Overnight, that weekend, John F. Kennedy Place and Street and Bridge burgeoned in
Germany, just as Adolph Hitler Avenue and then Karl Marx Boulevard burgeoned overnight in Beethoven Alley. (Burgeoned with
massed torches that some of us had trembled to see there a generation
ago.) Would West Virginia and Indiana both be renamed before the
weekend was over? Would every airport in America be Kennedy
Airport? A newspaperman carefully covered his irony by reporting
a nameless proposal to rename the Lincoln Memorial.

The placards in Dallas that read Hail Caesar! that Friday morning
disappeared in a hurry. The fallen flag was hung everywhere—or
almost everywhere: At the Santa Barbara Republican Women's Club
it flew at full mast. The Birchers—children and fathers of fear—were
afraid. There were anti-Catholics, too, and they galore, who had their
fun (or was it fun?) with the "Irish Mafia," plunged now into the
guilty gloom their fun had excavated to receive them when the man
they wanted gone was gone. The few who said they were glad he was
gone only underscored the general pathology, for Mr. Kennedy was
no more ardently hated than he was ardently loved.

Ninety days after a million Negroes wept unabashed for Father
Abraham in 1865, the "Illinois ape" was fair game again North and
South. So, too, at the death of That Man, in 1945 (for whom one
weepy acquaintance of mine wept abashed). And these were wartime
chieftains and warm men. But in 1963 all the strangers cried and
cried at the funeral—how marvelously wrong Murray Kempton had
been, and how much more marvelously right—and there was none to
say to them, as the dying Socrates said to his friends, "What is this
strange outcry?"

What was this strange outcry? What is this mute lament that per-
sists, to be broken so raucously by the Democrats in Atlantic City
who roared their mechanized delirium at every mention of the dead
man's (or any other live or dead Democrat's) name? Even in Barry
Goldwater's cheapshow "the Kennedy failures" were instantly translated into "the Democratic failures" and then "the Johnson failures."
Goldwater, in his mad campaign, made every political mistake but
one: He did not invade the sanctum.

What was it that happened, that day in Dallas? What was this
wound that bled torrents of tears? An able man died violently and
untimely; a man, moreover, rich and famous and powerful who had

savored richly of all his gifts. Too bad, too terribly bad, truly, that he died; but are most of our lives any more satisfactory or better (if later) rounded?

Of course he had had to sacrifice the pleasant blessings of men more inconspicuously situated. But the measure of their sacrifice is the value he himself put upon them, and many men have eagerly forgone them for less than a mighty place. As for the burden of his office, he had panted for it as breathlessly as he ever panted under it. And he had his reward of it each kaleidoscopic day.

Who was he, that his assassination unstrung us all?

Hard to say so soon, and it may not be easier when the market for the hurrying memoirs has been wrung dry of the last maudlin dime.

He was above everything else a sinner (like the rest of us). We should never have known it—certainly not that weekend or since— had it not been for the Requiem Mass in which the Cardinal Archbishop of Boston prayed for the forgiveness of his sins above everything else. But the Cardinal Archbishop's testimony, though it is unsupported by any other public authority, and though it still stands alone in violation of the injunction, *nil nisi bonum*, may be taken to be authoritative enough.

The petrifactive fiction of history doesn't assess such men as Mr. Kennedy; it fixes them, Caligula in his place, Cato in his. Who today or tomorrow would hear (or expect to hear) that the sainted Lincoln bought convention delegates, that the devilish Hitler provided free milk for every hungry child at school? History written is already history rewritten, and the book is closed.

John F. Kennedy did possess the brightest virtue in the modern American lexicon: bright youth. The vigor (no longer called "vigah") of youth has always been our hallmark. But youth is not a father figure, and since August 6, 1945, we have been afraid of the dark that we ourselves hung between man and the sun that day. We have groped—having shucked a venerable God—for a venerable man.

But venerability wants a settled preoccupation with grand purposes, purposes that evoke commitment, contagion, and passion from the depths. Four years ago the Editor of the *Progressive* found (as did everyone else) "an absence of the kind of contagious passion and deep commitment. . . . Most Americans see both [Kennedy and Nixon] as men who are cool and calculating. Men of measured merriment . . . and of measured tears."

Tears again . . . and who would supply them when they were wanting in a man in whom "what we miss most" (I am quoting the Editor again) "is a militant dedication to something greater than the single-

minded pursuit of power"? Who would supply the tears? The other
180 million of us, four years later.

A newspaperman traveling with Hubert Humphrey in West Virginia
in 1960 asked him what kind of man his opponent in the primary was,
"in one word." "In one word," said Humphrey, "cold"; and it was
clear that, had he been allowed a second word, it would have been
"ice."

No *charisma* in this cool and calculating man at whose death a
whole people cried and cried and cried. No identification with what
we were and are. No adoration, no madly-for-Adlai following. No
magic and no mystique beyond the mystique of competent power.
Here was the Boss with his hand on the tiller, and the methodologist
with his eye on the computer he used to be elected.

"In my family," he once told *Time*, supererogatorily, "we were
interested not so much in the ideas of politics as in the mechanics of
the whole thing." "A Kennedy-Humphrey ticket," said Walter Reuther
before the 1960 nomination, "would be a liberal ticket, and a Kennedy-
Symington ticket would be a conservative ticket." John F. Kennedy
once said he wanted the Presidency because "that's where the power
is." "A man of his age," the eulogists called him (and who, apart
from the Cardinal Archbishop, wasn't a eulogist?). But the age is not
the age of obstinate principle. It is the age of adjustment to reality,
the age of fast footwork, of the streamline and the hot line, of the
hard sell and the soft, of the adman and the admass, of the "people
machine" and the polling of polls and motivational research. "A man
of his age."

I see a brown photograph of Woodrow Wilson at his obstinate
typewriter, an Oliver, if I remember, a real photograph of a real man
writing a real speech on a real typewriter. A still photograph. Now
the speeches are written by many and rewritten by still more and put
on a moving prompter and read by the man whose name is given them.
And they are not such speeches as that given at Gettysburg by a man
in whom there predominated the mysterious dread (as Lowell said)
of praise, not blame. The words and the phrases ring on the counter
all right; they're pretested; but you who have teeth to try them bite
into the lead: "Ask not what your country . . ."

For three years the Editor of the *Progressive*, and everyone else,
waited for the emergence of "what we miss most"; and it never
emerged. Three years' time is too short, surely; but not too short for
a man to make himself, and not his image, clear. Not too short to
define a slogan. But the first two men escorted across the New Frontier

were J. Edgar Hoover and Allen Dulles, and the last was Adlai
Stevenson; and Mr. Kennedy was shoved and hauled across it by
four little Negro Sunday School girls in Birmingham. The test ban
was irresistibly pressed by the Russians and the English and the howl
here at home. The country didn't "get moving again." There was no
war on poverty or on wealth (including Bobby Baker's). And there
was never a mumbling word, in three years, on the un-Americanism
of the Un-American Activities Committee.

The country, and with it the world, was not much better and not
much worse after three years of vigor. In the December 1963 issue
of the *Progressive*—gone to press just before Dallas—the Editor said
what the other independent editors around the country were saying:
"There is more than one mess in Washington. . . . The President's
lame response [in the Korth case] falls far short of measuring up to
his campaign concept that the White House 'must be the center of
moral leadership.' . . . Nor was it civil rights opponents who shot substantial holes in the Subcommittee's bills, but the President himself.
. . . He preferred to put politics above principle."

His tenure was impeccably stylish: Chiang Kai-shek's was "the
only rightful government of China," and the people of Cuba would
"have their freedom restored." (Whose China? What freedom?) He
spent a couple of billion a year more for war, like all the Old
Frontiersmen before him, and on October 22, 1962, he took the
step to the brink from which Dulles himself had recoiled: No more
freedom of the seas (for which we had gone to war every time out),
and the Russian missiles ninety miles from Florida would have to go
(and the American missiles ninety kilometers from Russia stay) or
we would burn up the world. He united a dumbfounded country;
politics ends at the water's edge, and the grave's.

But the Kennedy computer, like all computers, was not infallible.
It had failed him when he turned his courageous profile to the wall
of a Boston hospital instead of casting an absentee vote in the Senate
censure of McCarthy. (The censure was already acceptable, even in
Massachusetts.) A premonitory failure, for as President he was unable, for all his computations, to carry his own Congress with him.
And the crude and clumsy aggression he ordered at the Bay of Pigs
in 1961 turned out to be a—quick! the right word for the image!—
"fiasco." The fiasco went into the computer and the "missile crisis"
of 1962 came out. (But Barry Goldwater could have plunged the
country into both the fiasco and the crisis without a computer.)

The computer is a capricious as well as a ruthless master. Forty-
eight hours after he found himself at American University, urging
coexistence, Mr. Kennedy found himself urging a perfectly rabid

anti-Communism at the Berlin Wall (rejoicing an audience that had learned its anti-Communism under Goebbels). He found himself alternately *for* humanity and *for* the starvation of Cuban humanity; *for* the Bay of Pigs and the Caribbean blockade and *for* international law and "our solemn agreements;" *for* peace in London and for *"Guerra! Guerra!"* in Miami.

Of course he had to be pragmatic—is this what pragmatism is?— because he was President by the skin of his teeth. More people actually voted against him than for him in 1960; and he squeaked through to victory over a man known by the two epithets "tricky" and "slippery." It was the first American election in which the candidates had been fully exposed to the electorate; in our spectator society we look men over and size them up; and we found these two to be of a size. There were even bumper stickers that read, Vote No.

What kept us all sitting on our hands in 1960 and for three years thereafter—until the day we all began wringing them? We had reason aplenty, after Ike, to admire Jack Kennedy's at-homeness as manager of the national enterprise. But we didn't cotton to him. Why not? We didn't know precisely. He didn't remind people—as Ike and Harry always did—of somebody they knew. He reminded people of an actor, on stage. (And at his side, on stage, Jackie.)

The family itself—the whole proliferation, including hidden "old Joe"—seemed to have a fine corporate flair that seemed to be busied with arranging the multi-million-dollar set for the leading man. The Lincoln rocker was a real help to his bad back, and ineluctably a stage prop (never more so than the night it was taken away from the White House under the klieg lights). The "Lincoln-Douglas" debates of the campaign were real—and a prop whose ham falsification on Cuba and Quemoy and Matsu seems to have been made for the medium whose forte is ham falsification. Robert Frost—the idea of using him was not Mr. Kennedy's at all, but Stewart Udall's—was splendidly real and an incomparable prop.

Was something going to be played out here, on both sides of the lights, to the very end? How right it was, after Ike, to bring culture into the White House, and how right the Housekeeper (and her stylists and designers). Was Jacqueline Kennedy hanging lace curtains? Well, aren't we all, these days? Not all of us: There was once a White Housekeeper, and not so long since, who was ridiculed because she went into the factories and the mines and the fields and let the lace curtains take care of themselves; Eleanor Roosevelt.

To the end, and beyond. Under the headline, "The Kennedy Sense of History," the *New York Times*, in one of its two accounts of the

incident (one placing it on the plane itself), reported that immediately upon landing from Dallas, Mrs. Kennedy summoned the Chief
of Protocol and said, "Find out how Lincoln was buried," and the
Chief of Protocol summoned a team of seven researchers who did
"ten hours of fast and furious work" in the Library of Congress and
had the report ready for the former First Lady before dawn. And so
the ritual was staged, under the direction of those masters of grand
illusion, the military.

Dallas, too, was on stage in the most amazing of all TV spectacu-
lars, to the end and beyond. "Grandma," said a lady I know, "is not
quite right in the head any more, and she's always phoning us to turn
on the TV. Usually it's Martians or Nazis. When she called and said
that President Kennedy had been assassinated, we paid no attention
to her. A couple of days later she called and said that the assassin
had been assassinated, and we paid no attention to her. She lives in
a dream world." To the end, and beyond: "The assassin," *Life* called
the suspect; in the midst of Death we are in Life.

John F. Kennedy's death and burial were possessed, like his life,
of a formal magnificence. "Ritual alone holds society together."
Everything he did and suffered—including the loss of his baby—seemed
to be transcendentally timed. He was the player, but he played a
script that might have been written on Olympus; a script that carried
us all with it, that weekend, in its elegant, almost Roman, rightness.
The Greeks had a word for it—a word that means both neccessity and
destiny.

We may be sure that this was a good man, as men go. He appeared
to have great qualities that other men do not appear to have. He was,
for instance, a man of apparent captaincy, unlike the man who said
to his friends in 1864, "I claim not to have controlled events, but
confess plainly that events have controlled me." He was a man
of apparent unambivalence, unlike the man who said to his enemies in 1864, "If God now wills the removal of a great wrong, and
wills that we of the North, as well as you of the South, shall pay
fairly for our complicity in that wrong, impartial history will
find therein new cause to attest and revere the justice and goodness
of God." He was a man of apparent aplomb, unlike the man of
unmeasured tears who was more of a myth a hundred years after
his assassination than he was a year after it.

President Kennedy was nonetheless a martyr, and nonetheless
did the most that a man can do for his country. His death was—
as Chief Justice Warren said at the bier—an awful lesson to the
purveyance of hatred and distrust among us. But the lesson went
unread; hatred and distrust rolled on.

For fifteen years we have not known what to do but keep our finger on the trigger. We put our faith in the Big Bang—we invented it—to purge us of the troubles with which wealth and fat and strength have paid us out. In Dallas something went bang. In Dallas we did what great power enables a great people to do: Destroy, and then weep like a little girl in a pet who has torn her doll to pieces.

For the Man Who Has Two of Everything

A few years ago M. Georges, Couturier in Furs, took an eighth-page ad in the *New York Times* for "the Georges Kaplan natural Russian crown sable": "It took us four years to gather them, but we now are in the position to offer what we believe to be the most expensive and the most beautiful natural Russian crown sable skins in the world. Just enough skins to make one coat, for only one woman, in time for Christmas." The price—this was before the inflation—was $125,000.

One warm woman, in the whole wide world, inside those skins at Christmas. What would you give to be that woman? (Your all?) What would you give to have her?

I dream of that woman, and it isn't lilac time.

It is Christmastime, time to pause amid the caroling canned goods and ponder Marx and Aristotle. "It's people's possessions," says Marx, "that get them into trouble." "It's not their possessions at all," says Aristotle. "It's their desires." (Guilty as charged: maunder in the first degree.)

What do I desire at Christmastime—the most beautiful sable skins in the world, *or the most expensive?* Has a society which has one fur coat, for one woman, in time for Christmas, at $125,000, or one such woman, or one such man who desires one such woman, got itself into trouble or hasn't it? Or the Personal Rolls Royce at $31,600? ("The paneling is of rare Circassian walnut. The carpets are wool, rimmed with hide.") (Whose hide?)

I would not buy the coat or the car, not at those prices. Not I.

What I would buy, at Christmas, for one warm woman, is an electric can opener to open a can or two a day. Or a genuine cow chip from the LBJ Ranch, offered locally for twenty-five cents. Or a canister of hot lather. Or, at $119.50, a Liquid Crystal Clock with "more than 1,000 transistors"—1,003? 1,009? 1,999? What's a transistor, Pop?—"to give you accurate time. The Liquid Crystal Digital Read-Out also gives you A.M. or P.M. indication."

"Read me out the time, Mother."

"11 o'clock."

Reprinted from the *Progressive*, December 1973.

"A.M. or P.M.?"

Or a cheapie (no Rolls, it) with not two, not four, not six, but eight lights in back. Or a pair of "Sperry Top-Sider" Jogging, Boating, All-Purpose Shoes for $14.50 (plus $1.75 for Shipping and Handling). Or a pair of gym shoes for $1.45. I will buy a Technoramic Razor from Schick, and heave-ho the old Gillette Technometric. I will go to the Holiday Inn, with one warm woman, to see the advertised Waitresses in the Briefest Attire.

What I would buy is that M. Georges coat or that Personal Rolls if I could lay my hands on the money. Unless Spiro got there first. "Charge or check, Mr. A?" "Cash."

It is Christmas time.

Half the world is hungry, hungrier, hungriest. Christ is crucified, without 1,000 transistors to tell Him when it's the Ninth Hour. "Who crucified Him?" "Nobody here but us finger-lickin' chickens, boss."

Who's going to save the country from me? Professor Cox?

I desire a ten-dollar, twenty-dollar dinner at the Inn. Who's going to save me when I haven't the money to pay the ten-dollar-twenty-dollar-dinner-gorging doctor? The Lord, whose injustice keeps the prostate in and lets the teeth fall out?

We girls will not be liberated by antiperspirants, no, *sir.* (Or enslaved by M. Georges's coat?)

Who will liberate us boys from the Touch-of-Gray Formula (Hi there, Dickie) and the Wide Necktie? (*Off* the narrow necktie, boys.)

What needs to be taken out of life, at Christmas time, is the jollity. Jollity at Christmas prices is no jollity. If it's jollity you have to have this Christmas get yourself the Amazing Talking Toilet ("Hey, I'm working down here!") for $5.98. That's your speed, soldier, this Christmas.

The beatniks of San Francisco's North Beach had the revolution going a decade ago. Its slogan was, Stay Out of the Market. It was the real revolution, the right revolution, the only revolution. It miscarried when the hippies came along with their $50 boots and then the Weathermen with their $50 bombs.

Going into the market for your Christmas jollies is a futile exercise in one-downmanship. There is nothing you desire that the slob next door doesn't desire two of, except *one* coat, for *one* woman. Are the Russians out of royal crown skins? No more Grand Dukes in the woodwork? The Personal Rolls Royce takes "a whole week's work to the tailoring of a single top"; that's fifty-two a year. Who desires to be one of fifty-two? Not I.

One of these Christmastimes I am not going to get out alive. If the B-Hong-Kong flu doesn't get me, the fire-bomb must, and that's for the birds if there's nobody left alive to bury me (or for the worms if there is). Next season may be that season. It would have been this season if God were watching His p's and q's.

God is watching His p's and q's, brethren. He is watching to see if Ibn Saud, and the Ford Foundation, and the slob next door, and I will give the $125,000 (or the $5.98) to the poor and then let go with a Pater Noster.

The efficacy of prayer is guaranteed: It saves you somewhere between $5.98 and $125,000.

The Lake

This," said Bob Vogel, "is it."

"Is what?" said I.

"Is Lake Elsinore" said Bob. "Beautiful Lake Elsinore, The Largest Fresh Water Lake in Southern California."

Before us stretched a long bed of gray mud, maybe five miles long and a mile wide. On the far shore, across the width of mud, was a narrow strip of gray water, maybe a foot deep. "That," said Bob, "is where the gnats breed."

"And where does the smell breed?" said I.

"I don't know," said Bob. "Lake Elsinore is—*was*—highly mineral. They say it's the minerals that killed all the fish when the water went down.

"That smell isn't minerals," said Jane (who is also Mrs. Mayer). "That smell is fish."

"The fish have been gone for two years," said Bob. "But Lloyd Lafler will know about the smell. We'll ask Lloyd."

He swung the car around from the shoreline—that is, from where the shoreline used to be and the mud is now—and drove down Lake Shore Drive. Most of the bungalows and cottages facing the mud seemed to be empty, and they had For Sale or For Rent signs on them.

"It's spooky," said Jane. It was.

It was spooky long before we got there, coming up Highway 395 from San Diego, out of the richly irrigated orange and walnut groves and into a stone-and-shale-strewn country of poor little clapboard farms and corrugated shanties with names like "Good Hope Chicken Ranch." A potato valley turning to wasteland; subsurface water pumped out, diverted out, lowered out, dried out.

It was spookier still, as we approached Lake Elsinore, to see all the For Sale signs along the highway, the closed motels and hamburger joints, and the signboards rusted, splintered, and fallen; spookiest of all when we got into the little town and didn't see anyone in the streets. "If I was going to Elsinore," said a man in Palomar, when I told him we had to be in Elsinore before dark, "I'd rather get there after dark."

Elsinore, California, was one of a series of one-night stands that

Reprinted from the *Progressive*, August 1951.

Jane and I were doing for the American Friends Service Committee. That night—it was six o'clock then—we were to lead a panel discussion at the Elsinore Union High School Auditorium. The subject of the discussion was "The Declaration of Independence and the Communist Manifesto." The panel members were to be twenty Elsinoreans, including a bartender, a Catholic priest, a Negro schoolteacher, a Jewish lawyer, a public utilities man, and the mayor's wife, Mrs. Edson D. Washburn.

The local sponsors were billed as the Elsinore Lions Club, the Elsinore Veterans of Foreign Wars, and the Elsinore American Legion. Bob Vogel, of the Service Committee, was along as general manager and to take the free-will offering, if any, for the work of the Service Committee. Lloyd Lafler, the parson of the Elsinore Methodist Church, was to be chairman of the meeting.

"Things are bad," said Lloyd, when we got to his house. "The town is terribly tense, and maybe we'll have a meeting and maybe we won't, and maybe we'll begin the meeting and maybe we won't finish it. I've arranged for the doors to be left open for the first fifteen minutes, but the doors are at the back and you're at the front."

"It Can't Happen Here," I said.

"It's happening," said Lloyd. "I don't know how many of the panel members will show up. I've been begging them to see it through, but they're scared. Everybody in town is scared."

"Of what?" said Bob.

"Of Communists," said Lloyd, "since the Lake dried up."

"Do you mean," I said "that the Communists dried up the Lake?"

"I mean," said Lloyd, "that the Lake dried up. Nobody knows who did it. The geologists don't know. The hydrologists don't know. The hydrotherapists don't know. The theologists don't know. Nobody knows."

"*We* didn't do it," I said, "we just got here."

"It isn't funny," said Lloyd, "and they don't say you did it, because they don't know for sure. They don't know anything for sure any more. So they're scared. They're scared of Communists. They're scared of the American Friends Service Committee. They say it's Communist. And they're scared stiff of the Mayers. I heard down at the Lions Club today that Jane was one of 'those women Communists.' They say that you two are a brother-and-sister team. That comes from your being billed as Jane and Milton Mayer, instead of Mr. and Mrs. Oh, I know the Quakers always use first names, but Elsinore doesn't. They say you aren't even married."

"Not," said Bob, "if they're brother and sister. At least I hope not."

"It isn't funny," said Lloyd, "and I'm scared, too." He was. "I'm not scared for myself," he went on, and he wasn't, "but I'm scared for you, and for the people on the panel, and for the town. The town's got it bad. The whole police force—all four men, including the Chief and the Captain—will be there tonight in plain clothes. The members of the Civilian Defense Organization—it's the biggest thing in town now—will be scattered through the audience. And the whole town will be there, scared and smelling blood."

"Blood and fish," I said.

"It isn't funny," said Lloyd, and it wasn't. It was spooky. It was spooky about the Lake, and spookier still about the fish. "The fish all died one day summer before last," said Lloyd. "One morning the whole surface of the Lake was solid with dead fish. The whole town turned out to haul them away and bury them, but they kept coming, and they had to get convict labor to haul them to the fertilizer factories in Los Angeles. But the smell never went away, and they're scared it never will."

"Gosh," said Jane.

"And then the gnats came, and they've sprayed everything, but the gnats keep coming, and the entomologists, immunologists, meteorologists, and philologists don't know why."

"Are they gnats," said Bob, "or locusts?"

"It isn't funny," said Lloyd.

"You bet it isn't," said Bob.

"Lake, fish, gnats," said Lloyd, "and this is a resort town, 'The Year Around Resort Town of Southern California.' That's its industry, always has been; mineral waters, mud baths, hot springs, reducing diet, and, above all, the Lake. We keep telling ourselves we aren't ruined, but—"

"You are," I said.

"How do we look?" said Lloyd.

"You don't look good," I said.

They didn't. We drove through the darkening town to the Wreden Hot Springs Hotel, "Famous for Food," "Visit the Elbow Room Bar and Lounge," "Nature-Heated Mineral Water," "Television in the Lobby." The town was hot—"360 Days of Sunshine Every Year"—and empty. The blinker light at the main intersection blinked at the emptiness. The Wreden Hot Springs Hotel Dining Room—"Famous for Food"—was empty except for us and the waitress. The food was not famous, but it was cheap.

It wasn't funny. It was spooky. I was scared. Not for the town, not for the panel members, not for Lloyd or Bob or Jane, but for me. I was scared that maybe I wasn't a pacifist.

We asked Lloyd about the Lake.

"First I've got to tell you something," he said. "Down at the Lions Club today somebody said we'd all have to take the pledge of allegiance to the flag tonight. Everybody looked at me and I said we would. I shouldn't have. I don't mind, myself, but I know you Quakers don't believe in pledges and oaths."

"Look," I said, "do they know that I'm a Jew, and not a Quaker?"

"No," said Lloyd. "At least they haven't said so. But they wouldn't. There are about 400 Jews in this town of maybe 2,000, and they are good customers, so nobody talks anti-Semitism. And there are about 400 Negroes."

Bob said he never heard of such proportions, and how did it happen? Lloyd said that in 1940 there were one or two Jewish families in town, and then some Los Angeles Jews who succeeded in getting their old folks out of the Old, or Hitler, Country started settling them in Elsinore, where they could sit inexpensively in the sun and the mud baths, and one old Jew told another and now there were 400. There had always been a few Negroes across the Lake, and along about the same time as the Jews came, Negro families from Los Angeles started building summer cottages there, and now there were 400 Negroes.

"Are there any Communists in town?" said Bob.

"Of course not," said Lloyd. "And there are 36 churches—in a town of 2,000 people—including the Holiness, Pentecostal Holiness, and Assembly of God. Mayor Edson D. Washburn is a trustee of my church and a fervent admirer of Gerald L. K. Smith and a leading authority on Communist activities."

"Any Klan?" I said.

"Nope," said Lloyd.

"Gerald Smith organizers?"

"Nope."

"Employers' outfits?"

"Nope."

"But who's behind it all?" I said. "Who's pushing it—the Legion?"

"Nope—the Lake. The Lake dried up. I've already told you. Something terrible is happening to us, and we don't know who's doing it, and we're scared. Acheson and McCarthy tell us the Communists are everywhere, so we know they're everywhere, so we're suspicious of everybody."

Bob said he guessed we'd better take the pledge of allegiance to the flag, because Lloyd would be in a bad spot if we refused. Jane said she didn't like to take pledges under duress, but she agreed with Bob. I agreed with both of them.

Then Lloyd told us about the Lake. Beautiful Lake Elsinore was about seven miles long and two and a half miles wide when it was a Lake. "What makes it spooky," said Lloyd, "is that the hotels are all named Shore Acres and Lakeview Hotel and names like that, and the Chamber of Commerce stuff and the signboards all still say 'On Beautiful Lake Elsinore,' and the ads all say 'Private Beach,' 'Water Sports,' and things like that and show pictures of bathing and boating and fishing and water skiing. The Lake was Elsinore and Elsinore was the Lake. And then the Lake dried up. Like that."

On the way to the Elsinore Union High School we didn't see anyone, and it was spooky, and the smell, or the sense of smell, was stronger in the dark. The school was on a knoll, and the auditorium, which was also the gymnasium, was up a long, wide flight of stairs. The big double doors were at the back; the dais for the panel was at the front; and between the doors and the dais were rows of folding chairs. Every seat was taken; an audience of 300 adults out of the town's total population of 2,000.

But there wasn't any chatter in the audience, as there always is before a meeting of any sort. The audience sat there facing us and looked at us hard, especially, I thought, at Jane.

"They looked scared, all right," I said to her.

"They're scared of *us*," said Jane. "Do you think they'll do anything?"

"If they're scared enough," I said.

"Or if *we* are," said Jane.

Half the members of the panel—including the mayor's wife, Mrs. Edson D. Washburn—didn't show up at all. The whole meeting stood up and took the pledge of allegiance to the flag, and I wondered what would happen to anybody who would refuse to, but nobody did, including me. Everybody was then given a copy of the Declaration—which we were going to discuss, along with the Communist Manifesto—and the Declaration was printed on red paper by some fool printer. The discussion was like taking candy away from babies—almost impossible. Jane and I threw our discussion outline away and did what we could to ease the tension by being jocular, but the jokes were painful. Every time we asked a panel member a question—any question—we got a Fourth of July oration by way of reply. The Jewish lawyer, no matter what we asked him, said that this was the greatest country on earth, and the Negro school teacher, no matter what we asked her, said that everybody had an equal opportunity in America, regardless of race, color, or creed.

The panel members were preoccupied. The leaders would ask a question, and the panel member addressed would ask to have the question repeated. But by that time the leaders would have forgotten the question themselves; they were preoccupied, too. Panel members and leaders, as they turned their heads to address one another, studied the audience, as unobtrusively as possible. The audience sat there, staring hard.

After 45 minutes like that, I interrupted the meeting to introduce Bob Vogel, who made the appeal for the Service Committee. The offering, among 300 Elsinoreans, was $21. Then I opened the meeting to questions from the audience. Usually half the audience leaves before the question period begins; that night, in Elsinore, everybody stayed.

The questions from the audience were slow in coming and didn't amount to much when they got there. There were long silences between questions.

Then a big, tall man in a sports shirt got up and said he wanted to ask Mr. Jack Norvell a question. Mr. Norvell, a member of the panel, was a roofer by profession, and was said to represent one of the handful of votes—most of them came from "Colored Town"—that Henry Wallace got in Elsinore in 1948. Mr. Norvell was one of the two or three panel members who had not delivered a Fourth of July oration during the discussion.

"I want to know," said the big, tall man, who turned out to be the high school athletic coach, "what Mr. Norvell thinks we ought to do with the people who won't fight for their country."

I think I nudged Jane.

You could have heard the head of a pin drop.

Mr. Norvell, a little man with a hearing aid, got up.

"Do you mean," said Mr. Norvell, "people who believe in religion?"

"I mean," said the coach, "people who won't fight for their country."

"If you mean people who believe in religion," said Mr. Norvell, "and their religion tells them not to kill anybody, why, I guess they don't have to, if that's what you mean."

There was a silence—just a few seconds, I suppose, though it seemed a lot longer at the time, and then the coach said, slowly:

"And how would you like it if some of us came out to your house some night to burn it down?"

Mr. Norvell, the little man with the hearing aid, said slowly:
"Come on out and try it."

An elderly man in the front row had his hand halfway up and I
called on him fast. He made a long speech about religion being communist among primitive people. He was hard to understand and he
talked a long time, and after a while the coach slowly sat down and
then Mr. Norvell slowly sat down. The old man ended with a favor-
able reference to God, and Lloyd Lafler popped up fast and adjourned
the meeting. There was scattered—thinly scattered—applause, and the
people started drifting toward the doors, very slowly, and then a fat,
red-faced man, in the second row, on the center aisle, jumped up and
hollered, "Wait a minute," and came to the front of the hall.

He was carrying a book in one hand and a long roller—of the sort
calendars are mailed in, but five or six feet long—in the other. He
stood half facing me and half facing the audience, and hollered:

"Are you the Milton Mayer who's a professor at Chicago University?"

I was sitting, so I stood up.

"I'm the Milton Mayer who *was* an *assistant* professor at the University of Chicago," I said.

"All right," the fat man hollered, "and now I want to ask you another question. Were you at a world government conference in Syracuse, N.Y., on February 13, 1947?"

Then I recognized the book he had in his hand. It was *Let's Abolish the United States*, by Joseph Kamp of the Constitutional Educational League, which, according to the American Legion, "makes
malicious and irresponsible charges against responsible and respected
groups and individuals" and "is a personal vehicle of Kamp's which
sells its pamphlets at profiteering prices in order to assure a good
living for him." According to Kamp's book, I, a responsible and respected individual, had advocated desecrating the flag, and that in
Syracuse, N.Y., on February 13, 1947. I hadn't.

But since Kamp had been put in the penitentiary, word seems to
have gone down the line to be a little careful of him. I sensed that the
fat man was being careful of Kamp, so, instead of talking about the
flag, I took the easy way out. Since the conference I attended in
Syracuse, N.Y., on February 13, 1947, had not been a world government conference, I said:

"No."

I was right; the fat man was being careful of Kamp. "All right,
then," he hollered, and laid the book down. Then he pulled out of
the long paper roller a big American flag and started waving it and
hollered:

"I'm a descendant of Admiral Perry, who sailed the Great Lakes and said, 'Don't give up the ship.' And I'm here to—."

Lloyd Lafler had been standing at the side of the hall, looking at me with eyes that said, "What shall I do?" I couldn't tell him what to do, at that distance. If he had been standing next to me, I couldn't have told him, either.

He came to the front of the hall and said to the fat man:

"I'm sorry, but you're out of order. The meeting is adjourned."

A low, hard voice said, somewhere in the audience: "Let him talk."

Lloyd stood there. So did I. More than half the audience was still there. They sat there, staring at me.

"And I'm here—" the fat man went on. And on. His hollering was all about Communism in Elsinore. Instead of attacking me, or Jane, or Lloyd, or Bob, or somebody, he was attacking Communism in Elsinore. But Communism in Elsinore is disembodied, and you can't lynch a disembody. And all the time he was talking, he was waving the flag, and you can't lynch a disembody with a flag. "Let's all sing," he hollered, and he sang, or hollered, the following World War I song:

If you don't like your Uncle Sammy,
Then go back to your home o'er the sea,
To the land whence you came,
Whatever be its name,
But don't be ungrateful to me.

If you don't like the stars in Old Glory,
If you don't like the Red, White and Blue,
Don't be like the dog in the manger
Don't bite the hand that's feeding you.

But you can't lynch a disembody with a flag and a song; nobody in the audience sang with the fat man. But they all sat there, and stared at me.

And then—the fat man was still hollering—my wife stood up next to me trembling. But her voice wasn't trembling, and she said, "Admiral Perry"—she says she said "Mr. Perry," but I say she said "Admiral Perry"—"I'd like to say something, if you don't mind."

The Admiral didn't hear her, and then a low, hard voice said, somewhere in the audience, "Let the lady talk," and Jane started talking to Admiral Perry, who stood there, with his mouth open, staring at her and waving the flag slower and slower as she talked. She said something like this:

"It's very hard to believe in God, Admiral"—or "Mr."—"Perry,

but we Americans want to believe in God because we want to be
protected and we're afraid that we can't protect ourselves. And
we're right. And believing in God is what makes the difference between the Declaration of Independence and the Communist Manifesto. If we take God out of the Declaration of Independence,
Admiral"—or "Mr."—"Perry, then we're left with a sort of polite
Communist Manifesto on our hands. But if we leave God in—and
leave Him in our lives—then we don't need to be afraid of Communism or anything else. We don't need to be afraid in Elsinore or
anywhere else."

Something like that.

And when she finished, and sat down, trembling, the people started
getting up and walking out of the hall, out of the big double doors at
the back, which were still open, and Admiral Perry stood there with
his mouth still open, and the flag waved slower and slower, and lower
and lower, and then the Admiral furled the flag and put it in the roller
and started out of the hall, looking around, but nobody said anything to him, and he went out.

The members of the panel had, some time during the Admiral's
hollering, faded away, all but the Negro schoolteacher and the bartender and the pastor of the Presbyterian church and the Jewish lawyer, all of whom came over and shook hands hard.

On our way out of the hall, Lloyd and Bob and Jane and I, we
heard some of the local toughies wrangling, and doing a little shoving
among themselves, in the back of the hall, just inside the big double
doors.

"And what would *you* say we should do?" one of them was saying,
"stick our heads in the sand?"

"What I say we should do," said a man in a T-shirt, who turned out
to be the local milkman, "is stick them Communists in the sand, head
first. They were all Communists."

"Ah, nuts," said the other man.

The high school janitor was turning the lights off.

The next day we learned that Mr., or Admiral, Perry lives in Murietta, according to the Elsinore people, and in Elsinore, according to
the Murietta people, and is a friend of Mayor Edson D. Washburn of
Elsinore. We learned that Mayor Washburn, trustee of Lloyd Lafler's
church and admirer of Gerald L. K. Smith, had been at the meeting,
along with Mrs. Washburn, who had failed to show up for the panel.
We learned that Mayor and Mrs. Washburn had witnessed the proceedings through an eye-slit in the movie projection booth at the back
of the hall. And we learned that as Mayor Washburn left the hall he

said to Chairman Habenicht of the high school board, "We shouldn't
have things like this in Elsinore," and Chairman Habenicht said, "I
don't know why not, it sounded all right to me."

That's what we learned the next day, before the *Lake Elsinore
Valley Sun* reported that Mr. Jack Norvell had, at the meeting, held
up a copy of the Communist Manifesto, printed on red paper, and
said, "I was born under this document and I'm going to live under
it."

We learned about that the next day. But we didn't stay overnight
to learn about it. We drove on to Riverside, for the next one-night
stand, and went to sleep, Jane and I, in an $8 room at the Mission
Inn, amid the palms and the orange blossoms, and forty miles behind
us we left Elsinore, The Year Around Resort Town of Southern California, where the Lake dried up, and the fish all died, and the smell
hung on, and the gnats came, and the people were looking for Communists.

Hollow Men, Hollow Laughs

The light fantastic has gone out all over America. No more people like my Old Man to ask the railroad depot ticket agent for a ticket to Springfield and when the agent says, "Ohio, Missouri, Massachusetts, or Illinois?" to say, "Whichever is cheapest." No more ticket agent. No more depot. No more railroad. Up and away.

Up and away up tight, and nobody up tighter than the dreary young enemies of Dreary Dick. I got into a plane in Cleveland last spring—the same Cleveland where Gene Debs once said, "A man can't live sober in a world like this"—and a collegiate drab took the seat next to me and tried to get her suitcase under it and couldn't. She turned to me and said, "What will they do?" "Call out the National Guard," I said. "That's not funny," she said.

That's not funny.

What is any more?

This side-splitting, skull-splitting society deserves its comeuppance for taking the joy out of the lives of its young. Gone the sweet smiling candor of the hippie who, when the judge said, "Take those stupid beads off," said, "As soon as you take that stupid robe off, your honor." Gone the hippie who cadged a dime from a straight and put it in the parking meter and lay down to sleep in one piece of street rented from one city for one hour. Gone the saturnine social commentary of the hippie buttons: "Jesus Saves Green Stamps," "I Am a Human Being—Do not Fold, Staple, or Mutilate," "Support Mental Health or I'll Kill You," "Kill a Commie for Christ," "God Is a Teeny-Bopper," "Smoking is Safer Than Breathing," "Help Stamp Out Thinking."

Gone the goofy good time they were having—was it only two or three years ago? Moping mum the merrymen of the Hashbury now. Gone the garlands, come the rocks. Gone the V sign, come the fist. Gone the curbside communion, come the confrontation. Gone the tinkling temple bells, come the pigstickers. Gone, all gone, and come all the sullen young men (and the furious young ladies demanding liberation from electric dishwashers and tossing their brassieres to the winds in protest against their being sex objects). *That's not funny.* What is?

Reprinted from the *Center Magazine*, January/February 1971.

It isn't only power that is not funny, but the struggle for power, the struggle to increase it, and the mortal struggle to hold on to it. Who wants power wants trouble. Who has power has trouble. Trouble isn't funny. Revolution isn't funny—Lenin is purest pain—and the Counter-Revolution of Declining Expectations isn't funny. The barricades aren't funny. And, though the Beatific Vision might be an improvement on Martha Mitchell, the end of the world isn't funny, and the young alone are intrepid enough to face it (and intrepidity isn't funny).

There are only True Believers standing eyeball to eyeball to eyeball now, massively reacting to their massive meaningless apothegms like "All Power to the People," or "Love It or Leave It," with Pavlovian inexorability; members all of what Peter Viereck calls the Salivation Army. The central element of True Belief is its unrelieved earnestness, the hallmark of the Vision in all its standard and revised forms. Marx is no jollier than Mark; ponderous Protestants (O! Wittenberg!) preaching the unglad tidings of great joylessness to an excruciated world whose only relief is the *Reader's Digest.*

Man is not only an animal, and a rational animal. He is (being an animal) a laughable and (being rational) a risible animal. If he isn't grotesque, his posturing ludicrous, his capers contradictory, there is nothing to be discovered in him. There are more chuckles in the tragedy of Hamlet than in all the triumphs of Socialist Realism, more realism in the chin of Philip IV as Velasquez saw it than in the ten tallest statues of Spiro Agnew. If man was ever going to be good for a giggle or two, it ought to be now, when he has come apart at the seams and John Kennedy turns out to have contemplated the advisability of assassinating Fidel Castro, a head of state. But no—that's not funny.

What's funny? What ever was?

Men who are reduced to extremity and know it—such men are humorous, and no others. Negroes are humorous; not blacks. Jews are humorous; not Israelis. Czech Communists are humorous; not Russian Communists. The reason they are humorous is that they have nothing else to lose and nothing else to live by. Humor is man's survival kit. If all Hitler ever wanted to do was destroy the world's joy, he had only to do what he did and put an end to the Jewish jokes (yes, of the Jew's own "anti-Semitic" jokes) that rejoiced the world so salubriously (and so harmlessly to the Jews). End of Moran and Mack, the Two Black Crows. End of the *Lumpenbourgeois's* Moran and Mack, Amos 'n' Andy. If my Old Man had not listened to Amos 'n' Andy, he would have been much more of a bigot than he was.

A last look at Dreary Dick's nomination of G. Harrold Carswell to the Supreme Court. One of the counts charged against G. Harrold Carswell was a joke he once told about a "Nigra" who was asked if he was from Indochina and said, "Nope—I's from outdawh Gawgia." A cornball joke, but a harmless joke; and Carswell's deadly, deadly enemies took it as evidence that he was a racist (as I don't doubt he was). Ridden out of town, as he should have been on his demerits, by a country that could not take a joke.

What such a country can take is entertainment. Never have so many provided so much entertainment for so many who laugh themselves silly enough to buy the product that produces the laugh for the sake of selling the product. But what has laughter—which can be evoked by the flagellation of a corpse like Mussolini's—got to do with humor? Laugh, and the joyless world laughs with you; smile unseen and unheard, and you smile alone. The country's smartest entertainer, S. J. Perelman, announces his departure into exile in a far land, and he is all bitterness; others he can entertain, but not himself. The worst thing that ever happened was television, which does our enjoying for us.

I suppose I am subject here to the charge of mixing two separate, or at least separable, phenomena. Enjoying oneself is one thing, humor another. But whatever further and loftier (or lower) purpose humor may have, its immediate purpose is pleasuring. If I do not have the capacity to pleasure myself, am I not still profited by other men's capacity to pleasure me? But then I must be pleasurable. I must be capable of being diverted from the doldrum which incapacitates me from doing my own enjoying, and unless I am, the immediate purpose of humor is frustrated. My thesis here is that we are losing our capability of being diverted from our daymare. The hollow man laughs a hollow laugh.

A culture which can take round-the-clock entertainment and get up every morning more morose than it was the day before can only be humored: it cannot be humorous. It cannot enjoy itself but only other's enjoyment—or others' representation of enjoyment; humor thrice removed. It is not having, but watching, a good time. This is the vicarious life. As we all know, the vicarious life is not worth living.

Tell me it isn't all that bad. Tell me that the landscape still jumps with Dickenses and Clemenses and Wildes and Gilberts and Dooleys and Cohens on the Telephone and Chaplins and Brothers Marx and Fieldses. Tell me that it jumps, not with reflexive pandemonium, but with the music of square pegs in round spheres.

Tell me that I shall live to see another *Beggar on Horseback*, hear another Englishman say, "Some say that life is the thing, but I prefer books." Tell me that Aristophanes and Rabelais without the raunch would be a drag and that Cervantes is a period piece. Tell me that *Twelfth Night*, if it weren't Shakespeare, wouldn't double me up, that I'm confusing fashions in humor with humor itself, and that we are as readily diverted as grandpa and a lot readier than Cotton Mather. Tell me that a clever divil like Swift—and what a bad time *he* had—can always get a sadistic rise out of people and that one or two comedians a generation (or a century) have always been par for the course in any case. Tell me that it is pleasant to read anything but the squibs at the bottom of the page in the *New Yorker* or that our columnists and commentators sparkle.

Or tell me that it is about time we took ourselves seriously and that he who can't live sober in a world like this is the butt of a very bad joke.

Enemies

About crime in the streets," I said, "I hear the statistics are down."

"Way down," said Alderman Leon M. Despres of Chicago's Fifth Ward. "We are waging a relentless war on crime statistics. And we're winning it."

"So," I said, "it's safer on 56th Street than it was."

"I wouldn't say that, exactly," said Alderman Despres. "You asked me about crime *statistics*, not about *crime*. The situation around your old haunts hasn't changed much since we began our relentless war."

It got to be 10 P.M.—time to wash my drugstore teeth—and the rest of the company had gone. I told my hostess that I'd toddle over to the Illinois Central suburban station and catch the 10:26 downtown. "Oh, no, you won't," she said. "Nobody 'toddles' down 56th Street after dark any more, and nobody, but nobody, goes up on the I.C. platform except in a phalanx."

"My strength," I said, "is as the strength of ten because my heart is pure."

"Better it should be bulletproof," said my hostess. "On the I.C. platform after dark you'd catch your death—not of cold, either. What you do is take a cab from here downtown."

"The Mayers," I said proudly, "did not get rich taking cabs."

"The Mayers," she said, "far from getting rich, barely remained alive. If you want to continue barely to remain alive you'll take a cab. I'll call you one and you wait downstairs inside the *inside* door and watch for it."

She called a cab and said, "They'll have one soon. Go down now and wait inside the *inside* door."

"Why not here?" I said sociably. "He can ring the bell."

"He can, but he won't," said my hostess. "They don't like to get out of the cab any more after dark. Not on 56th Street."

Fifty-sixth Street—land where my fathers died, land where I lolled and strolled my youth away, summer, autumn, winter, spring, baby, every evening, everybody lolling and strolling to and from the Univer-

Reprinted from the *Progressive*, May 1973.

sity campus. Loll and stroll no more. Fifty-sixth Street—klieg-lit like ghastly ghostly daylight now and nobody on it. At 10 P.M. on that rarest of all Chicago phenomena, a balmy evening, and nobody on it.

It was so balmy, and I so unterrified, that I decided I'd wait outside —the devil with inside doors and capitulation to popular panic. I leaned against the doorpost, insensibly turning up my coat collar insensibly to look terrifying. An occasional car went by with a swish. No patrol cars. No patrolmen. No nobody. (Off the pigs.)

Ten minutes passed. Fifteen. No sound. No footstep. Nobody. No body. Ghastly klieg light, a city abandoned before the Mongol hordes. No hordes. Nothing.

I sank my head deeper into my coat collar and lounged terrifyingly against the doorpost.

A car came along slowly and stopped, twenty-five feet or so up the street on my side. The driver—there were no passengers—began maneuvering it into an open spot at the curb and his headlights caught me. He stopped his maneuver and sat there, halfway out in the street, with his motor running, and held me in his headlights. Five minutes passed. Ten. I sank my head deeper into my collar, but I didn't feel terrifying. I felt less and less terrifying all the time. The driver sat there looking at me in his headlights.

The building door opened and my hostess came out. "I called again," she said, "and they said the cab's on the way," and she went back in. As she went back in, the driver began maneuvering his car again and parked. Then he turned off the lights, turned off the motor, got out of the car and locked it and with his house key let himself into the building next door.

He had been terrified sitting there with me in his headlights.

I had been terrified standing there in his headlights.

"It's a good thing," said Alderman Despres when I told him about it, "that neither of you had a gun."

My Country Wrong

Here is a woebegone burg, if ever I saw one. Its very ruins are fallen in ruin; and that, in a country whose principle product is visible ruins, means that Pharsala has no reason for being visited or, indeed, for being. Its 6,000 denizens bestir themselves in the manufacture, by ungloved hand, of a nougat so sticky that it is not very popular (not even in Greece). The *Guide Bleu* puts the kibosh on the place by saying, "Nothing of particular interest to see."

But the *Guide Bleu* is wrong. What the *Guide Bleu* means is "look at," which is not the same thing as "see."

You have only to sit in front of the Pharsala Café, drinking an American Nescafé, which is now the national drink of Greece, and open your back issue of the *New York Times* and read the words of the late Secretary of State Dean Acheson: "In the final analysis, America is the engine of mankind and the rest of the world is the train." Then you have only to raise your eyes to see something of interest in Pharsala.

The first thing you see is a small boy of godly mien playing King of the Mountain in front of the Pharsala Café. He is Dean Acheson's spiritual forebear, and his name is Achilles. His father is Peleus, the ruler of rich and mighty Pharsala. The nougat-and-fly-specked calendar on the wall of the café says, with marvelous foresight: 1242 B.C. Little Achilles is dancing around on top of a mound of donkey-dung and waving his wooden sword and crying: "Pharsala is the engine of mankind, and the rest of the world is the train."

The patrons of the Pharsala Café stare at him mesmerized: What will he do next? What will become of him, and of us with him? (It will all end twenty-two years later on V-Day in far-off Troy with his being mortally wounded in his unguarded heel and his falling off the engine of mankind, whose name is Greece.)

But there is something of more particular interest still to be seen in Pharsala. You have only to sit here, sipping your Nescafé for another twelve centuries, and *two* forebears of Dean Acheson draw up their forces in front of the Pharsala Café. One of them is Caesar,

Reprinted from the *Progressive*, September 1965.

the other Pompey, and they are going to fight it out, right here on the dungheap, to decide which of them, Caesar from the West, Pompey from the East, is to be the Imperator, or engineer, of the engine of mankind, whose name is now Rome.

The two Roman forebears of Dean Acheson prefer (like all Achesons) to fight it out as far from home as possible, and thus Pharsala in Greece is the Roman Vietnam. And thus you may see—if what you want is to see, and not look at—the Battle of Pharsala and the final analysis it provided: Caesar (who is soon to be assassinated) is the engineer of mankind, and Pompey (who is still sooner to be assassinated) is thrown right off the train. All in front of the Pharsala Café where the foresighted calendar now reads 48 B.C.

But it may be that the Pharsala of A.D. 1965 provides the *final* final analysis and that there is more of a particular interest to see in front of the Pharsala Café than there is from the White House window. To see, and even to hear; for here comes the café's proprietor, who tells you that the Americans are wonderful people, and when you say, in diffident reply, that all people are wonderful, he says no, only the Americans, and when you ask him for the evidence, he shows you what his *baba* brought him back from America: a transistor radio.

The engine of mankind.

The Americans used to be loved in Europe. The love was not, to be sure, unmixed with opportunism, envy, and cultural contempt, but the mixture was preponderantly affectionate. The Americans were open-handed, happy, and innocently idealistic. The land of the juke box and the Big PX and the hard sell was also the land of the four freedoms, the last best hope of earth.

But the European love of America has been a slowly wasting asset for the past fifteen years or more. Now one finds it nowhere— nowhere, that is, where I have talked with people on my return to Europe after an absence that dates from the Cuban missile crisis. It was on that occasion that fear (still inchoate after the Bay of Pigs) began to take the form which now seems to have hardened: the fear that the Americans can't afford peace and don't want it, concomitantly with the persuasion that the Russians don't want war and are doing OK without it. Since last February the fear has escalated into the ubiquitous suspicion that the Americans *want* war.

"Ubiquitous" is a big word. I speak of a sampling, and a small sampling, but an off-the-record sampling of independent persons, journalists especially, in Spain, Italy, Switzerland, Germany, Austria, Czechoslovakia, Hungary, Yugoslavia, and Greece. In some circles a thoroughgoing cynicism prevails. A holidaying Polish pundit—or pundish Polit—in Yugoslavia wanted to know, over a *vivoslitz*, why the Americans didn't attack China before it was too late; had they learned nothing from Potsdam?

But more pervasive than the cynicism and, for the first time, as common in the West as it is in the East, is the dread of a cowboy America gone beserk with Dean Acheson's doctrine of the engine of mankind. Europeans West no less than East are mesmerized, like the patrons of the Pharsala Café when Dean Achilles was waving his wooden sword atop the dungheap thirty-two hundred years ago. *Stupor mundi.* What will he do next? What will become of him, and of us with him? How will it all end? If Achilles' heel, then Acheson's.

The Communists over here can understand the Vietnam ploy as capitalist imperialism; they can get that right out of the book. But they can not square it, any more than the non-Communists can, with Medicare, integration, and the war on poverty. Nor can I; nor can you; nor could the people sitting outside the Pharsala Cafe listening over the transistor radio in 431 B.C. to Pericles telling the Athenians that he would not insult them by talking gobbledygook to them and that they had to maintain a tyranny abroad in order to maintain a democracy at home.

The only answer to the contradiction is, I suppose, implicit in Dean Acheson's "final analysis": What the engineers up in the engine are doing is none of the passengers' business in the train behind, an implication which the *New York Herald Tribune* explicates by revealing that "history has assigned the United States the grueling, often thankless but vitally necessary role of world policeman." The Greeks had a word for it as long ago as Achilles. The word was megalomania.

My country—my own, my native land—is morally wrong. And I can not, unlike the people of Eastern Europe, pass the buck by saying that it is ruled by a tyrant. I am its ruler. I should prefer to keep my country's scandal in the family and defend its name abroad even while I chastise it at home. But what am I to say to the European suggestion that it is as wicked as it is witless to send white killers with napalm to Asia—white killers, what is more, from one of the world's most notoriously racist societies?

Vlasta Petranik of Prague, the old Communist who has, Stalin in, Stalin out, proclaimed her feeling for America, asks me if educated men like Rusk, Humphrey, and the late Adlai Stevenson did not know that the Americans are the residual legatees of two centuries of Asian hatred of the white devils of Europe. She asks me if none of them dares to point out to President Johnson that the German invaders were in Czechoslovakia for seven years "and we hated them even more at the end than in the beginning."

The pro-Americanism of Europe is become non-Americanism, and the non-Americanism anti-Americanism. The British government is, aside from the vassalate of Bonn, the only "ally" supporting the American Imperium. But the British government does not love America; it loves Malaysia, so it has to say it loves America. The British and their government are bitterly divided on the issue. Like the French, who have no reason for playing the hypocrite, the British know the fatuity and the fatality of arguing that they have to stay where they don't belong because they are there. *Stupor mundi*, like Rome and like Greece; and what happened to the British, the French, the Romans, and the Greeks is to be seen in Pharsala, plain as a pikestaff.

Stupor mundi, and what will he do next? But there is a darker, deeper sentiment brewing beneath the mesmerization of Europe: the conviction, in hangover sorrow, that America is not the last best hope of earth. There has been no other in the post-Christian era, and now, with the recrudescence in nuclear America of Pharsala's megalomania, the delusion of the Renaissance, the Icarian delusion, is exploded. Man can not soar. The world is what the Greeks and Romans ended in—a mangy old tank town like Pharsala.

The meat on which the new Caesar feeds—anti-Communism—is tasteless and dry. It does not hold body and soul together, only body. It moves the Americans to the same thing it moved the Germans to not so long ago, *Kadavergehorsamkeit*, dead-man's-obedience. The next step is the advent of the wretched consciousness of the Europeans that "the king makes war and the people die." The next step: J. Robert Oppenheimer has only just discovered that his dream that his atomic bomb would "blackmail man into peace" has miscarried; he has yet to discover why.

To have to say these things in Europe in answer to the questions of Europeans is, as I say, a hard thing; hard to have the hooks thrown into one and to have to hang one's head. And to voice agreement, and disclaim responsibility, is a harder thing still; one sounds like an expatriate. "I notice," said one of my old Swiss friends, "that you say 'the Americans' these days instead of 'we Americans.'" I hadn't noticed.

The German elite should have been ashamed of their government thirty years ago, and some of them were; but too few, and too late. The massive shame of the American elite today is not too little, and every European I have met is aware of it and happy with it; the European question, posed in dread earnestness, being only, "Is it too late?" American resistance to American aggression is, certainly since last February, quite the thing and quite the spectacle to the generally servile European, East or West. For the first time since the Abolitionists it is now respectable at home to disavow the Establishment; indeed, whoever does so finds half the Establishment with him overtly or covertly. But to be a citizen-ruler abroad, and abroad to have to confess no defense of one's country is a dismayed, and not just an embarrassed, experience.

Sitting here in front of the Pharsala Café, I have asked the proprietor, him of the transistor radio, if he knows a fellow Greek named Herodotus. He can't place him, he says, though the name sounds familiar. Despairing, then, of finding a copy of the book in Pharsala, and having left my own in my other suit, I have to quote the final analysis of the Father of History from memory: "Those places which are now great were once nothing, while those which are nothing were once great; and so, I suppose, it will be in the future."

The Europeans seem to be saying, and many say it, that it is America's turn now to go over the falls, as it was once the turn of each of the engines of mankind that succeeded one another in Europe. That is why there is something to see, if nothing to look at, out here in the Greek sticks, where Caesar KO'd Pompey in front of the Pharsala Café for the Championship of the World.

A Diamond Is Forever

S. Zangara, the man who tried to shoot President Roosevelt and shot Mayor Cermak instead, when he was asked why he did it, said that he got black blood in his stomach sometimes and when he had black blood in his stomach he didn't know what he was doing. That's my trouble, only I know what gives me black blood in my stomach. It's the advertisements in the *New Yorker* magazine.

Once in a while the magazines, including the *New Yorker* (and the *Progressive*) have something good in them, but only once in a while. And then they are sure to be called to your attention, and you can go to the library and read them. That's how I got to read the condensation of William Bradford Huie's *The Execution of Private Slovik* in *Look* magazine and from there I read the book. The book is the best reporting job I have ever seen, and one of the most important books of our time. It did not win any prizes, because it lifted the lid a little on the national shrine, which is war.

My friend Ephraim Doner, who paints pictures, gave up reading the newspapers several years ago. Ephraim is now the best-informed man in the neighborhood, because everybody, knowing that he doesn't read the newspapers, hurries over to tell him what is going on. Magazines are for coffee tables and newspapers for wrapping and, in the absence of kindling, for rolling into scotch twists to start the fire. Fielding's *Tom Jones*, Dostoevski's *The Possessed*, Melville's *Billy Budd*, and Proust's *Remembrance of Things Past*—these are for reading.

So it was that somebody called my attention to Edmund Wilson's wonderful report on the Dead Sea Scrolls in a recent *New Yorker*, and, as I turned the infinite pages, infinitely filled with two columns of advertising to one column of content, my eye, which is poorly fastened, fell on the advertising, and my stomach filled with black blood.

In the advertising, Rise Stevens, the singer, was shown plugging Air France. The ad said: She's Air-Wise, She Loves Luxury, She Pays No More. I translated the first assertion to read, She's Money-Wise, and

Reprinted from the *Progressive*, July 1955.

the last, She Pays Nothing. But my black blood boiled when I read, She Loves Luxury, and, like S. Zangara, I didn't know what I was doing. Miss Stevens should not love luxury. At least she shouldn't say so. She should love God. At least she should say so.

Then there was an ad, full-page, in forty-seven colors, for De Beers Consolidated, and the ad said, A Diamond Is Forever. Now forever is a long time, and, if it is true that all things shall pass except the truth of the statement that all things shall pass, then a diamond is not forever. But my black blood cooled when I remembered that General Electric had just succeeded in manufacturing the first manufactured diamonds. Diamonds will soon be a dime a dozen, and that will take care of De Beers Consolidated and their claim that a diamond is forever. At least De Beers Consolidated isn't forever, and that is some satisfaction.

On the next page was an ad for Union Oil Company, and at the bottom of the ad it said, Your Comments Are Invited, Write: The President, Union Oil Company. So I am writing mine.

"Dear President, Union Oil Company: In your ad, you say, ' But if—as in Russia today—government had a monopoly on all business, there would be no incentive to bring you anything better.'

"Now, Dear President, since there is no incentive to bring you anything better in Russia, you may rest assured that there is nothing in Russia now (including atomic bombs) that wasn't there in 1917, at which time the government obtained a monopoly on all business. In 1917 Russia fell apart, and since things must be the same there as then, there is no reason for a war scare here, and if there is no reason for a war scare here we will just take the government out of the business of buying oil and the Union Oil Company will fall flat on its face. I remain, but not yours, etc."

On the next page was an ad—for the American trade—for the Austin-Healy sports car, only $2985 fully equipped. It showed two dolls looking at a guy with an enviable amount of enthusiasm, and the ad said: "For some people distinction is a gift conferred at birth. More often though it is something aquired with maturity as tastes become more discriminating. But however it is achieved, the unnamed owner in our advertisement seems to have attracted an enviable amount of enthusiasm. That he is identified by his Austin-Healy '100' is no coincidence."

You bet it isn't. He's a sap, with pimples retouched out by the advertising agency artist. Without his Austin-Healy he would attract no enthusiasm. Without $2985 he wouldn't have an Austin-Healy. He's a sap with pimples and $2985, and the dolls who are enthusiastic about him are tramps.

I couldn't finish reading Edmund Wilson's report on the Dead Sea Scrolls because my eye kept falling on the advertising and my stomach filled with black blood.

The editorial content of the magazines and newspapers is so much better, at its worst, than the advertising content that the Man from Mars will never believe that they were prepared for the same people. But the editorial content isn't as good as Fielding, Melville, Dostoevski, and Proust, so why read it until you have read what is better? The *New Yorker* stories pass the time, but so does sleep, and more profitably, because what my old man said of the Alps, "When you've seen one, you've seen them all," can be said of the *New Yorker* stories, while there is no such thing as enough sleep.

But some of the things the newspapers report are as black-blood-curdling as the Union Oil Company advertisement. On last February 28, e.g., the Associated Press reported from London in the *Baltimore Sun:* "Prime Minister Churchhill finished today the draft of a speech which informants said outlines the horrors of nuclear warfare and explains Britain's decision to build hydrogen bombs."

This looked like a misprint, at first. The second clause, to follow the first, should have read, "Britain's decision *not* to build hydrogen bombs."

But it wasn't a misprint. Nor was the United Press report, a few weeks earlier, from the capital of the United States, Augusta, Ga.: "President Eisenhower today hailed French Assembly approval of West German rearmament as a 'decisive' signpost to world peace." I should have supposed that if any kind of armament would be a signpost to world peace, it would be *dis*-armament. Uh-uh. A diamond is forever. In Russia today there is no incentive. She loves luxury. He seems to have attracted an enviable amount of enthusiasm.

Black blood.

The Wheel of Hate

American democracy has just been saved—again—by the American Veterans Committee, the American Jewish Congress, the Jewish War Veterans, the Anti-Defamation League of the B'nai B'rith, and the National Council of the Arts, Sciences, and Professions. May their tribes decrease.

The enemies of American democracy consisted, this time, of two aging male musicians, one of them, Wilhelm Furtwaengler, the third, or perhaps second, greatest living conductor, the other, Walter Gieseking, the third, or perhaps second, greatest living pianist and by all odds the greatest living interpreter of Mozart and Debussy. Their weapons consisted of a wand and a piano. They have both been repulsed by the saviors of American democracy and they will both continue to perform in France and England, where they are welcome.

The French and the English suffered less, presumably, at the hands of Furtwaengler's and Gieseking's Nazi friends than we did. Or maybe France and England are antidemocratic and pro-Nazi. Or maybe our democracy is so enfeebled that the invasion of a conductor and a pianist would destroy it. Or maybe the United States has been made a fool of by the AVC, B'nai B'rith, et al.

Furtwaengler, the conductor of the Berlin Philharmonic since 1922, was invited to conduct the Chicago Symphony Orchestra next year, and he withdrew his acceptance after some of the blood-drinkers listed above threw the whole book of Nazi horrors at him. Gieseking arrived to conduct a sell-out concert tour and left with a *Vive la France!* when the pack turned on him.

Neither of the men was a Nazi, both of them had been cleared of Nazism by the American Military Government fumigators, and both of them had been certified as harmless by the State Department. The testimony that Furtwaengler actually saved the lives and the freedom of Jewish musicians under the Nazi heel was uncontradicted.

But let's say they were both Nazis, just to make it easy for the blood-drinkers. The American State Department and the American Military Government are both so asinine in these matters that we should not be impressed by their seals of either approval or disap-

Reprinted from the *Progressive*, March 1949.

proval. Let's say that Furtwaengler and Gieseking, instead of being dumb, compliant, and weak-kneed musicians were full-blown Nazis who actually thought that Hitler was Wotan and who condoned the unspeakable bestialities committed by the Nazi regime.

What then?

What did we gain by letting the blood-drinkers repel them from our shores, and what did we have to lose by letting them in, the one with his wand, and the other with his piano?

In the gain account, I find not one item. Not one. Two Nazi musicians—we're saying they're Nazis, mind you—who do not make speeches could not in any way imaginable have injured American democracy, American morals, American freedom, or American culture. The war is three years over, the Nazi regime has been destroyed and deracinated, in so far as force can destroy and deracinate, and Furtwaengler and Gieseking are Nazi musicians who were musicians before they were Nazis and were never engaged in any other occupation than music during the Nazi regime.

In the loss account, I find, first, that American democracy has testified to the world that its fabric is weaker than that of England and France; second, that America has repudiated both its Judaic principle of equal justice before the law and its Christian principle of redemptive love; third, that those Americans who wanted to hear it have been deprived of hearing some of the best music in the world, and that all of America has been deprived of a serious contribution to its culture; fourth, that, by treating as monsters two Germans who are adored by their countrymen, America has played into the hands of the Russians.

This is the gain-and-loss account in the Furtwaengler-Gieseking matter, and none of the blood-drinkers listed above can, nor will any of them try to, maximize the gain or minimize the loss. What they want is more blood, and whether or not a liquid diet is good for them they are too drunk on blood to care.

Instead, they will reply by reciting the list of unspeakable bestialities committed by the Nazi regime, under which Furtwaengler and Gieseking were compliant musicians, and, while they deny they hate the two musicians for being Germans, they will crucify them for the same crime, namely, weak-kneed compliance, that was committed by nearly all the Germans in Germany.

Furtwaengler and Gieseking were not heroes, though there may actually be a trace of heroism in their refusal to join the Nazi Party. Germans are not heroes, although there may have been traces of heroism in untold millions of them who, while they did not dare open their mouths, dared to smile a friendly smile on the open street at

Jews whom they had loved. Americans are not heroes, though there
may be a trace of heroism in the feeble protest of millions of them
against the bestial atrocity of Hiroshima.

The spokesman-in-chief of the blood-drinkers, just for the record,
is Walter Winchell, the darling-in-chief of the original and persistent
native American fascist, William Randolph Hearst. When American
democracy is saved by Winchell, the rights of the workingman will be
saved by Pegler.

Apart from Winchell—the most scurrilous figure in journalism—
the blood-drinkers appear to have found few confederates in their
effort to keep the wheel of hate turning, with all of mankind chained
to the rim. Newspaper opinion—such as I saw—was almost uniformly
against the pogrom. The *New York Herald Tribune* was eloquent, and
the *Chicago Daily News* rose to mournful beauty:

"Many Germans who were not vicious men acted like Furtwaengler.
Sometime, the rest of the world must reestablish relations with them.
It is important that those who can be brought actively to share in the
common culture of civilized humanity should do so. If they will
share in its common political and ethical traditions, so much the better. It will not be wise always to cry 'untouchable' to those who are
willing."

But the blood-drinkers weren't taking any chances on the American people. Carnegie Hall was sold out for Gieseking's first concert—
which was canceled two hours beforehand—and Orchestra Hall in
Chicago would have been sold out for Furtwaengler. The blood-
drinkers didn't care whether the American people agreed with them
or not. They did not want democracy; they wanted German blood to
drink.

The Anti-Defamation League, whose single function, so far as I
have been able to discover, is defamation, explained to the *Chicago
Tribune* that the League had gone to work on Gieseking "out of a
sense of duty." The *Tribune* asked: "Duty to whom?"

The question went to the heart of the matter. And of course it
went unanswered, because the answer is, "Duty to hatred."

Now, we can understand, without justifying, the hatred that Artur
Rubinstein has for his fellow Germans, and his refusal to appear in
concert with Furtwaengler. Five members of Rubinstein's family
were murdered by the Nazi regime. We do not expect him to behave
normally toward his fellow Germans for a long time to come, if ever.
What is more, he and the rest of the Jewish soloists who said they
would not appear with Furtwaengler are exercising the same right as
those Americans who, for any reason or for no reason, would not

attend a Furtwaengler or a Gieseking performance. If a Jew does not want to associate with a German in activities that do not involve the common good, there is no reason why he should.

But nonassociation is not the same thing as segregation, and segregation is a form of pogrom. The Jews have been on the receiving end of so many pogroms that you would think they would not want to have anything more to do with them, but the smell of one's very own blood seems, in this instance, to whet the appetite for another's. And so they keep the wheel of hate turning, ignoring the fact that the one way *not* to save the Jews—or any other small minority—is force.

If you ask the American Veterans Committee, the Jewish War Veterans, the American Jewish Congress, the Anti-Defamation League, and the National Council of the Arts, Sciences, and Professions whether they want to keep Nazis out of this country, they will say yes. If you ask them whether they want to keep Nazis off the U.S. Government payroll, they will say yes, indeed. But if you ask them why they don't get up on their hind legs to protest the importation of Nazi scientists and engineers to work on bombs and rockets for the U.S. Army, they will tell you that that is different. Nazi musicians produce music, but Nazi scientists and engineers produce bombs and bombs produce blood.

The doctrine in the counterpogrom against Furtwaengler and Gieseking combines the pernicious fallacy of collective guilt—the fallacy on which the Nazis slaughtered the Jews—with pernicious infantilism of revenge. When the unspeakable bestiality of the Nazi regime has been avenged on all the Germans, where shall we be?

The wheel of hate was turned at Potsdam; then, in spite of MacArthur's great words on the *Missouri*, at Manila in the hanging of Yamashita, then at Nuremburg, and then at Tokyo. In our duty to hatred, we manufactured a fraud called international law, in the prosecution of which we have thrown out the window the very first principle of Anglo-Saxon law, namely, that no man shall be a judge in his own cause; out the window, too, the Constitution of the United States, which forbids the passage of an ex post facto law; the Declaration of Independence, which asserts that government rests upon the consent of the governed; and, just in case it, too, should turn out to be an American document, the Holy Bible, which enjoins us to forgive those who trespass against us.

The tragedy of the Jews is their imitation of the Gentiles, who have sacrificed Christianity and the Constitution to the duty to hate. A Jewish musician like Yehudi Menuhin, who pleads for Furtwaengler, goes unheard and himself goes into the blacklist of the pretended Jews who will not remember that Job asked God to grant him consideration for the fact that he never gloated over his fallen enemy. The Jews learned the counterpogrom from the Gentiles. The Gentile answer to Chancellor Hitler's Nuremberg Laws was Justice Jackson's Nuremberg Laws, both based on force without justice. In this perpetuation of hatred, in this increase of sorrow and suffering, in this Hitlerism turned inside-out, the American Gentiles who engage in destroying Furtwaenglers and Giesekings are destroying American liberty and love, and the Jews who join them are destroying themselves.

Part Four

If You Keep Moving . . .

The Turn of the Year

Christmas is the hinge on which the year turns. The world is suddenly quiet for the event, as quiet as the world can be. The sun, the source of tumult, is farthest and palest; the wind, which blows creation into its holes, is coldest; and the things that grow grow slowest. It is a time for quiet, in which the pagan ear is open for the sound of a snowflake pushed aside by the crocus. The liquorous celebration of merchants and statesmen only contributes to the quiet, for when they are making merry they are not making mischief. Suez is quiet; Main Street is quiet; Holy Russia is quiet. The year is going to turn, and who, whether or not he knows it, is not brought to prayer that he will find less hate and more love within him next year than last?

There is no time like it for man, no time so well and so widely known as the time of change and the time to change, if change there will be and if to change is possible. Each of us has his own private birthday, coming any old time in the year, and which of us remembers the birthdays gone or, as we grow old, anticipates the birthdays to come the way we wait for Christmas? At Christmas the English eat, the French are hospitable, the Germans joyful, the Americans generous; it is the time of times, of redemption from the solstice dark, from the atomic age, from the hypocrisy which drives us to succor the victims of Communist bullets in Budapest and ignore the victims of Democratic bombs in Port Said.

It is a time to be young, a time of skates and sleds and Lebkuchen and lights, and a time to be old and welcome the Spirit of Christmas Past, of skates and sleds, Lebkuchen and lights, to the table.

Leaves have fallen which hung on through the sunless solstice of the turning years of yore. This year the Spirit of Christmas Past brings new companions of his own to the table—my old teacher, Anton Carlson, rightly called Ajax, who knew the living organism so well that nobody doubted that he would live forever, and he almost did; Carroll Binder, patiently particularizing the flash of current history in solid editorials; Noel Sullivan, bringing Negroes to swim in his swimming pool because why else, he wondered, would Christ give a man a swimming pool; Al Widdifield of the bull sessions of a quarter

Reprinted from the *Progressive*, January 1957.

century ago, disappeared into business, reappeared in an unlucky
plane over the Grand Canyon, the Vice-President in Charge of Advertising of the Sunbeam Corporation, insured for $650,000 against
unluckiness; Ike Rosenfeld, 38, young enough to have been a student
of mine, too fat for his heart.

At one of the turns of the years it became the time to be old, and
to talk a new kind of talk, talk of cancer and smoking, of wills to
write and places to settle down in, of things you never did, and meant
to, and had better do now. Maybe when you're thoughtful, or senti-
mental, or Jewish, the time comes a decade ahead of its time, and the
thoughtless, the reasonable, the gentiles are rolling along as merrily
as ever and going ahead and cutting down trees, competition, men;
maybe. The new head of NATO is exactly my age and he says that
the Russians understand nothing but force; he must be half my age,
or twice my age, but he isn't my age, where, when the year turns, the
lifetime turns. You've been going through, say, the Sonora Pass, up
and up and up, and then there's a sign that says SONORA PASS
9624 Ft., and you know, even though you've been in the pass for
miles, even though the road ahead has its ups and downs, that this
is the summit, and now you're over the summit and onto the slope.

A settled melancholy is upon you now; whether you wanted to be
a saint or a satrap, the chances against you have changed categorically
from one in a million to one in a billion. You are what you are, and
all your contemporaries are what they are, and this is the way it will
be, give and take a little luck here, a plane crash there, every Christmastime from now on. You can fight it, by drinking a pint or chasing a
girl or playing three sets of tennis, but you can't fight it off; it's upon
you, the last of life for which (the poet said) the first was made, and
if you try to slop the first over into the last you are only sloppy. Or
you can do your work, and know your place, and smile and read and
gossip and go to the movies, but home (now that the kids are old
enough to leave them without a sitter) seems to be the best place to
be in the evening. You're not unhappy, not in the least; it's just that
you aren't a tomcat on a tin roof any more.

Joe Schwab's Jill got married; Cecil Hinshaw became a grandfather;
and ladies whose necks are lined (their grandmothers would have
worn real or false pearls right up from the clavicle to the chin) tell
you how becoming your hair is with gray in it. The leaves are falling.
More of them are gone every Christmas time. And those that are left
in the garden of your life are all sere, or just on the verge.

Somewhere way back there you quit drinking, ostensibly for religious or financial reasons, but somewhere up here you know it's because it was bad for you, meaning your organism. Chuck Sills had a

heart attack, and how easily he gave up smoking. Bill Dickinson quit smoking because he likes to play tennis, and his leg hurt when he played, just a little. Did you know that you've got to lay off milk (and you've always loved milk) because its fat is saturated with hydrogen-producing cholesterol and cholesterol is the insulation that the little carpenters are tacking up inside your arteries? The oculist says you haven't a sign of glaucoma *or* cataracts, and at *your* age (he says) that's unusual, but, still, you shouldn't wear your distance glasses for reading any more, and it won't hurt (he says it like that) to quit typing, just for a couple of minutes every hour, and rest your eyes. You can still carry two suitcases and a rucksack on your back in Europe, but you can't laugh any more while you're doing it.

You've been dying, physiologically, since you were twenty-five, but now you know it. You've got a few good years in you yet. So has your automobile, if you take care of your automobile, and if you take good enough care of it you haven't got time for anything else. Some nice people gave us an old automobile a couple of years ago—they felt sorry for us because we didn't have one—and it had a little ridge of rust around the trunk lid. Now the doggone thing is eaten away completely. You've got to take care of it or it will go to pieces on you. Of course you can always trade it in on a new one; that's one nice thing about an automobile.

Now that you know how to beat the world, or save it, whichever you wanted to do, it goes tearing by you. And it isn't a matter of running as fast as you can just to stay in the same place. Not at all; you mustn't run as fast as you can any more, and that's all there is to it. It was two years ago that Dicken—he was nine then—beat the pants off me at tetherball and waited while I came up the hill to the house after the game. He doesn't even suggest any more that we play. He's the Sunset School tetherball champ, is Dicken.

You're not unhappy. No, you're not. You're never been happier, and the Spirit of Christmas Past is not a gloomy companion, just a quiet one. You've had a jolly good time and you've been a jolly good fellow and you might have been and done worse. Think what might have happened to you over Hiroshima, or in Madison Avenue. Think of the trouble you've seen, and it doesn't add up to a fraction of the trouble that others have seen—or shut their eyes to. You're going great. You're in the pink. "You're in wonderful shape," says Bob McCabe (who's on a diet now), "but don't shake your head or it might fall off." If you want to go to Athens—you always wanted to go to Athens and find out about Socrates—you'd better be think-ing about doing it. You'd better be learning Greek right away.

As the year turns I've been learning Greek. An old man—he seems
to be much older than I am, but Dicken's big brother Rock looked
at the class the other night and couldn't tell who was the teacher—
teaches it free. Which is reason enough for learning Greek. Then
there's the Oxford boy who, a couple of centuries ago, asked the
Dean of Christ Church what good it was to learn Greek and was
told, "Not only is it the original language of the Holy Ghost, but it
leads to great dignities and emoluments." I was telling the teacher,
last time, that I was so tore up over the first and second aorist that
I couldn't remember the accusative singular of *potamos*, which was
the first word we learned, and an old lady in front of me turned
around and whispered, "The trouble is, Mr. Meyers, that we're not
as young as we used to be."

A time to be old, at forty-eight, older than you will ever be again.
What did it? Do you know what did it? The children did it.

It was the children that kept me young, while they were young.
That's why I kept them young as long as I could. It was their de-
pendence on me that made me independent; a little like a bunch of
drunks going down the street, the drunks on the outside leaning on
the drunk in the middle and, by doing so, holding him up. And now
the children are independent—they really are, you know—and I am
dependent again. I can't stand up the way I could, and there's no one
to lean on. We want Grandma to come and live with us, to be dependent, but Grandma won't come; she's gone past forty-eight and
learned how to stand by herself; so we have no one to lean on us to
hold us up.

I remember when my father was forty-eight. I remember the gray
in his stubble before he shaved late (just as I do) on Sunday morning.
He was the oldest man in the world. I could not imagine being so old.
I can't imagine it now. But I am. What, at forty-eight, could he tell
me when I was a kid? What did he know about the phonograph? What
do I know about television? What did he know about Gallagher &
Sheen? What do I know about Elvis Presley (including how to spell
it, if I've spelled it wrong, and I'm ashamed to ask Rock)? What did
he know about the Charleston, except that it ought to be banned,
and what do I know about rock'n'roll, except that it ought to be
banned? What good could he do me?—He was a salesman and, in the
great mobile democracy of America, I was going to be a writer. And
I am a writer, and my kids, in the faster moving democracy than ever,
are all going to be something else.

What?

Aristotle wasn't a fool clear out to the rind, and he said that all men want to live forever, and, since this is impossible in themselves, they try to do it in their children and to make their children in their image. So I love Little Julie the best, because she is most like me; and I love Little Manda the best because she is most like what I wanted to be, deep and beautiful; and I love Rock the best because he is most like what I tell the sinners to be, kind and forgiving; and I love Dicken the best because he is most like the men I most admire, tough-fibered and tough. But of them all, only Dicken (he's eleven now) still feels for my hand and takes it in his, instead of the other way around.

They have their lives and their secrets. Good lives, but not mine; innocent secrets, but not mine. They have their problems, but they are not overwhelmed, or at least not overwhelmed enough to come crying to me with them. Amanda is away for a year at a time, at a school in England, a good school, she says, and it's fun there, but— my Little Amanda, how can she grow up without me? Quite easily, that's how. Little Julie, my firstborn, is finishing college; scatter-brained Little Julie; how can she *finish college* without me? Quite easily, really. Rock has a newspaper route, and with his first month's take bought a $25 television set at a rummage sale. Well, we would never have a television set in the house, and Mommy and I wondered, before the fact, just what we should do, and then I remembered that when I peddled bills for Spivak & Stein's Grocery on 51st Street, I stuffed them down the sewer and wanted worse things than a TV set.

They know I'm a pretty nice fellow, for all of my hollering, but I don't hold their attention. They don't think I'm funny. That's the worst. I think I'm a riot. My gags are great. But the kids go right on snouting their soup, and when Mutti, who loves me, laughs at the gags, the kids raise their pink little snouts from the trough and say, "What's up?" Nothing's up. I'm down. I'm a displaceable person. I feel like Cicero getting home from his proconsulate in Spain and saying to the old keeper of the city gate, "What has happened in my absence?" And the old gatekeeper said, "I didn't know you were away, Cicero." My kids don't know that I'm here.

I had a dream. I dreamed that my babies left me outside the super-market in my wheelchair while they went in to do their shopping, and got to talking, the way babies will, and ignored my whimpering and my drooling, and then the Spirit of Christmas Past came down the street and snatched me out of my wheelchair and made off with me, and I cried to my babies to save me, and I heard them say, and it was the last thing they said before I woke up, "He doesn't really want anything—it's just an attention-getting device."

There's still Dicken. He reaches for my hand. He calls me for his
prayers. He walks to the post office with me. But the other evening,
on our way home from the post office, he said, "You know what I
think? I think the Russians will never be forgiven for what they did
to Hungary." "Who told you that," I said, "Mr. Jones?" I knew doggone well it was Mr. Jones. "Yep," said Dicken. Mr. Jones, who's
supposed to be teaching seventh-grade subjects to seventh-grade kids
at the Sunset School, ought to be canned for saying that, but I can't
tell Dicken that his teacher ought to be canned, so I say, "Did he
say anything about the English and French attack on Egypt?" "Nope,"
says Dicken, "he didn't." And I know that Dicken is slipping away
from me and into the world of the Joneses. I want him to be a pacifist. Well, maybe he'll be a pacifist some day; I was told once that the
Germans would never be forgiven for what they did to Belgium.

Slipping away, without ever a notion that they're pulling the props
out from under me. Making me old by growing up—and then pushing
me playfully down the stairs. Oh, I'm still good for a little tame football or basketball when there's nobody else around; still good for
three, four, or five squares a day; but I'm not good enough to go
steady with any more, the way I was when I was leaning on their
baby carriages. Let 'em go, let 'em go, God bless 'em. I know better
than to try to hang on to them. The heck I do.

So Christmastime is a sorrowful time. They let me sit at the head
of the table still, but it's only out of respect for the aged. Say, listen,
I'm still in my prime. At the top of my powers. I've got twenty,
thirty years in me yet. Providing I take care of myself and forget
about everything else. Not on your tintype. None of your chain saws
for me: I'll go through that pine like a knife through butter; but I'll
sit down for a while, in between logs, and be sorrowful.

Is what I'm saying that I want to live forever? No, *Ma'am*. I want
to be born again, but I don't want to live forever. Just look at the
damage I've done and think of the damage I'd do. But I don't want
to be cut off in my prime, and I tell you I'm just really *approaching*
my prime. I believe I *will* have a second cup of coffee, thank you.
It keeps me awake nights, and nothing else does.

A sorrowful time, not because I would be made a child again, but
because I want my children made children again, and it was only a
few little years ago that they were. Only a few little years ago that I
could hold them in one hand—and get my hand wet. A sorrowful
time, the turn of the year; more crowded than last, and the next one
more crowded than this, with the companions of the Spirit of Christ-

mas Past. But the Spirit of Christmas, Present, Past, and Future, consoles me with glad tidings of great joy, the good news of salvation. And salvation is better than nothing.

An Extra Pair of Laces

Did I ever tell you how my Old Man made it? No matter if I did; if Mozart's *Vesperae Solemnis* is worth hearing twice, so is the story of my Old Man's making it.

He didn't make it good, but he made it. And so have I. And so will you, if you do as he told me and as I tell you.

My Old Man was as honest as the working day was long in those days. But he had his own idea of honesty. Taking a little something from what Wendell Willkie (before he turned pious) called "public utilities, privately owned," was the bounden duty of an honest man. It wasn't taking a little something at all; it was taking a little something back. For the utilities were—as they still are—bleeding the poor.

It was a case of we or they—"them or us" were my Old Man's words. They gave no quarter and took every nickel in sight. If you got one back, by whatever means, you were performing an act of rough rectification, or distributive justice. And you were the same man who would walk a mile to bring a widow a jar of hare's-foot jelly. There was no contradiction between uprightness and downright robbery of the rich, Nottingham or no Nottingham.

The American way provided many blessings then, but one of them, known as higgling and haggling, had already given way to the Quaker doctrine (which had made the Quakers rich) of O.P.O., One Price Only. A pair of shoes was a dollar-and-a-half, take it or leave it. You could not get them for less—or be sandbagged for more unless you were an immigrant or a darky who could not read the price tag.

There was half a dollar's profit in a pair of shoes, and my Old Man did not see why there shouldn't be forty-eight cents. So, when he bought us our shoes, he would say offhandedly to the clerk, "Just put in an extra pair of laces, will you?" And the clerk, though he stood rock-ribbed, four-square, and copper-sheathed on O.P.O., was nothing loath in those happy-go-lucky days.

That extra pair of laces was the foundation of my Old Man's fortune. It was not a large fortune, but it was enough to bury him. Par for the course.

A penny here, a penny there; and thus my Old Man made it, with

Reprinted from the *Progressive*, April 1969.

an occasional Pullman towel, an expired streetcar transfer, a coin in
the Coin Return box, and a seven-year-old on his lap who (as he and
the conductor agreed) was big for three.

I am a chip off the old block, an old chip now, curling fast and
more than a little brown around the edges. But I have made it the
way my Old Man did, a penny here, a penny there. A lot easier, because a penny is easier to come by. In the supraverbal society anybody who can string two words together can sell them to anybody.
My Old Man had to hustle his paper-box samples on the streetcar
the whole day long, including Saturday mornings, and he took in
forty dollars a week. (He called them iron men.)

Me, I would not stop rocking in my rocking chair for forty dollars
a day. (I call them lettuce leaves.) I'm a contemptible hack, of
course. I will never write the *Ode to the West Wind*, which would
take me a year and pay me five dollars and immortalize me. But I
cannot afford immortality, and neither can you. These are the times
that try men's bodies.

I made it by holding before me the image I commend to you.

It is the image of my Old Man, slicing it thin at the dinner table
and saying, with affected amazement, "Why, there's enough left
over for another meal." And if there wasn't, to Ma: "Lou, buy a
pot roast tomorrow and ask Art if he has a nice soupbone he could
throw in, and then go over to the grocery department and tell John
that you got a nice soupbone from Art and you wondered if he had
some soup greens"; a nice soupbone being one with enough meat
on it for a meal.

The rest of the Armenians were starving, but the Mayers, though
they were eating low on the shish kebab, were eating. When my Old
Man said, as he did, "You only live once," he, like you, was talking
through his hat; but unlike you he did not mean that you should
spend. He meant that you should save, a penny here, a penny there,
in order to stay alive in case you only lived once.

Saturday afternoons the spenders were in the saloons, feeling
flushed. My Old Man stayed home feeling flush. Saturday afternoon
was the best time to hit him for an extra penny. Since he slipped
me my weekly five on Sunday, when Mrs. Wispy's School Store was
closed, I was, at the rate of a penny a day, fresh out by the following
Saturday. So I would rub his back for him—those samples were plenty
heavy—and he would slip me the extra penny, pretending he was
joking when he said, "Don't spend it all in one place."

I would tear down the street to Mrs. Wispy's and luxuriate in front
of the showcase, choosing among an embarrassment of riches—a yel-

low marshmallow banana, a likrish whip, a cornucopia of candy corn
or peppermint hearts, a whole miniature package of Necco wafers, a
whistle, a print-paper for my sun-picture slide of the Empire Express.
I would then ask Mrs. Wispy what else there was, and she would say,
"What do you want for a penny—the world with a little red fence
around it?" And I would say, "Let's see it." Having made my choice
and insisted on a striped bag, at which point Mrs. Wispy would say,
"You boys are driving me to the poorhouse," I would tear back home
and my Old Man would ask me what I had done with the penny. I
would say, "Spent it," and my Old Man would say, "Boy, you don't
know the value of a dollar," and I would say, "What's a dollar, Pop?"

My Old Man knew what a dollar was. A dollar was a conglomerate
of one hundred highly productive enterprises, a holding company.
Its operating subsidiaries produced all sorts of valuable commodities—
a penny postcard, a newspaper, a top-string, a half-pair of shoelaces,
or *two* carmels at the Greek's. You could bet a penny, lend a penny,
borrow a penny, steal a penny, lag a penny, play penny ante. There
wasn't anything you couldn't do with a penny, including burning a
hole in your pocket. My Old Man, surveying, of a Saturday evening,
the hundred operating subsidiares of each of his forty weekly con-
glomerates, knew the value of a dollar.

As I do now.

And of a penny.

True, the only two things you can buy with a penny nowadays are
a much thinner stick of greatly debased gum out of a slot or ten minutes in a small-town parking meter. Instead of chewing gum I chew
my gums now, and if you drive around the block you'll find an empty
parking place with ten minutes left on the meter by a crazy spender.
You may have spent a nickel driving around the block, but that's not
the point. The point is that you know the value of a penny, and unless you do you'll never make it.

Still another thing you can do with a penny is stay home and
fondle it until the first of the month and then take it carefully down
to the bank and put it out at interest. There is nothing more
un-Christian than taking interest, but I can not afford salvation, and
neither can you.

You go to the bank via the back streets, and return via the shopping
streets. You don't go into the shop lest they give you credit and re-
plevin the junk the day you can't make the last payment.

With leopard coats at $10,000 and wood-pulp tomatoes a dime
apiece, you have been priced out of the market. Stay out. You won't
make it otherwise. Don't repair and don't replace, unless it's a
cooking-pot. A man who doesn't have a pot to cook in needs one.

Buy what you need, and never anything else. And stop talking about need being relative; today Biafra, tomorrow the world, so Be Prepared.

Consider the things you think you need. Half of them you can borrow and return "some time"; books, for instance, at $6.95 for a thin one. There is no evidence that books have ever done anybody any good, but that is not the point I am making here; the point I am making here is that you can borrow books and you can most easily borrow those books about which your tasteful (but profligate) friends are most enthusiastic. The other half of the things you need not only do you no good but do you positive harm, television, for instance.

It takes time, but time is nothing; money is everything. It takes time to soak an uncanceled stamp off a letter; it takes time to squeeze every coconut in the supermarket until you have got the biggest one; it takes time to root around in the crannies for a penny you either lost or think you lost. But time is nothing; money is everything.

Once you decide that time is money, you are done for. My big brother Howard once tried to persuade me to cross the country by Pullman instead of by day coach. I would, he said, arrive refreshed instead of exhausted, having got a couple of good days' work done in my Pullman compartment; three days saved in all, "and your time is worth fifty or a hundred dollars a day." I didn't argue with him; he was right; but once I decided that time was money, I'd be done for (and never play another game of chess, besides).

It takes time to find "yesterday's" bread at half price instead of "today's" but time is what you've got and money is what you haven't.

Most of the people who get hooked on the fantasy that time is money get coronaries, and then they have time. Take it easy. The only place you can take it easy is home, once you have broken your wife's spirit. Don't go anywhere unless there's money in it. Don't play golf or tennis or Ping-Pong unless somebody else furnishes and refurnishes the equipment. You can't afford equipment. Take up sports like walking or jogging or yoga, providing you don't have to buy a sweater for them. Don't buy a book on yoga; one book leads to another. Borrow one.

It is false pride (and you can not even afford true pride) that makes people make long distance calls, leave the lights on, take taxis, go to steak joints, buy other people drinks, travel first class (or second, if there's a third), and see the plays and the concerts and the movies five or ten years before they're shown on television. It is the falsie of all falsies to keep a bowl of fruit on the table until it starts rotting and you have to throw it away. You can live without any of these indulgences. You can not live pleasurably without them, but you can not afford to live pleasurably.

You can not afford not to be a piker. You can not afford to go to a restaurant at your own expense. Go, if you must, with people who can. If you don't know people who can, stay home. Your wife will complain. Let her complain, you can not afford an uncomplaining wife. When you go to a restaurant with people who can, don't reach for the check. Say, "Let's make this dutch," but don't wound the other fellow's false pride by being a pigheaded dutchman about it. Lose the argument and don't insist next time that this one's on you. There need not be a next time. If he is the kind of small-minded person who entertains with a view to being entertained, cut him off your list. You don't want friends like that. You don't want friends who cost you money.

The principle of nonreciprocity applies with equal force to your being invited to somebody's home for dinner. Whenever people entertain you and you entertain them "back," both parties lose money; it's what A. A. Stagg used to call a viscous circle. Stay home. Stay home and look at—I didn't say "enjoy"; you can't afford enjoyment —the nice Westerns. Or save the electricity and contemplate your navel, if you have one. The life of contemplation is the highest life, and it was Aristotle who said so in the *Nichomachaean Ethics*.

If you make friends, make rich friends who do not count the cost, or poor friends who provide you with Quaker hospitality, however lumpy the bed and the mashed potatoes. You'll survive, and if you don't—well, do you want to live forever? Not if it costs money. Under present wartime conditions, with the whole world at war with you, you have got to live off the land or you won't make it. When would Sherman have got to Atlanta if he hadn't foraged, or Grant to Richmond?

On the whole, the rich should be avoided, partly because they count the cost (how do you think they got rich?) and partly because they think that you love them for their money. (They may be right.) They want you to love them for themselves—and to prove it by spending money on them. But what you want is a free flop or a free meal. With the poor, you can lay it on the line and tell them why you want to visit them; besides, you love them. The rich will suspect that you are using them—as, indeed, you are, and as you are using the poor— and its winds up with a lot of heartbreak. You cannot afford a broken heart if it costs you money.

Stick with your own kind of people. Drink, if you must, but drink

Gallo's; you can not afford wine. And don't ever drink with people who, when they get drunk, get so drunk that they say, "Let's go out and get something to eat."

Your inability to remember birthdays and anniversaries will break your wife's heart and, ultimately her spirit. Remember, it's her spirit you've got to break. Your refusal to celebrate the Great Gouge of Christmas will take the exuberance out of your children. If the present uproar on the campus tells us anything it tells us that children should have the exuberance taken out of them when they're young.

Don't celebrate your wage raise; according to the Bureau of Labor Statistics, wages rose by 5.5 percent in 1968, but "increases in consumer prices eroded most of this gain"; plus taxes. Don't consume and don't celebrate. There isn't anything to celebrate, and the only thing you can celebrate is the Mass. Celebrate the Mass, if celebrate you must; the best things in the *next* life are free.

Enter the next life precipitately. Die, but don't get sick. If you get sick, you will find, when you get done with Blue Cross (or *v.v.*), that you were afflicted by an exotic affliction (such as a broken leg) that wasn't covered by the policy or, if it was, was covered up to a maximum of twenty cents a day when the daily cost was twenty dollars (or, more likely, up to twenty dollars a day when the daily cost was two hundred). Don't buy glasses; go blind; you've seen everything. Don't go to the dentist; milk toast is cheaper than porterhouse. The lives these Manslaughterers in White save are outnumbered by the deaths brought on by stroke suffered by people who got their bills.

Stay out of the market. Don't buy anything. Don't buy anything pink. Don't buy anything blue. Don't buy anything borrowed. Don't buy anything new. Don't buy anything retail, and don't buy anything wholesale. Don't buy napalm, and don't buy it for the Government by paying your taxes. Don't buy anything from Dow or anybody else. Don't—but you're not *that* stupid—buy a car no matter how much it costs you to keep the old one going. My '59 Volvo is so crumpled and crummy that I'm ashamed to be seen in it even when (as is usually the case) it is standing still. I can't afford to be unashamed. And neither can you.

Like my Old Man, I've made it. I've made it by being a cheapskate and, what is more important, by being known as a cheapskate. Carlyle was right. Carlyle was right because he said that of the three great goods of life, money, health, and reputation, the one a man can easiest live without is reputation.

If you start doing things for the sake of reputation, such as making money in order to help the poor, you are *tutto kaputo*. Nobody cares about the poor except the poor, and nobody is going to do anything about the poor except the poor. Comes the revolution, and the man the poor are going to go after is Mr. David Packard, who, for all I know, makes money in order to help the poor. Mr. Packard is a Merchant of Death. Upon taking up the post of Assistant Secretary of Death under Mr. Nixon, he said that he had no intention of living on his salary of $30,000 a year.

You may say that Mr. Packard is a fool; I wouldn't know. But if you think that you can go on racing down the primrose path without becoming Mr. Packard, you are already a fool. The profligate society, living it up and shooting 'em down, spends as if the bottom were going to drop out in the next ten months or the next ten minutes. It is going for broke with its increasingly nonnegotiable currency the way the kids—God bless them in general, but not in particular—are going for broke with their increasingly nonnegotiable demands.

Comes the revolution, you and Mr. Packard, unless you listen to me, are going to wish you had never been born, while I go right on making it, like my Old Man, a penny here and a penny there, a nice soupbone, an extra pair of laces.

I Do Not Want an Automobile Just Now. Or Ever

Automobile Manufacturers Assn.
New York, N.Y.

Gentlemen:

I yield to no man, and to few women, in my admiration for the automotive industry. The very phrase rolls on my tongue like tokay. But I do not want an automobile just now. Or ever. I don't want a hydramatic, ultramatic, or numismatic automobile, a powerglide, dynaflow, airflow, -flight, -flyte, or fleetline automobile, or even a Cadillac Debutante like the one I saw covered with leopard skins and white sidewall tires optional— optional like death and taxes.

I've had an automobile. There's a Ford in my past. I bought it for $100. It ran halfway out of the used-car lot and stopped. The used-car man had a tape measure, and the tape measure showed that the car was more than half-way out of the lot; it was mine. I pushed it to the J. B. Johnson Automotive Service. J. B. Johnson himself was there. He opened the hood, wrinkled his forehead, and said, "It's the compression." "What's that?" I said. "Fifteen dollars," J. B. replied.

This happened once or twice a month. It wasn't always fifteen dollars, but it was always the compression. Then J. B. retired to Palm Beach and bought the old Flagler Place, which he renamed "Compression Cove."

I bought a Buick cabriolet for $200. This was an interesting model of a type you may not remember. You could look out of it both to the front *and* to the rear. You could even wear a hat while looking.

I walked this one into the S & S Garage one day in late April. "I think it's the starter," I said to Sam Schenck, the co-proprietor. Sam opened the hood, wrinkled his chin, and said, "It's the points." Points turned out to be half the price of compression, but twice as often. I suppose Sam calls his Florida Place "Point Comfort."

After the Buick I traded my inheritance *and* my pottage for a $975 vehicle. About the time the engine block cracked, my banker,

Wormley, dropped in to tell me my loan would be called unless I put up more collateral. "You have my right eye now," I said. "You still have your left," said Wormley, polishing his gold-handled cane with the palm of his glove. I got to my feet, took a few tentative steps in the direction of Wormley, and found I could walk. *"I can walk,"* I said wildly. "You no longer interest me," said Wormley frigidly, and he waved to his man to carry him to his car.

All that was some time ago. But I am still on my feet, I am happy to say, and in spite of your blandishments I am going to stay there.

Gentlemen, the automobile made a fool out of me. I got so I called people bad names—not just pedestrians and policemen, but my own little children, when all they wanted to do, in the middle of Sunday afternoon traffic, was go to the bathroom. I got into two wrecks mastering the overdrive in the city and two more using fingertip touch control in the country. I got into another one trying to wear a hat.

I have taken note of the "integrated" fender. You nick a fender and you buy a body. And now, they tell me, you're taking the clutch out. So all right, you take out the clutch and the left foot joins the tonsils, the adenoids, and the appendix as evolutionary vestiges. But, like them, it hangs on, with nothing to do. It gets nervous. It starts beating time to the music coming out of the dashboard radio. Then the right foot absentmindedly joins the left, and the road is strewn with flaming wreckage.

I have been thumb-and-forefingering through the four-color advertisements for your 1950 models. I see them now for what they are. That beautiful woman leaning on the front fender (it *is* a fender, isn't it?) of the new Nash Airflyte—what will she look like ten years from now? What will she look like now, if the brake slips? That couple getting out of the new Lincoln Cosmopolitan in front of the big red-brick house with white pillars—where did she get the ermine throw? Why have they been invited to the boss's house for dinner? I had a car, and the boss never invited me to dinner. Not only that, but when I told him I had to have a raise, he said, and his voice was like ice, "You manage to keep up a car on your present salary, I see." Ermine throw, indeed.

My brother has one of your automobiles. He told me it costs a man $1000 a year to drive a car. He had it down in black and white— not just depreciation, but wear and tear *apart from* depreciation; not just wear and tear, but repairs *apart from* wear and tear. He told me about things I had never heard of, things you never advertise in four colors, such as the interest on the purchase price, compounded.

I asked him how long it took him to figure this all out. He said he

did it in three or four hours one Saturday while driving around looking for a place to park. I asked him how much his time was worth.
"Ten dollars an hour, time and a half on Saturdays," he said. It cost
him $60 to figure out how much it costs a man to drive a car (and
$2 to park it when he finally found a place). I say that a man who
doesn't drive a car is putting money in the bank—$2 here, $60 there,
$1000 here and there.

Gentlemen, I am in the middle-income bracket, or vise. People
like me are doing well if they make *one* end meet. On top of not
having a car, I haven't got all that money it takes to drive one. I
don't want you to take this personally, gentlemen, or to think that
I'm a small-minded old fogy. I'm aware that the automobile, like
the flying saucer, is here to stay. I simply don't want one. I've had
one. I bought it for $100. It ran halfway out of the used-car lot . . .

Yrs. rspy., &c.,
MILTON MAYER

Not Making It

On December 2 last, President-elect, now President, Richard M. Nixon wrote me a personal letter.

I know it was personal not because it began, "Dear Mr. Mayer"—they can't fool me; that's done by machine —but because it ended, "I will appreciate greatly, Mr. Mayer, your taking time from your busy schedule to participate in this all-important program." If they can do *that* by machine, I'm a chump.

And I'm not a chump. If I had been, President-elect Nixon would not have been asking me to recommend for the new Administration "men and women who by their qualities of youthfulness, judgment, intelligence and creativity, can make significant contributions to our country. I seek the best minds in America . . ."

Now, I am no sunshine patriot who could not take time from his busy schedule to help his President-elect seek the best minds in America. Nor am I suspicious of other men's motives—Mr. Nixon and I both learned simple trust from our Quaker forebears. So I did not ask myself how Mr. Nixon knew that mine was a busy schedule and whether he had had somebody watching me to find out.

His letter was not marked Confidential, but he enclosed copies of a Confidential Résumé for Federal Government Appointment. I was to have my recommendees complete the forms and return them to me to be forwarded to Mr. Nixon with my comments. The completed forms would not be Confidential from Mr. Nixon *or* me, but both of us learned from the Quaker taciturnity of our forebears how to keep our mouths shut on certain subjects at certain times in our lives.

The Confidential Résumé required recommendees to reveal the number of their marriages, to account for "all time since High School," to confess whether they had ever been charged with or convicted of a felony, and to disclose their present and past "political experience . . . and affiliation." They had also to admit the purpose of their foreign travel in two countries, Russia and China.

But Mr. Nixon and I both know from our forebears that Quakers have nothing to hide. Why should other people have anything to hide?

Reprinted from the *Progressive*, February 1969.

In shouldering the burden that my country laid upon me in the person of President-elect Nixon, I found myself possessed of an embarrassment of riches. I had four youthful and very creative children to recommend. My cousin Moe (known lovingly as the Doppis) is no longer in the first blush of youth, but he brings creativity to whatever job he gets—and is looking for one. My local police chief has never been charged with or convicted of a felony. My intelligent superiors in academe have had plenty of political experience, all of it outside Russia and China. And my Aunt Liz can account for all time since High School; she was sixteen when she got life-and-99 for judiciously taking a meat cleaver to her Ma and Pa.

In the end, I submitted fourteen candidates. None of them was appointed—or, at least, hasn't been so far. Meanwhile, President-elect Nixon had selected youthful, judicious, intelligent, and creative men for his Cabinet, including, as Secretary of the Interior, a Mr. Hickel, who announced that he was against "conservation for conservation's sake." How creative can you get?

I had recommended the best minds I know, and I could only conclude, when Mr. Nixon made his appointments, that he knew still better minds. So I was at rest as regards the safety and security of our country.

Or would have been if it had not been for my confounded wife. My confounded wife, who conned me into *Who's Who in America*, said she had read somewhere that every one of the 60,000 best minds listed in *Who's Who* (including my cousin Moe the Doppis) got the same personal letter from Mr. Nixon. (*There's* what I call a busy schedule.) If each of them recommended fourteen best minds, that's 840,000 best minds for Mr. Nixon to have chosen from, or an even 900,000 including the 60,000 recommenders.

That ought to make me feel even safer and securer except that Mr. Nixon and I were both brought up on the words of George Fox, who in 1652 was moved to tell the people of England that "the mighty Day of the Lord is coming upon all deceitful merchandize and ways."

A Much Better Mousetrap

I went down the mountain—no small matter—to see Herr Michel because Herr Michel is the hardware and implements man in Meiringen and I had to have an implement right away. I had to have an implement to keep the mice out— or bounce them if they kept coming in. Or, as a last, always regretful, resort, show them that the white man was master by adopting a pacification policy of search-out-and-destroy.

It was the middle of November, and the snow line was descending from the high meadows of the Berner Oberland. The mice were coming down ahead of it, just a-looking for a home. Some of them, and some of their sisters, and their cousins, and their aunts, had found Chalet Flühli, which I was renting. They were gnawing their way into my investment and coming up from the cellar (which was cold) by way of the rotted wood around the water pipes.

Mind you, I didn't blame the mice for coming down, and in, and up. But I'm afraid of mice.

Don't ask me why.

It could be because I'm a city boy (or was, before I rented Chalet Flühli). Or because their tails are naked (I'm not afraid of squirrels). Or because they scamper and I'm afraid that they'll scamper up my pants leg or down my collar.

"Afraid" is the wrong word, of course. Make it worth my while and I'll wrestle any mouse in the house. But I don't *relate* to mice the way I do to, say, butterflies and some people. Put it that way.

What I am of mice is shivery. *Unbequem*, is what I said to Herr Michel in Meiringen; uncomfortable. But I said it of Mrs. Mayer, not of me.

I'm just as shivery of them dead as alive, what's more. The formerly-five-cent mousetrap is not supposed to be disposable. You're supposed to remove the mouse and then pour boiling water over the trap so that the next victim won't smell anything untoward, and then bait it again. Instead, I pick it up by the end farthest from the mouse and heave it as far as I can into the woods from the nearest window (which I have opened before I pick up the trap). Then I keep away from the woods for a while.

There is a finer side to my shiveriness. A mouse is something to be killed. I don't like to kill (or even be killed). I don't mean that I'm physically afraid—that, too, of course—but that violence is as unendurable to me morally and religiously as it is (to anyone in his right intellect) intellectually. It isn't manly (not to say Christian) to kill, or even injure. Self-defense? A just war? Against mice? Come off it. It isn't, above all, fair play to set a trap for man or mouse. There was a time—or should have been—.

Not a word of these vaporings to Herr Michel in Meiringen. Herr Michel is a countryman and he calls a rat a mouse (and doesn't understand my German anyway). He says that there is no way to keep mice out in the late autumn. And once they are in, and warm, they get to feeling neighborly, and paying calls, and the next thing you know the place is all over mice. Herr Michel shrugs his shoulders. He has lived a long time and always in Meiringen—whence the word *meringue* was derived when a former Meiringener first baked meringues in Paris.

The night before I went down the mountain to see Herr Michel I was setting a formerly-five-cent trap and caught my thumb in it. I always do; intentionally, I dare say, since it is an article of my faith that he who sets the trap will perish in it. The next day I was brandishing my bandaged thumb at Herr Michel—who didn't see how I could possibly have caught my thumb in a mousetrap—and telling him that I had to have an effective implement. He handed me another formerly-five-cent mousetrap and when I said, "They don't do any good; the mice keep coming," he said, "That's right. But sometimes," he added, "after a while they stop." "Why?" I said. He shrugged his shoulders. Then he said, "I heard of a better mousetrap recently. An American invention."—I puffed up.—"It's supposed to *keep* catching them somehow. And then they go away." "Why?" I said. Herr Michel shrugged his shoulders.

He said he'd get it for me in a day or two—meaning a week or two —and meanwhile I should try something else. Something else was a deadly powder with an ingredient that created a maddening thirst. The thirst drove the mouse outside and there he died. In agony. Internal contact was fatal, to mouse or man, pets, or farm animals.

The instructions were to spread the powder thickly along all regular routes of mice in the cellar. The mouse picked it up on his paws and tail and ingested it the next time he washed himself. But when would that be? As frequently as an American schoolboy? As an Uzbek goatherd? As a German dentist? The instructions didn't say.

Holding the dreadful box in two fingers, and away from me, I

went to the cellar and tried to figure out the regular mouse routes.
They weren't marked. Then I pondered the agony I was supposed to
spread thickly—and proceeded to spread it thinly along the routes *I*
wouldn't take if *I* were a mouse. Then I retired sedately.

The next morning we had a mouse in the formerly-five-cent trap
in the kitchen.

I wondered whether he had picked up the deadly powder and
dusted the kitchenware with it. (I also wondered whether he had
mistaken the drip of the kitchen faucet for the old millstream outside.) But I didn't let on to Mrs. Mayer, who, when it comes to taking
umbrage in the kitchen, yields to few women, and to no man. I hove
the whole thing, neck and crop, woodswards, whistling a tuneless tune
the while.

Small shades gnawed at my sleep the next couple of weeks, and I
awakened desperately parched between times. But there were no
more mice upstairs, and I saw to it that I had no pressing business
in the cellar. December came, and the fields and woods were white.
Then the better mousetrap arrived, via train from Meiringen to Brünig
and post bus from Brünig to Goldern and sled from Goldern to Chalet
Flühli; a distance, all told, of about a mile as the mountain goat flies.

The better mousetrap looked like a miniature barn with a silo (a
topless tin can) slid into one end. At the other end was a low entrance,
mouse-high. Just inside the entrance was a tiny tin ramp operating
on the seesaw principle. Suspended by stiff wires above the entrance,
and resting on the banisters of the seesaw ramp, was a tin portcullis,
which fell into slots, closing the entrance when the seesaw was tripped
from inside.

On each side of the wooden barn, near the entrance, was a little
latticed gate. Inside the rampway, opposite each gate, was a little
latticed window. The gate was raised by human hand, which hand
installed a small slab of Swiss cheese (which the Swiss call "cheese")
between the gate and the window. The hand then closed the gate,
leaving the cheese, but not its smell, inaccessible; the condemned
mouse did not even get the steak dinner.

So far, so good.

Meanwhile, back at the mouse route, the mouse comes scampering
along and smells the cheese. All unwary—or wary, for all I or anybody
else knows—he tries to get at it from the outside and can't. Recon-
noitering, he smells it from the inside at the entrance. If he stops at
this point, and studies the better mousetrap, he no more recognizes
it as such than you or I. So he enters without batting a whisker, goes

up the little ramp, trips the little seesaw, and the little portcullis falls behind him.

What then? What would you do?

Nothing for it but to scamper through the barn. When he gets to the other end he finds a semicircular tower going up the side of the silo. The tower entrance is open and the tower is perforated all the way up, to give him a foothold, maybe (or to persuade him that he is on his way out into the open air). Up he goes through the tower—and at the top he falls into the silo, which the householder has filled with water.

Lackaday. Mice can't swim, as the Rättenfanger von Hameln well knew.

Lackaday and *finito*.

Capito. "Marke Capito" is what is inscribed on the front of the tin silo. Under "Marke Capito" is the name "Lauchs." "Marke" and "Lauchs" indicate that the American invention comes from the Teutonic world. (Herr Michel thinks either that the Americans invent everything or that I think so.) The "Capito" doesn't mean any more than does "Charme de Nuit" at Woolworth's perfume counter. The berry-box wood construction of the Marke Capito is pleasantly primitive, however sophisticated its concept. I see Lauchs at his modest workbench in Modesto, or perhaps Munich.

But Herr Michel had said that "it *keeps* catching them," and I couldn't see how. Once the portcullis fell, there was no way into the trap until it was raised again. It was child's play to raise it—but not to confine a child to the cellar to do the raising. There was something here that didn't meet the eye. One thing that didn't was the terminus of the stiff wires that held the portcullis above the entrance. They disappeared into the top of the tower running up the silo, but where they went, and what they did there, was beyond me.

The next morning I went to the post office and phoned the intrepid Herr Michel in Meiringen. Sure enough, he had worked it out. It seemed that the mouse, as he plunges to his watery doom from the top of the tower, goes through a plate that pulls the wires down and opens the portcullis for the next victim. The cream of the whole Teutonic jest.

Herr Michel told me that I ought to find half-a-dozen mice in the better mousetrap every morning, and, he added, after a few days they ought to go away. Again I asked why, and again he shrugged his shoulders.

I found one drowned mouse in it every day, except once, when I found two.

The queasiness wore off by and by. Apparently a man can get used to doing anything. But *being* anything is something else. I had been a neck-breaker and then a poisoner and now I was a drowner. But I kept at it for two or three weeks and then, one morning, the silo was empty and I up and quit. I had reached the point where I'd rather see—aye, be—a live mouse than a dead lion.

Mirabile dictu, there were no more mice to be heard or, worse yet, seen, upstairs or downstairs after that. By that time, of course, winter had frozen over hard and the mountain was immobilized except for householders scampering like mice to the store and back. I comforted myself by saying that by now every mouse on the mountain must have found a home—other than mine. If only this world's mice would go somewhere else! So war the better angels of our natures against the worse; and so, after many a megrim, dies the swan in us all.

I suppose the better mousetrap has some advantages over the formerly-five-cent implement—if "advantage" may be said of the ability to kill the mostest for the leastest. It operates (or is supposed to) on a self-cocking basis. It relieves the apostle of nonviolence of the nightmare horror of the snapping spring and substitutes the ever so slightly more tolerable vision of the victim's walking the plank. It lasts indefinitely and conserves Swiss cheese. It doesn't catch more thumbs than mice. It doesn't powder the kitchenware with poison or endanger pets or farm animals. And it is a triumph (though only one, these days, among many) of human ingenuity, and, as such, an instructive object of contemplation.

But it leaves the fundamental problem unsolved.

The fundamental problem is the mouse. The first law of psychological warfare is Know Your Enemy. Nobody in the Berner Oberland—beginning with Herr Michel—seems to know anything about the mouse *in se*. And if nobody there, where man and mouse have been at it for a thousand years, then nobody anywhere. There is nothing about the mouse *in se* in the encyclopedia. Nobody anywhere seems to know what everybody everywhere ought to know about mice.

This, I suggest, is why a really better mousetrap is still wanting. Everybody knows why mice (and people) come in and why they stay until all hours. Nobody knows why mice don't come in, or why they don't keep coming in, or why they go away, if they do, or, if they don't, how to get them to go away, or what the effective counterpart is of yawning, turning off the TV, carrying the glasses to the kitchen and leaving them there, and saying, "It's been wonderful seeing you folks again."

Why did my mass production (or consumption) mousetrap characteristically catch only one mouse per night? Why did it catch two one night? Do mice, like men, learn from experience—or, at least, like man, from fatal experience? Did the fate of the one mouse in the better mousetrap warn its friends away, and, if so, (1) how, and (2) why not the friend that followed the first one up the ramp that one night? I quizzed Herr Michel sternly on these and related points. He always shrugged his shoulders and at last began looking at me as if I were odd. I put it to you: Given the prospect that mankind might beat a path to his door, is it I who am odd or he and his shoulder-shrugging likes?

Mice are in long, and ever longer, supply. They are pests, and you can't keep them out by pulling down the shades and pretending not to be home. Besides, they are known, in a pinch, to eat anything. In Chalet Flühli they ate the *Neue Zürcher Zeitung* in which Mrs. Mayer had wrapped the things in the cellar. The scientific spirit (though I'm no more than a dabbler) moved me to rewrap everything in the *Financial Times* of London, which is printed on pink paper; and it seemed to me they ate a little less of the *Financial Times* than they did of the *Neue Zürcher Zeitung*. That is the kind of empirical investigation that is needed on a better-controlled basis than I am competent to undertake without a government grant.

No self-respecting laboratory scientist would be caught dead without his warren, and no psychologist without his maze. We study mice, all right, but we study them to find out about man and not about mice. What is man, that we should be uniquely mindful of him? The mouse has been with us as long as we have been with each other—longer, if Genesis is to be believed. Mice fanciers—except for cats—are few. At the same time Brother Mouse is one of God's creatures. We have got to come to grips with the mouse in his very nature and resolve his right relationship to man. If, on ultimate balance, it should be resolved against him, then I say off with his (or should I say "its"?) head.

It is unthinkable that Space Age Man can find out whether the moon is made of green cheese and can not invent a much better mousetrap. *Or that a much better mousetrap has not been invented and suppressed.* "To whose advantage?" the Romans always said (when they weren't saying *Mirabile dictu* or *in se*). To the advantage, in this case, of the worse mousetrap manufacturers.

Twenty years ago I was told (by a Nobel hydrokineticist) that there was nothing to the desalinization of water; he said that the Water Monopoly had put the kibosh on it by getting hold of the patents. Thirty years ago I was told that a coated razor blade had been invented and swallowed up whole by the Razor Blade Mob. Forty years ago I was told that the solid rubber automobile tire, attached to the rim by springs, had been perfected and bought up and buried by the Rubber Trust. Going on fifty years ago I was told that an old process for beating swords into plowshares had been pocketed by the Armaments Combine.

Now we have the "new" stainless-steel razor blade that shaves fifteen smiling barbers but (if my own experience is indicative) only five scowling laymen. And as I was rewrapping the things in the cellar of the Chalet Flühli I came across a report in the *Financial Times* of London that the stainless-steel market was now saturated and the Razor Blade Mob—the *Financial Times* didn't use that expression— was readying a new "new" blade that will shave fifty sneering sergeants major without turning a hair.

I can apprehend, as a dedicated and conscious free enterpriser, the wholesome motivation for built-in shoddy and planned obsolescence. As a New Testamentarian I can apprehend why there is no break- through—nor ever will be until the Great Getting-up Morning—in man's understanding of man. What I can not apprehend is why there isn't a breakthrough in man's guerrilla warfare with the mouse. A civilization which can not master its environment has no squawk coming when it is blown apart or nibbled away.

No Coronary, No Corona

I don't suppose that the Lord Himself ever had it so good—not even in France (as the Germans say). Just look at me. I don't have to run the world or run after it. I don't even have to look at it. All I have to do is inhale, exhale, ingest, digest, exgest, and maybe metabolize a little. I am sick unto death and feeling (as usual) no pain. Radiant with ill health.

No Visitors. No visitors to cheer me up or get me down, to catechize me or console me. No bill-collectors, no pollsters, no hipsters. No metal can touch me; no fall-in, no fallout. I am (again, as the Germans say) *hors concours, sans souci,* and *au plat.* Wonderful days, these last ten—one like another and never a moment's monotony. I put it to you, my friends: Is that having it both ways, or isn't it?

Idle rich, idle poor, what does it matter as long as you're idle? All power to the workers; if they want it, let them have it. I have everything else. I have only to grunt—and a Registered Nightingale comes running with a wiggle on. I'm an attention-getting device, with bells at my fingers and bells at my toes and nothing to do but jingle them. "Here's your pillow-control," and the Nightingale hands me a space-capsule dashboard at the end of a wire. "And why," I say, on my horizontal high horse, "should *I* have to control the pillow? What am I paying *you* for?" "Pillow-control," says the Nightingale, "is to control your TV from your pillow. Be quiet now and watch the nice Westerns."

What did people like me do in hospitals before the Big Picture with pillow-control? Scalp, Seminole, scalp. Scream, Sabina, scream. Snarl, sadist, snarl. Depilitate, demoiselle, depilitate. Keeps you *quiet*? It keeps you *numb.* And with hours left over to reread *The Wings of the Dove* to test your recollection that it doesn't matter whether you turn one page or two. (Sure enough, it doesn't.) And reread and reread Haniel Long's *Interlinear to Cabeza de Vaca.* (If you've got a good book, why change?)

Maybe I'll write a postcard or a paragraph today. I'll see how I feel—if I feel like taking the trouble to see how I feel. Tomorrow is as good as yesterday. Don't work. Don't think. Don't worry. Just swallow this. 1984 is what you've achieved, twenty years ahead of

Reprinted from the *Progressive*, July 1964.

your time. You're a built-in man. They ought to put your bed (with you riding it) into a bottle and send you around to the schools on a Freedom Academy stipend.

"Get well soon," the well-wishers write. What's so good about well? Get well and you get up and out. Malinger, friend. Recover, if recover you must, as slowly as possible. Let them unensconce you and see you hobbling and they'll send you back into the trenches. No sir-ee-sir. "Feeling any better today, my boy?" Pallidly: "About the same, doc, just about the same."

My ancestors used to say, *Gam zu l'tovoh*—this, too, for the best. But why did I wait so long? Why didn't I bring it on twenty years ago, before I'd outlived my uselessness? Where have I been all my life? The answer is, Nowhere for more than ten minutes. And now, for no more than ten minutes, I've been to the brink (brinkmanship's the thing these days) and seen Dulles and Dante and Grandpa. I can cross that one off my list of musts and get out my list of near places to travel.

For years I've been ready, not to die, but for death. My affair (I have only one) is in order. Why, pray, shouldn't a man be ready for death instead of planning to build himself a bigger barn tomorrow and then hear the words, "Fool, this night thy soul shall be required of thee"? We suppose that the man on the scaffold is ready. He may as well be. And what, pray, do *we* think we have under our feet?— The floorboard of a tomato-colored convertible. We *chase* death and plan bigger barns.

Does it ever occur to anyone any more that he has to die of *some* thing *some* time? Oh, we are a God-fearing people; afraid, above all, of seeing Him face to face. Nobody wants to go to Heaven; everybody wants to be there, but as far in the future as possible and without the trouble of taking the trip.

Of course there's a difference between my readiness and my neighbor's on the scaffold: I was ready to die happy because happy was the only way I knew how to be. A small difference, though; not enough to plunge me so head-over-heels in love with life that I ever supposed I couldn't live without it. I didn't want to die just yet— but that was because I owed the world a living and wanted to pay off a little something on the chit.

I never got around to it. No time. According to Maritain, a capitalist is a man who has no time. I was a capitalist's capitalist. Not for me the stately tempo of the rat race; I was a pack rat, an entrepreneur, defined by Senator Bill Benton as a man who would rather go broke working for himself than get rich working for somebody else. Your

organized rat-racer takes excitement as something adventitious, acces-
sible only from five P.M. on. Your entrepreneur has to be excited
around the clock or he's what the Italians call *tutto kaputo*; he has
to keep eight balls in the air because he's sure to lose four.

Now I have time. Time, which the capitalist's capital isn't money
enough to buy. Andrew Mellon is said to have dreamed all his life
of taking a year off to paint. He left the country an art gallery instead. And *he* lived long.

If I died tomorrow—if I'd died yesterday—I'd still be ahead of the
game. My life's been a bowl of *seedless* cherries; an American life,
whose very sorrows come in a do-it-yourself kit. Fly now and fry
later. All excursions and no alarums. Never a sling. Nary an arrow.
A loaf of cake, a jug of bubbly, and thou all over me in the lavender
wilderness of a Tuscan afternoon. And now—. The world is sweet
in every weather, if you have but a window on anything man hasn't
made, or even, without a window, to hear the fluted roar of the kids
at recess, to see the buds go bang or the sky peopled with stars, or
one spring to have planted a tree.

A charmed life need not be a long one, but mine has been both.
Look at me, I say, and see perversity personified; drydocked in de-
light and peevish to be up and out. The hand of Fred X. Fry, M.D.,
restrains me. Nay, liberates me: Fred Rx. Fry tells me that exertion
just now will be the death of me or, worse yet, the sickness.

Worse yet, for death is a dream. A man might be alive, and then
dead, while a bee zeroed in on a flower, while a fly washed a wing.
But to sicken to death is a prospect from which I understand that
even Christ crucified shrank. I shielded myself when Pete Loomis
threw a rock at me on Calumet Avenue an aeon ago. I didn't want
to *suffer* death. Being dead—who knows? But dying—the known—
is a fearful thing.

Every time I leave home to catch the evening airplane, I turn
around once and look at the lights in the house and wonder if I'll
crash *and be hurt* and die. But being dead—? I've eaten, drunk, been
merry enough. What have I to lose—for sure—being dead? Some
more of the same (which is dandy) for the possibility (to be "faced"
late or soon) of something peachy. In the event, I left home to
catch the evening air. I turned around once—home at night, with
the lights lit—and a half block from the house I crashed. It had
never occurred to me that I might conk out on my feet.

We used to say on Calumet Avenue, "You're dead—lay down."
It's taken me a baker's half century to get the idea, and now I've
lain down in state. Oh, it isn't all beer and skittles, but those are

the only things it isn't. The actual discomfort (apart from the bills, which are merely disastrous) is in all at once throttling all the way down and eventually doing sixty on the freeway instead of ninety. *That's* the hard part.

"Be still and know that I am God" is not the national motto. To be doing nothing is the great American offense. To be doing anything is the thing. What profit it a man if he gain his whole soul and lose the round-the-world tour? What's the Free World free for, anyway? To lie *quiet*, like a child who knows that the sooner he sleeps the sooner today will be tomorrow, like a prisoner who knows that the sooner he sleeps the sooner today will be yesterday—*that's* the sin against Enterprise itself.

Entrepreneur, do you the Lord's work or Mammon's, you have led the titillated life, the breathless discontinuity of deadlines dotting an eight-day week. The expanding life that the advertisers advertise and the climbers climb—you have lived it because, you leaky balloon, you had to expand or shrivel. Yours the appearance (to you, too) of variegation which produces the reality of brilliance. Yours the life in which something good or bad—but *something*—is likely or liable to happen, the expectation of the unexpected.

Yours the deliciously disordered life of the solid citizen's dream of electric shoeshines and surfboards on Sunday. Yours not the charmed life; yours the solid citizen's idyll. They the many who derive their suspense from watching which way the cat will jump; you the few who do the jumping, who prowl the ledges and choose, on the instant, liberty and insecurity. The form of society has nothing to do with it, either; there are as many cats, maybe more, in China, as here, and more ledges.

On Calumet Avenue my mother (alias Grandma now) used to call me Mr. Fidget. And as I crashed the other night, my whole future life passed before my eyes. I had to be in Ann Arbor next week, in Palo Alto tomorrow, next month Istanbul, and from Istanbul on the double to Warsaw, and from there hotfoot to Haile Selassie I University. The notices were all out, I "had" to be there; there was no way to change it.

No way but one. One way to stop the All-American Boy: The Lord lays a hand on him and says, "Let's stop, my boy." "But I have the world to save," says the All-American Boy. "All by yourself?" says the Lord. "Just about," says the Boy. "It must be a heart-breaking job," says the Lord, "heart-breaking." "Well, help me up, I've got to get going." "I can't," says the Lord, "you've broken your heart. You should have had someone to help you save the world, you know." "I couldn't think of anyone." "I noticed that," says the Lord. "No time," says the Boy. "Well," says the Lord, "you'll have time now."

The thief suddenly shows himself and cries, "Hands down!" and no man knows when he cometh. So (say we all) must every man live every day as if it were his last. Half of my last day I spent working for money, money I didn't need for that day. One-fourth of it I passed like a true householder—paring my nails, twirling my mustache, wiping my chin, and moving my income tax return to the bottom of the pile on the top of my desk. And I am giving myself more than a little when I say I spent one-fourth of that day in the service of people who needed help and thought—mistakenly, but no matter— that they could get it from me. And what did I read that day? Not a chapter, not a verse.

So I went out batting, at the very most, .250—and yet there are those who say that there's no rest for the wicked. I regret that I have but one septum to give for my country, and, more than that, that I gave only one-fourth of it. For I am a man of faith, and the man of faith knows, every day of his life, that he's in the foxhole and in line of the Enemy's fire. But he knows that the hand of the Lord (hasn't Isaiah said it?) is stretched out to him still on the last day. And on the last day he hit .250—and a week or so later lied about *that* by maybe .050 or .075.

But he had no time.

We live long enough, on the whole. But we value our little lives so low that we let them slip through our fingers like a baby with a jewel. Oh, we're active; but at what? At pursuing the unavailable objective of making ourselves indispensable to somebody, anybody. This (and not money at all) is what the frenzy is for, to have it said of us, by the Lord, wringing His hands on His throne, or by Mammon, wringing his in his fat leather chair, "I don't know how I'll get through the day without him."

To be important is to be important enough so that *it*—the company, the country, the club—can't do without you. But it can. We are dispensed with and things go on nicely. Rome without Caesar, Washington without Kennedy, Bailey without Barnum, Junior without Senior—and all their enterprises prosper (along with the man who letters the names on the door). The Organization by definition has got to have another man, and still another, to put in every man's place.

But everything that happens to a man is instructive if only he be *docilis*, teachable. Does it involve some discomfort? So much the sharper its instruction, let him only be docile and study the ruins. The Cherokee-rose-choked traces of the cemetery where Cahaba once stood on the Alabama River. Germany at the end of the war, when the hand of man, the builder, was finished with it. The ghost town at the time of the ghost's siesta. If you want the peace and quiet my Old Man bellowed for on Sunday afternoon, go to the ruins.

So my own ruin instructs me. Decomposition has it all over composition when it comes to reading the soul a lesson. The sere has something to tell a man, not the green. What does the bud know about fruit? Go to the ancient leaf. But, you say, if you want the comforts of ruin you must undergo the discomfort of ruination. So you must. No Cross, said William Penn, No Crown. No coronary, no corona.

But this, too, is for the best. Best for my children who thought they had to think that Pop was God and who know now that they need no longer dream guilty dreams of destroying him. Best for my contemporaries, whose secret solace that it is I, not they, is sullied by the secret certainty that if I, then they. Best for my elders, whom I never called by their first names without a sense of audacity (and whom I saw myself burying). And for my old Greek professor, Fred Farley, who now comes toddling (so suddenly spry!) to my sickbed with his Crosby & Schaefer Grammar under his arm.

This, too, for the best. My friends all at once overvalue me. Being honest men, they insist that their tenderness is tenderness for themselves, like the young man who gives an old lady his streetcar seat in the prepense that he'll be an old lady himself some day. But what really moves them is their supposition that I've had a squint down the long valley of the shadow, and how does it look, and what's it like looking? The answer is of course, *Gam zu l'tovoh*.

All these years I've been strutting and fretting from hall to hall, trying to dampen the ardor of the ardent few by telling them that the problem is not to change the world but to keep the world from changing them. And all the while the world was changing for the worse and changing me with it. Now I can cut down on the preaching and step up the practice. If I'm impatient to be up and doing now, I need only a twinge (not a spasm, just a twinge) to bring me to heel.

Let us, then, be down and doing the things we can do and wean ourselves from the self-indulgence of those that we can't. We are punk utopians when we reach for the stars with a toothbrush. See the puniness of princes, doing the things that can't be done. Why shouldn't I be wiser than they—and more effective to boot?

There's my chess game, for instance; like the world, it gets no better. There's my vacant chair (the fourteenth and last) in the second fiddles of the local band, wholly within my power to polish. There's my Greek; O tempus, tempus, as the Greek said. And my garden, untended, Pangloss, and my beard running rampant, steel filings now among the iron. Let the graybeard tend his beard and it will be as Basil's.

Nor is mine the contemptible counsel of this-little-pig-stay-home. It is the realistic counsel of the-world-too-much-with-us; which in turn is the consequence of nothing but our refusal to concede that the world is too much for us. There are things beyond, but just beyond, a man's toothbrush, and to reach for them is paradise enow without a man's making himself ridiculous.

But they want time. To write, for instance. All my nine lives I've wanted to try my hand at writing. Who writes? Who immures himself writes—and none other. Descartes in bed all morning, Proust in bed all day, Santayana in a nunnery. Me, I've never seen my way clear, on the jet, to try to write; not the way a writer writes. "Any year now; I'm young yet; prematurely gray is all. Just see me go."

See me go. Now see me gone. See the long-lived, lifelong member of the Universal Volunteer Fire Department. I should have had sense enough to resign long ago. No credit to me now that I can't come down the pole. But it gives me time to try my hand at writing if I get my chess, my fiddle, my beard, my Greek, and my garden all tended to. So *Carne vale!* Let the decayed gentleman brandish his toothbrush at the aorists and aphids he can reach from his rocker.

Oh, I've had my young dreams of being a hero to my valet, a pirate (on sea or on land), an engineer (of the Pony or Empire State Express), a lady's man or a man's. But none of them soared to the reality of the truly entrepreneurial life in the age of servile enterprise; with the right friends and the right enemies (and not too many of either), with lovable loved ones, and with some of my own teeth. My neighbors have in the main appraised me correctly and, in doing so, spared me that floating resentment that, more furiously than the fire, consumes the soul. As for money, Socrates told the Athenians that it comes from virtue, and so it does; I have as much money as virtue, and no more.

You don't hear *me* complaining, except to mutter, "No time, no time." And there is—*was*, now—nothing to do about that. It's the entrepreneur's Eumenides. The thinner the ice, the faster you have to skate. But *Gam zu l'tovoh*, they can't hit you if you keep moving. I've got away with murder and known it. And knowing it, I've never been tempted too much to cry when my turn came to be coshed.

Who has suffered enough? The innocent? Herod himself could not punish me adequately for the evil I've done—and what about you, you red-handed bystanders? Hitler himself could not punish me adequately for the evil I'd have had to do (that good might come of it, of course) had the wind blown me to, say, midtown Manhattan or Massachusetts (or Connecticut) Avenue. "Take care of yourself," the cards in the mail all say. When have I ever done anything else?

"Take care of yourself," the Devil says, and there is nothing like a good swift kick in the chondros to induce hypochondria. The rubber man of India is, overnight, the spun goblet of Venice. Will you baby it lest it break, and all the more delicately when you're up again and no one babies it for you? Will you find yourself possessed of a new alibi for your old derelictions?—"I'd do it in a minute, but my heart—." Will you bat .000 from now on, spending all the time you have left getting (and keeping) all the money you can get to meet the illimitable claims of the next crash and the next? Will you keep reminding yourself that the entrepreneur has to pension himself and provide for his babes? Or will you (ye of little faith and reason) rise to the faith that considers the lilies of the field, to the reason that knows that a good man's friends, and they only, will provide for his babes? If the soul turns brittle with the body, then, this, too, will not after all have been for the best.

Aye, there's the rub. But forewarned is—or is it? We shall see, we shall see—to be forearmed. Be forearmed, then. Go to the snail and eschew the ant, thou entrepreneur. Midtown is more than ever the menace. You thought that if you kept moving they couldn't hit you. You found out that you could still hit yourself. Hit yourself again, then, rather than let them hit you, and don't complain, now or next time, that you didn't have it coming to you; neither beguile the time by saying you did. You've bought the time and taken it home with you, the time that Mellon didn't have enough money to buy. It's yours. Use it. Don't let it use you.

Time, with, at last, a measured urgency, and time, at last, to investigate the nature of the measure.

An intimation of mortality pulls a man up. I have never understood why people took me seriously, and the universal penchant for pomposity I have turned to strictly entrepreneurial purposes. The bishop who invites me to take his pulpit—me, a Calumet Avenue boy, fit, maybe, for Midtown—is a calumny if he isn't a dotard. And so, as the black of my visage narrowed to my eyebrows, I had either to give up taking other men seriously or maintain that they were right to listen to me; and I knew better than that. If I would never grow up, neither, though they didn't know it, would they. We were all young and fair—well, fair to medium.

Nor was I wrong, now that I've had a gander at Dulles and Dante and Grandpa. What does Churchill know? What did great Goethe, confessing that *What man knows not is needed most by man. And what man knows, for that no use has he*? What did great Goethe know except that he needed more light? He was grown. And now I'm as grown as I shall be, and lo! as grown as he. Getting to be five feet was nothing, and six not much more; it was getting to be seven that threw me, and Goethe, and Churchill.

Our dance is danced anyway, Goethe's, Churchill's, and mine. Yours, too, if you're fifty, or forty, or thirty. You and I passed when Einstein wondered if E might be equal to MC^2. There was the watershed; and we on this side of it have been swept back and away. We are ancestors now; half a century younger than Engineer Herbert Hoover, and with him we say, as he said of Telstar, "I belong to a generation that just doesn't grasp all that." What difference whether we came in with the Mesopotamian ox cart or the internal combustion engine, we fogies of the jet set? Our hour is struck, ill or well. There's a *button* now to press the button; what has great Goethe to say to *that*?

The doctors I used to meet socially—why should a lad past the measles like me meet them otherwise?—used to say, "Low blood pressure type. You're lucky. You'll never have a heart attack. You'll live to indulge your New Year's Eve passion to sit home and snarl at the turn of the century." I had a forty-dollar phaeton once (with a bud vase in back) that ran and ran and ran, slow and easy, with a cracked block until the moths finished the upholstery—and *then* I sold it. What's a blown gasket these days?

These days we are made of spare parts. Homer sang—great Goethe, too—of hard-hearted and soft-hearted and heavy-hearted men, of faint-hearted and lion-hearted and black-hearted men. And now the heart turns out to be a console of electric charges and a vermiform nuisance, and a man would be better off without one. What is wanted is the light-metals-and-plastic-hearted man. And the artificers have him ready for us. They have everything ready for us. Pretty soon the genetic code will be broken, and then we shall need no more light. We shall be, not as Goethe, but as gods. But perhaps it will take twenty-five years.

I have twenty, fifteen, ten good (good enough, good enough) years in me yet. Time enough and to spare, to do the few little things that *I* can do; to sip instead of gulp. I know how (and even that) I am going to die and, home being where the heart is, where. And when—unless I take better care of myself than a man with even a false pretense to decency has a right to. Where, and when, and how; and now I shall take the trouble, for time is an alibi, to find out why.

There is no wondering now whether the summit is behind or before. I have always told whoever would listen (and whoever wouldn't) that we would leave the world worse off than we found it. Now I know that I knew what I was talking about. Bed teaches a man to grow old gratefully instead of gracefully; a cocoon again, it teaches him to curl up to size and practice the gestation that prepares the babe for the life to be. To learn to be prone—this, too, if a man but consider the long run, is for the best.

Have you heard—hear it again—about the two old *Chassidim*? One said, quoting Heine, "Better to be dead than alive," and the other went on quoting Heine and said, "Best of all never to have been born," and the first said, "But who has such luck?—Maybe one in fifty thousand."

A Hell of a Way to Run a Railroad

What do they sell for new?" "This one was $130,000." "What are you asking?" "Twenty thousand." "I'll give you ten." "Sold. Take it with you or send it out?" "I'll eat it here."

What else can you do with a Pullman car?

They had wonderful names, on a lighted sign at the hind end of the observation car, the City of this and the City of that, days away, the Sunset and the Empire and the Chief. The Century had a barber and a manicurist and a secretary and *showers*. They were as wonderful to watch as they were to ride, across the prairies and over the grades—two engines, three engines—and around the horseshoe bends.

Carolyn Teetzel and I, at Englewood High School, sat on a baggage truck at the Englewood Station, where the Central and the Pennsy and the Rock Island crossed, and watched them pulling out in the late afternoon, one after the other. We held hands and ate licorice.

Spurlos versunken—gone without a trace. "The States on time today?" "There isn't any States. It's 427-27 now, and it's never on time." The Century is 61-27—merged with the New England States— and it's never on time. (*It* used to pay *you* when it was late.) The Overland is dead. The Commodore is dead (and the Advance Commodore is dead).

I sat out on the railing of the old brass observation platform and hooked my feet so I wouldn't fall off. I was Douglas Fairbanks, El Cid, Beau Geste. You could hardly lift the silver in the dining car. The waiters were black and the napery—you heard me—white. It was worth waiting an hour to get a seat by the window facing forward in the dining car.

"A pig can cross the country without changing trains—but you can't." The last of the campaigns for passengers, and the C&O got cars switched at Chicago and St. Louis and people and pigs (and policemen) could all cross the country without changing trains.

Three days and three nights. You could get a room and take a book or a girl or a typewriter with you—or a book and a girl and

Reprinted from the *Progressive*, August 1969.

a typewriter—and nobody knew where you were or who.

The Albany Union Station cost $37,000 to heat last winter. Finito. Now you grab the rattler in the freight yard across the river, in Rensselaer. Nobody can spell—much less find—Rensselaer.

There was a line—a passenger line—that ran from Opaloosa to Tallapoosa, Alabama. It was called the Wetumpka and West Point.

The Consolidated Railway Guide had three more pages than Webster's Unabridged.

The Central and Pennsy are trying to kill the St. Louis-New York Spirit of St. Louis. They're trying to kill the Spirit.

They had to agree to take over the New Haven; no New Haven, no merger. They took it over and cut the "service" by 40 percent.

Seniority. Old, old boys doing their time. End of the line. Help the company kill off the passengers. Help the company, hell. The passengers, hell, too.

Springfield: "Check it to Santa Barbara, please." "Can't do it." "Can't do it? How come?" "SP won't handle it beyond Frisco. Got to recheck it there." "That's terrible." "Wait 'til the Central gets action on its application to close ten thousand baggage rooms."

The California Zephyr is the nicest train in America, scheduled for the scenery of the Rockies and the Sierra. Burlington runs it to Denver, Rio Grand to Ogden, WP to S.F. The last two each put a $20 interline surcharge on their tickets to kill it, and the SP filed with the ICC to kill the City of San Francisco (already down to a couple of cars off the City of L.A. at Ogden). If they get rid of the Zephyr and the City, there will no railroad train between Chicago and San Francisco.

The trains in Europe go in all directions all the time, with coordinated national and international connections day and night. Small countries, nobody takes planes. Government-owned railroads, no competition. Communism. Swiss Communism.

The American air lines compete by advertising the sky and the costumes they've got for their baby dolls. They take us for slobs. They take us for what we are. Listening to plastic baby dolls chant their plastic litany, eating plastic food and looking at plastic relief maps. Plastic slobs.

Use Lower Back Seat Pad for Floatage.

Floatage.

You know what we used to sing, to the tune of "Humoresque"?—

Passengers
Will please refrain
From flushing toilet

While the train
Is standing in
The station (I love you).

"I'm going to buy some railroad stock," said Pa. "Isn't it risky?" said Ma. "Risky?" said Pa. "When the railroads go, the country'll go first."

On the Passing of the Slug

When I contemplate the things that happen in Chicago, such as the Fire, the Haymarket Riot, the Eastland Disaster, and Colonel McCormick of the *Chicago Tribune*, I wonder how any man with a mind of his own could ever choose to live anywhere else. This week I have another Chicago phenomenon to report, and it will give you an idea of what I mean.

The use of telephone slugs in public places has been abandoned in my city. I am not positive for sure, but I think that Chicago was the only city in the U.S. of A. where you could not make a telephone call from a pay station without first purchasing, for five cents, a conversation tablet, or slug. Each place had a differently carved slug, with an apparatus hitched on to the nickel hole of the telephone so that only that particular breed of slug could be used.

The idea, obviously, was that Chicagoans were crooks, who, if the nickel hole accommodated nickels, would use nickel-sized slugs purchased at, say, a penny apiece. The total effect of the slug system was to make telephoning difficult, and to load down the jeans of the citizens with slugs which fitted a telephone the location of which they had forgotten.

The system had another, more sinister, effect, besides. Like the Prohibition Law, it not only got people mad, it also broke down their respect for law and order. Chicagoans resented the implication of the slug system, the implication being that Chicagoans, in contrast, say, with New Yorkers, were not to be trusted. Whether or not it was the telephone company that invented the slug system, the system bred in the heart of every Chicagoan a violent resentment toward the company.

This resentment was handed down from generation to generation, as such things are, and by the time it reached my generation it had taken the form of an unrelenting feud. I was brought up to fear God and hate the telephone company, and I was forgiven my derelictions in the former matter if I stood fast in the latter.

By the time I got to college I was an adept at beating the company. I knew, for instance, that if you had a two-party line and the

Reprinted from the *Progressive*, January 1945.

operator, after you gave her the number you wanted, asked you what *your* number was, you had only to give her the number of the other party on your line and she would never know the difference. Of course, the other party was then charged for your call, and the company did not lose a farthing. But you had the blind satisfaction of somehow having deceived the company.

In addition, I knew that you could, every once in a while, get a free call by rousing yourself to a bogus state of fury and insisting that you had dropped your nickel when in fact you hadn't. It often worked.

But my bright college years made a finished artist of me. I learned, among other scientific matters not taught in the science department, the dime trick. The dime trick consisted of opening the box that contained the guts of the telephone and touching two adjoining screws with a dime. This contact signaled the operator that a nickel had been deposited, and she gave you your number.

The company had only one way to beat the dime trick. When it found a phone, as it did in the office of the college paper, where a goodly number of calls would normally be made, and approximately three nickels in the box at the end of the month, it put some sort of special operator on the job and, evidence of guilt being established, yanked out the phone. That is why the Chicago *Daily Maroon* had no telephone in my last year.

Still another common college prank was the plugged nickel. One end of a piece of thread was tied to the plugged nickel and the other end held scientifically in the hand of the man who was beating the company.

You let the nickel down until it established the contact which signaled the operator, held it on the contact until you finished talking, and then withdrew it. The objection to the plugged nickel system was that a nervous man might jiggle the nickel while he was talking and tip off the company. That is how my fraternity lost its phone.

The best of them all, while it lasted, was the flattened penny. Since the flattened penny device involved not merely the ordinary criminality of the other tricks but, in addition, the violation of the Federal law against beating the life out of U.S. currency, it was especially attractive to those collegians whose view of life was not bounded by the local community, with its petty police ordinances, but embraced the entire sweep of a great nation and challenged the Department of Justice and the Army and the Navy.

The penny had to be flattend with consummate skill. If it was too flat, it would go right through, like sassafras through a blue goose, and come out the coin return chute. It had to be flattened just to the degree that would enable it to rest delicately on the contact screws.

If it was not flattened enough, it would go into the coin box, and there would be the evidence when the man came around at the end of the month. Flattened just right, it lay, as I say, on the contact screws while the call was in operation. At the conclusion of the call, you gave the box a terrific whack and the penny came out.

The flattened penny was a wonder while it lasted, and I would guess, if I were put to it, that it had more devotees than the plugged nickel. It had, besides all the beauties mentioned above, a higher degree of fidelity performance than any of the other tricks, and it demanded a higher degree of skill.

But it did not work forever. One day one of the boys, Jim Cusack, if I remember right, was using the flattened penny. Now Jim was a giant of a man, and a man of quick and stormy temper besides. He whacked the phone at the end of the call, but the penny did not come out. He whacked again, and it didn't come out, and Jim began to get mad. About the fourth or fifth try, he kicked the box, and the box came off the wall. And that, I am sorry to say, is how the office of the Student Honor Commission lost its telephone.

Now the incentive to all the ingenuity I have described has been removed. Why the company discontinued the slug system I no more know than I know why it started it, if indeed it was the company that started it. But it is gone, and Chicagoans, no longer mutely accused by every telephone of being crooks, no longer hate the telephone company.

This is too bad, and not just because the hatred inspired the invention of the flattened penny. It is too bad because the company is still a monopoly, which regulates, instead of being regulated by, the Illinois Commerce Commission. And if you do not like their rates, your only recourse is to communicate with people by Indian runner.

Last Man through the Loophole

Awhile ago my admirers convened in a kayak and sent me a cable to Europe: "Why don't you come home and save the country?" I replied that the country would need me still worse in another six months and I was staying on to gird my loins for Armageddon.

I was lying, as usual, I was staying on for the purpose of saving $5,000 in taxes. All I had to do for the $5,000 was to stay away from God's Country for "at least 510 full days during any period of 18 consecutive months." (*Tax Guide for U.S. Citizens Abroad*, Publication 54, Internal Revenue Service.)

"At least 510 full days" living (as the Germans say) like God in France, and the U.S. Citizen (or Taxpayer; that's how you know he's a Citizen) is exempt from taxation on $20,000 of earned income his first year abroad (or $25,000 a year if he stays on).

The catch is that he has to earn the income, but that is one of the disadvantages of this sordid life anywhere. I earned like crazy. Nobody ever earned so hard for 510 full days or earned so much more than he deserved. (And still I managed a haul of only $15,000. I could have got another $5,000 tax-free if I could have found somebody more to con.)

Having loved it and left it, I stayed away from the U.S.A. for 512 full days—the extra two to celebrate—and then caught the first scow for home. Sure enough, the country needed me even worse than it needed me 512 days before.

This, my friends, is one of the loopholes through which the cunning camel passes en route to the eye of the needle which leads to the Kingdom of Heaven. It is one of the littler loopholes designed to accommodate a little looper in comfort—"not so wide as a church door, but 'twill serve, Horatio." The big loopers have church doors and barn doors and manholes and craters. And the whole world's a loophole for the loop-the-loopers like ITT.

It isn't everybody's loophole. It's not for the poor, for instance, or for people who sit around watching sunsets or television. It is for sharpies. You have to be sharp to know about it and stay sharp to keep up with it. You have to be a sharp student of fine print and

Reprinted from the *Progressive*, September 1972.

give up being a student of anything else. You have to be able to bear 510 full days far away from the ashes of your fathers and the temples of your gods. And you have to be able to work abroad and be paid from home. (Nobody abroad will pay you for anything.)

At the end of the 510 full days, having improved each shining moment of every one of the 510, you come looping home loaded to the scuppers and take your stand again for righteousness, refusing, for example, straight-faced to pay half your income tax for war. It is hard on your character, but you can do without character in a pinch; you cannot do without money.

The rationale of this spectacular little loophole is, or was, imperialism. It was designed to induce American businessmen to tear themselves tearfully away from God's Country and endure the barbarian terrors of Paris or London or Geneva in the interest of American business. Nowadays every American who can conjure up a way of getting there tears himself tearfully away from Paris or London or Geneva, where it's cheaper, cleaner, and safer to live, and the rationale has hardened into a tax dodge.

And that, my friends, is the way (in a small way) that the tax system cuddles the rich (big and little) and lays the lash on the poor in God's Country (and in every country). And among the people who had the system taped was that filthy old atheist Communist Karl Marx—not, in this company, to mention Jesus Christ, who promised the greater damnation to the scribes and Pharisees who devoured widows' houses. (I'm a scribe, myself.)

And that may be—at least I hope it is—why the young detest the system and despise the foxy gran'pas (like me) who batten on it and make long prayers for a pretense.

And as long as I have my hair (or hairs, nowadays) down, that is why a good man named Albert Gore was knocked out of the U.S. Senate in the 1970 election and replaced by one of Friend Nixon's Young Dobbins. Albert Gore had spotted the $20,000 loophole and swore that he'd plug it if it was the last thing he did. He didn't get to do it, because I put an anonymous million dollars into Young Dobbin's campaign kitty.

A man has to live, I always say. But when the late O. K. Bovard of the *St. Louis Post-Dispatch* was firing a reporter for elbow-bending in the line of duty and the reporter said, "But a man has to live," Bovard said, "Not necessarily."

Happy Old Year

I t was a great year, 1972. They're all great years, but this was the greatest in years.

It was the year of the massive demonstration—at the polls November 7—in support of the Watergate Two. It was the year that George McGovern (along with Richard Nixon) fearlessly spurned the Arab vote by declining to denounce the Israeli massacre of innocent Arabs in "retaliation" for the Arab massacre of innocent Israelis. It was the year in which the foundation was laid (in living color) for the 1984 Congressional investigation of the question, "Who Lost Taiwan?"

A great year, too, to come home from Weary Old Europe to Weary New America and witness the great democratic clash of ideas between the Pentagon under the banner of Burn, Baby, Burn, and the populace under the banner of Yawn, Baby, Yawn. The year of that trinity of miracles—inflation controlled (and prices uncontrolled), law and order achieved (and a record crime rate achieved), and war with dishonor rechristened peace with honor. The year, too, in which the Reverend Robert Schuller of Garden Grove, California, preached his sermons at America's first and biggest drive-in church in his "twenty-two-acre shopping center for Christ."

A great year for Christ to shop around for souls reduced for quick sale before they spoil.

It was a great year around the house, too, at the Mayers' new $250,000 home which cost them $45,000 to buy and $205,000.49 to get the leak in the cellar stopped (temporarily); the year, oh, great, that the Berkshire Gas Company, *Your Gas Company*, sold the Mayers a hot water tank for $205 whose apparent counterpart Sears sells for $80.

The year, ah, yes, the year in which the crick in my neck did not go away no matter what I did to get it to go away; the year the Lord found Himself with time on His hands when He numbered the hairs on my head; the year my dentist decided he could afford to replace the mahogany on his yacht with teak.

It was the year in which a lassitudinous bevy of college freshmen arrived in college with 27,000 hours of watching 30,000 dots behind

Reprinted from the *Progressive*, January 1973.

them—and twice as many of them wanted to learn something as wanted to two years ago (and nobody knew why, including them). The year in which a college freshman wanted to know, "Which came first—World War I or World War II?" The year in which a college freshman said, "King Lear was a Jewish mother" (and was right). The year in which a college freshman sued the local school system for having graduated him without teaching him how to read and write.

An A-Number-One year.

It was the year, with my four little hay-burners off my back, and a fat salary, that I had no time to do the only things I ever wanted to do—and used to do when I was the jobless father of four little hay-burners; play chess, fiddle, garden, study Greek, and work for the American Friends Service Committee.

The year I wondered whether I'd have time on Social Security.

But it was a good year, too, and not just a great one. A good year the day I got a letter from R. M. Hutchins reading, in full: "I have always been a great admirer of your work. Have you done any lately?" A good year the day after the Presidential election when a bumper sticker in Cambridge appeared reading: Massachusetts— Love It or Leave It. A good year the day a little old lady who ran a little old grocery store around the corner from the supermarket, when I said to her, "I suppose the difference between the forty-nine-cent brand and the fifty-nine-cent brand is the quality," said, "No— the forty-nine-cent brand is the better quality."

A good year on two or three such occasions, and not just a great year all year.

And a Happy Old Year to you.

Sit Down and Shut Up

I talk too much, and so does everybody I have ever met who knows how. Yap, yap, yap; yammer, yammer, yammer. Meetings, conferences, committees, lectures; street-corners, parlors, bedrooms, and baths; playgrounds, poolrooms, love nests, and funerals. As soon as I let the fellow next to me get a word in edgewise, he will jabber his head off; and he bores me. I have never been anywhere yet where everybody wasn't trying to talk at once, and I have never heard or said anything that did me or anyone else any durable good.

I have actually wondered, on occasions when I came home inordinately hoarse, what it would be like if a lot of people, meeting as friends, just sat still and said nothing for an hour together.

Now I know.

I have been to a meeting of friends. To a Meeting, I should say, of Friends.

The other Sunday morning, while the hypocritical preachers preached hypocrisy to the hypocrites, and the honest pagans lifted themselves on one elbow and swallowed the Alka-Seltzer, I went to Meeting.

Nobody opened the Meeting. It opened with silence. Living silence, they call it. Nobody closed the Meeting. It closed with silence. When the living silence gave way to dead silence—the kind you and I know —the people got up and walked out.

When, in the course of the living silence, a Friend felt moved to talk, he got up and talked. Not like you or me, though his words were no more pretentious than ours; less so. He felt moved; not, like you or me, driven. In the course of an hour, three Friends rose and talked—the usual number is smaller—and none of them talked for more than two minutes.

No Mr. Chairman. No By Your Leave. No We Are Fortunate to Have Brother Jones among Us on This Auspicious. No We Will Now Hear a Few Words from. No larruping of the Mighty Organ to rouse the House to Attention. No House. No Head Man or Hind Men. No frock coats, censers, holy water, crypts, crosses, kaddishes, or choirs. Just Friends.

Reprinted from *Common Sense*, April 1945.

The Quakers' denial of all this apparatus as indispensable equipment on the Stony Road is, I know, a horror to all the sacramental sects. The Kingdom of God is supposed to be a kingdom, not a democracy. The purple harberdashery of the Episcopalians, the cold-water dunking of the Baptists, the Wafer of the Irish, and the Tablets of the Jews are the standard targets of the incredulous moderns, who mock the faith by mocking the paraphernalia. But they can't mock the Friends; and the Friends mock neither the mockers nor the mocked.

One evening, long ago, I was walking down the boulevard with Ludwig Lewisohn. He paused, in the darkening daylight, in front of a great cathedral. "This," said Ludwig, "is the third we have passed in three blocks. If our civilization were to pass leaving nothing behind but archaeological evidence, the next would conclude that ours was the most religious that was ever on the earth." "Ah, yes," I replied, "and this particular spire, the tallest hereabouts, was erected by non-union labor at the expense of the most hardened sinner of his time, who, as his arteries grew brittle, thought that he could make the Ascent by offering God a nickel out of each quarter he had stolen from his fellow men." "Ah," said Ludwig, and we hastened on.

But the Meeting I attended was held in a small, garish, sub-ballroom in a smoky hotel in Pittsburgh. If the Pittsburgh Friends paid more than $1.50 for the hire of that particular hall, they were gypped. And it could have been held, for all that went on, in the park, on a hillside, in a basement. All that went on was a living silence, a silence that made inaudible the clatter in the immediately surrounding lobbies and kitchens.

My first feeling, as the silence began, and I studied the plank platform, the plain pine chairs, and the blue-serge suits acquiring a shine on them, was, "Dear me, what a saving on overhead." Then I focused on the clatter outside and wondered how, in or out of God's name, these people could expect living silence to hold its own against living noise. Then, with proper pagan disdain, I scrutinized the ceremony of nonceremony before me. Only I was self-conscious. Only I was *looking*.

I saw, though, that some of the faces were black, and I recalled that the Quakers were the first, and perhaps to this day the only, religion formally to denounce human slavery, to oppose it, to fight it, and to have no traffic in it. Some of the faces, including mine, were, I guessed, Jewish. The man on my left told me afterward that he was a Methodist, and that the Methodists never kept quiet for more than 15 seconds. I asked myself, after the manner of Milt Gross, "Is diss a system?" Apparently it is.

All unconsciously, it must have been, I folded my arms and bent my backbone in my chair, like most of those present. And the next thing I knew, I had been considering my misspent life. The living silence had got hold of me, and the clatter outside had let go of me. What brought me to was a slight shuffling on the platform, as one of the Friends arose to his feet.

"I read in the paper this morning," he said, as if he were talking at home, "about a Negro soldier being refused a sandwich at a canteen. I thought: you can't legislate a man a sandwich. It will have no taste. I thought: what will help the Negro who is hungry for the *taste* of a sandwich? The answer seemed to me to be spiritual aid. *Certainly nothing but spiritual aid will help those who refused him the sandwich.* 'He who drinks the water at his feet shall be thirsty, but he who drinks the water I offer him will never thirst, it shall be as a living well unto him.' "

He sat down. This time I was conscious that the silence had hold of me. *I wanted to think.* But the silence, after what seemed like fifteen minutes but was only five, let loose its embrace on me. *I wanted to talk.* I was halfway off my chair when I found myself saying to myself, "Mayer, you want to talk, all right, but you have nothing to say. You just want to make your face go, shoot your cuffs, and put 'em in the aisles. You've been doing this all your life, and so has everyone else. Sit down and shut up."

The living silence embraced me again, and it was on the train that night, long after the Meeting, that I grinned and said to myself, "The boys will never believe you when you tell them that you had a couple of hundred people sitting still and ready to listen to you talk as long as you wanted and you never unbuttoned your chin."

A Friend got up on the floor and said, "I can't get it out of my head that this world organization we are all talking about is trying to make us all members one of another, and I do not see how it can succeed without the conviction that we are so created by God."

He sat down.

This time the silence slipped up on me like my mother's arms. If you asked me how I felt during this third stretch of living silence, I would say that I do not know, but I would guess that, for twenty whole and successive minutes I had realized Aristotle's definition of happiness: *I wanted for nothing.*

A man got up. "I'm not a Quaker," he said, "but it seems to me that it would be worthwhile to study the causes of war, to learn just who it is that profits by war."

The day before, or the day after, I'd have leapt to my feet and said, "You fathead, Oscar Ameringer answered that question for once and all: *The sharks and the buzzards.*" Today I said nothing.

I don't know yet how the living silence, and the Meeting, ended. I think two of the Friends on the platform made the first move by shaking hands, but I'm not sure. All I know is that at some point I found myself walking out in the crowd, neither a sadder nor a wiser, but a stiller, man.

What do I know about the Quakers? I know that they were persecuted, not merely as dissenters, but for many of their positive tenets, such as their denial of special priesthood; their indifference to sacrament, including their refusal to take oaths; their complete democracy of organization, down to the point of determining action on any issue by the "sense" of the Meeting and not by vote; their historic opposition to war, though in this, as in all temporal issues, they refuse to try to bind individual conscience; and their recognition, as original as their opposition to slavery, of the complete equality of women with men. I know that no one, including their own apostates, ever hates them; that Franklin was influenced by their manners and by some, if not all, of their morals; and that Jefferson, in one of his letters, wondered why men were not satisfied, as were the Quakers, to live at peace with one another. And I know that the American Friends Service Committee, unlike the Red Cross, will have nothing to do with racism or nationalism and does not, so far as I have been able to discover, understand the term *enemy*, even in wartime.

It all adds up. The only thing I know, or *think* I know, that bothers me is that Quakers have a tendency to get rich. Now industry and thrift are characteristic of all persecuted and exiled people, and the Quakers have, in their time, taken a lot of pushing around. But it is still generally, if roughly, true, as it was in the beginning, that the man who says, "That rich man's a fool, but when I get rich I won't be a fool," is a fool already. If the Quakers have got disentangled from their vestments only to get entangled in their investments, they are going to wind up with windy cathedrals and the straight Republican ticket. I will try to talk them out of their money. I feel moved already to get up in Meeting and talk for an hour and a half. And I don't want to be interrupted.

Jackpot

We pulled up to the motel in our waterless cooker, Ms. Baby ("My Name Is Jane") Mayer at the wheel. Seventeen dollars for a flop and don't argue—it's the only flop in town and there's no other town around Wendover, Utah. While Baby unloaded—easy there, woman, with those suitcases—I pondered the grand strategy. (Baby always handles the details, like the driving, and the cooking, and the laundry, and the cleaning, while I take care of the grand strategy and decide whether to impeach Nixon, who's to pitch the World Series opener, and when to raise the Prime Interest Rate.)

Wendover is one street wide and half a mile long. It consists of the motel at the eastern end, a continuum of gas stations in the middle, and the State Line Casino at the western end. Hidden among the gas stations is a sign: "Welcome to Nevada—Where the West *Really* Begins—Entertainment Unlimited." Wendover is famous for being in two states. (The only other such town I've been in is Texarkana, where you can buy a postcard showing a man pulling a mule through town, with the legend, "Man in Texas—Ass in Arkansas.")

The grand strategy in Wendover involves the decision to patronize the greasy spoon at the eastern (or Utah) end of town or the State Line Casino Coffee Shop down the street in Nevada. It used to be that you could get a half-dollar dinner anywhere in Nevada, the idea being to get you inside the joint at any price. No more; nothing cheap anywhere any more. But everything in Nevada is open all day and all night, and you can split a $1.75 breakfast at any hour; which, it being the dinner hour, I decided we'd do.

But that decision involved the further decision—such is the life of the grand strategist—to go inside the Casino. Inside, everywhere in Nevada except the ice chest, or morgue, are the slot machines. Row on whirring row the iron sirens sing their song to the wayfaring Christian.

Nevada is one great gambling hell, always has been. When the Comstock Lode played out there was nothing left there, not so much as the low profile of a coyote in the sagebrush. In 1931 the state

Reprinted from the *Progressive*, November 1973.

legalized what it calls gaming, but the only game to be seen in Nevada is the wayfaring Christian. Nevada makes sure of seeing him by refusing to let Interstate 80 bypass any town in the state. The freeway becomes a rut, and the Christian has got to stop and get gaffed on the game of chance.

He hasn't a chance. The Nevada aborigines spend their whole lives psyching out the machines and wind up in the County Home. If you go on playing, you are sure to lose everything. How otherwise, you Christian chump, do you suppose the big hells in the big towns manage to stay in business and offer you a free ride from L.A. to Vegas or S.F. to Reno? It's like all the other games people play—stay out, get out, or you're dead.

The grand strategy came clear as Baby and I wended our way through Wendover to the State Line Casino Coffee Shop. With one $1.75 breakfast, plus an extra coffee for appearances' sake, we could afford, should Satan, as he usually does, have his Satanic way with us, to sink a dollar in the slots.

But at that hour of the evening Baby sips tea with her half breakfast and I savor a twenty-cent Sanka. The chiclet handed us the check and dove. We'd been billed for twenty cents *each* for the tea and the Sanka. I assailed the management and lost on a technical knockout; "coffee" on the table d'hote breakfast meant coffee, not tea or Sanka. (It wasn't until we got back to the flop that I remembered that in the heat of combat I had forgotten to leave the chiclet her two-bit tip.)

Taken for fifteen cents net by the two-armed bandit in the Coffee Shop, we undertook to make our intrepid way through the Satanic array of one-armed bandits in the Casino. I had to hold Baby tight; once up from the laundry tub she tends to get frisky. Baby tugged at my sleeve, and larceny tugged at my heart; all around us creatures that once were men (and women) were pouring their ready into the ravening maw of Satan.

Always before me on such occasions I hold, and on this occasion held, the memory of Simon O. Lesser, whom I dragged into Rudy's speakeasy in Chicago forty-fifty years ago. Simon O. Lesser had never gambled; he put his paper-route money into the stock market. He stood fast at Rudy's until I staked him to a quarter, I to stand the loss, he to take the winnings. Temptation unstrung him and he reached for the quarter, bit it, and put it into Rudy's illegal slot. He hit the jackpot, scooped the money out of the trough, put on his hat, and walked out of Rudy's and never returned. He knew when to quit, and ever thereafter stuck to sure things like Insull's Middle West Utilities.

But Baby was tugging at my sleeve and the tinkle in the trough (and the occasional clatter) was tugging at the Christian wayfarer's wayward heart. A good Baby, Baby, manning the quarterdeck all these years while I strode the bridge. A good Baby, and a good clatter and tinkle. The memory of Simon O. Lesser faded and the memory of Jerry Nathan supervened—Jerry, the college penny-matcher, whose motto was, Speculate and Accumulate.

I handed the Change Girl a dollar and called for five dimes and ten nickels and gave my good Baby the dimes.

Baby hurried over to the dime row to play the field. I pondered the grand strategy and, from a decent distance, waited until a creature that once was a woman lost her all on the last nickel machine in the third row. When the woman left for the Powder Room to take her strychnine I leaped to the nickel machine, played, won a few, lost a few, won a few, and lost everything. Baby's petty strategy fared her no better in the dime row. Entertainment Limited.

The machine that had whammied me now had a discernible lipoma, or fatty tumor, in its side, and a creature that once was a man stood at an indecent distance watching me *and* the machine. Baby told me it was time to go. I told her to take a stance at an equal and opposite distance from the machine and watch the cad while I sauntered to the Powder Room. On my return my good Baby informed me that, sure enough, the cad had begun playing my machine as soon as I'd sauntered. I told Baby I was going to see the Change Girl and to give me the high sign when the cad was wiped out.

Baby asked me what I was going to see the Change Girl about. I said, "In for a dollar, in for a dime." Baby seized my sleeve and said, "I beg of you"—she always says "beg of you" instead of "beg you" —"not to. I beg of you. You've given up that fancy-pants professorship of yours to gratify your independence fantasy, and we have nothing between us and the strychnine but our meager savings. What would become of me if you should be hit by a streetcar here in Wendover? I'd have to sell my scrawny old body." "Sell it dearly," I said, recalling the dying words of the restaurateur to his sons, "Slice it thin, boys," and tore myself away. She was weeping softly.

I pirouetted up to the Change Girl and commandeered a dime's worth of nickels. Baby, still weeping softly, gave me the high sign. The cad who had thought to reap where I had sown had been wiped out. The machine was unmistakably tumescent as I sauntered back to it. Baby hurried over to me, her weep rising to a wail. I thought I was going to have to whale her, quarterdeck and all, and then, in my grandest strategic manner, I said, "I got two nickels, and you can play one of them." Her wail sank to a weep, and then to a sob, and she grabbed the nickel and played it. Lemons. I put the other nickel in, and it came up—not three bells, nor yet three bars, but three watermelons.

100 to 1.

The nickels cascaded into the trough—but only twenty of them—and the buzzer sounded all over the Casino. The Change Girl came running up and said, "Put a nickel in to clear it." I said I wanted my winnings, 100 to 1 and not 99. She said I had to put a nickel in to clear the machine. I said I wanted my winnings. The buzzer rose to a scream. She said put a nickel in. I put a nickel in, and Baby wailed, but the buzzer subsided. "Here," said the Change Girl, muttering something that could have been "piker," "is your money," and she handed me two one-dollar bills and two one-dollar rolls of nickels. (Baby had already scooped the twenty nickels from the trough.)

Hand in hand Baby and I converged on the Cash Desk and said we wanted two one-dollar bills for the two rolls of nickels. The Cash Man hissed on behalf of the House, which figures that the Big Winner will unroll the nickels and put them back in the slot. But the creatures that once were men and women gazed after us in envious despair, as I had gazed at Simon O. Lesser when he walked out of Rudy's forty-fifty years ago.

We slept, that night, the untroubled sleep of the justly treated Christian, and as we left the ruts of Nevada behind us we thought we heard the howl of a low-profile coyote in the sagebrush.

There Is a Doctor in the House

Pa hustled his paper-box samples on and off the street-cars for thirty years to keep body and body together. Anything left over, nickels, dimes, an occasional quarter, went into the sock to buy a college educa-tion for his little boy. With a college education his little boy would be better off—not better, but better off—than he had been.

Helas! the little boy never got the college education.

The nickels, dimes, and quarters went to the University of Chicago, which offered, but did not require, the education. Exploiting the distinction, the little boy flung roses around the campus for a few years and was then placed on Permanent Probation for conduct un-becoming a junior.

Ten years later the little boy was back on campus as Toady to the President. One day the President, whom we shall call Robert M. Hutchins, said to him, "We ought to regularize your employment so that I can answer the people who keep asking me what you do around here. If I could tell them that you were a professor, they would keep quiet. Nobody ever asks what a professor does."

I pointed out that I was still on Permanent Probation for conduct unbecoming a junior.

"I'll tell you what I'll do," said the President. "After I have done everything else I can think of around here to antagonize everybody, I'll confer the P.P. degree on you."

He never did. (He never ran out of other things to do to antago-nize everybody.)

Nobody has ever called me "Doctor" (except the President whom we shall call Hutchins, and in his case it was the second most con-temptuous thing he could think of to call anybody; the most was "Professor").

I never got the contemptible degree, and nobody ever called me "Doctor."

A couple of months ago Windham College in Vermont informed me that it was conferring a Doctorate upon me *honoris causa* (i.e., like everything else I have ever got, unearned).

Reprinted from the *Progressive*, June 1973.

I have always supposed that I would not want an honorary degree from any college that was willing to give a fourflusher like me an honorary degree. But Windham is a liberal arts institution that keeps the faith and keeps the faith alive, the last best hope of education going.

President Winslow of Windham asked me if I had any preference among doctoral designations.

Well, there was D.D., which could be Doctor of Divinity *or* Dishonorable Discharge—a little too close to P.P. for comfort. D.Wt., for Dead Weight, was a possibility, as was D.O.A. for Dead on Arrival. Pa would have settled for D.F. for me, little knowing that it means, in addition to Damn Fool, Dean of Faculty and *Defensor Fidei*. Now D.B.A.—Doing Business As—pretty near encapsulated my career. Not bad.

But this would be a serious occasion, and I must be a serious man, especially if, after I got my Doctorate, I was going to stroll into the operating room somewhere and perform a heart transplant or two. There was Lit.D., but I remembered enough of my Englewood High School Latin to know that that means Doctor of Literature, while Litt. D. means Doctor of Letters.

That reminded me that I am a great hand with a postcard; but D.C.V., or Doctor Chartae Vecturae was not in the book.

I settled for Litt. D.—I have doctored a few letters in my time—and borrowed a robe from a colleague who had done his doctoral dissertation on (and I quote), "The Bacteriological Content of the Cotton Undershirt."

Myself the Dokteh.

But I'm still on Permanent Probation for conduct unbecoming a junior.

Chucking It

I went to "my" office and cleaned out "my" desk. (Jar of spurious coffee, stale; jar of spurious milk, coagulated; spurious plastic cups, encrusted; bottle of real ink, what's ink, Pa?) (Notes from students saying they'd get their papers in as soon as possible, "possible" misspelled on two of them.) Then I got into my cabriolet (campus parking violation tag) and toodled on home—an Ex-Professor.

I am still trying to figure out why I chucked a job that paid a $5,000 man $20,000 plus Fringe Benefits, Cost-of-Living Increases, Old Age Pension, and Lifetime Tenure.

It wasn't on principle—though a hustler can always hustle up a principle. The $20,000 hadn't done me any good. What it had done was make me want $25,000. I never told the bosses that I wanted the $25,000 because I did not want to draw their attention to the fact that I was doing $5,000 worth of work for $20,000.

My friends—Job's comforters—all tried to dissuade me from quitting. They spoke to me of security—they whose friendship constitutes my security. They did not speak of our common consecration to education. They spoke to me of security. Well, sir, when the late Moe Annenberg was on trial for tax evasion, Judge Wilkerson asked him why he had named those five corporations after girls. Moe explained that the five girls were his daughters and he wanted them to have security. The corporations had five million dollars apiece in them.

Maybe it was bigness, nothing but the bigness, that finally frightened me away. The place is so big that it has to be run by computer (which was what enabled it to become so big in the first place). You dream that you have forgotten your number and wake up moaning like Prometheus. My beloved colleague Murgatroyd, who knows all about Swinburne, and can't sell what he knows outside a university, found himself computerized into teaching two sections of a flim-flam (or film-flam) called The Gangster in Film. The students are serviced by computer, and the computer declares that The Gangster in Film is the servicing they want. There is nobody to tell them that the servicing they want is not the servicing they need.

Reprinted from the *Progressive*, October 1973.

It's a great big state university and, oh, how I wanted to love it. But who can love a State or any subdivision or agency thereof? Not I, and oh, how I tried.

Your stem-winding hustler is always uneasy in the neighborhood of the State. He blooms best in the cracks in the pavement. So maybe it was the icy breath of Big Brother that finally frightened me away. Last Spring the faculty senate interrupted its interminable argument about campus parking fees—that's what faculty senates argue about— to reverse the decision it made three years ago ('mid the rockets' red glare) to remove university credits from the balmy "courses" in ROTC. Nobody said so—nobody needed to—but everybody knew that the craven reversal was the consequence of Big Brother's jaundiced view of those institutions which live on Federal grants and fail to maintain the right attitude toward National Security as represented by ROTC.

For my loving, lovable colleagues Big Brother is one of the costs of doing business. They are as good men as I, my colleagues, and more learned far. But they are caged. They are genuine professors; for them it is Swinburne or die. I am a bogus professor, and a hack. You name it—and I've got it in my bag or I'll get it for you around the corner. An earthquake in Tierra del Fuego on Thursday?—I'll have a ladies' club lecture on The Home Life of the Fuegans ready by Friday.

In my youth I had four little beaks to fill and one little woman crying for Butane. Up, up, and away I went and came back to the nest with an occasional rabbit skin and an occasional rabbit. A fellow once slipped me a sandwich after my Tierra del Fuego lecture. Ansley Salz saw the little woman pushing the groceries in a go-cart and slipped me an old Cadillac. Meyer Kestnbaum of Hart Schaffner & Marx saw me in my ravels and slipped me an overcoat.

Nobody slips a $20,000 professor an overcoat or a Cadillac, or a sandwich.

The four little beaks are filled and flown now, on one wing, three kidneys, five tires. Lots less Butane now, a rabbit skin for two.

Robert Morss Lovett (*alav ha-sholom*) used to say that his university was his club and he'd like to remain a member if the dues didn't go too high. Back, then, to the cracks in the pavement, where the hustler blooms best. Back to trying to learn how to learn and teach. Back to the ancient (I didn't say honorable, only ancient) family motto of the Mayers: If You Keep Moving, They Can't Hit You.

Part Five

Displaceable Person

America the More or Less Beautiful

I have crossed this country, or this here country, a hundred times, or a thousand, in every which direction and by every kind of common conveyance except the surfboard. The summer of my sixteenth birthday, when I ran away from home, or pretended to, I even walked, and got hove into jail in La Junta, Colorado, not for running away from home, but for walking; so long ago was an American expected to use his feet for shoe trees.

There were only twenty miles of macadam between the outskirts of Chicago and Los Angeles that summer, all twenty of them in one piece running west from Garden City, Kansas; why Garden City, Kansas, I couldn't imagine then, and I can't imagine now. Maybe the governor came from there, or from twenty miles west of there.

Automobiles went twenty to twenty-five to thirty miles an hour (with an occasional wild man, or that Garden City stretch, doing forty). They went so slow that they could hardly help stopping to pick you up. You could fix the driver with your doloriferous eye, and he, in turn, could give you the double-O as he passed you and stop a few feet up ahead if you looked (as I took care to) like a nice boy.

You got to see the country, or at least look at it, and smell it and taste it and hear it. You got to talk to people, of whom there weren't so many; to strangers, who became friends when you went into the ditch or your tire went boom or your radiator boiled or you couldn't walk any further in the Mojave Desert in July. You depended on people, and they on you in the same fix or its prospect.

No more, nevermore.

A couple of years ago I stood outside Modesto, California, on the freeway, trying to hitch a ride to the coast. I looked like a nice man. The cars, usually one person to a car, went by me at a million miles an hour. I could see the air conditioner in the front window and the clothes hung on hangers in the back. After two hours or so a jalopy with two migrant workers came tea-kettling along and took me into Gilroy, where I got a lift in a pickup truck from a fellow who recognized me.

Reprinted from the *Progressive*, November 1966.

Last summer the companion of my sorrows—at the wheel; we divide the labor, she driving and I looking at the scenery—and I did the round trip coast-to-coast, in our old four-cylinder, mile-high microbus. Freeway half the way between Chicago and San Francisco—Your Tax Dollars at Work—and more in September than there had been in June. Thruway all the way between Chicago and the East, spelled (unless it's spelled "turnpike") "thruway," so don't be a perfessor of English. Minimum speed 40, maximum 10,000.

The heap broke down at Milepost 371, smack at the Milepost, near Rochester. It cost us $22.75 (plus a $3 service charge) to be towed into town. No mechanics—it was Friday night—until we found Bernd Schrodt, just over from Germany. Bernd was supposed to go out with his wife that night. Instead he worked on the heap all night, and all day Saturday, and Saturday night, when he was supposed to go out with his wife again. If I were his wife I'd leave him. But she's a foreigner, and he's a foreigner, and he charged us an un-American $30.

Brother Schrodt, a German, was just about the only American we got to talk to from one coast to the other except for three truckers at a Wyoming truck stop, one from Bekins in Seattle and two from Lyon Van in San Berdoo (San Bernardino on the map). Before I could tell them about Vietnam, they told me. One of them said it was a shame when you had to be ashamed of your own country; another that his boy was thinking of emigrating and so was he; and the third, a twenty-year Army man, that nobody he knew was for it.

That's a big change. A big change. America is supposed to be where everybody stands united—for what?—and politics ends at the water's edge. A big change, when people tell strangers that they're against the wartime government; first time since the Spanish-American War. Apathy has become the property of the prowar faction, whose prowar morale consists of their saying that we *have to* back up our boys. It's the first time since the Russian Revolution that the Red Menace hasn't "taken"; Joe McCarthy wouldn't know the old place.

That's good, you say. But it's bad, too, when such fervor as there is in a society is against something. America is Vietnam, all right. But it isn't Vietnam and nothing else. America is where two of those three truckers have sons in college, something that couldn't happen anywhere else in the West. America is where, of a sudden, the downtown streets of the cities are crowded with Negroes with purchasing power and the confidence to go downtown and use it—or withhold it. We didn't see a Negro, not one, in a motel along the way both ways, but we saw all the integrated ads on TV, on the billboards, in the newspapers and magazines, self-consciously saying that what the

well-dressed woman is wearing (or scouring or hair-dressing with) is
what she's wearing (or scouring or hair-dressing with) whether she's
white or black—unheard of, or, rather, unseen, two years ago, or
even one.

Changes galore, big changes. The bar was well lined at eventide
in Elkhart, Indiana. I climbed aboard and watched the barflies watching the news on the swivel TV. Vietnam—here's how we were winning there today, folks—was followed by the evening's race riots and
the peace demonstrators trying to keep Vice-President Humphrey
from talking. (Fat chance.) Not a peep out of the barflies from start
to finish or after the finish. A big change, when Americans don't
know what to say about gooks and niggers and beatniks. A big
change, when Americans don't know what to think about their
country or their kids. Me, too. A big, undreamed-of change, Americans bewildered.

Not all of them. Not on the road to Reno. As you come turning
along the Truckee River into town from Winnemucca, where the
Safeway Supermarket has a row of slot machines, there's a billboard
with a big flag on it and the legend, "Save Our Republic—Impeach
Earl Warren," and on your left a trailer slum called Happy Valley
(which turns out, on a raid a week later, to have been a multiple
portable bordello). Then you pass a truck on the up-grade, the biggest truck you ever saw, loaded with slatted crates of bomb casings,
westbound, whence, whither; no identification on the truck or the
crates. And another billboard on your right: "Fun Jets—Los Angeles
—Las Vegas—Reno."

America is a great country—they're all great countries—but it
isn't settled yet. Doesn't look as if it ever will be now. Just about
beginning to get settled back there, when the tin lizzie rooted it up
again. Mobility jerrybuilt it, and there's more mobility all the time.
A beautiful country, too—they're all beautiful countries—but it
isn't getting any more beautiful and it doesn't look as if it ever will.
Land of plenty of land to waste and lay waste and put prodigality
into the national bones. We're not staying anyway. Who lives where
his folks lived? Whose children live where he does? Illinois's "Here
I Rest" ought to have "But Not for Long" tagged on to it, and California's "I Have Found It!" "Guess I'll Move On."

There isn't anything in Nevada, not even in California, unsightlier
than the big New England towns, the mills abandoned, the village
green faced on four sides with red-brick "blocks" converted to gim-
crack store-fronts below and left to the loft rats above. A beautiful
country, some of it. Going into the beautiful Donner Pass on the
eastern slope of the Sierras a "don't-litter-$100-fine" sign and along-

side, on the beautiful river, a beautiful car dump. Only where unimaginative people stay put, or used to stay put, is there self-imposed order, uncontrived, unimaginative beauty. Germans, Swedes, Dutch. Where it is still a little like that—Iowa, for instance—is where the political stability is, too.

Where the action is, and where it isn't beautiful, is Nevada. Without the action Nevada would be abandoned to the gypsum plants and indomitable Basque shepherds and end-of-the-roaders spawned by the people who didn't make it to the end of the road. But the action, a nickel at a time, is barely enough as it is to keep Nevada from falling off the map. The really big gambling money, which doesn't come out of the machines or away from the tables, goes back where it came from—to the eastern hoods who own the joints under delirious disguises like the XYZ Company.

It isn't just in Nevada that the Company has taken over and stamped its implacable stamp on the place and the people. K. Ames's little old-timey butter-and-egg store in Northampton, Massachusetts, turns out, in small print, to be a part of the Kennedy Butter-and-Egg Chain, and what ever became of K. Ames? In Chicago we saw a man behind the counter of a North Side motel, and when we got to a South Side motel a half hour later, looking for a cheaper "unit," we saw the same darned man behind the counter *there*, and he explained that he works for "the outfit that owns all these places along here." At Howard Johnson's (which is on the New York Stock Exchange) they no longer put free matches out on the counter. The girl at the register explained that the Company efficiency experts ordered them not to.

The soulful corporation provides the facade and décor, and the boss, like the busboy, is a hard-pushed hired hand bucking for a few cents more an hour. Soulless people, trying to keep body together. It's plenty bitter in Nevada in the wintertime when the fun is over, and plenty bitter in the summer when the fun is on. The people who peddle the fun don't have it. I asked the bald man at the gas station in Battle Mountain if he was permanent there—of course he was—and he said he couldn't get enough together to be anything else. Then I asked him how many of the permanents played the slots. "Ninety-five per cent," he said. Then I asked him how many of them win. "They all lose," he said. They look like losers, too, working at Harrah's Club ("For Fun") or at Harold's Club ("For *More* Fun").

Every time Baby and I cross Nevada we watch the fun lovers playing the Generous Slots until they've lost everything they have to lose, or more, after the tantalizing little wins; who in his right mind would quit when he'd put ten nickels (or dimes, or quarters, or silver dollars) in and the bells all ring and ten come cascading out? Then

Baby and I get steamed up and take a dollar apiece out of the food
kitty and have fun and get out of Nevada. Two dollars is too much
for fun, though a fellow might lay out that much for happiness.

"Reno for Fun," where, the book says, there are six times as
many marriages as divorces, was always squalid and is getting squal-
ider fast. Vegas has taken the play away, two hundred miles closer
to Los Angeles, where the people live who need the fun the most.
The stucco Wedding Chapels on Fourth Street are falling apart, a
crumbling contribution to the world's cathedral architecture. Fun;
it's hard to believe that there are schools and grocery stores and
dentists' offices and funeral parlors and babies in Reno, but I suppose there are. And a state university (where, I suppose, they have
teaching machines that take nickels, dimes, quarters, and silver
dollars). A great state to travel by night, Nevada; everything's open
around the clock.

Big changes across the country. Indications getting more insistent
that the bloom is off the boom. Less spending for Fun, for new cars,
new houses, new boats; at least less *carefree* spending for them. The
air of hilarity is down. People seem to be beginning to un-enjoy putting out $3.95 or $4.95 for a dollar dinner. Got to pay 15, 20, 25
cents for a cup of coffee; 50, 75, or 85 cents for a hamburger with
an even bigger bun and an even smaller "patty." Got to build and
crash a $600,000,000 bomber—yep, $600,000,000. Got to keep
Your Tax Dollars at Work: "Rest Area—State Funds $15,000. U.S.
Department of Commerce Highway Program $220,000." Long, low
rumble of bewildered discontent across the land, all of it focused on
Washington.

No more, nevermore do you see the country or talk to the people.
No need to, no time to, no chance to. "Fill 'er up." "Gimme a room."
"Ham and eggs—scrambled." And away you go, sealed in your car,
grooved on the freeway, and, at the end of the day, locked in your
"unit." The motel is the ultimate triumph of impenetrability. You
don't have to talk, or listen, or look. You can walk in, and walk
around, and walk out with your eyes shut. Same plastic-and-formica
furniture, won't scratch, burn, mar; same doge's lamps, same sani-
tized king-and-queen sanitation; same hand-wrought-by-the-million
fixtures, which some fellow-Kilroy, trying to hang on to his sanity,
has tried, with success, to pull out of the wall; same plastic drapes,
same plastic management, same plastic guests, same concrete floor,
same concrete patio, same concrete television program.

The traveling salesman used to complain about having to sleep in
a different bed every night; now he sleeps in the same bed every night,
no matter how far he has traveled. You wake up in a Cheyenne motel

room and you think you're in Chattanooga. On the return trip you
know you're in Cheyenne because you've learned that the ice cubes
are square in Chattanooga and round in Cheyenne. At the cast-iron
Holiday Inn in Grand Island, Nebraska, there's a sign saying to notify
the management if you want to move the TV set because it's connected to the burglar alarm. Well, that's a *little* something.

You buy the local paper to see if you can't locate the American
pulse, and sure enough. It's J. Y. Castle Day in North Platte. Mr.
Castle, the President of the McDonald State Bank, will receive a free
meal from Tucker's Restaurant and a free tie from J. M. McDonald's.
It doesn't say what for, or whether there's a connection between the
McDonald State Bank and J. M. McDonald's; everybody in North
Platte doubtless knows, and the paper isn't published for outside
agitators.

Vietnam is nowhere near Page One in the small-town papers and
there are no editorials on the war. The Omaha riots are the world of
the *Omaha World-Herald*, and the *Cleveland Plain Dealer* deals plain
pictures of the Cleveland riots. Same as North Platte: If It Doesn't
Happen around Here, It Doesn't Really Happen. In all of them the
AP and UPI dispatches refer to whoever opposes Ky (whoever Ky is)
simply as "Communists," to make it easy for North Platte, Omaha,
and Cleveland. In the driest interior of the country the Navy makes
its recruiting pitch with Burma-Shave-type signs. Get out of the dust-
bowl and bite the dust at the bottom of the deep blue sea.

The whine and hum of the highway outside the soundproof motel
unit conspires with the grind and the roar of the trucks to drown out
the whirr of the air-conditioner that controls you instead of you it.
Magic Fingers—a quarter in the machine by the bed—jiggle you if you
aren't up to jiggling yourself. No movable lamp lest you steal it (along
with the TV set) or else no lamp cord long enough. Across the road
something is being built—another motel, or a church, or a gas station,
or an emplacement for another one of Big Brother's Direct Early
Warning Stations. (Twenty-six minutes to evacuate North Platte or
New York.) You'll never know. Property of U.S. Government—Keep
Out. By and by, you'll never care.

The independent American at last, without the inconvenience of
either self-reliance or reliance. People-processing in the homogenized
society. We got into Willoughby, Ohio, late and got hooked for a $13
catacomb (plus tax) with a candlelit restaurant with wall-to-wall car-
pet and wall-to-wall people. Baby, knowing better than to ask if they
had bulk tea in the house, asked the waitress if the tea bag could be
put in the pot *before* the hot water. The waitress said that the only
thing they had was instant tea.

But she said she was sorry, too; and the other day I was walking along a high-speed highway south of Brattleboro, Vermont, and a truck with a No Riders sign on it passed me and stopped and backed all the way up and the driver asked me if I needed a lift; and on the way home I saw a beaver working like a beaver on a tree beside a pond. So I figure there's a little life in the old land yet.

Socialism with No Face

There was a knock—a peremptory knock, I decided afterward—on the hotel room door. I got one eye ungummed and said, "Yes," in Czech (the Czech word for *Yes* being *Ano*, pronounced *No*). "Hotel clerk," said the voice on the other side of the door. "Gentleman to see you—Police." Instead of saying, "Make up your mind which," I said, *"Ano."*

Mrs. Mayer, or, as we say in Prague, Pany Mayer, was, as usual, half awake. She couldn't have heard the clerk's last word. "Who is it?" she said. I said, *"Ano."*

You can't tell the difference (if there is one) between a Czech soldier and a Czech policeman. They all wear baggy brown uniforms with epaulets and stars. "My" policeman had four stars; private first class, maybe. And no gun. They don't need guns in Prague; all they need (as Moran & Mack used to say) is your name and *add*ress, and they had mine.

My visa, my policeman said, was not in order: "Our Embassy in Bern made an administrative error when they changed the date on your visa from last Spring. They have no competence to do that." "But," I said, "we were allowed through the Passport Control yesterday." "That," he said "was *our* error. We must telephone to the Foreign Ministry—from Ruzene Airport" (which is where I came in, the night before).

He said he would gladly wait for me; they always do. I went to the dining room and, with the premonition that I was condemned, ate a hearty breakfast.

As I ate hearty, I reflected that there might just be a little something here that did not meet the ungummed eye. Though I had been back in Prague in '69 and again in '70, I had published a great deal, in the *Progressive* and elsewhere, since the Soviet invasion of August 20, 1968: *inter alia*, a little book called *The Art of the Impossible: A Study of the Czech Resistance*, and, what was perhaps worse, a long interview in England with the condemned philosopher of the Dubček movement, the man who had spoken of "socialism with a human face," Professor Eduard Goldstücker.

Reprinted from the *Progressive*, December 1971.

My policeman wanted to know if I wanted to take Pany Mayer
with me. I thought fast and said no (not *Ano*)—I'd leave her at the
hotel. Pany has a somewhat lower boiling point than mine, and in
the face of any injustice tends to tear the place apart, something
that, under the circumstances, would never do. Besides, they might
go easy on me if they had a hostage for me—this on the false assumption that the police in Prague or Attica are only human after all.
Besides, Pany would, and did, bid me an extremely fond farewell—
which is not to be sneezed at, and wasn't.

My policeman had both our passports, which we had left (an old
Socialist custom) with the hotel desk on our arrival.

En route to the airport I explained that Pany and I had got our
visas (at four dollars each) from the Czech Embassy in Bern last May
—it was now September 26—to attend the *Praske jaro*. (The *Praske
jaro*, or Prague Springtime, is the great music festival whose name is
now synonymous with the eight-month liberation that ended on
August 20, 1968.) A few days before we were to go we heard on
the West German radio that no more foreigners would be allowed
to enter Czechoslovakia in May. (The Congress of the Czech Communist Party was scheduled then—the devil with the *Praske jaro*—
to put the seal on the "normalization," now called "consolidation,"
of the Russian invasion of three years before. No running dogs of
capitalist imperialism wanted.)

The Czech Embassy in Bern put forward our visas to fall, and
now my policeman said that they were *neplatne*, or no good, and
six or eight hours after he and I got back to the airport he remembered to borrow the passports and so stamp them.

Now we were illegal, but Pany was illegaler than I was, because
she was in Prague, crying her baby-blue eyes out, eating all our Swiss
chocolate, and counting all our money (which, except for ten dollars,
I had made the mistake of leaving with her). That Pany.

My policeman took me back through Passport Control, where
everybody, including me, saluted everybody else, and suggested that
I make myself at home for a few minutes. I was in the Departure
Lounge, watching the planes come and go, a diverting variety of
ancient props and less ancient turbos and jets and an occasional monster Tupelov leaving for Moscow, Bombay, or Baghdad. What was
especially interesting was the shiny new *French* Caravelles of the
Rumanian Air Line. What was less especially interesting was the rust
of all the Czech ground equipment, dilapidation everywhere; you
can't Build Socialism and Polish the Brass at the same time.

What was poignant was the jam-packed observation deck outside—

thousands of Czechs looking at the passengers coming and going (especially going). During the "terrible twenty years" before Dubček, amazingly few Czechs tried to get away. They loved their country, and they lived in hope. They live in hope—at least in short-term hope— no longer. Some 40,000 got out after the Russian invasion, and stayed out, losing their jobs, their property, even their citizenship (and a steady procession sentenced to prison in absentia). Now the borders are sealed tight, and 14,000,000 caged birds can watch the uncaged of the world taking flight.

Ruzene Airport was completed in 1966, with great runways ideally suited to the midnight landing of the Russians and their tanks two years later. It is a small replica of all the wall-to-wall airports all over the world, except that there is not a book, a magazine, or a newspaper to be had in the place.

Nothing to write on and nothing to read. Some of the nonresidents had left Czech, Russian, and Polish newspapers on the benches, but I had read them all before; twenty years before. I watched a man reading a German magazine. He got up to get a beer and I grabbed it, but it turned out to be an *East* German magazine full of stories of happy, heroic workers and peasants. I had read them all twenty years before.

Three hours after he'd left me "for a few minutes" my policeman— by now I thought he'd defected—shuffled up and said he was sorry but it would be a few minutes yet; it being Sunday, the Marxist Sabbath, it was difficult to reach the Foreign Ministry, I thanked him and went up to the second level of the Departure Lounge. There I studied the goodies all the happy people leaving Prague were buying at the Duty Free Shop, including Russian and Czech vodka. ("They're both the same," I heard a salesgirl tell a customer.) Everybody smokes in airports, the way everybody used to at theater intermissions, and I was out of tobacco. I had to break my ten dollars to buy a package, and the cashier had no silver and gave me bubble gum to make up a dollar.

The bubble gum reminded me that it was well past lunchtime.

I went down to the lower level of the Departure Lounge and struck up a lively conversation with the nice girls at the Czechoslovakian Air Line Transit Desk. I asked them if I could use their phone, on the ground that the one pay phone was always busy. They said yes, and in the course of my stay I used that phone fifty times; at a quarter-crown a call, that would be eighty-seven and a half cents; a penny saved is a penny earned.

The penny reminded me to telephone Pany. She said I'd better buy some lunch. I told her I had only nine dollars left and I thought

I ought to save eight dollars in case the administrative error was nothing but a bourgeois device to get another eight dollars out of me for new visas. Pany said, "I don't think it's an error at all, I think they're after you." I told her she was of little faith and proceeded to the dining room, where I ordered (what else?) Russian borscht and Czech *pivo*, beer. Now I was down to eight dollars.

I went back to the Transit Desk and called the Christian Peace Conference whose assembly from September 30 to October 3 I was planning to attend. The brethren at Prague headquarters, they of great faith, said that they would protest vigorously.

The afternoon waned. There was a Kino, or cinema, on the upper level, but it was locked. I went back to the Transit Desk and bummed some Czech Air Line paper. I was reduced—something I have avoided for fifty years—to writing. After I wrote I started looking for my policeman again. No luck, until I bethought me to stroll through the Passport Control. My stroll produced my policeman. He was sorry, but he had not been able to reach the Foreign Ministry. (Later a nice girl at the Transit Desk said, "That's a joke. He doesn't even try. He must wait, just as you must.")

I asked him what I should do, and he said, "Wait." I told him I was a heart patient—I didn't tell him that the statute of limitations had long since run on that one. He said, "Wait." I said, "I may die on your hands." He said, "I am going off duty. But my colleagues know all about the matter."

This was a lie. None of his colleagues knew anything about the matter, and each time I buttonholed one I had to tell my story from the beginning again. A whole world of interchangeable nonpersons with baggy pants and epaulets. ("They have no authority," said one of the nice girls later. "They are only organs.")

My policeman suggested I fly to Vienna and apply there for a new visa. I told him I was a poor man, and he said, "That is all right. When you get back to Bern, you make those people at our Embassy pay you for everything." I told him I'd tell them he said so, and what was his name? He had none. And then he was gone.

Evening, and traffic picked up. The incoming planes were filled with French and Italian hippies in outlandish American costumes, all coming to Prague to debase the socialist morals of the Czechs. (Czechoslovakia needs the hard Western currencies, among which the dollar is still stupidly numbered, worse than it needs to protect itself from Western contamination.)

The happy, hash-laden hordes of Western contaminators queued up at the Passport Control and, after being sent back to pay $5 a day, in advance, for their stay in Czechoslovakia, were pushed through Customs without an examination. The same thing had happened to Pany and me the day before. We could have brought a bomb in. We could have brought Solzhenitsyn in. We could have brought Lenin in, saying, as he did, "While the State exists, there is no freedom. When there is freedom, there will be no State."

Evening faded. I phoned Pany from my office at the Transit Desk and asked her if she missed me. She said she did and could she bake a cake? I thought not, though she had been trying for twenty-five years. "Why don't you talk that sassy to the police?" she said. "Why don't you tell them you're sick?" I told her I'd told them I was dead, and it didn't help.

Pany was beginning to worry. She had phoned an American friend who hangs around Prague and he had suggested that I buy a nice Bohemian cut-glass vase at the Duty Free Shop and give it to my grandmother if I ever got out. She phoned some of our Czech friends and they suggested I call the American Embassy. Pany said, "He doesn't like embassies." But our friends were insistent, so Pany was insistent, so I called the Embassy.

"It's an outrage," said the American Duty Officer. "They can't hold you. They have got to give you a twenty-four-hour permit and take you to the Transit Hotel in town until the visa matter is straightened out." I thanked him, strolled halfway through the Passport Control, told a new policeman my whole story, and demanded to be taken to the Transit Hotel. "It is impossible," he said, and I thanked him.

Now the big guns, or *grosse Kanonen*, of the Christian Peace Conference went into action. "We will get you out of there," said one of the biggest of them. Then the American Embassy phoned me at my office at the Transit Desk. The only nonperson they had been able to raise at the Foreign Ministry said he was the porter—this turned out to be a lie on the so-called porter's part—who knew nothing about the matter. "I'll get back to you," said the nice Duty Officer. "Don't move." I said I wouldn't and, indeed, couldn't.

Night, and Czechoslovakia beyond the airport searchlights was barren and forbidding and a man making a run for it could be potted like a partridge. Out there somewhere—you can't see Prague for the smog—was Pany abandoned. In here, abandoned, was I. My upper lip was numb from having been kept stiff since morning.

The cake talk with Pany reminded me that I was hungry. I might need my eight dollars for two new four-dollar visas—I could not get it out of my bourgeois head that the whole thing was a dirty bourgeois trick—but I was hungry. I repaired to the lunch counter—not to the restaurant—and bought a small sandwich, a small *pivo*, and a small package of Nabiscos, which the Czechs (unable to pronounce Nabisco) call *oplatky* and claim to have invented. Now I was down to $7.40. Maybe they'd give me the new visas wholesale.

Midnight. The American Duty Officer called again and said that the "porter" at the Foreign Ministry now told him that it would take several days to straighten things out. "This is no 'administrative matter,' " said the Duty Officer, "it's political." "It's an outrage," I said. "A scandal," he said.

Casing the Control lanes, around 1:00 A.M., and wondering if I might slip through them during the night (and go where?), I espied two officials of the Christian Peace Conference arguing with a non-person with *six* stars. He let me approach, and I kissed my friends, not once on each cheek, Czech style, but, since 1968, three times for the Holy Trinity of the Russian Orthodox Church.

They told me in despair that nobody had been able to reach anybody in authority—and that I'd have to spend the night in the airport. It was a scandal. "An outrage," I said. But the nice Passport Control, understanding that I was sick and might die, was going to let me sleep in a room for Nursing Mothers. I asked them to lend me a baby, but they said it was all right, and we kissed good-night, three times.

I waited an hour and then went up to the lunch counter where all the policemen were drinking Coca-Cola (which is now bottled in Prague). I bought a Czech nightcap called Karlovy Becher. $7.05 left. An hour later one of the nice girls hove into sight and told me that they hadn't been able to find the key to the Nursing Mothers' Room but there was one other place that was possible, the anteroom of the Health Control Office.

She took me down the stairs and thither, and there was a cot. She apologized, and I soon saw why. The planes kept roaring in and out across my chest and the searchlights had me pinpointed. I thought I would sleep on my passports and then decided to hell with it. Then I thought I would sleep, and then decided to hell with that, too.

My friends, I am a newspaperman by trade, albeit unemployed, and if anyone had ever asked me where and when, as a newspaperman, I should most like to have spent a night, I'd have said, "Ruzene Airport, August 20, 1968." I had got my wish three years late. It was a drag. No toothbrush, no sheets, no pillow, no pills, no Pany. Stiff'per lip.

If I'd never got into Prague and had never been there before, I'd
have known, on the basis of that night's adventures, how bitterly
the Czechs hate their tyrants and their tyrants' tyrants. I was, for
the first time in my life, an *innocent* victim, and the word had got
all around the airport. Some of the civilian personnel dared do no
more than smile at me, some with their eyes alone. One put a hand
on my arm as I passed. One wanted to know if he could do anything
for me. One sat down next to me and said, in slow English, "We have
nothing in commune [sic] with them." *Them*, always *They* and *Them*.

Their tyrants' tyrants are now providing them with Western goodies,
in the fond, foolish hope of buying their allegiance; as if to say, "See,
we deliver what Dubcek promised." But the great goodie that Dubček
promised was freedom, which is in all-time short supply. There is a
somewhat greater variety of clothing, shoes, and food. And automobiles galore; at long last it is hard to find a parking place in Prague.
The Czechs know how to take it: deadpan. They are the grand masters of psychological retreat in depth. Always yielding and never
surrendering, they have worn down their every conqueror. They will
wear down this one too, in ten years, or a hundred, or a thousand.

I hauled myself back up to the Transit Desk with the resumption of
heavy traffic at dawn. The nonresidents were beginning to arrive. I
went to the lunch counter and ordered coffee *bez blata*—without
mud. Soft rolls, Praha style. No jam on hand this morning. $6.15 left
—not enough to get in *or* out of Czechoslovakia with—and 6:15 A.M.

There was, of course, a whole new cast of characters at the airport.
I was the only old-timer left. I told the nice new girls at the Transit
Desk that in the unlikely event that anybody should ever look for
me I would be in my *lanai* outside the Health Control Office.

An hour later a policeman with two stars got me up and took me
to the Transit Desk. He needed my passports "for a few minutes,"
and I gave them to him. That was a mistake an American should
never make, and especially this one. I had fought for that passport
and won it from the Supreme Court when I refused to take an anti-
Communist oath. By now I was uttering anti-Communist oaths one
after another.

Two hours later a policeman with eight stars ordered your Roving
Editor to rove: "You must leave Czechoslovakia immediately. You
can return on October 6." October 6. Three days after the all-
Christian Peace Assembly would end. I said to a nice girl, "What
does he mean, about my returning October 6?" "He doesn't know
what he means," she said, "he is only an organ." He certainly was,
and a specific organ at that.

Now the American Embassy and the Christian Peace Conference were both calling me on the Transit Desk phones. I told the Embassy man what had happened. "Don't move," he said. I told the Christian Peace Conference man what had happened. "Don't move," he said.

Fifteen minutes later the Embassy man called again and said, "Don't move, I think it's breaking." Five minutes later the Christian Peace Conference *Kanone* called and said, "We have reached the highest authorities. Don't move." Three hours later, high noon, the policeman with eight stars said, "Come with me. They have changed their mind." *They.*

I was issued an invitation visa—no charge—and escorted through the Passport Control and Customs. The outcast was incast. A young man with a car, from the Christian Peace Conference, was waiting for me. He grinned, and I grinned—three times.

Nothing in the papers, of course. The difference between freedom and unfreedom is the press. I know that the American press is not a very good one. But at least it's a press. In Prague (and Saigon and in Athens and Moscow) it isn't a press at all. In Prague, where the newspapermen have all been fired since 1968, it is edited and written by semiliterate slobs, and whenever a decent piece of writing appears in it its readers (and no doubt its editors and writers) know that it was written by a "former" newspaperman under a cover name. (I am told that the regime knows it, too, but is so insecure that it doesn't dare pursue the matter.)

But the Czechs are a literate people, with nothing, now, to read. (In the bad old Stalinist days of the 1950s and the '60s anyone could buy the Western papers at the newsstands of the luxury hotels. No more.) One night we walked into the biggest hotel in Prague and found the lights out. In the anonymous dark I said amiably, "Just like New York." "Except," said a Czech voice, "that it happens once in a hundred years in New York and a hundred times a year here." "That's not the difference," said another Czech voice. "The difference is that it's always in the newspapers in New York and it never is here. That's how we Build Socialism."

I should like to know—idle curiosity—why the police held me in Prague. Maybe it was all a mistake, tyrannies being inefficient as well as imbecile. But none of my friends in Prague would buy the imbecility hypothesis. One of them who has "contacts" said, "It is said that you once compared Soviet Communism to German Nazism." "More than once," I said, "Still," he said, "it was not you who on August 21, 1968, chalked the walls of Prague with the hammer-

and-sickle and the swastika with an equals sign between them, was it?"

In the Czechoslovakia that has dug in for the long term the incomparable Czech stories à la Schweik flourish again. *First Czech: "A Swiss soldier stole my Russian watch." Second Czech: "A Swiss soldier stole your Russian watch?—You mean a Russian soldier stole your Swiss watch." First Czech: "You said it—I didn't."* One of my friends said, "Somebody vetoed you in Moscow—and somebody vetoed the veto."

A week or so later Pany Mayer and I were leaving Prague and I showed her around the Ruzene Airport telling her how they had pulled my fingernails out, how they had strung me up by the thumbs, how they had given me the Green Beret water treatment (with, I must say in fairness, *pivo*), and what they had done to me in the anteroom of the Health Control Office. *"They?"* said Pany. *"They,"* said I. Then we boarded the plane for Zurich.

The plane rolled to the end of the runway and sat there. Pany was eating a piece of Swiss chocolate, courtesy of Swissair. I was looking steadily out the window. A red car drew up to the plane. A policeman got out, the door was opened and the steps let down for him, and he came aboard.

He handed the stewardess a paper, left the plane, and drove away. The plane went roaring down the runway and was airborne. Pany and I had made it, just like the lovers in *Casablanca*.

A few days later I toddled off to Bern to bug the Czechoslovakian Socialist Republic by telling their Embassy that their Foreign Minister said that they had no competence to prolong my visa. I demanded my eight dollars back—and the man smiled, three times, and gave it to me.

The Grace of God in Spain

Alicante, Spain

If I was going to see Harry—and I was—I was going to have to see him in Spain. Harry cares not who makes a country's laws, let him but strum its guitar and sop up its sun and its sherry. Harry doesn't worry about the Caudillo, whose picture is on *all* the coins (the few that there are) with the superscription that the Caudillo is Caudillo "by the grace of God."

Thirty-five years ago the people of Spain, or most of them, tried to save their poor republic from the Caudillo and his Nazi and Facist patrons, choosing to die on their feet rather than live on their knees. Now they live on their knees, and after thirty-five years of it there is a new generation to whom Guernica is the name of a provincial town up north somewhere.

A new generation, too, of American tourists, who never did much care who made a country's laws. And a new generation of French and British tourists—and British pensioners settled in the sun—people who (or whose fathers) once stormed the Quai d'Orsay and Whitehall shouting shame at the neutrality policy that let the Nazis and the Fascists carry the Caudillo to Spain. Germans, too, of course; always Germans.

I didn't want to go to Spain again, not as long as the Caudillo ruled by the grace of God. After thirty-five years I was still shouting shame, now at the Nixon mob, all but two of whose cabinet members have gone to pay their homage to the western anchor man of the sea in which they think they might fight it out with the Russians sometime. (Their eastern anchor men, in Greece and Turkey, are of course anti-Communist despots, too.)

But I had to see Harry, so I had to go.

I suppose this kind of secondary, or tertiary, boycott is ridiculous; who cares (if I don't) whether I go to Spain? The Caudillo? He had 24,000,000 other foreign visitors this summer (to a country of 34,000,000), and Spain is now the top tourist country in Europe. I have American friends who thought I shouldn't go to Germany after the war—but I had German friends in Germany, tottering out of the concentration camps and the prisons. And how could I "teach

Reprinted from the *Progressive*, September 1971.

the Germans a lesson" by not going to Germany to teach and to learn?

Now I have Czech godsons in Prague, and I'm on my way to see them again. My godsons don't understand secondary boycotts, and they don't like walls. And neither do I.

But Spain stuck in my craw. But I had to see Harry, so I had to go.

I suppose it meant something (at least to him) when Thomas Mann left Germany and said, "Where I am there is Germany," and when Pablo Casals left Spain and refused to go back. But these were famous men, and it was their own, their native lands they were boycotting. But where is there then to go? Casals, living in American Puerto Rico, by that fact "supports" worse in Vietnam than the Caudillo did in Spain.

And the Caudillo's is a tired old despotism now, and, as despotisms go, an easy one. The foreign papers are available; the Spanish press is allowed to report objectively on *foreign* affairs (and it does); and there is no censorship of the mail.

Of course, there is no real liberty. The constitutional rights, like Russia's, are a joke, and their "suspension" in times of emergency a bigger joke. When there is protest, it is violent; there are far fewer graffiti on the walls than anywhere in the West except Switzerland, where there is nothing to graff about. At seventy-nine, the Caudillo, under the influence of the lay Catholic organization Opus Dei, represents autocratic moderation against the generals who mean to outlive him.

This past summer the foreign tourists were pouring into Spain so fast that the border-control police were waving them on with a get-the-hell-into-here gesture, without letting them stop to show their passports. The solemn country is incongruously full of jerry-built junk, like New Jersey or Phoenix, and incongruous fun-lovers from you-name-it. A Spanish friend of mine likes to go into the restaurants along the tourist *costas* and say, "Do you serve Spaniards?" or "Do you speak Spanish?"

Spain is the only cheap country left in gung-ho Europe, and a European can be rich there (an American fabulous). A solemn, stony country, and a dry one; "the water flows uphill," from the barren fields of the Castilian peasants to the flower gardens of the rich up above. A country of dreadfully poor people on whose backs the tourists ride cheap. By the grace of God—and of Truman, Eisenhower, Kennedy, Johnson, and Nixon, and before them of Hitler and Mussolini—you can live and laugh in Spain, providing you have forgiven and forgotten Guernica.

You don't even have to have forgiven it, only forgotten it.

Sunshine, Flies, No Wind, and Death

Costa Plenta, Spain

The Spaniards like to say—I didn't say they said it; I said they like to say—that the Franco *dictadura* was a *dictablanda*, a mild dictatorship. Under the centuries of the Romans, and then the Moors, and then the Church, they have known worse, and never much better. Under Franco they said and did as they pleased—provided, of course, that it didn't please them to say or do anything about politics. They didn't hate Franco—or love him. There is no charisma in Spain, except (among bullring aficionados) in an occasional torero.

In 1974 the tourist boom was off by perhaps 25 percent, after 1973's unbelievable 34,000,000 pouring into a country of 34,000,000, but it still sustains the economy. A revolution is inevitable, of course, but most unlikely, because the Spaniards are as rich and happy as they have ever been (which is not, to be sure, very rich and happy).

I am rich and happy, too, in Spain for a couple of weeks to see my old friend Harry. It is always pleasure before business in Spain, and I swim every day, sometimes twice a day, at Harry's club. Harry's club is up above the Mediterranean beaches. It has three magnificent fresh-water pools with almost nobody in them, a first-class bar, and a fastidious restaurant (and lunch is served, besides, in the lavishly tended gardens). The sun shines and shines and shines, the breeze is gentle, and in two minutes from Harry's villa we're there.

Harry's villa, like those of the rest of the richer expatriates, mostly American and British with a scattering of Germans, Dutch, Belgians, and Scandinavians (and, in the holidays, Frenchmen), is in the flowering hills with a splendid view of the sea above the teeming condominiums that now run the whole length of Spain's coasts, Costa Brava, Costa Blanca, Costa This, and Costa That. Harry bakes in the sun, and then paddles in the pool, and then visits around and eats and drinks the lowest-priced vittles and booze in Europe. Like all the richer (but not very rich) expatriates, Harry and his wife have a servant who goes to the market with them and does the cooking and cleaning at a dollar or so an hour.

Reprinted from the *Progressive*, October 1974.

I envy Harry, and whenever he observes that I seem to be gloomy I tell him it's because I envy him.

I don't tell him that the reason I envy him is that he doesn't know (and I wish I didn't know) that $6 a month sent to the Fellowship of Reconciliation (P.O. Box 271, Nyack, NY 10960) will feed and clothe a Vietnamese orphan and that two cents sent to the American Friends Service Committee (160 North 15th Street, Philadelphia, PA 19102) will provide a hot meal for an orphan in Orissa Province in India.

Harry has worries of his own. Spanish inflation is running 20 or 25 percent (or 30 percent) per annum. (In Spain nobody knows anything exactly, except what time the bullfights begin.) Though the expatriates pay nothing but nominal taxes, they are worried, the British even more so than the Americans. The British could not survive, much less keep servants, if they went back home. That's one worry.

"So we live here," says a sharp Englishwoman whose much older husband seems to like fascism. "We don't like fascism, of course, and being isolated from everything and having nothing to say—. Well, we don't belong in England any more, it would be difficult there, so we might as well stay in this fascist country." (None of these expatriates ever emigrates to where he might say, "So we might as well stay in this communist country.")

Harry has another kind of inflation to worry about besides. He is overweight; he doesn't know how much, because nobody (not even the expatriates) knows anything exactly in Spain. He asks me how I keep my weight down, and I don't tell him that I take the edge off my appetite by thinking about the Vietnamese and Indian orphans— just thinking about them, not doing anything about them.

Harry doesn't read any more, except for the *International Herald-Tribune*, where he watches the daily fluctuation of his Eurodollars. He doesn't write. (He used to be a writing man.) He says he'll never go back to America and doesn't care what happens there, or in Spain, or anywhere else. And it's just as well that he doesn't care what happens in Spain, because he'd be invited to leave Spain if he did; and he used to be a free-swinging American loudmouth like me.

Like Harry, the rest of the expatriates I meet are in their healthy sixties or seventies, or in their fifties or even in their forties. They are almost all of them, like Harry, doing nothing at all in sunny Spain. There is the smell of dead money in the sunny air, of just enough, or not quite enough, dead money. Harry, in his prime, sits in the sunny patio above the Mediterranean and smiles and chuckles and seems to be waiting. But I am darned if I can see what he is waiting for. Unless he hurries home (and Spain takes the hurry out of a man in a hurry) he is going to die some day sunburned in Spain.

It's an isolated country, Spain, its millions of foreign tourists heed-
lessly unattached to it. Franco's was the last and the longest-lived of
the old strong-man tyrannies that used to disturb us. France, to the
north, came within a squeak, in 1974, of voting to admit Communists
to its government. The Portuguese, to the west, overthrew the oldest
fascist tyranny of them all, forty-eight years in the saddle, and
within a month the Communists emerged as the strongest party in
the country. When Franco's prime minister was assassinated, presumably by the Basques, who consider themselves Basques first and
Spaniards second (if at all), nobody in Spain was visibly glad or sorry.
Who knows how the Spaniards feel, or what they are going to do,
those most voluble and taciturn, demonstrative and sullen, of people?
Nobody. (The Russians wrote off Spain a quarter-century ago, just
as they wrote off Portugal.)

But Spain has always been isolated: "Africa begins at the Pyrenees."
When President Eisenhower threw his arms around Franco in 1953,
Spain's isolation from Europe was supposed to have ended. Fascist
Spain was America's front door to the Mediterranean, with fascist
Greece the back door, and Europe, in 1953, depended on America.
But ten years later, and twenty, the isolation hadn't ended. The
Americans have had to go it alone. They cannot get the Europeans
to admit Spain to the happy family of NATO—Greece and Turkey
(holding the nose) *si*, Franco Spain (even holding the nose) *non*.

Spain has always been isolated. Untouched, in its peninsular illit-
eracy, by the three Rs—Renaissance, Reformation, Revolution—that
schooled the modern world, it leaped from the arms of the Moors
into the arms of Holy Church and conquered the world over two
centuries of unexampled cruelty and devastation, its ramshackle
Christian imperium (Inquisition and all) extending from the Sahara
and Sardinia to Brussels and Amsterdam, from Port of Spain to
Tierra del Fuego and Luzon. Then its Invincible Armada was destroyed by the New Spaniards from England, and three whole centuries later the last of its poor wooden boats were burned at Havana
and Manila by the Newest Spaniards from America.

And still, in its fall, it remained and remains Spain, the legendary
mother country of the whole Hispanic world, a sentiment of bygone
grandeur and bygone pride, providing asylum to rightists and leftists
"returning" from Latin America, to a Peron, to a Juan Bosch, and
maintaining diplomatic and commercial relations with the Cuba of
Fidel Castro. The grandest manner of a mannered nation in an un-
mannered world, legendarily resisting the "Europeanization" of industry and urbanization and socialization.

The reality, not the legend, is a reality of extremes, the jerry-built *costas* with their *supermercados*, the foreign factories looking for, and finding, cheap docile labor, the competing modernization of the competing capitals, "European" Barcelona and "Spanish" Madrid, and the dreadful interior of barren plateaus and dry rivers, blazing and windswept, skeletal mules threading the passes, the most irresistibly underdeveloped land of Europe, the tourists, everywhere in Greece to dig the remains, nowhere in Spain except on the coasts.

Always excepting Portugal. Death knocked at the door of the Presidential palace in Madrid when the contemptible Portuguese toppled their seamless dictatorship. If the contemptible Portuguese, how secure was the palace in Madrid? The palace had no way of knowing, because no one in Spain has any way of knowing anything.

Potentially significant was the broadcast in Spain of all the details of the Portuguese revolution. Potentially significant was the daring of the press (which is not precensored) to carry all the news of it; but only potentially significant, because there has never been any censorship of foreign news, since Spaniards don't care all that much about it. But—*Portugal*. Did it mean liberalization in Spain?

The government talked about permitting "political associations," whatever that might mean, and the election of local mayors. And then Franco (or somebody acting for Franco) abruptly dismissed the Chief of Staff, Gen. Manuel Diez Alegria (whose tenure would have expired automatically a month later). After the assassination of Franco's prime minister, the supposedly moderate Diez Alegria had successfully resisted the blood bath projected by the *Guardia Civil*, the national police who have the habit (if not the legality) of acting independently of the army. Diez had been receiving monocles in the mail; the man who overthrew the Portuguese tyranny, General Spinola, wears a monocle.

More significant was the permission for public opinion polls to be taken—for the first time in Spain—on carefully delineated social issues. Unreliable as they had to be, among a people so long habituated to the avoidance of serious discussion, the polls revealed that while two thirds of the respondents professed "no interest whatever" in politics, a majority wanted to see key industries and banks socialized, a majority of the laity wanted to see a divorce law (in this last True Catholic country of Europe), and a majority of the priests under forty were (of course, nonparty) "socialists." Most significant was the 26 percent who would not like to see "the present political situation" continue for another thirty years—and the 31.5 percent who said they were undecided. (42.5 percent said yes.)

But no revolution after Franco. When I first went to Spain, in the early 1930s, the saying that "every Spaniard dies of hunger or over-eating" was more than hyperbole. There was no middle class what-ever. A servant got not a dollar an hour, but a dollar a day (without, however, having to spend anything on shoes). There were no social services of any kind—wasn't that what Holy Church was for?—and only the children of the rich went to school. The improvement of the thirty-five years of Franco has been phenomenal. Spain has com-mon schooling and social security and wage and job guarantees—no unions, of course—and skilled workers have cars. There is no urban unemployment, and agricultural prices are high. The boom depends upon three contingencies wholly outside the country's control—foreign investment and development (the U.S. is now Spain's number one trading partner); tourism (which brings in a quarter of the nation-al income); and the remittances of cheap unskilled labor exported to northern Europe (and replaced by still cheaper labor from North Africa).

But the prosperity, contingent as it is, is the opiate, as it is of all peoples, of the Spaniards, and the Spaniards do not need much of it to be tranquilized. It is radically uneven. The traditional poverty of the south, Castile and Andalusia, has been only marginally affected, and where the subjection of farm tenancy has given way to owner-ship the independent peasant moves, as he always has, in the direction of anarchy in paradoxical conjunction with the prosperous industrial workers of "European" Catalonia in the northeast. Barcelona, Cata-lonia's capital, is the first outpost and the last bastion of romantic anarchism, a Spanish marvel compounded (and confused) with social-ism. Catalonia, where no newspaper is permitted to be published in the Catalan dialect, despises Madrid, and the separatist Basque prov-inces of the northwest detest Madrid.

The Spain on which the new "reality" rests is not the impoverished south or the radical north but the *costas*, which have been sold out to the foreigners, with every imaginable inducement and no restric-tions. This is green Spain, the only Spain that is not somber and suspect. The Spaniard who happens to have been born here—Span-iards are still the least mobile of Europeans—never wants for work and overtime work building for the foreigners, fishing for the for-eigners, growing for the foreigners, and serving for foreigners as a flunky. This is Spain debased and desecrated by the camper-condominium-pizza-hamburger-bikini-gin-and-tonic-pleasure-leisurites. It is still, for all the inflation, the best buy in Europe. The sellout has produced some of the finest high-risk gimmicks on earth: For $10,000 you can have a villa any one month of the year you want, for ten years, and then get your money back.

Until the boom collapses completely, Madrid is probably safe from revolution after Franco. Still—there was Portugal, where the young officers staged a revolution *from the left*. In poor, backward countries like Spain, in contrast with "civilized" countries like Germany, or even Italy, the army is everything. The strong man is not an ex-corporal, but a general. If he can keep the army in line, he can keep the country. Still—there was Portugal, Hispanic Portugal, and Hispania has a character of its own.

There is, of course, no such thing as a national character—except for the Spaniards. Out of the welter of Spanish contradictions there emerges a shrug of the shoulders which, having nothing else to go by, the tyrant has to try to interpret. He knows his countrymen's tragi-comic preoccupation with dignity (or its appearance) and the "anarchistic" attachment to one's own and one's family's survival. (The Spaniard will tell you, with dour irony, that the national motto is, *Viva yo!*—"Hooray for me!") The nation is nothing to him, he is a foreigner in it, as every Spanish artist has been, from Cervantes right up to Picasso and Casals. The village is something to him. The individual is everything to him—*Viva yo*! All government is misgovernment. Honor and honesty, deeply involved with dignity or its appearance, by universal consent end where the government begins.

Life has always been short and hard in the sun, and death so soon, in a world of black-weeded widows, that the robust expatriate, living on and on, his back unbroken, is not so much a class enemy as a dream. A man or woman who works from 7 to 7, or from 7 A.M. to 9 P.M. with two hours off for the siesta, does not want to bother or be bothered. He wants to eat and drink and sleep and, eating and drinking, talk incessantly in his hard, harsh tone about nothing at all. He is not an organization man. He is not a Rotarian or a Little League coach or a deacon. (There are no deacons.) There are no Cub Scouts or Campfire Girls, no Junior Fallangista. No political posters or graffiti, no confrontation or contestation (the lifeblood of the Frenchman), no alacrity or exactitude (the lifeblood of the German). Life itself is enough to keep a man moving as fast as it compels him to move. The *dictablanda* is the best of all worlds possible to him just now, with nothing but the bullfight to punctuate the short, hard survival in the sun.

The Spaniard's contradictions are profound and visible. The natural colors of Spain are all dark, black and brown and blue and the deep green of the pine and the olive tree—and the mad clash of yellows, oranges, and reds of the fiesta, the flag, and the bullring is like nothing anywhere else. The saddest of songs and stories and art, the harshest to the hard life, the flamenco, the poetry of Lorca, the *Vida Breve*

of de Falla, Unamuno's *Tragic Sense of Life*, Velasquez's bitter por-
traits, the gloom of El Greco, the stark terror of Goya, and, at the
beginning, the really woeful countenance of the Knight of the Woeful Countenance—here you have Spain and, alongside it, the wild
castanet and the shrill and the whirl of the Spanish dance. The
courtliness, the punctilio, the sweeping bow, the kissing of the hand
—and the cast-iron stomach enables the Spaniard to cheer the bull
as it goads the picador's blindfolded horse and to round up the "suspects" in the ring at Badajoz and shoot them because there are too
many for the garrote. The splendid machismo of the peasant, the
worker, saying, only to a male, never to a female, *"No me da gana"*
—"To hell with it"—and the blindfolded acceptance of a cast-iron
despotism in Madrid.

Don't ask me how "Francisco" becomes "Pacho," but there you
are. "The contradictions," says my weather-withered old friend
Pacho, "the contradictions are what make the Spaniard and what
make him an interesting fellow. Name me another race with such
contradictions, and, yes, I say 'race.' You must combine a monk,
a torero, a macho, a grandee, a slave, and a bum to get a Spaniard."
But why this wholly humiliated people under tyranny? Was it only
thirty-five years ago that they fought to the death in unruly passion
to hold on to what few liberties they had?

"Yes," says Pacho, "the same. This Spaniard is a singular man.
Excess is his humor—a fatal humor, of course. You would think, to
come here now, after you and I first met in the 1930s, that Franco
fascism changed his character. No. His fury sleeps, and then it awakens,
and then sleeps again. In the Civil War you could not imagine a quiet
Spain, unless you were a Spaniard. The Spaniard is a civil war that
cannot end."

But one institution is changing sides in that war. In the 1930s the
Catholic Church—of *Spain*; Spaniards have no interest in what an
Italian Pope says, or does—was the bulwark of feudalism, fascism,
and Franco, and was rewarded with government stipends and special
privileges for the clergy. In the past ten or fifteen years, with the
maturation of young priests, that relationship has crumbled away,
and the "rebel priests," openly taking the side of social protest, are
heavily, if cautiously, supported by their bishops. When the esteemed
Bishop Anoveros of Bilbao was arrested in 1974 for the issuance
of a pastoral letter appealing for cultural and linguistic rights for
the Basques, the Franco government threatened to deport him for
his "subversive attack against national unity." A Papal remonstrance
against the threat was ignored in Madrid—and then Bishop Anoveros
announced that he would excommunicate any official who laid a

hand on him. He was set free, with the support of all but three of his fellow bishops and of the whole country's "worker priests." "The Church is the only agency in Spain that reaches the people," says my friend Pacho, "and it was on the wrong side of the people in 1936. It does not intend to be on the wrong side next time."

We talked, Pacho and I, as sooner or later we had to, about the bullfight as the hallmark of the Spanish character. It is the one sport, of all national sports, that has no market outside its own boundaries, the Hispanic world of Europe and Latin America. "It is not a sport at all," said Pacho.

"People speak of the hypocrisy of the foreigners who cannot stomach the bullfight—and at the same time people say that it is the foreigners who keep the bullfight alive. All this is nonsense, although it is true that, in keeping with everything else, in Spain and everywhere else, the bullfight is now so commercialized that it has no heroes. Even the 'brave bulls' are not trained to the bravery of fifty years ago.

"Still, the bullfight is Spanish. In its way it is Spain. People do not realize that because they think of it as a sport. They compare its 'inhumanity' or its 'degradation' with fox hunting or prizefighting or cockfighting, and they say it is only a difference in sports. But there is no sport in which death is the centerpiece, in which the opponent or the quarry is doomed from the start to fight to the death and to die. That is not a sport.

"The bull is bred to die, and the bullfight is a celebration of death, a Spanish celebration. It is in the bull, not in the torero, that 'the Spanish character' is to be found. The torero is partly brave and partly cunning. The bull is wholly brave. The torero, if he is killed in the ring, dies like a sportsman. The bull dies like a Spaniard. You know, we say that for the bullfight you must have four things. You must have sunshine, flies, no wind, and death."

Pacho could be wrong, or right. Perhaps we are all bred for death, the bull, the Spaniard, Harry, and I, with no other purpose (all other purposes being intermediary) than to die bravely in front of the world. The bull is bred to try to kill and (unless there's an accident) to fail. But Harry and I kill the orphans of Vietnam and India and elsewhere, without being brave.

The bull is brave because he doesn't know any better; he doesn't know that some things are fearful. But he doesn't sit in the sunny patio smiling and chuckling and waiting to die. At the end of his short hard life he comes charging out of the pen and into the ring, to earn his death.

The Swiss

Wasserwendi/Hasliberg, Switzerland

He found himself—he who was destined to be the first Swiss—on the top of a world of walls. Walls all around him. On the north walls, glaciers that never got the sun; on the south, snows that came roaring down as avalanches and then as torrents. Here and there, in the distance, a pass through the walls, open three months a year, maybe four, but no way to cross it. (Hannibal tried it with elephants.) It was the place that everybody wanted to cross (to get at the kingdoms beyond) and nobody wanted.

He who was destined to be the first Swiss found himself (and all the Swiss after him) dour. "I am," he said, "*steinreich*, rich in rocks," and he was desolate, and he prayed.

And the Lord appeared before him and said, "What can I do for you, my child?" And he said, "All I want is to survive, Lord. I came here because there was no place else to go, famine in Sweden, plague in Italy, war in Germany and France, and this was the only place that nobody wanted. If only I had a tree and an ax . . ."

So the Lord gave him a tree and an ax and said, "Take care of them. Take very good care of them. They're all you've got." So he took very good care of them and became a careful man (and all the Swiss after him) and got firewood from the branches, boards and pegs from the limbs, and a bed from the leaves. And every night he carefully sharpened his ax (and all the Swiss after him). And he prayed.

And the Lord appeared and said, "What can I do for you, my child?" And he said, "If I had a little black dirt between the rocks, I could have something to eat besides acorns." And the Lord gave him a bushel basket of black dirt and said, "Take good care of it. It's all you've got." So he took good care of it and had some hay, and he put the hay in the barn in the evening, and he prayed, and the Lord appeared and asked him what he wanted, and he said, "I've got this hay, Lord. If I had a cow I'd have milk and I'd want for nothing." And the Lord gave him a cow and told him to take good care of it because it was all he had.

Reprinted from the *Progressive*, December 1974.

And he who was destined to be the first Swiss took good care of
his cow (and all the Swiss after him) and fertilized his bushel basket
of black dirt and sharpened his ax and dried his boards and built his
chalet with a fence around it and saved and scraped and made do and
learned (as he had to, and all the Swiss after him) to put bits and
pieces together with a marvelous degree of ingenuity and precision,
because they were all he had. And he prospered in a small, hard, and
hardening way and never wasted and never wanted. And the walls
rose all around him in the place that nobody wanted, but he never
looked up. From dawn until dark—and after dark—he took care of
his property because it was all he had.

And one day the Lord appeared before him and said, "My child,
you have actually survived in this Godforsaken place." And he who
was destined to be the first Swiss was proud, very proud, of what he
had done, and said, "I've been very careful, Lord, and wasted nothing
and saved every scrap and learned how to put bits and pieces together
with marvelous ingenuity and precision." And the Lord said, "And
how is the milk from your cow, my child? Is it good milk?" And he
said proudly, "It's the best in the world, Lord. Would you like to try
it?" And the Lord said, "Don't mind if I do." And he measured out
a quarter litre of milk, precisely, and the Lord drank it and smacked
His lips and said, "Thank you, my child." And the first Swiss said,
"That will be twenty centimes, Lord."

And all that was before Ms. Baby Mayer and I took the 10:56
from Lucerne to Zurich one morning. At 10:55:50, precisely, the
bell rang, and at 10:56 the stationmaster raised his green wand, and
with never a jerk or a squeak or a rattle the train slipped ingeniously
out of the station, propelled by electricity purchased (at the cheap
night rate) from Germany and even from Sweden because the Swiss
had learned to put bits and pieces together so marvelously that all
their waterfalls did not generate enough power to power their precision industries. (This winter the Swiss will have to cut their electricity consumption 10 to 20 percent because their energy-squeezed
neighbors will not sell them all the current they need.)

And the 10:56 train from Lucerne slipped noiselessly into Zurich
at precisely 11:46 and Ms. Baby and I got off and went into the spotless station (which was being cleaned, even though it was spotless),
and Ms. Baby remembered that she had left her cigarette lighter and
cigarettes in the second-class car. So we went to the Lost and Found
and the man took a chart of the train from under the counter and
said, "Which car were you in, and which seats?" And we showed him
on the chart (as best we could) and he said, "How many cigarettes

were there?" And Ms. Baby said, "Only two." And the man said (without looking it up), "That car has gone back to Lucerne and Basel. It will be back here at 1:52 and be cleaned by 2:02. You can get your things here after that."

So we came back at 2:03 and got our things there—including the two cigarettes—in a bag marked with the train, car, and seat numbers, and the time they were found, and the number of the cleaner who found them, and the time they had been delivered to the Lost and Found, and the man said, "That will be one franc [Lord]," and I said, "How much would it be if it were a string of pearls?" and the man said, "One franc."

All that was before Herr Steudler, the Village Clerk of the Hasliberg, phoned me one afternoon and told me to call a number in Bern, the national capital, immediately. I didn't ask him what it was about, because he would answer, not in German, which (like all Swiss) he had learned in school, but in Swiss-German, which is a spoken, not a written, language and which all Swiss use with one another but (except for Herr Steudler) not with foreigners.

I called the number in Bern immediately and was connected with a man whose first words were, "What language do you speak?" Instead of saying, "None of your business, and who the devil are you?" I told him, and he said, "You claim to be a professor, but you leave Switzerland and return without notifying the Village Clerk." Instead of saying, "None of your business" again, and "Who the devil are you?" I explained that I'd left Switzerland the day my residence permit expired and returned to stay less than ninety days as an ordinary tourist. "You will be in this office at ten o'clock tomorrow morning," he said. Now I had to say, "What office?" "The Commandant of the Foreign Police," he said. "It is impossible to get there from here by ten," I said. "You will be here at ten," said the Commandant, "or be out of Switzerland by five P.M."

I got a lift down the mountain and rapped at the Commandant's door—*FREMDENPOLIZEI*—at ten. It was a handsome building, like all the buildings in beautiful, slumless little Bern. The Commandant's office—and everything in it, including the two men, one at the desk, one on a chair in the corner—was strictly typecast. The room was large and dark and heavily doored and furnished. The Commandant, at a large desk with one dossier, and nothing else, on it, was thin and old with a long, lined, "sinister" face, French-Swiss or, likelier, Italian-Swiss. (His name, which I did not get from him, was something like Modriani.) The man in the chair in the corner never spoke. He was young and fleshy with (so help me) a trench coat with the collar turned up and a felt hat with the brim turned down.

"When you left Switzerland," said the Commandant, who did not introduce himself to me, "you did not inform the Village Clerk that you were going—or that you were coming back." "I informed everyone else," I said, "the postmaster, the innkeeper, the baker . . ." "Why not the Village Clerk?" "Because I cannot communicate with him," I said. "He always speaks Swiss-German instead of German, and I do not understand Swiss-German." The Commandant did not smile (or frown). He said, "You have been in Prague several times, Professor." (The sneer in "Professor" would be undetectable in a tape recording; you'd have had to be present to catch it.) "Yes, sir," I said. "Would you mind telling me your politics?" Instead of saying, "None of your business," like an American, I said, shaking like a would-be American, "I am a free man." "There are all kinds of free men. You are one who has gone often to Prague." "On religious business," I said. The Commandant said, "On religious business"—tonelessly, not a question, or a contradiction, or a do-your-expect-me-to-believe-that: on a tape recording a mere repetition of my words.

I dove, unhopefully, into my briefcase. In it by (like everything else in it) accident was a German theological journal, *Junge Kirche*, with an article of mine on the state of the church in Czechoslovakia. He looked through it and handed it back; on or off a tape recording, nothing. "In your application for a residence permit a year ago, you said that you had to be back at your university post in America in January. This is March." "The university extended my leave." "In writing?" "Yes, sir." "I want a copy of that writing tomorrow morning."

Back up the mountain lickety-split by late afternoon, I dove, unhopefully, into my "files." I found the extension of my leave, scrawled in pencil on a half sheet of scratch paper by my department head. It read, in full, "Don't ever come back. We won't miss you. Love, Buzzy." I dove—hopelessly—into my briefcase and pulled out the official extension notice (which I had never opened), went sliding down the snow to the post office asafetida over appetite, got it into the mail as the postmaster was closing the door, and never heard another word from the Commandant. The only other words I heard (that I could understand) were from the Village Clerk when he extended my residence permit: "*Feef-ee-zwahnsk Frahnkeh*" for *fuenf-und-zwanzig Franken*, or twenty-five francs [Lord].

And all that was before my friend Peter explained it to me. "So you didn't know," said Peter, an Un-Swiss Activities type, "that we have a police state here. A very tidy police state, a very neutral police state (especially against the Communists), but a very thorough police state."

"But," I said, "one never sees a policeman on the Hasliberg—or anywhere else." "That," said Un-Swiss Peter, "is because we have a very democratic police state. Every Swiss is as much a policeman as every other."

"Informers? Spies?"

"Oh, no, nothing like that. It is just that all Swiss, or maybe I should say most Swiss, for this, too, is changing, take it upon themselves to keep order in Switzerland. This must seem strange to an American, where the only people who keep order are people hired to. We Swiss are very—very proprietary about our country. It's all we've got."

Twice in my adult life—that I can remember—a mere citizen policed me. (I do not count the ostentatiously threadbare civilian, a Party Block Captain, who, with the power of arrest, chewed me out for driving the wrong way in a one-way street in Budapest.) One occasion was in Tbilisi, or Tiflis, in the U.S.S.R., when I knocked my pipe dottle out into the gutter and an elderly man told me I shouldn't have done that and handed me an empty matchbox (which he put back into his pocket) to accommodate the dottle I scraped up from the gutter. The other was in Zug, in Switzerland, when an elderly woman, expensively dressed, caught up with me after I'd crossed the street against a red light to inform me angrily that what I had done was forbidden.

In the U.S.S.R., forgetting for the moment the ostentatiously threadbare civilian, you don't see a policeman except en masse at government-organized demonstrations or singly, in the crowd, and apparently off duty, listening to two truck drivers arguing (non-pugilistically) the right of way. In England you see individual policemen, unarmed, sauntering everywhere, answering tourists' questions, helping old ladies across the street, stepping out to untie traffic knots, or breaking up a fight by saying, "Now, now, gentlemen." In the ceremonial Mediterranean countries (all of them police states) they walk in pairs, sometimes with swords intended, unsuccessfully, to intimidate the crafty populace. In Germany they turn the traffic signs from green to red, fiercely. In France, a shaky police state, they are everywhere in overwhelming numbers, clubbing, gassing, and shooting. In America they, like everyone else, ride around in cars—and between cars there is always time to mug, slug, slash, slit, and run.

1. You don't need policemen to have a police state, and policemen can't keep a state policed.

2. Don't kid yourself in Switzerland.

When I reminded Peter that I had been coming back to the Hasliberg for twenty years—"They ought to know me by now, they ought to trust me"—he said, "Oh, they do, they do. But you're a foreigner, and you've been accumulating residence permits. Once you have twelve years of permitted residence you can apply for Swiss citizenship—first to the village, then, if you're accepted, to the canton, and finally to the Helvetian Confederation of Switzerland. You are suspected of wanting to be a Swiss citizen."

"Me?"

"You and every other foreigner."

"Why would I want to be a Swiss?"

"Why wouldn't you want to be? Why wouldn't everybody want to be? You yourself once told me of a representative social gathering in Prague where you asked what country the people there would like to have been born in, and most said Czechoslovakia, of course, but a few said Switzerland, and none said America or any place else. If you had asked how many would want to leave their country—under the circumstances you wouldn't ask such a question—a few more would have said Switzerland. It is true of every country, truer all the time, in the 'free' world or the 'slave.' Almost 10 percent of the Americans have said in a poll that they would like to emigrate, almost 15 percent of the English. Where do you suppose they would like to live—among starving people in a sun-kissed dictatorship like Spain?"

"But more Swiss citizens would mean more . . ."

"More what? We have 6,400,000 Swiss citizens, not quite enough to do our skilled work and none at all to do our really dirty work. We import more than 1,000,000 workers—most of them dirty-workers from around the Mediterranean. And we can get all the skilled people we want from abroad on the same basis. We are afraid of foreigners—*all* foreigners, except tourists. Every year we have a 'xenophobe referendum' measure proposed in Parliament to limit foreigners in the country, even on a temporary basis, to 12 or even 10 percent of the population. (They're 17 percent now.) In 1970 it went to the people, and 46 percent voted for it in spite of its denunciation by the politicians, the press, the church, the unions, and the intellectuals. This year the Federal Council yielded partially to the xenophobists and abolished the unlimited immigration privilege of doctors and teachers and set the 1975 overall immigration quota at 20,500. Of 1973's 31,000 immigrants, 26,000 were doctors, teachers, and artists.

"But that little sop didn't satisfy the xenophobes. They came up with the most barbaric proposition since Nazism, to deport half the country's foreigners in the next three years. And they had no trouble getting the 50,000 signatures requiring a referendum. It would have wrecked our economy and shattered our country's image, but these considerations didn't touch them. They lost two-to-one, carrying the rural areas where there are few or no 'guest laborers.' "

"Who supports the xenophobe movement?"

"Most of the farmers and villagers and some of the workers."

"To protect their jobs?"

"Not at all. They don't need their jobs protected. In 1974 we had a total of seventy-four persons unemployed."

"Here on the Hasliberg?"

"No—in the whole of Switzerland."

"Why, then?"

"Pure xenophobia. The foreign laborers, most of them Italians, are 'noisy,' 'dirty,' 'disorderly.' (And by Swiss standards a majority of them certainly are.) But that's not the heart of it; it wasn't the cities, where most of them live, that voted for deportation. The heart of it is xenophobia. They're a threat to our Swissness—which we're selling out ourselves, of course. Remember the Bürgermeister of the North Sea town where there were no Jews, who sent a telegram to Göbbels reading, 'Send us a Jew for our boycott'?"

"But Switzerland is the most open-hearted country on earth."

"Yes—to people who stay where they are or who (as in the Hungarian affair in 1956) can go back. The behavior of some of the northern cantons to German refugees from Hitler was a great disgrace, which we don't like to talk about. If they were penniless, they were turned back or expelled."

"But I am a rich foreigner."

"But a foreigner, and therefore suspected of wanting to be a Swiss. Or at the least of wanting permanent residence, of wanting to buy, and build, and live here and 'dilute' Switzerland. In the mid-sixties rich Germans bought up much of the best land in our Italian canton, the Ticino. Germans are all crazy about Italy, but not about the lira. In the Ticino they got Italy with the Swiss franc. Then rich foreigners like you started buying up pastureland all over the country, a building lot with a magnificent view for a couple of thousand dollars, for a summer or winter chalet or a place to hide from the next war. And a couple of years ago, first in the Ticino, and now everywhere, foreigners were forbidden to buy land. That stopped it, but not all of it: For a price you can get a Swiss intermediary to buy and 'own' it. Then you're at the mercy of the intermediary—you have no title."

". . . hide from the next war." A few years back, my friend Luethi, the innkeeper, doubled the size of his inn and replaced all his beautiful old tile stoves with central oil heating. I wanted one of the old stoves, which were now in the barn, but Luethi hemmed and hawed and finally said, "In the last war we had oil rationing in Switzerland. Now they keep talking about another war, and we may have oil rationing again. Then I'd want to put my tile stoves back." It took me a couple of years to educate Luethi on the probable character of "another war," and when he was finally persuaded that it would involve something more catastrophic than oil rationing, he let me have one of the stoves (for $35). ". . . the next war ."

And ". . . the mercy of the intermediary." Corruption—in *Switzerland*? "Oh, yes," said Peter, "more all the time. Already we feel that 'the foreigners' are ruining the country, even its character. An old farmer will refuse to sell his land; he doesn't own a car or want one; his house needs restoration; his toilet is on the porch . . . but his land is 'all he has' and 'all his children will have.' Then the speculators offer him, or his children, first ten and then twenty-five thousand dollars for a corner of his land that grazes a couple of cows and brings him in a couple of hundred dollars a year. But the kind of corruption that 'Watergate' suggests . . . no . . . not yet."

I once asked my friend Dr. Schild about "the politicians," and when he realized that by "politicians" I meant public officeholders, he said that a public office was a public trust. So I asked him about the Swiss Senate committee that controls the Swiss National Railroad. "If, say, a nephew of a member of the Senate Committee applied for a job on the Railroad, would he stand a better chance than another applicant?" "Of course not." "Your civil service examinations . . ." "Not at all. That has nothing to do with it. It simply wouldn't happen, not in Switzerland."

"Not in Switzerland." Corruption?—not in Switzerland (except as "foreigners" induce it). Crime?—not in Switzerland. (There was a bank robbery in Zurich a few years ago, and the press at once ascribed it to "foreigners, thought to be English," and a bank robbery in Geneva a few months ago, at once ascribed, and, in the event, correctly, to "foreigners, thought to be French.") Accidents?—not in Switzerland. (An *Italian* tour bus ran into Lake Lucerne a few years ago. But—a Swiss postbus ran off the road a few years ago, and an American with a residence permit took some pictures of it and was called on by two Swiss gentlemen who wanted to know if he would be so kind as to give them the negatives and all the prints and sign a paper saying he had done so.) Do you want to fly safely?—Swissair. Do you want to ride the train punctually?—the *schweizerische Bundesbahn*. ("The train is eleven minutes late in Brig [Lord] ; it is coming from *Italy*. But it will be on time by the time it reaches Biel.")

There are, of course, foreigners—and foreigners. The despicable "guest laborers" from the impoverished Mediterranean world are Switzerland's (and Germany's, and Scandinavia's) niggers. They do not need to be watched or guarded, only herded. They live in hidden bunkhouses. (Tenements?—not in Switzerland.) They earn almost nothing and spend nothing and go home "rich" to the families they leave fatherless for months, even years, at a time. They are exported by their countries, which have no work for them; and when the economies of Switzerland, Germany, Scandinavia slow, they are sent back home and, unemployed, live on their "riches." They make no trouble in Switzerland, Germany, etc., apart from their being "noisy," "dirty," and "disorderly."

Foreigners—and foreigners. Foreigners—"That will be twenty centimes, Lord"—bring great gouts of money to Switzerland and spend it on the precision products that, like the Swiss, the Japanese and the Germans once made. Now the Japanese and the Germans make American junk, but "Made in Switzerland" still means precision. The foreigners make the Swiss richer and richer and heat up the economy and, in every way possible, muscle into it: Swiss workers are the world's best and most "stable," i.e., least Communist, least ideological. The Swiss fight off foreign industrial and commercial takeover with their own capital and their rigid controls. But they want that twenty centimes, Lord.

The "gnomes of Zurich" fight a defensive fight and always win. *They* know how to manage an economy: In the year preceding March 31, 1974, the annual inflation rate was stupendous everywhere—U.S., 10.2 percent; France, 12.2 percent; Britain, 13.5 percent; Japan, 24 percent. Germany's was an alarming 7.2 percent, and Switzerland's an alarming 9.7 percent. But 1974's first quarter was fantastic—U.S. up to 14 percent; France up to 18.2 percent; Britain up to 19.6 percent; Japan up to 39.8 percent. During that quarter Germany managed to get its rate down from 7.2 percent to 7.1 percent. *Switzerland reduced its from 9.7 percent to 2.4 percent.*

Instability abroad—and there has never been any like the present—sends the speculators, the wide-boys, into the Deutschmark. (And out of it, when Volkswagen shuts down; the Swiss know better than to make cars, which are not precision products and are made by everyone else.) But the *investors* and the *depositors*—the sound men—flock to the Swiss franc, and stay there, with their numbered accounts that defy identification back home. (The world hates the Swiss for this dirty form of banking, but the Swiss don't mind being hated; and, besides, who knows better than the Swiss that all banking is dirty?)

All the sheikhs of all the teetering Arabies, including America, keep their money hidden in Switzerland—but not, as Bernie Cornfeld, Robert Vesco, and Mr. and Mrs. Clifford Irving discovered, hidden from the Swiss. In 1972, to cool the economy and fight foreign control, the Swiss put an end to interest on foreigners' deposits. The foreigners—*these* foreigners—don't care about interest at a time like this. They care about capital; it's all they've got. (When the money continued to pour into the franc—even without interest—the government slapped a *40 percent* penalty on the conversion of foreign currencies into Swiss accounts.)

Xenophobia and chauvinism are more than obverse-reverse sides of the coin. People who hate their own country (or themselves) may be xenophobes. People who, like the Swiss, love their country, may also be xenophobes. There is a nonchauvinist xenophobia in Switzerland, directed, now as ever, against the Germans. "We're afraid of the Germans," said my friend Peter. "Chronologically the last segment of Hitler's Greater Germany was to be the 'German' two thirds of Switzerland. He wouldn't get it the way he got Austria and the Sudetenland of Czechoslovakia; he'd have to fight for it, and he never figured out how."

"But such a small country . . ."

"Such a small country, yes. Such a small country of nothing but mountains and passes. The passes are all mined electrically. They can all be exploded to seal us off, for ten years or a hundred. We have the world's longest military service; the conscript has to train (at the end, a week a year) until he is forty-five, and then keep his gear in readiness all his life. 'Prussianism?'—pooh. Look at even our *new* highways—and the circular insets you see across them, wherever there is a steep rise on one side and a steep fall on the other. Tank traps, operated electrically. We can never be invaded . . ."

". . . unless somebody invents the airplane."

"I said," said Peter, "that we can never be invaded. We can only be destroyed. But we are also aware that the airplane has been invented. We have the world's best fighter force in the air. (We spend nothing for bombers, nothing for a navy, and almost nothing for a citizen army always at home.) We are a completely militarized police state, completely nationalist, completely chauvinist. Why do you think you see the Swiss flag flying everywhere here?"

Why, indeed? In France the flag means a public building, nothing else. In England it is not to be seen unless a king is being crowned or buried. The Swiss fly the flag all the time. To prove that they're

Swiss—or more Swiss than the man next door—the way the Americans do? Hardly; they have been there for a thousand years, and for five hundred "melted" into their trilingual, tricultural melting pot. Every Swiss is a Swiss. Why, then? "Pure chauvinism," says Peter. " 'We' are the people who really conquered Switzerland, conquered this *land*, created this *country*."

Everywhere else, even in Germany, once a planned country with planned cities, now an arrant imitation of planless America, people build for themselves however they want to, or build to make a profit for themselves. In Switzerland people still build to build Switzerland because, building Switzerland, they build for themselves. Zurich, Bern, Geneva, Basel, Lucerne, Lausanne, and every town and village, are the only cities left that aren't hideous, that are beautiful cities right out to the rind. Almost three years ago the Lucerne railroad station was gutted by fire (from the station-restaurant kitchen, where "foreigners" were working). It took a year or more to make the award in the architectural competition for the new interior, to be built behind the restored facade. The construction is still going on, and nobody knows when it will be finished. The workmen are the world's best—but there's no hurry. In Switzerland primary building materials have to be guaranteed for 200 years; on the Hasliberg there's a handsome chalet, still occupied, with the date 1492 (yes; 1492) burned into the lintel.

An irrelevant land that reads us movers and shakers no lessons, neither of federalism nor of war and peace, nor of economics nor of ethnology, nor of topography. There is no land anything like it, a land wholly of mountains and rivers and waterfalls and lakes. There are no wastelands, no scrublands, no swamplands, no badlands. A singular place, this place that nobody wanted, and all other places partake of grandeur and serenity only insofar as they partake of Switzerland, or, in Europe, shade off from its borders across their own.

An irrelevant society which, if it had not been born organically, would have had to be invented, to be what it is and serve what it serves; no part of the "Europe" that fights America or itself, no part of the ruinous swagger that overtakes and, in their time, overcomes all the empires. No part of the League of Nations, the United Nations, the Nations. No part of the European Economic Community or NATO or the Grand Alliance. No *part* of any alliance—and the meticulous broker to them all. "The representatives of the Shell companies of the countries now at war today established a world clearinghouse in Geneva." "The Swiss have been asked to handle American interests in Cuba." "On Sunday the European finance ministers will gather for a crucial meeting in Zurich."

Irrelevant to the bourgeois dream of a currency that always floats and never fluctuates, never collapses, never rockets and plummets; irrelevant to the proletarian dream of a tree and an ax and bushel basket of black dirt and a cow. Relevant only (and only perhaps) to the ultimate critique of utopianism, Marxist utopianism in particular: Here, on this mountaintop and between these walls, is the man who has what the proletarian wants, and in spades: a piece of the inaction. Here, on this mountaintop, is the man who has what the singers of the Brotherhood of Man and the Parliament of the World would all of them have (and what many of them would trade the Brotherhood of Man and the Parliament of the World for). What is it like to be this man?

Or the ultimate critique of capitalism: Here, on this mountaintop, is the Man Who Has Everything the bourgeois heart should (if not could) desire. Here, in a world where most (and more all the time) are hungry and the few fight them off (more furiously all the time) is the truly rich man. What is it like to be a Swiss, who has what the capitalist openly and the proletarian secretly, both of them forever called (or calling themselves) to the barricades, dream of, what my father and your father, and his, her, and their father dreamed of on Sunday afternoon after Sunday dinner—a little peace and quiet, neutrality?

The man who was destined to be the first Swiss—did he get to be happy after the Lord gave him twenty centimes for a quarter litre of the best milk in the world? He's a dull fellow, to be sure, producing no passion except his comical chauvinism, a dull materialist whose dullness alone enables him to live in the exaltation of his mountains without going to pieces like a Californian. As dull as that other rich materialist, the Swede—that other, and only other, neutralist. *Duller* than the Swede (whose climate drives him to drink and, via drink, arouses some passion in him). "Four hundred years of Swiss democracy have produced the cuckoo clock"—and in our time a total of a half dozen names in the arts (Duerrenmatt, Max Frisch; who else? What else?). Neutralist—neuter? Is this what the mover and shaker, the hurler of missiles and paving stones, has to hope for? "It's all you've got, my child." Is it all any of us have ever got a Chinaman's (or an American's) chance of getting?

Let him be dull, so long as he's happy, and what else does a man want for happiness? Several years ago the Swiss satirical weekly,

Nebelspalter, the Fog-Splitter, carried a full-page cartoon in color of an agonized Swiss on his mountaintop, the great peaks around him, the great stars above him, and the caption: "I've got a house and a car, life insurance and health insurance, a job and a pension, a radio and a television—I want for nothing. I ought to be happy." This master of the masters of precision, ingenuity, survival, conquest, stability, neutrality, with no one (except his wife? his child? his neighbor? the "foreigners?") to discharge his aggressions on—is he happy? He seems to be glum, dogged, stiff, close, tight, safe, sure, small, like Switzerland.

He ought to be put in a bottle, this lineal descendant of him who was destined to be the first Swiss, and sent to Harvard for analysis and the answer to the ancient question, "What is man, O Lord, that thou art mindful of him?" Soon, though, for Switzerland, too, is going to go the way of the world which, tearing itself to pieces, laughs at Swiss locksmiths and Swiss watchmakers and Swiss tank traps and Swiss passes ready to be blown sky-high. Ten years ago some developers from Zurich—purest Swiss—made their way up to the Hasliberg and proposed to build a ski-lift funicular. "I don't know whether I'm for it or against it," said my friend Luethi the innkeeper. "If it's built, I'll get rich—but the Hasliberg will be ruined." Now there's a network of ski lifts on the Hasliberg, and Luethi and the rest of the Hasliberger are rich.

The Last Time I Saw Selma

The first time I saw Selma there was a sign at the north edge of town that read, THIRTY THOUSAND WHITE FARMERS IN DALLAS COUNTY BY 1930, and another at the east edge of town, on the Montgomery highway, that read, SELMA—DALLAS COUNTY'S FASTEST GROWING WHITE COMMUNITY. Both signs were signed, Chamber of Commerce—H. Hohenberg, President.

It was crowding 1930 then, and it didn't look as if Dallas County would make it; and if Selma was Dallas County's Fastest Growing White Community, all the others were shrinking, because Selma wasn't growing fast or slow. There were stores and houses for rent a-plenty, and this was just before the Crash. The bottom was out of Alabama cotton (which couldn't compete with Texas), and the train in and out of Selma had one dirty old day coach which was running nearly empty.

Selma was dying, a dying town on a dead river. The mighty Alabama—and it was and is mighty to see—had been killed long ago by the railroads. Selma was poor, and Selma was seedy, living on its antebellum gentility.

And its gentility was fading fast away. The sons and daughters of the big old families in the big old houses were going away to school and they weren't coming back. Some of the big old houses had one elderly widow or spinster in them and old Negro servants who came by the day. Roof-gutters and outbuildings and porches were sagging, siding and fluted columns peeled, and broken windows in the rat-ridden attics unmended. Five thousand dollars bought you a block of Selma with a porticoed mansion on it and a stand of live oak and magnolia, and there were no takers.

As I read the papers nowadays and see the names of Selmians like Clark, Smitherman, Wilson, and even Connors, I can't find a name that I recognize. Yes, one: Sheriff Clark's lawyer, W. McLean Pitts. Must be a son or grandson of Old Judge Pitts; there are a few lawyers, I suppose, and a banker or a doctor or two, who maintain the old family practices. But I don't see any Boyds or Pettuses or Owenses or Kings—or Hohenbergs or Hagedorns—mentioned anywhere. The Selma of 1965 is not the Selma of 1929.

Reprinted from the *Progressive*, May 1965.

Nor is the Selma of 1965 the Selma we read about in the papers; nothing is, I guess. Selma is just another town except for its above-average record on race. The papers don't bother to tell us that the Hotel Albert is long since desegregated, and the restaurants and the movies, and all without demonstrations or violence. Selma is better than a thousand other towns in the South. But nobody tells us about that.

Nobody tells us about that any more than anybody tells us that a generation ago Franklin D. Roosevelt listened to Walter White's assertion that the only Negroes in the Navy were messmen and turned to his Secretary of the Navy, Frank Knox, and said, "Frank, maybe we could have some Negro bandsmen in the Navy." We don't want to hear about what we were twenty-five years ago any more than we want to hear about what Selma is today.

What we want to hear about is the black-hearted wickedness of white Selma, so that we may be whiter-hearted free of charge. We had a big Selma demonstration on the Monterey Peninsula in California a few weeks ago. None of the speakers said that we Californians, by passing Proposition 14 for segregated housing, had put the club in the hands of the Selmians who attacked James Reeb. Nobody said that two of the Peninsula's five towns, Carmel and Pebble Beach, are Jim Crow towns. One of the local beats carried a sign reading, WHY ARE THERE NO NEGRO POLICEMEN OR FIREMEN IN MONTEREY? And one of the highest officials of the Peninsula said that the sign was unfortunate. "This demonstration," he said, "is about Selma."

So we thank God that we are not as other men are—in Selma. We thank God that nobody tells us to see the Selma racists as they see themselves or the California racists as the Selma racists see them. And we thank God that nobody tells us what we don't want to know. So the Selma racists hate us the more for our hypocrisy, as we hate them the more (just as we hated Hitler) for pulling the skeleton out of our closet. And so the wheel of hate turns.

We Americans are hysterical these days, and I reckon we should be. We cannot bear the spectacle of our naked condition at home or abroad, in Vietnam or in Alabama. And by "we" I mean you and me and Walter Lippmann, who says (and the italics and the exclamation mark are both his), *"Selma is not only an American tragedy. It is an American disgrace. Selma is happening in a country which is engaged in defending freedom throughout the world!"* But we are not defending freedom throughout the world, least of all in Vietnam, where Walter Lippmann doubts that 30 percent of the South

Vietnamese support the government. Nor is Selma either a tragedy or a disgrace. Selma is a looking-glass—and a triumph. And it symbolizes the only triumph "we" have achieved in a long time. But the "we" who have achieved that triumph are not you and I and Walter Lippmann, but the poorest and worst oppressed and most inarticulate and most religious minority in our gung-ho secular society. Its religion has even moved the white church.

Everybody knows that the integration battle is won. It will take another half century or so to mop up, and another two or three centuries to eliminate the bigotry that has its last-ditch stand in the opposition, North no less than South, to interracial marriage. But the battle is won. Meanwhile the hatred and the fear and the frustration that create racism go on mounting as "we" go it alone in attacking North Vietnam with our conventional weapons of napalm and phosphorus and gas.

What we have won in Selma is the battle. What we are losing in Vietnam, and everywhere else in the world, is the war. For we are the minority rich, we Americans, and we cannot think of a better way of stopping Communism than to kill the uppity poor. And so it was in my day in Selma long ago. We were the white minority, and we could not think of a better way of stopping integration than to keep the uppity Negroes walled up.

I wasn't a Selmian, or a Southerner, but I spent many a long, languid week and month in Selma over a period of fifteen years. A big old home, across from the Hotel Albert on Broad Street, where Miz Julie ruled a large family (or let it rule itself) from a sickbed; and with her four sons and her other son-in-law I carried her to her grave. But I mean to write about Selma here, and not about me.

Nobody had ever heard of Selma then, or ever would. The last battle of the War had been fought there—but it was a week before Appomattox and it wasn't anything like the big battle we're now told it was. And nobody outside of Selma had ever heard of that battle. And that was the last thing that had ever happened in Selma, or ever would.

Out on a washboard turn-off from the Marion Junction road was Old Cahaba, the first capital of the state, a tangle of Spanish moss and Cherokee roses, tumbled with fallen and worn-away tombstones and, among the still-standing chimneys that mark the burned shanties all over the South, a few great chimneys of the great houses of Old Cahaba. Old Cahaba was drowned out—the Alabama at flood backs up into the Cahaba there—and the capital was moved to Montgomery. I used to go out to Cahaba to commune with death and decay, in company with Rabbi Joe Gumbiner of Selma and Sampson Lightning,

Cahaba's only centenarian and only citizen. "It be a mighty place den," said Sampson, "but it done gone down."

Selma, too, was done going down, without even having been a mighty place. But a few years after the last time I saw Selma we got into the Second World War to Make the World Safe for Democracy, and Craig Field, a flight training center, was set up outside Selma, and Selma done went up a little. And in the news pictures of Selma these days I see the names of low-wage and nonunion manufacturing plants that weren't there at all in my day or in the day of M. Hohenberg, President of the Chamber of Commerce. Selma done went up a little more; enough to bring in all kinds of new people.

Maybe mostly one kind, country people and boomtown people and people possessed of neither antebellum nor postbellum gentility. I hope that somebody some day takes the trouble to find out who they are.

I suspect that they are the rootless rednecks, rooted out of the canebrake by the war and the collapse of cotton and the promise of industrial jobs—in which last the Negro might have his only opportunity to move up and compete with them for work. The Selma Negro in my day was, as I'm sure he is for the most part still, a house servant or a janitor; the county Negro a fantastically miserable cropper whose crop was "advanced" before he ever made it. The house servants in the home on Broad Street got up to $2 a week and "takin's" from the kitchen; my little girl Amanda is named after one of them, Amanda Lark.

Amanda Lark held that home and that family together, at $2 a week. Mistuh Ben, the patriarch, paid no attention to the house, and Miz Julie, the bedridden matriarch, never saw her own purse. Amanda Lark, joyous, virtuous, and wise, managed the money, the house, the kitchen, and the six children at $2 a week. And when Amanda Lark said, "Y'all pick up dat stuff dis minnit," or "Outa mah way, chile," or "Go on, now, Ah ain't got no time fo' studyin' y'all," the six children moved to it. She was the head man, at $2 a week. If she said to Mistuh Ben, "Ah needs money, Mistuh Ben," and Mistuh Ben said, "Go get it out of my wallet," it meant that she needed money to run Mistuh Ben's house.

Was Amanda Lark happy? Were any of them happy? Of course they sang and they laughed, and they prayed and they shouted, and they never committed suicide (or murder or rape). Of course some of them (but not most of them) pilfered a little (like poor white folks), and some of them (but not most of them) got likkered up a little (like rich and poor white folks) on Saturday night; and you

heard, on occasion, when a servant or a janitor didn't show up, of a
cuttin' on Washington Street. But nothing ever appeared about the
cuttin' in the *Selma Times-Journal*, or about anything else that any
Negro did or was done by. Were they happy?

A believer would say yes, and a nonbelieving psychiatrist would
say yes. But a political philosopher would say that that was not the
question. If man is a political animal, he is not a man unless he par-
ticipates in his governance; and that no Negro in Dallas County (or
any other county down that way) ever did. And having no part in his
governance, he had no human part in his community. No truant officer came to see if his children were in the Negro school taught by
near-illiterates. (The white schools looked better, but they weren't
much better taught.) For the Negroes, there were no health measures
or police protection, no sanitation or sewage system, no water, no
paving or pavements; nothing. Between five P.M. and eight A.M. the
Negroes of Selma did not exist. But they were a majority of the
people of Selma and the county.

Their complete squalor was completely isolated. But out of that
squalor, on Sunday morning, came the whole resplendent Negro
world into the Resplendid Presence. They existed, all right; not in
Franklin Roosevelt's New Deal or Lyndon Johnson's Great Society,
but in the New Jerusalem and the Great-Gettin'-Up-Day, in the one
Society that admitted them and admitted them first that were last.
The Kingdom. Clean and dressed in their finest—though the children
in their finest might be shoeless—they went to Church. Rabbi Joe
Gumbiner and I, two Northerners, marveled. How did they do it,
without water, soap, or money? The white Selmians didn't know or
care.

What could the white Selmians have done if they had cared? Here
was a borderline economy, the city's, the county's, and the state's.
To relieve the squalor of the Negroes—not to say hiring them at
white men's wages—would have wrecked that borderline economy
in ninety days. Selma, and Dallas County, and Alabama were (as they
say down that way) just too po' to tote it.

What could the whites of Selma have done? What can the whites
(and blacks) of America do in all the world's Vietnams, besides stop
killing the Vietnamese? If we Americans were to substitute justice
for the scandalous pretense of aid, in a world two thirds of whose
people are hungry, we'd sink the American Standard of Living in
ninety days. We have no intention of letting justice *or* Godliness
touch the American Standard of Living. Neither had the white Selmians in the thirties; and theirs was much lower than ours.

So you see how it was in Selma, and how it is outside Selma.

White Selma survived on the backs of the unlimited supply of dirt-cheap Negro labor, town and country. And just survived. The stores sold the Negroes bright-striped shoddy. The landlords and the banks double-compounded interest on the advance the Negro lived on, and the money men took a fat mortgage on his skinny cow. The Negro didn't understand the white man's cal'atin' and would have had no alternative if he had. The insurance companies issued him policies consisting of nothing but loopholes. When Rabbi Joe Gumbiner squawked on behalf of the synagogue's janitor, the insurance agent, one of the new men moving in, said, "What do you want to mix up with the Niggers for?"

Mixing up with the Niggers was really beyond comprehension in Selma (as where wasn't it?). The Niggers were happy, weren't they? They weren't complaining, were they? No-*suh*, boss. They weren't pushed around, or made to get off the sidewalk, or clubbed or lynched; not in Selma. I never heard of the Klan's being in town in those fifteen years—and I'd have heard if it had been. No redneck rabble posse was needed; there was no more "white leadership" than there was Negro leadership, and the black and white pulpits (except for Rabbi Joe Gumbiner) were as mute on race as they are today on Vietnam.

The mythos was all that was necessary, the mythos of what the whites called "social distance." But social distance didn't mean that the whites did not feel a responsibility for "our own Nigras" when they were starving or dying; at the behest of their white patients the white physicians took care of Negroes as a matter of course. Within the absolutely formal isolation there were nevertheless the vestiges of a community, half ex-slave and half free; and within the community was an always amused concern, but a real concern, of the whites for our own Nigras, who got all the cast-off clothing and food and shoes, and who, inside the homes where they worked, got the love that bridges social distance. Most every home had its Amanda Lark, and if the wet-nursing of white babies by mammies was gone, a good deal of the rest of the antebellum lived on. Births and birthdays and weddings and funerals of our own Nigras commanded the observance, and even the attendance, of their masters and mistresses.

There was a lot more love in Selma then than now, and, I trow, a lot more in slave times than in my day. Without love men fight for justice. And when men fight—whatever they fight for—there is always less love. And without love there is no durable justice in peace. A melancholy circle. But the love of a man for a Nigra—at his mercy, like his dog—is not the love of a man for a man. So the love had to go, in Selma, and the Negro had to settle for justice finally; and maybe lose himself something in the process, and maybe lose us something too. If he is equal to us when he is equal, he won't be equal to much.

If Selma was better than most towns like it—and it was—it may have been because it was newer. It didn't go back much before the 1850s, and almost as far back as it went there were Jews there, and a Jewish synagogue. These were prosperous Jews of the "right," i.e., German, kind, whose cultural level was higher than that of most of the antebellum gentiles. Mistuh Ben's partner in Tepper Brothers, "Where a Child Can Buy," was Max Hagedorn, Miz Julie's brother, and Max Hagedorn was just about the weightiest man in town. He read the *New York Times*, the only man in Selma I ever knew who did. He thought that things would change in the South, not, of course, in his time or mine, but some time, and in some unimaginable way; and so did his cousin, Mayor Leon Schwartz of Mobile.

Like the Hohenbergs and a dozen other Jewish families, the Hagedorns belonged to the Selma Country Club; this, mind you, in the thirties. They belonged to everything, and they hadn't to stoop to get in. Being in, and being Jews, they had reason to keep away from "trouble," if trouble should ever appear, and to worry about Rabbi Joe Gumbiner's radicalism. But being Jews, and having once been in Egypt themselves, they supported Negro charities (including Tuskegee) far heavier than the gentiles did. Happy, oh, happy, those Amanda Larks who, in Egypt, had jobs in the homes of those who would never quite forget their own Egypt. But the Hohenbergs and the Hagedorns, like the Pettuses and the Kings and the Owens and the Boyds, sent their children away to college; and when Rabbi Joe Gumbiner of Berkeley went back to Selma (and to jail) a few weeks ago, the old Jews of Selma, like the old gentiles, were far to find.

The last time I saw Selma it was immobile, with nothing to move it or mobilize it. Nothing moved. Nothing could, except gently down. Keeping cool, eating and sleeping, and talking. Talking always about the old days, and talking about the Niggers, old times and new, in always amiable mockery. The Niggers were the conversational staple. "Theah she is, sittin' on th' copin' scretchin' huh haid, en Ah say, 'Aunt Mary, yo haid eetch?' En she say, 'Sho' do, Mistuh Harry.' En Ah say, 'Whyn't yo' scretch it hahduh?' En she say, 'Ah *do* scretch it hahduh, but it *eetch*.' " Under the slow, creaking ceiling fans on the veranda in Selma in the evening, that was the way it went, and the young whites who stayed in Selma gew up less literate than their elders; "culture" meant what the whites were, not what they had.

Keeping cool, eating and sleeping and talking and visiting. And hunting and fishing and swimming and bowling and poker. A physical world, slipping further and further back into the physical. Wartime or peacetime, it gave a disproportionate number of its sons to the Army—any army. The religion, art, books, and music of the antebellum rich were losing ground fast. I talked with the librarian, the editor, and two of the teachers occasionally; there was less reading in white Selma, per capita, than there had been fifty years before. Books cost money, and the library was too far to go in the heat.

A generation before Northerners got into their cars to go around the corner, Southerners did. But they would stand half the night in a cold, wet duck-blind, and walk through the fields and the swamps for partridge three days in a row." "En Ah say, 'Oncle, wha' kine uh boid dis heah?' En he say, 'Da's uh kildee, boss,' En Ah say, 'Ent no snipe?' En he say, 'No-*suh*, boss, da's uh kildee.' En Ah say, 'Dey good fuh eatin'?' En he say, '*No*-suh, boss, Ah gives 'em tuh mah chillun tuh eat.' "

And that's the way it was in Selma when Selma was dying and I was young. And I didn't see how I could change it or how I could help change it; and neither did you, and neither did Franklin D. Roosevelt, and neither did Theodore Roosevelt, and *he* had Booker T. Washington to the White House for lunch. And neither did Booker T. Washington. But the Negroes thought that God could change it and would show them how, because he had said to Isaiah, "You shall walk in my path, *and I will show you my way.*" And that, in their unutterable ignorance, they believed.

And in 1965 they came pouring out of the doors of their crumbling churches—churches the white Christians had sold them at a price that built new churches with parking lots in a better part of the new Selma. They came pouring out of the doors of their churches, clothed finer than their finest this time: clothed in the whole empty-handed armor of the Lord. The Niggers. And they stood on the white man's pavement in Selma and waited (*so the Niggers say*) on the Lord.

Selma is not a tragedy. It is a triumph of faith in a faithless age and among a faithless people, South and North, who tell the Sheriff Clarks to go sic 'em in Vietnam and don't go sic 'em in Selma. Selma, Alabama, the Selma I knew, is an historical accident as the focus of that triumph. It could have been anywhere in America, and maybe, except for the spectacular splendor of it in Selma, it should have been somewhere else altogether: Jim-Crow Carmel, California, say; or in Vietnam, where, if we only allow the Niggers to live and stop killing them and let them make a crop and eat it, they may some day have the strength to stand on their feet and register to vote.

Where Was It I Wanted to Go?

Nice day," said the mailman, and so it was; they all are. And then he whipped a letter out of his bag and a premonitory cloud hid the sun. "Registered," he said solemnly, "with return receipt required. You gotta sign twice." I always do what I gotta do, so I signed twice. The letter was from the Department of State of the United States of America.

It contained a shiny new blue passport, in my name, issued on July 13, 1964. It was delivered to me on September 21, 1964, and it enclosed a letter from Frances G. Knight, Director, Passport Division, apologizing for the two-month delay in delivery and explaining that it had been placed in the "will call" box in Washington by mistake.

That wasn't the first mistake of Miss Knight's life.

The first mistake of her life was to tangle with me. For I am a tiger with teeth, and Miss Knight is a tidbit. In my immoderate love of liberty I yield to no man—and to very few women.

The passport was in order.

It was two months late, but it was in order.

It was two years late, not two months. It was the passport I had applied for on January 17, 1962.

I had needed it in a hurry then. My tattered old passport—green, until Miss Knight moved in and redecorated the place—was expiring of age. I was in Europe and hurrying home for a lecture tour and then back to Europe for a half dozen assignments. I had to have a new passport to hurry back to Europe.

But I didn't get one. I didn't get one because Mr. Robert C. Ode, the American Consul in Bern, where I applied, had given me an oath to take and I didn't like the oath. The oath had just been slipped into the passport application and had not yet been printed on the forms. On a separate sheet, which Mr. Ode handed me, it swore me to innocence of membership in the Communist Party of the United States. I proceeded to take the immoderate position that a man is innocent until he is proved guilty, and the burden of guilt is on the accuser. Mr. Ode took the moderate position—as did Eichmann—that he was just doing his duty.

Reprinted from the *Progressive*, November 1964.

So, on that winter afternoon in Bern, Mr. Ode returned my passport fee to me and I got into my snowshoes and out.

A man with a country for a prison—a country he loved because it was free.

I still have the fee. And the passport. I have the cheapest passport in town—yours will cost you ten dollars—if you don't count the couple of thousand I spent suing for it. ("I" is a figure of speech here; it was my friends who put up most of the money. If I had had to pay my chief of counsel, Francis Heisler, for his services, the thousands would have been more than a couple.)

I am not planning to use my new passport just now because I can't remember where it was I had to go in such a hurry two years ago. The assignments are all by the boards long since. Europe is still intact, and none the worse for my nonappearance. And I am eating more regularly than a good man should. It doesn't seem, in the end, to have mattered.

But it mattered, all right.

It mattered because Miss Frances G. Knight and her superior, Mr. Dean Rusk, the Secretary of State, were trying to scare the lights and liberties out of us with that unholy oath. Mr. Rusk is eloquent on the subject of our glorious allies of the free world, but he is mute on their glorious ally right here. He is a lover of liberty in Vietnam— and of test oaths at home.

I don't know if Mr. Rusk is a good Secretary of State (or what a good Secretary of State would be or do). But I do know that he knows that the test oath, by which the citizen is compelled to disclaim guilt of an offense with which he has not been charged, is a blunt instrument of terror and nothing else. It is not intended to catch traitors and has never caught one; it is intended to intimidate the people as a whole and to reduce dissent to the kind of craven mumble we associate with dictatorship.

Why, then, you ask, would an American official attempt to impose such an oath upon his countrymen to his country's, and therefore his own, disservice?

The answer, in this instance, is probably to be found in the late Senator McCarthy's threat, way back in 1950, to unveil 212 homosexual Communists in the State Department. The personnel of the Department was terrified. Valentines started flying through the mails and everybody got married and took to waving the bloody black flag of the Red Menace. The State Department became a hotbed of heterosexual anti-Communists. McCarthy won, and is still winning, as witness Mr. Rusk; there is nothing like terror to teach a man terrorism.

Close to thirty-five million Americans have now taken one test oath or another on pain of occupational ruin. And I dare say that every one of the thirty-five million—Mr. Rusk included—is a little bit less loyal than he was before he took the oath. For disloyalty is inspirited by twisting men's arms to make them say that they are loyal. As a loyal American—not a brave one, for my occupational ruin was not really involved—I had no choice but to say no when Mr. Rusk sent his little boys (and girls) in blue around to twist my arm, and to take my chances of being confined forever in what had once been my country and would now be a great big stockade.

I got the passport, and I got it without taking the oath (which is still on the books). But I got it on a fluke, and if this government is going to deal with the rest of its sovereign citizens in the devious way it dealt with me, it is not going to enjoy their respect much longer. It enjoys less of mine than it did when it was standing up in court and fighting me. It will enjoy less of yours when I tell you how I got my passport.

There came a day—this last June 17, to be precise—when Mr. Rusk was so anxious for me to have a passport that he offered to slip me one under the counter. Yes, the same Mr. Rusk who, up until then, had been so anxious for me not to have a passport that he had mobilized all his minions and myrmidons, an army with banners, to stave off my peashooters.

It was on June 17 that the United States Supreme Court, in a six-to-three decision, held for one *Aptheker* in the case of *Aptheker* v. *Rusk*. Mr. Aptheker was a professed Communist whose passport had been lifted by Mr. Rusk under Section 6 of the McCarran Act, which forbade passports to Communists. The Court majority held Section 6 unconstitutional. The Court could not see why a Communist should not go abroad—to take the waters at Baden-Baden, for instance—unless it could be shown that the purpose of his travel was the furtherance of the Communist conspiracy.

You are aware, of course, that wherever the Communist conspiracy seizes power, it forbids *anti*-Communists to travel, just as the anti-Communist conspiracy here forbids Communists to travel. There is, to be sure, a difference: the Communist here can sue, as the anti-Communist there can not. But the difference becomes ever more formal and ever less substantial as a free people throw their freedom to the winds in their panicky pursuit of the illusion of security. The difference is, indeed, nonexistent unless the Communist (or non-Communist) declines to be put to the torture by Mr. Rusk and sets up an expensive and uncomfortable holler when the Rusks, who grow fast to monstrous size, are yet no bigger than a man's hand.

In the wake of the *Aptheker* decision the Court reached into its
"In" box and got hold of *Mayer* v. *Rusk*, which was on its way up
from the court below. The court below had upheld the State Department's claim that the Rusk oath was simply the implementation of
Section 6. If, then, Section 6 went, the oath went, too, and the
Supreme Court in *Aptheker*, without adverting to the oath, remand-
ed *Mayer* to the court below with instructions to reconsider it in the
light of *Aptheker*.

At this point Mr. Rusk was in for a licking in the court below,
which had no choice, upon reconsideration, but to reverse itself. Mr.
Rusk did not want to be licked; or, rather, he did not want to be
seen being licked. Besides, a judicial decision against him would tie
his hands when, one of these days, he came up with a new oath based
on some law other than the defunct Section 6.

True, if Mr. Rusk forced a passport on me without the oath, the
oath would be dead under the equal protection clause of the Constitution. But who would know about it? Passport applicants would go
on taking the oath until it was quietly dropped in the next printing
of application forms. They wouldn't know that they didn't have to
take it under the equal protection clause, and Mr. Rusk figured that
what they didn't know wouldn't hurt them.

It was, as I say, on June 17 of this year that *Aptheker* was decided.
Within a week I received, in writing, through a mutual friend, an
offer of a passport from Mr. Rusk. All I would have to do, said Mr.
Rusk, was to file a new application *and strike out the oath* and I
would get the passport immediately. (The proposition was made
orally to our mutual friend; you will understand that the Secretary
of State of the United States prefers not to put a proposition of this
sort in his own writing.)

Now I have, I am sorry to say, a suspicious, or journalistic, nature.
I asked Mr. Rusk's and my mutual friend how it was that Mr. Rusk
had so suddenly turned so cozy and what his coziness augured. "It
augurs as follows," said our mutual friend. "Mr. Rusk wants to plant
a passport on you in order to send his Chief of Counsel, the Solicitor
General, hotfoot into court to claim that the case is moot, that is,
that there is no case before the court since the plaintiff was suing for
a passport and can now be proved to have one."

"In one word," I said, "a low dodge and a shabby assault on the
American Constitution and the Rights of Man." "In one word," said
our mutual friend, "or two." I told our friend to tell Mr. Rusk thanks
just the same, and I cal'ated that I'd be puttering around the old air-
conditioned fatherland for another year or two while justice crept its
crepitatious, crepuscular way.

The next thing I knew, the mailman was saying, "Nice day," and there I was with the passport I had refused to ask for. Finessed. Conned by the Secretary of State of the United States of America.

The mailman waded away through a sea of autumn leaves. There I stood with a passport which, when I needed it, I couldn't get and now that I didn't need it, I had. Alone in the ring, throwing left and right hooks at the empty autumn air. Mr. Rusk had been groggy; one eye was shut and the other on the main chance. Now he had melted away in the melee. Nobody here but us passport clerks, boss.

But it wasn't a passport that I needed, nor a passport with a ten-dollar tip left furtively in my hand as the donor disappeared. Neither I nor any other denizen of this fair land has to have a passport. My grandpappy got along without one, and so did yours. What I have to have, and every American with me, is my grandpappy's liberty to come and go or, if I feel like it, stay. Without that liberty I might as well have a passport to Russia or Mississippi.

It was the liberty from Mr. Rusk's unholy oath that I had to have; and not I, actually, but those of my thirty-five million countrymen who had to take test oaths or starve. And Mr. Rusk had managed, as he ducked out, to hide the oath where the court could not get at it.

I had been prepared to go out with a bang, and instead I was in with a whimper. Associate Counsel in Washington informed me that the court appeared to be helpless to proceed when the Solicitor General came in with my return receipt for the registered letter. I had sued for a passport, and now I had it. The intervening two years were on me and my friends who paid the court costs—another lesson to upstart citizens who think they can argue with City Hall.

"You have, of course, won," said Associate Counsel. "You got your passport without taking the oath and in doing so you killed the oath."

But I didn't want to kill—or, in the event, merely wing—the oath. I wanted to deliver a Sunday punch to those domestic invaders of our country who cannot resist using the individual as an expendable means to the general welfare which they think, mistakenly, that they and not he provide for.

Who are they? They are each and all of us when we get our hands on public power. These Rusks are men, grubbing away like the rest of us, and overnight they are become as gods, and, since their experience as gods unfits them for the life they led (and the rest of us still lead) they will do whatever they can to continue their experience. They will not resign on principle, or even protest on principle, because they can no longer contemplate the grubby business of private life.

Mr. Rusk may never have had his hands on this case; a passport is a trifle to a man who has to fix everything up right away in Vietnam, Berlin, and the Congo. But I charged him with it because he is charged with the acts of all his subordinates in their line of duty. It is not Departments that perform acts but men; not "we" but "I." This is the Nuremberg Doctrine, which we impose on conquered criminals whose defense is "the Department." And this is the juridical doctrine of the United States, which required me to sue Mr. Rusk, and not the Department, and prove if I could that a man had wronged me. For all I know, it was one of Mr. Rusk's heterosexual anti-Communists who proposed that unholy oath in the first place, but it was Mr. Rusk who ordered it engraved.

Knowing whose vengeance is—the Lord's—I say that I had it not in my heart to discomfit Mr. Rusk, but only to get a decision that would protect my country from the future depredations of him and his moderate likes, of whom we have not heard the last or ever will. You may say that he means well (and that Senator McCarthy meant well), but you will have to show me. Mr. Rusk himself will not peep; he will see to it that he is kept busy with bigger things.

I don't say I'm unhappy with my shiny new blue passport which forbids me (and you) to travel in "those portions of China under Communist control" (lest we discover just how horrible Communism is). But neither do I say that liberty rings throughout the land or that eternal vigilance is the whole of the price we have to pay to protect it from those who proclaim it the loudest from the highest places.

This England

London

Take an adulterated (and adulterous) nobility, a walk-on monarchy, a gentry that lived off the land (and lives on the cuff), and a mulish yeomanry marinated in pale ale;

Mix *very* slightly, to an immovable consistency;

Work in a hand-me-down disdain of the lesser (i.e., all other) breeds, a pleasant repugnance to innovation, an equally pleasant proclivity for muddle, miscalculation, and misinformation, and a humorless dignity (repression of wholesome emotion may be substituted);

Sprinkle steadily with gall and wormwood;

Add equal parts of stiff upper lip, gluttony for punishment, over-cooked vegetables, and understated principles;

Top with a policy preoccupied with precedent and precedence, a socialism of Rolls Royces, and a capitalism of Free Dentures for All;

Prepare separately an inflexible, inefficient, *and* incompetent complex of obstructions to production, distribution, travel, and communication;

Pour together, season plentifully (according to local taste) with rain (or coffee—no one will notice the difference), stir as slowly as possible for a thousand years over the lowest possible burner, brown in deep fat (which may be used again and again), serve in chipped Spode, my dear, with tea whitened to calcimine, "Ah" to be said with feeling after each gulp of the tea.

This irresistible concoction is, of course, the British Isle-and-a-Half more formally known as the Disunited Kingdom. (Cymru, as the Welsh call Wales, wants out now; Scotland always has.)

England.

(The audience breaks for the Exits before it has to stand still for God-Save-Our-Gracious-Noble-Queen played by phonograph at the end of every performance.)

It is not an admirable country. It is only the most admirable country in the world today. (The only such, if you dismiss the Scandinavians and the Swiss as uninstructive miniatures.)

Reprinted from the *Progressive*, October 1968.

The outlook for England is glum—which is to say, excellent. The worse things are, the more English are the English. When they never had it so good, they were execrable; when they were being blown to bits by the Germans, they were nobly nonchalant; falling apart, as they are now, they are pleasant, and to be an alien in their midst is to be in pleasant places. (Even a "coloured" alien is never detested out loud.)

Their problems are, of course, like ours, insoluble. Like us in our Eden—and who all else—they were centuries late in acquiring the knowledge of good and evil. But once they discovered it, a few years ago, they became dourly fanatical about doing the right thing, unlike, say, the French and the Americans in Indochina or the Germans anywhere. When they could no longer stomach what they were doing, they quit. India was (according to Churchill) "the brightest star in the Emperor's crown"—and the first dark-skinned colony ever to be given its freedom by the honkies.

It is some time since that Herodotus said that those cities which once were great are now nothing. Trafalgar, the Mall, the Palace, the Abbey—the whole magnificent (and, for the toffs, magnificently cultivated) cosmopolis that was is wistfully outsized now, like a concert grand in a kitchenette or a lion's mane on a terrier. The Mother of Parliaments debates the Minimum Standard Waiting Time of Outpatient Clinics ("Not more than 3 percent should wait more than an hour"), or the division of London's four telephone books into thirty-six ("Most people call their near neighbors"), or the Egg Board's operation (BBC gag: "The British Egg Board assures you that your egg has been in a Testing Station for a month being tested for freshness"). The Bank of England, having hocked the country, stands outside the bank with a few British Made pencils in its cap begging for a dime (not for a shilling). And the Queen Empress bestows the Royal Warrant on marmalade and confers the Royal Accolade on the salesman who sells the most of it outside the Pound Sterling area.

Insoluble the problems of a beaten people who won all their wars (except one which was just too much trouble and too far away). Their island—for which read their majestic city—brought considerably more than a fourth of the whole human race to its knees. The Republican Kingdom on which the sun never set—down now to a drab dab on which the sun never rises.

England is a body of land entirely covered by water. It reigned; it is rained on. It thundered; it is thundered at. It was Queen of the Seas; it is awash. London had 7.4 hours of what the English call sunny intervals in the first nine days of August 1968. "Theoretically impossible," said the *London Times*, and Mr. Peter Chapman wrote a Letter to the Editor: "On the morning of the 2nd August inst., I saw a small area of blue sky over that part of London known as Elephant & Castle."

"Mass hallucination," Mr. James Chambers retorted in *his* Letter to the Editor. "Mr. Chapman sounds quite sincere in his belief that what he saw was real, but I must warn him that the whole weight of scientific opinion is against him."

This wonderful whimsy, England.

The pub in Marylebone—pronounced, of course, Mary-le-bun—High Street called The Old Rising Sun and the pub in Portobello Road called The Sun in Splendour. And the Lancashire pub (established by a hangman) called Pity the Poor Struggler. And the Fulham Road hardware store called Do-It-Yourself & Timber. And the venerable bathroom fixtures establishment—it held a Royal Warrant from Elizabeth—of Thomas Crapper in King's Road. And, in Liverpool, where the Liverpudlians live, the Liverpool Residence for Decayed Gentlewomen.

This England.

Or would you like to tour the countryside and spend the night in Wyre Piddle or in Piddletrenthide—a stone's throw from historic Tolpuddle—and thence on to Appletreewick, Birdlip, Blubberhouses, Goosey, Hope-under-Dinsmore, Maidenhead, Mousehole, Mumbles, Nempnett Thrubwell, Nether Wallop, Petts Bottom, Sheepy Magna, Unthank, or (I kid you not) Barton-in-the-Beans?

This England.

At the entrance to the Meadow of Christ Church—Christ Church is a college of Oxford, but one doesn't say Christ Church College—is a sign that reads: "The Meadow Keepers and Constables are hereby instructed to prevent the entrance in to the Meadow of all beggars, all persons in ragged or very dirty clothes, persons of improvident character or who are not decent in appearance; and to prevent indecent, rude, or disorderly conduct of every description. . . ." On a plaque in the Poet's Corner of Westminster Abbey are the words (and no others), O RARE BEN JONSON.

This (as Shakespeare *also* said) England.

England is theoretically impossible. If we wanted to create *de novo* a civilized country on the reasonable supposition that England is about the best we'll ever do, we should have to set up an aeon of totally untutored savagery such as scandalized the visiting Romans, to be followed by an aeon of bloody, brutal, bawdy disorder (to be called Merrie England), to be followed by an aeon of unconscionable

conquest and perfidious exploitation of the conquered at home and
abroad, to be followed by the instant loss of all these stately goodies
and endearing young charms and the supervention of soggy democratic doldrum.

Nobody in his right head would call it Merrie England today.
Swinging England, yes. The world's miniest miniskirts on the world's
unbeautifulest birds, their bare-faced buttocks tossed into the eye
of the unbeauty-beholder like the bursting bosoms of Good Queen
Bess's days which transfixed the Tudor dinner table by their immi-
nent threat to pop out of the decolletage and into the potage. Drugs
prescribed free by your Friendly Family Physician and available at
the twenty-four-hour drugstore (called chemist's). Pink velvet skin
trousers and maxi-hair to the male knee and wide boys in variety.
All sorts of sexes, rampant and couchant, including the hetero. A
virginity study—by an American sociologist, natch—awards England
first prize as Liberty Hall.

If liberty is the barometer of stability, England's is indeed the
stable society. An Englishman lives and speaks (and sleeps) as he
wants to. A phenomenally tolerant theater censorship has just gone
by the boards altogether, and there is a terrible dust-up now over
the right of metropolitan police to stop and search drug suspects.
(The resistance to the "breatholator" test has evaporated with the
radical decline in traffic accidents since its adoption.) The British
press, unlike ours, is taken seriously, and unlike ours is as vigilant
and pertinacious as Speakers' Corner. The lower courts, unlike ours,
are untouchable. Parliamentary debate, unlike ours, is downright.
When a Tory lord demands stern measures to protect the police
against demonstrators, the Home Minister begs to inform His Lord-
ship that the police will not use tear gas or water cannon as long as
the present Government is in office.

The world's only unarmed police have long been a lesson—and as
long unread—to the world. "If we carry guns, they will"; so we don't
and neither do "they." The death penalty is out (except for high
treason in war). There are more murders per day in the United States
than there are in England in ninety—and in England they are not
connected with robbery or public (as against private) passion. Hold-
ups are sharply on the rise, but its victims are usually those antique-
shop branch banks. The streets are safer than they were fifty or a
hundred years ago; everyone, of all sexes, walks alone at all hours.

The civilization of this "socialist" country derives directly from
its obdurate individualism. Once the Englishman got his rights—in a
few famous punch-ups—he held on to them against despots lured

away from domestic oppressiveness by the prospect (dear to all sea-coasters) of colonial fun and games abroad. The rest of the English-man's rights, in his crowded island, all flow from one: the right to privacy. He is not a mass man. He is not to be swept away by tub-thumpers. He is not to be whistled into that boneyard of all rights, the ethnocentric fold. Every Englishman is as much an Englishman as every other, and homogeneity spares him suspicion or surveillance of his neighbor. He can let the other fellow alone; behind his small wall (and England is the greatest place in the world for walls) the Englishman's life is his own.

Thus liberty out of privacy, and order without a trace of the lock-step conformity of the Germans and, yes, of the French. The *self*-government that requires the queueing-up at bus stops, shop counters, ticket windows—what else in the world is civilization but this? Don't shove. Hear the other man out. Stop for pedestrians at unpoliced crosswalks. Your right derives from everyone's. The "fair play" that Thomas Arnold introduced at Rugby in the 1830s went on up to Oxford and Cambridge and thence down, by slow stages, to the Eng-lish schoolboy; the civilizing virtue badly calculated, alas, to hold an empire or run a modern (or an ancient) business. The Labor Party's "fair shares for all" was unarguable in British theory, however inade-quately achievable in British fact.

Self-government: Whitehall—the legal owner—would no more tell "its" great BBC what to broadcast and what not to broadcast than it would tell "its" great universities what to teach or whom to hire or fire. *Self*-government: The Press Council is a private kind of Royal Commission, a body of men so far above partisanship that its tooth-less condemnation of a newspaper—any citizen may submit a com-plaint—carries the weight of shame which is so much more potent than law. A civilized journalism, presupposing a civilized people, tells it like it is (including what is not good about the dead):

> Mr. Randolph Churchill, M.B.E., son of Sir Winston Churchill, died yesterday. . . . At social gatherings he was liable to engage in heated and noisy argument . . . exacerbated by an always generous, and occasionally excessive, alcoholic intake. His public persona could seem irascible and arrogant, if not absurd. Yet, however irritating, or, in certain circumstances, despicable he might appear, his intimates knew that he was a sensitive, perceptive person, easily wounded, very unsure of himself. . . . However appalling his be-havior, he never lacked invitations or guests. . . . It was because of something original, something distinctive, perhaps clownish, in his own disposition that he failed so signally.

And what is wrong with this England?

Everything.

Rigid resistance is the hallmark of every undertaking—one hesitates to say enterprise—public or private. The one immutable law of British life is that nothing should ever be done for the first time, or, if it is, it should be done so badly that everybody will see that it shouldn't have been done at all. But isn't it true that the Giant Economy Size has been introduced in the stores? The Giant, yes, but not the Economy: The price is the same for the two-pound package as it would be for thirty-two one-ounce packages. Sorry, sir, but that's the way it's always been.

The way it's always been is the way of an immobile people of an island never invaded, never destroyed, never rebuilt, always restored. (Of an island, twenty miles from France, that doesn't know how to prepare a salad.) The way it's always been is a long, long way in England. St. Mary's Church in Harrow was "Consecrated by St. Anselm 4th Jan. 1094." In Parliament the Tories fought the substitution of majority for unanimous jury verdicts on the ground that it would "overturn six hundred years of established practice"; the Government carried the day by replying that the Scots had had majority verdicts for *seven* hundred years.

There have always been three or four small butchers (and as many grocers) in a block. A convenience, if not to themselves, to the trade; or it would be if they didn't all close at the same hour. Do you need medicine on Sunday?—There is *one* pharmacy in London that's open. Convenient, too, the overstaffing of all the shops: if one clerk doesn't know where something is kept, another also doesn't, and so you have two people (and sometimes a third, who also doesn't know) helping you. Sometimes it's really helpful: in my tea-and-coffee store the paleolithic coffee grinder operates electrically, with one clerk pounding it at the top and another jerking it at the bottom. *Two* ladies man the kettle at my favorite Buffet Bar. I order coffee with milk, and the only other customer orders tea without milk. In due season we are both served tea with milk.

I ask for five items from the grocery clerk. He puts them all in a very small, thin paper bag. The bag is too small and it splits. He picks up the contents and puts them much more carefully into another bag of the same size (which also splits). Then he totes up my indebtedness—not, like the Chinese, with an abacus, nor yet with a pencil, but in his head—and calls it out to the cashier. She doesn't hear him, in her glass cage, so I tell her, and she negotiates the change. Making change for pounds-shillings-and-pence is no quick trick, but after a thousand years of it the British are planning to join the human race by shifting to the decimal system. (And, to the metric system, which, come to think of it, *we* haven't got around to yet.)

If you are going to do a thing right, you do it slowly; everybody knows that. The English do it slowly—and do it wrong. But what you don't have much time for, when you do it fast, is decency. Added to his "blessed stupidity" (as Walter Bagehot called it) and his helplessness to improvise, the Englishman's decency is fatal to his country's desperate need to get going and get things done at whatever cost to whom. It's that last that doesn't seem quite right to him—he doesn't know why—so he digs in his heels quite politely and takes his time. I've never seen an ambling Londoner *tear* to get anywhere or do anything except catch the last bus or subway before midnight; which he'd jolly well better, because (I tell you no lies) he won't get another until six A.M. *O mores, O tempo.*

The conductor who punches my second-class ticket and says, "Thank you very much, sir," is neither obsequious nor subservient; he's as much of a second-class gentleman as I am, and the nearest thing I've seen, among urbanites, to a contented soul. He is pretty well satisfied to be what he is, to have what he's got, and to do what he's doing; the true un-American. What he lacks is the get-up-and-go that makes the great society greater and greater until it drops in its mad tracks. He loves his country—though he'd never say so—and its quiet dripping wet countryside and his city's ubiquitous little parks and squares. (For all its seediness London alone among great cities is a gently delightful place to live.) Give him his pub—"Closing time, gentlemen"—and the test match or the bangtails on his telly and he is not going to break his heart or cut your throat to get ahead.

The tempo accelerates; England may yet be saved. There's more pushing and shoving now, more scuffling and more shoddy, more corner-cutting (on and off the road), and more unhelpfulness among young clerks. There are some very bad manners and some very bad boys and girls. There isn't much booze—too expensive. There is still very little anger or explosion in public. But there is more loudness, vulgarity, and obscenity (though not on walls). The young are having a bad time of it and know it, and the minuscule 12 percent of them who are in school above the age of sixteen are sitting-in and squatting-in and generally bucking. (But no "student riots" yet, and the only country so far without them.) Tensions are building, pressures tightening, family life feeling the crunch; almost half the country's hospital beds are psychiatric. England may yet be saved.

A 2 percent down-the-line increase in productivity would solve the country's balance of payments problem. But with unemployment at 2.5 percent (not bad compared with our 3.5 percent—plus all our marginally employed), increased productivity, besides driving a man, sounds like fewer jobs. If the British worker's horizon is short, his memory is uncommonly long. He is descendant of the Luddites who smashed the first machines. He put Labor in power to protect his job, and the chairman of the Government's Prices and Wages Board says that British industry is 30 percent overmanned. Now Labor is trying to do him out of his job with its call for modernization. He's begun to vote Tory.

England's problem is economic, unlike ours. Our imbalance of payments is a political problem; no matter how much we export, we "import" more in the form of foreign war. England has had to give up war and move West of Suez, with no conscription and almost no military establishment (and not enough recruits to man it). But it has to import or die—it can't produce its own food or raw materials—and to import it has to export. But its "natural" market of empire is gone. Three of its four classic industries were decrepit before the war—coal, steel, and shipbuilding—and the fourth, textiles, is no longer dominant anywhere. Only the Dollar—itself shaken by the luxury import of war—keeps the Pound alive.

The Dollar is the "special relationship" that keeps the British Government in nominal line—not a farthing or a man contributed— on Vietnam and provides the encouragement of the "American takeover." Anybody who wants more money more than he wants more or less of anything else can take over from the English in England. One fifth of the whole American manufacturing investment abroad is here. It accounts for only 7 percent of the country's GNP, but for 18 percent of its exports. Americans make a bigger profit exporting *from Britain* than the British do.

Anti-Americanism is always tempered by the vivid recollections of 1917 and 1942 and by something like ancestral pleasure in seeing the Yanks pick up the Anglo-Saxon torch; resentment at being the fifty-first American state is partly compensated by America's being the forty-third English county. The transatlantic "brain drain" is an irritant. (Were it not for the 5,000 doctors drawn from still poorer countries, the National Health Service would have long since broken down.) But most of the hostility is directed against the doctors, scientists, and engineers who have hitched their wagons to the fast buck and gone giddy-ap. Attitudes are ambivalent. A decade or so ago America looked as unclovenly monolithic as Queen Mary's bust, but the appearance of cleavage over civil rights and Vietnam presents a less forbidding (if not necessarily more attractive) image. At the same time the "riots," the assassinations, the aggressions, and the Chicago police have given rise to the new dread that the United States is a weak reed; and England has no other.

The country might just have survived the loss of its empire. Or it might just have survived nationalization and socialization. But the cost of the two together broke its back. The Health Service—the "Communism and Bolshevism" of Morris Fishbein's A.M.A.—has enormously improved the nation's physique; twenty years ago an Englishman with four sound teeth was probably named Rhodes or Rothschild. But it has been murderously expensive. Public housing, too. The 1,800,000 slum units, no more hideous than ours, but, being British, more dismal, are being replaced at the rising rate of 70,000 a year; not bad for a poor country whose Government is given to the stodgy principle of a better than balanced budget.

Nobody believes that it will make a particle of difference if Labor falls and Tory comes back in; broken backs are not mended in talking shops. In both parties there is a real destitution of statesmanship. (As where isn't there?) But it is hard to see what statesmanship could do here except a more effective job of whistling in the dark. This summer unemployment hit a postwar seasonal high, and the National Institute of Economic and Social Research predicts worse this winter, plus a budget deficit and a slower growth rate next year. The struggle to hold down wages is frustrated by strikes (or strike threats) brought on by the unsuccessful struggle to hold down prices. Devaluation hasn't produced the export miracle, and the pressure against deflation mounts. Import controls impend, and the policy of "Buy British" means, as it always does, "And sell what?"

There is not much blood left in the British turnip. The base income tax (before much narrower deductions than ours) is eight shillings in the twenty-shilling Pound. The terribly rich are expropriated, and with the estate tax it's hardly worth while to have had parents. Not untypical is the $448,000 estate of Sir Myles Wyatt, an industrialist, which was taxed $440,000. The very rare Englishman who makes $50,000 a year keeps $19,500 of it. (The German keeps $30,000, the American $35,000, and the Frenchman $36,500.) Even by our standards living costs—except for medical care—are moderate rather than cheap. A young craftsman's top of $2,400 a year just doesn't make it, with two children; so, like everybody else, he's on "hire purchase" (the installment plan). One such (on one of those outspoken BBC programs) has $6 a week for food for a family of four after his "h-p" payments. And a pensioner has $1.55 a week after thirty years as a locomotive engineer.

Where except England wouldn't this mean revolution? The Englishman makes the best of it and asks, "What else is there to do?" The older men, who knew what it was to sing "There'll always be an

England" say they are willing to go on making the sacrifice "if it's for the country." But an increasing proportion of younger workers are what the English call bloody-minded. No "if-it's-for-the-country" for them; theirs the shiny new shibboleth of, "F—— you, Jack, *Ah'm orl raht.*" The English worker is worse educated than ours or any other Westerner. (It's only a century since he was educated at all.) He reads nothing but the popular press (which is just as bad as ours). Having lost his religion, he has nothing to look to but his cultural instinct, which means, in the class society that is still England, that he has to rely on the vestigial glimmer of what it is supposed to be to be an Englishman.

On that deliquescent reliance his country's fate depends. He is learning to hate the niggers, who are accepted at all job levels, are more industrious than he is, and cost the Treasury less (in health services, for instance) than he does. He is not impressed by their being only 2 percent of the population. He is not impressed by the fact that their limited influx of 60,000 a year no more than equals emigration. He is not impressed by their lawful behavior. Least of all is he impressed by the fact that the "tropicals" are his fellow citizens, Britishers from Commonwealth countries. On the contrary, he wants an even more callous immigration policy than he (and the Tories) pushed through Parliament six months ago. He is, in a word, getting to be the man we Americans see in the mirror.

But it will be a while yet before that vestigial glimmer dies and England is one with the New Brute. Empire was an awful thing; but it percolated a mythos of responsibility and incorruptibility, a mythos that held the whole thing together in the amazingly few "India hands" that traveled *posh* (*port-out-starboard-home*) on the boat to the East. The common Englishman never saw a high school (much less a college). His "betters" bought and sold him at the polls, and he was excluded from office as axiomatically as he was from Belgravia, polo, tennis, and hunting. He lived in a hovel—but *he* governed fifty-two Crown Colonies, Crown Protectorates, and Crown Dominions on all six continents. The mythos was as much his as it was the King-Emperor's, the mythos of the civilizer. The civilizer had to be—or at least seem to be—civilized. Good form.

It was only fifty years ago that the Imperial German Navy steamed into the Firth of Forth to surrender to the thirty-six battleships of the British Grand Fleet and the last threat to the Perpetual Empire was crushed. On the Big Scoreboard England was the Big Winner. Fifty years later—still the Big Winner—it is kicked all over the globe. By the Egyptians and the Chinese. By the "Commonwealth" Rhodesians and South Africans. By the ingrate French with their Common Market Club for Continentals Only. Yes, by Haiti's Papa Doc Duvalier, condemning to death a *British* official. (Fifty years ago it would have been enough to show the flag.)

The Big Winner. And what it has left is a Mediterranean rock (a great place for growing the fruit and vegetables the childless Mother Country has to buy abroad). And the miserable Spaniards, without an Armada, are in the process of kicking it off the rock.

This England that was only fifty years ago has faded fast away. The Island Fortress of only twenty-five years ago is dismissed by the next President of the United States as "an American airstrip." Its dignity gone, it is fighting to preserve its only remaining resource, its decency. But at least it has rid itself of the imperial indecency on which its domestic decency depended. BRITAIN IS GREAT, says the new pepper-up slogan around here this season. Well, it isn't. But it's greater than it was when it was Great Britain; and so, said Tiny Tim, may we all be when we have been cut down to size.

A Sense of Sin

We were packed, one Sunday evening, in one of the elevators in the lobby of the Hotel Ukraine. The Ukraine is twenty-three stories high, identical with four other rococo skyscrapers in Moscow, and there are not enough elevators to go around (or up and down). The young lady operator was pressing the floor buttons without looking up from the book she was studying, and the starter (an older young lady) was chattering with a friend. We just stood there, like an up-ended can of sardines with the lid off.

There was a sudden hubbub in the lobby, and two squads of square-faced soldiers came through on the double, carrying dismantled ack-ack guns, or bazookas, and steel cases of ammunition. We were all turned out of the elevator quick, and the soldiers with their munitions as quickly piled in. The young lady operator put her book down and without a signal from the starter the car shot to the roof, and then another, and another.

"This is it," the American lady moaned, "this is *it*. It's an air raid. It's started. We shouldn't ever have come. I didn't want to come," and she fell apart. Some of the other Americans fell apart with her; the rest, of sterner stuff, stood sternly awaiting the end.

But life, apart from the Americans, went on in the lobby. If this was the end, the Europeans and Asians seemed to have expected it. Only the Americans were surprised. But there's always a surprised American who wants to see the fireworks, and this time one of them got into the elevator after it shot back down from the roof and pressed the Roof button. The young lady operator thumbed through her book—it was an English grammar—and said, "No before ten o'clock. Everybodies at ten o'clock."

There was nothing for it, and everybodies at ten o'clock shot up to the roof. And then the fireworks began, simultaneously from the roofs of all five skyscrapers. Sweating grimly, square-faced, deadly automatic and deadly certain, the antiaircrafters loaded and fired their ack-ack; loaded and fired, loaded and fired. The whole sky was

Reprinted from the *Progressive*, June 1960.

ablaze. At ten P.M. one Sunday a month the Red Army produces a fireworks display. The crisscrossing colors and patterns were magnificent. Five million Muscovites—and fifty Americans—watched the ten-minute splendor.

Precisely on the dot of 10:10 the display ended on all five roofs. The ack-ack was dismantled with deadly automatic certainty and the powder-stained squads again commandeered the elevators and shot down to the lobby and out on the double. The American lady was no longer moaning. "Wasn't it wonderful?" she said. "Wasn't it just wonderful?"

Not especially; we do it as well at home on the Fourth; better, because we wind it up with the flag in red, white, and blue rockets. What was wonderful was the American lady. What is wonderful is America, alternately stupefied by doom and tickled pink to discover that "they're just like us"; and always spellbound. We are watching Big Brother.

Here in Peoria we have hula-hoops, ice-cream bars, Elvis on the juke, a drink before dinner, the icecapades downtown, and a late TV show to top it off; and in Debrecen, Hungary, a city the size of Peoria, we had every one of those blessings all in one day—hula-hoop, ice-cream bar, Elvis on the juke, drink, icecapades, and TV. In the Slave World it's a little further between jukes, and in the Free World you get the TV sell for soap instead of socialism. Confidentially, it's not so hot there—or here. It's so-so both places, though I like it better here.

And *they* see *us* in the same two contradictory and hypertense ways that we see them. The little girl in Debrecen thought that all Americans were cannibals; now she thinks that all Americans (including elderly males) are hula-hoopers like her. The questions most often asked me in the Communist countries were these: "Do you all have your dinner cooked by a restaurant and brought in on a tray while you watch TV?" "What happens to a Negro who can pass the examinations for a university?" "Do you really have insurance against a heart attack when you go to a horror movie?" They, too, believe what they read in the papers.

But what every schoolboy—if no alumnus—knows is that there is nothing we don't do that they don't do. There is nothing that they are that we aren't. There is nothing we want than they don't want. The differences are all historical or geographical accidents. Name it; whatever it is, including the chain gang or the slave labor camps, or the gassing of the Jews or the burning of the Indians, it is, or was, or will be everywhere.

If we could see that circumstances and not nature determine the

differences in human behavior, we could get a grip on our situation
and undertake the liquidation of the present processes leading to
disaster. If we can't, we must go on as we are, to disaster, because
good must undertake to overcome evil (whether with evil or good)
and people who think themselves better than other people are irresistibly compelled, and should be, to defend the good they embody
by destroying the evil embodied in their enemies.

The one Himalayan obstacle to our salvation in the present crisis
is the picture we have of other people. Can we change that picture
without having to change our human nature? I have it from my old
mother that you can't change human nature; but what if there is
already within our nature an element which would enable us to overcome the one obstacle to our salvation, if a way were found to give it
a chance to operate, an element presently repressed or uncultivated?

Two years after the bear launched the sputnik we still cannot
imagine his being a man like us. How could we? How could we, the
propertied, imagine this unpropertied man and what Marx called
"the naked condition of his existence"? How could we, the unpossessed, imagine this naked man possessed of a fanatical faith?
Balked by the limits of imagination, we settle *his* hash by describing
him as a madman or a villain—the only two creatures we can imagine
who do not conform to our propertied, unpossessed picture of man.

If we will reject reality, we ought at least to reject the imposition
of our moral judgment on it. We ought not to condemn a man whose
condition we cannot imagine. But our rigidity does not permit of
our being consistent: He is at once a sub-man and a bad-man. We
can only go on chanting, "He understands nothing but force." But
he understands the need to reconstruct society, and we do not. It is
we, not he, who are left understanding nothing but force. We are
traumatized into the monster of our own nightmare.

If the monster would only go away—. But the monster will not go
away. Or be blown away. It is not a bogey pasted up by a crazy Russian exile in a sidewalk café in Geneva. You would not expect the
retired Chief of Staff of NATO to say what it is, but he did: "It is a
world movement," said General Gruenther, "of the have-nots versus
the haves."

Communism is an ancient, profound, and profoundly religious
(and specifically Christian) theory of man and society. It has always
been everywhere in the world, in all of our lives, in perpetual contest
with capitalism. It is what we all practice in our homes—the burden
according to strength, the reward according to need—and what we
all preach in church. It is only when we go to our jobs that we take

it to be proper to practice and (in defense of the job-centered existence) preach anything else.

Communism is the response to man's wish to resolve the contradiction between the two lives we all lead. In its view man is so good
that he can lead the one life all the time—the life we practice at home
and preach in church. Marxism is this pleasant dream of man's nature
so modified by materialist rationality as to deny his Fall and relieve
him of the mysticism of grace in an age of unbelief.

Like all dreams, Communism—Marxist and non-Marxist—has great
gaps on precisely that level, the procedural, at which capitalism,
which is not a dream, is unanswerably specific. Jesus promised that
all these things—the rules of procedure—would be added unto him
who in faith accepted the Communist doctrine of burden and reward.
Marx, having no faith, was smart enough to leave the gaps wide open.
Plato had the dream, too, but, unlike Jesus and Marx, he tried to fill
in the gaps, and Aristotle tore him apart on purely procedural grounds:
"Everybody's business is nobody's business." But the dream remains,
always rooted in the perfectibility of man.

Marxist Communism substitutes belly-hunger for the Fall as the
obstacle to perfectibility. Denying grace in favor of bootstrapism it
spurns as sentimentality the spiritual call to men to care for one
another except insofar as mutual advantage is involved. Capitalism
accepts man's fall and says, "Leave him lay," which may be translated
into French as "*Laissez faire.*" But there its spirituality ends. It ignores grace and denies bootstrapism and limits itself to the ancient
but neither profound nor profoundly religious (nor specifically Christian) rules of the market based on the view that man is imperfectible
and not much good.

Capitalism, in theory agnostic, is in practice necessarily atheistic; a
capitalist who closes his shop on Sunday is simply a bad capitalist.
Belly-hunger may be reduced by the profit system, but that is not its
object; its object is profit. So, too, men's care for one another; the
capitalist is called to this concern neither spiritually nor sentimentally
but insofar, and only insofar, as he can not get labor cheaper or customers more dearly. In a buyer's market for labor or a seller's market
for goods the concern would ruin him. No matter how bad men are,
says capitalism, their bad impulses, providing they are left unhobbled,
will restrain one another.

In our historical, no less than geographical provinciality, we have
identified capitalism, not just with Christianity but with democracy.
The first is theologically false, the second politically groundless.
There is no necessary connection of democracy with either capitalism

or Communism, except insofar as belly-hunger may be an impediment to the free exercise of political choice; in which case there is a suppositious connection with Communism. But both systems have existed, and do exist, under political tyranny.

The power of Communism is not the reality, the procedure, the practice, but the dream. Whoever says in his old age that he was a radical when he was young means that he believed in some part of the Communist dream. Marx's "immediate program" for the Communist minority a century ago has become the actuality of every nation, including our own, which regards itself as progressive. Communism will always appeal to social idealism, capitalism to individual self-interest; and the unselfish advocate of capitalism will always be the man who sees it as the regrettable corollary of a regrettable human nature. And no matter how badly one or the other works, the realist (selfish or unselfish) will never abandon the necessity of the one, or the idealist the dream of the other.

To say, then, as Aristotle does, that Communism won't work, or that the experience of it in this or that society proves that it won't work, is to miss the point. We don't ask if it works in the home or the church; we say that, however well or badly it works, there is no other way to run a home or a church. The Communist—including the atheist Marxist—is a man of faith. And faith will always test itself and for its failure prescribe greater faith, and test itself again. There is no way to stop Communism. War—including victorious war—is irrelevant to it except insofar as it spreads the conditions under which the need to reconstruct society is more widely and deeply felt.

The American possibility here is, first, to recognize that there is no way to stop Communism, no more in other men's states than in our homes and churches, and, second, to try to correct its shortcomings in practice. Now nothing needs correction as badly as other people's shortcomings; but one of their shortcomings is their resistance to our good advice. If, however, their shortcomings turn out to be identical with our own, we can correct them by correcting our own. What Communism needs is a shining example.

Our task is to contribute our energies to the dream, so that it will work as well in society as it does in the home and the church. But we are chained fast by the nightmare, and this is where we came in. Unless we can dissolve the nightmare, we shall be able to recognize neither the fundamental good in the evil of the Communist world nor the fundamental evil in the good of our own. Dissolution of the nightmare, not armament, disarmament, technical assistance, or coexistence, is the condition of a détente. The cause of our immobilization has got to be eliminated before we can move at all.

Its elimination requires, not a change in human nature but a good, healthy, red-blooded and red-handed un-American sense of sin. Our earliest ancestors had it, and so did the Russians' latest. It is lost in both places, and in both places for the same reason: material triumph. We and the Russians both think we're wonderful. We're deeper in the pit than they are because we got into it first. And what we know in our bones—and show in our demoralized national behavior—is that we are not wonderful at all.

Our anti-Communist howl is the howl of a cry-baby. Without a sense of sin we are amazed at our being in trouble. It isn't *right* that superior people like us, who haven't done anything wrong, should be falling on our faces. It isn't right that Communist wickedness should prosper the way it does. Well, sir, God says to each of us, "Here is my creation. Take what you want from it—and pay for it." We have gorged in a belly-hungry world and the belly-hungry are presenting the bill, in behalf, of all things, of God.

It costs the American Friends Service Committee two cents to provide a hot meal for a belly-hungry child in the province of Orissa, in India. I was saying this the other night in a local saloon, where people were paying anywhere from $3.50 for a steak sandwich to $6.00 for a steak, plus, of course, drinks. I said that we couldn't be expected to change our habits—it's all a person can do to keep from getting to be any worse than he already is—but that the food and the drink ought at least to taste bitter. "You're breaking my heart," said a drunken lady in the audience, and she handed me a nickel. Two-and-a-half hot meals. She didn't know it, but I was breaking her heart.

Not to stop sinning, but only to know we have sinned and are sinning; to recognize that we've got it coming to us, whatever it is and whoever presents the bill in whatever form. No repentance, but confession. Not to change our condition, but only to know it. Is this outside our nature? I think not. And if this is possible to us, then daybreak is possible, and the end of the nightmare.

As long as I see myself sinless and my brother in Russia and China as sinful—as indeed he is—I shall pursue his destruction. I must. I should. Good should not, and will not, willingly coexist with evil.

When I can see in my brother in Russia and China the good that is in me, and in myself the bad that is in him, I can speak of coexistence without the hypocrisy that he, no less than I, discerns in my oratory. Which of us had the two cents to go to the belly-hungry child? Which of us went? I need nothing—nothing—but a sense of sin for my salvation here. They say that it comes in handy hereafter, too.

The Crisis-Eaters

During last month's Berlin crisis I was waltzing between the two besieged sectors of the city and I discovered what those three eminent students of human nature, Tom, Dick, and Harry, had known all along. I discovered that there is a kind of man—including all journalists, all welfare workers, all social scientists, all statesmen, and of course, all soldiers—who simply could not bear to go on living if a détente ever occured between warring worlds, nations, races, classes, or baseball teams. They are the crisis-eaters.

Their behavior is symbiotic; they eat crisis and feed it so that they will have something to eat. Nobody else wants any part of what is going on. Everybody else wants to be let alone and let other people alone. Nobody else cares about liberty *or* security, peace *or* justice, capitalism *or* communism; only these lifelong Eagle Scouts.

Their interests and their objectives are accidental; if they weren't thinking up liberty, security, and the like, they'd be thinking up Father's Day or penicillin or packaging. There is no real difference between Teddy Roosevelt and Teddy Khrushchev, or between either of them and Florence Nightingale or Trader Horn or Al Capone or me. They are the jumping-jacks-of-all-trades. The man they all differ from is Dwight David Eisenhower, who would like to practice his putting.

The tension in Berlin was acute last month; it was five minutes to midnight *again*. The West German crisis-eaters use Berlin for a slow burn—just as the East Germans would if they had a city in the West. It can be turned up to a fast boil whenever the awful threat of a lull occurs. This time it was a big exile-refugee "Day of the Homeland" rally of incendiary groups (like exile-refugees anywhere) calling for the return of Germany's lost lands in the East, which will never be got back without war (or with it).

The *East* German crisis-eaters responded—the way children used to and grown-ups do now—by forbidding West Germans access to East Berlin. I was careening around the East sector of the city in a car with West German license plates, and I made a wrong turn. A carload of the Dread People's Police came down on me, and I was

Reprinted from the *Progressive*, November 1960.

told to get out and produce the car papers. The papers were in order —but they had been issued to a Mr. Braun of West Germany. The rockets were at the ready all over the world.

"Identity papers," said the Dread People's Policeman, and the rockets all over the world came up from their hidden pits. I handed him my U.S. passport. He was frustrated. The rockets sank into their pits. There was nothing he could do but stand me against a wall and deliver a long lecture on how to drive a car. The Dread Policeman enjoyed it as much as his father enjoyed beating a Jew.

That's when it occurred to me that the Eagle Scouts—the average age of the Dread People's Police must be well under twenty-five— would rather have the world this way than be selling yard goods, or toting hods or punching streetcar transfers. Berlin is their dish—aye, their ambrosia—on both sides and at every level of importance. The crisis there has been unbroken since 1914 (except for the breather between the deflation of 1923 and the collapse of 1929). Only extremely old (and more extremely young) Berliners know what it is not to live on, or over, the brink all the time.

How have they done it? How do they do it? The only way for the temperamentally quiet man to live in Berlin—and name me the place that isn't Berlin—is to reject the crisis altogether. That is, to reject the world. This is what an Eisenhower does in the White House, sneaking out the back door with his putter. This is what the old lady does crossing Potsdam Place, between the East and West sectors of Berlin, with a baby carriage containing three cats. You have seen Ike and the old lady, and not just in Washington or Berlin but also in Oskaloosa and Pinsk.

These people are 95 percent of all people. Most of them have no stake in the lost lands—in any lost land. And even those who have would rather forget it than try to keep up with Laos, Lumumba, and the Lama. The 95 percent are vaguely aware—just as they are when the Freedom Fighters show up outside or inside the United Nations— that there is so much more than meets the eye in all these remote and unpronounceable matters that the only way to get any sleep is to shut the eye.

The 5 percent have their reward, win or lose. Theirs is the continuous titillation of brinkmanship. They would rather dance on hot coals than be wallflowers. They are partisans of peace and/or freedom to whom either, should it materialize, would be worse than anathema; it would compel them to face the humdrum, yard-goods reality of life and find something to do on a long-term basis, such as punching streetcar transfers, and confess to their pillows that they were sent here only to swell the crowd after all.

A world which is producing more history than it can consume has got to be rejected by the 95 percent who prefer (however mildly) the harness to the fire alarm. Your putter in Pinsk or your old lady in Oskaloosa at heart hates the Whites as much as the Reds because they are both ringing the fire alarm. Here he (or she) may think he hates the Reds and loves the Whites, but that is only a reflex. He never knew, or wanted to know, what went on in Hungary, or exactly what Hungary was, but he will cheer reflexively when you tell him that Imre Nagy is fighting the Reds there. You do him no favor when you tell him that Nagy is a Red himself; you drive him back to the apathy from which you had just aroused him. So you don't tell him; you don't want him to be apathetic, do you?

A man either rejects the crisis altogether or exploits it. And you need not be a clod to do the first (your artist rejects it, not just your yard-goods salesman) or a crook to do the second (your pacifist exploits it, and not just your Dread Policeman). In Prague last month I was one of two hundred selfless churchmen having themselves a ball, as one after another called upon God and man to save creation from the impending holocaust. Without the impending holocaust we selfless churchmen would be sitting in our separate holes and pasting up next Sunday's sermon to the hungover habituées who pay curled-lip service to their faith. Who wouldn't rather have a hand—even if it be burned, as it might be—in the holocaust? Who wouldn't rather be in Prague for a day than at Petosky's Resort for a month?

To be a Patriarch of the Church *or* a Policeman of the People— to be involved at the perpetual brink, at any level, be it a wooden-sword-bearer or water boy—is to live big, as big as you lived in knee pants playing King of the Hill. You were once King of the Hill, you 95 percenter. Now, by dint of keeping your mouth shut, or open, you are Vice-President of the First National at $50,000 a year, with a $51,000 house, with wall-to-wall carpeting, in a Gentile suburb.

Withdrawal from the 5 percent's hurly-burly—rejection of the crisis—is the 95 percent's way of defending the status quo. This is the hallmark of the established society in a world revolution. We call it apathy, but it is very energetic rejection; a man will drive a hundred miles at a hundred miles an hour to get away from it for a half hour at the slot machine. And he is free to do it, in the established society. The revolutionary society is unfree; every revolutionary society (including ours, when it was revolutionary) always is. And there the hallmark is the involvement of the individual in the crisis. There all the engines of revolution are stuffing the current overproduction of history down the citizen, together with all past history so that he will understand the necessity of the instant revolution.

There, as here, he fights it off as best he can; the 95 percenter, that is. He may have to buy *Pravda*, but he doesn't have to read it. He may have to look at the placards and the proclamations, but he doesn't have to read them. The Revolution is hell-bent on involving him, preferably on the side of the Revolution, but better a counterrevolutionary than a neutral; nonrevolutionary neutrality, "apathy," is the enemy the Revolution can not cope with.

And it is at this point, not at counterrevolution, that the pressure is most intense, here that the "police state," hell-bent on digging the 95 percent out of their age-old cellars, is most active and offensive. But it must not crowd the 95 percenter too far too fast. Every Czech village has a string of loudspeakers on the light poles, from one end of the village to the other. They are nearly always silent; the only thing I have ever heard coming out of them is music. When there's a fire or a flood—or the President makes an *important* speech—they are used.

But there are always meetings, always crowded with delegations. At a great peace meeting in Leipzig (imagine a great peace meeting here!) there was no room for individuals; they had to stand outside and the delegations filled the hall. To be chosen a delegate from a factory or a school is an honor which—well, which is not declined. The man is lucky who is allowed to bury himself in his craft. The supreme privilege in the revolutionary society is the privilege of privacy; a privilege as narrowly confined as the Revolution can make it, ordinarily to eminent specialists the importance of whose work transcends participation in the crisis.

I asked a bright young man in a Communist city—not in Russia—to tell me about the young people. "From Saturday noon until Sunday night they drink and dance and go after the girls," he said. "Freedom means freedom from having to hear about 'building socialism.' " Did this mean that they were counterrevolutionary? "Of course not. A big majority—young and old—support the system. But 'support' means 'accept.' Half of them because they accept every system, the other half because conditions are really so much better than they were. And this is really the whole of the matter in all the 'socialist' countries except the D.D.R. [East Germany].

"That's why the pressure is so much greater there than anywhere else, with meetings, meetings, meetings all the time, political slogans everywhere, and nothing allowed from the West (especially from West Germany). Everywhere there, it is 'Karl Marx Street,' 'Karl Marx

Park,' and so on. The old Opera Square in Leipzig is Karl Marx Square
—twenty years ago it was Hermann Goering Square—but the people
talking among themselves call it Opera Square. This is their escape.
If you ask a really ordinary East German what he thinks he would
like best in the West, he says, 'To be let alone.' "

It is hard to see, in the Communist countries, how any member of
the 5 percent gets any work of his own done. On the whole, he
doesn't. No matter what his profession, he always *seems* to be free
to engage in public work. One has the feeling that he'd better be. It
is the Communist test of loyalty; the Communists don't fool around
with loyalty oaths. Thus—except for the exempted specialists—creativity seems to be as dead there as here. Here we get what we
"want": diversion from the crisis. There they get what is "good for
them": immersion in the crisis. I like it here, where a man can duck
the diversion with no greater penalty than social ostracism.

It is not the fault of the counterrevolutionary segment—a very
small one—of the 5 percent that the Communist revolution has
failed. It is not the fault of the counterrevolutionary segment that
it is not socialism that is being built in eastern Europe. It is the fault
of the 95 percent whose self-interest is undisguised (unlike that of
the 5 percent) and takes the primary form of mere rejection of the
crisis. This self-interest unveils the high-falutinism of the 5 percent
and ultimately dominates it. The Revolution is trying to foist a
theory of human nature upon the 95 percent to which the 95 percent are resistant. Their resistance reveals the resistance of the revolutionaries themselves.

Every visit one makes to the Communist world displays increasing
prosperity all the way down the line—*and up.* A refrigerator here, a
motor scooter there, television everywhere (in the towns), and even
(in the most prosperous areas) a private car, privately bought and
privately owned. Communism is daily more triumphant—*in capitalist
terms.* And its triumph is the ruin of socialism.

In these poor lands, where, of course, real want still exists, and
where primitive living conditions are still the rural characteristic,
there are women in the cities buying expensive furs and jewels; more
all the time. Lenin's cap has been discarded for the homburg. The
elegance—and pomposity—of a Communist reception equals that of
a bourgeois France or England. Fancy food and sports shops and
luxury restaurants and hotels are proliferating in the national and
provincial capitals.

The New Marx seems to be having an increasingly hard time competing with the Old Adam. Atheist man alone is capitalistic, there as here. And there atheism is a virtue. Atheism (in theory there, in practice here) believes that man can be changed by man. The first principle there is that man's nature was corrupted by bourgeois production. The first principle here is (or was) that man was corrupted by Adam's fall. The second principle there is that man's nature can be healed by socialist production. The second principle here is (or was) that man's nature can be healed by the Second Adam called Christ.

It is the second of the two Marxist principles which seems to be falling on its face there—not the second of the two non-Marxist principles which is being validated. The Big Man in the revolutionary society (as it becomes stabilized) can not resist displaying his Bigness to other Big Men and, willy-nilly, to the Little Man. Why should the Little Man—the absorber of Marxism, not its purveyor—be different? If the Big Man wants and gets a car, why shouldn't the Little Man blunt the edge of his own resentment, there as here, by wanting and getting a scooter?

True, there's a floor (if only a dirt floor) and a ceiling there, as there isn't here. Here an able-bodied man can starve. There he can't. Here a man can have a million-dollar income (and hang on to half of it, via the tax dodges). There he can't. So the capitalist expression is less crude there than here. But where the average income is two thousand dollars, a paltry income five times that high is enough to procure all the symbols of capitalist status essential to *capitalist* man. The most un-American suggestion ever made was Henry Morgenthau's in 1942—Roosevelt put the quick kibosh on it—that dividends be limited to 6 percent and salaries to $25,000 for the duration.

True, too, there is an insistence upon *some* show of social equality there, but the insistence, compared with the first years of the revolution in Russia, seems to be declining, and perceptibly, as the opportunities for ostentation increase and the Old Adam remains. We were eating in an expensive restaurant in Prague, and a non-Communist admirer of the Communist drive for social justice pointed out to me a woman with a shawl on her head. "A peasant," he said, "just a peasant. That would have been impossible in a restaurant like this in the old days, even if she had the money." To which I could only have said—if I enjoyed argument with my meals—"And impossible today if she didn't have the money."

And so it is, not just as regards money, but as regards leisure. There's a cryptogram—with the incomes translated into something like American terms—quietly going the rounds in the Communist countries on a large scale. Life is divided into work, discussion (or "culture"), and representation in the control of society. The poor get lots of work and a bit of discussion and no representation; the middle-income people get plenty of work and discussion and a bit of representation; the rich get lots of representation and a bit of discussion and no work.

The cryptogram is a libel on the actual state of affairs, but a symbolic libel. Different brackets of income mean different kinds of life. Is this socialism? Is it "building socialism"? Can socialism be built by either the Marxist atheist materialism of the East or the non-Marxist atheist materialism of the West? Is the New Man emerging—or the same Old Adam? To visit West Germany, even after a few months' absence, is to get a newly exacerbated impression of deepening cynicism and bottomless despair. The heart of man remains locked—certainly in the West, where the dream does not ask to open it. And in the East?

What is being built in the East—at least in the "satellite" countries, where bourgeois life was wider spread than it was in Russia—seems not to be a revolution at all; *not a new kind of human society*, but a revolutionary reform of volcanic violence and stupendous, superficial proportions.

The West is going to seed, miserable as it sees itself forced to surrender both its free enterprise and its freedom to the interaction of technology and revolution. The East is planting its seed, which as it sprouts produces more and more tares of free enterprise and freedom among the rigid rows of healthy socialist wheat. The West, to "stop" the East, would have to be alive, like the East; and there is no way whatever for the West to come alive. But the East may be stopped— by its own contradictions.

The *theory*—dogmatically intact and incessantly intoned—only half sustains the practice. Communism seems to be purest when it is fighting for its life, and progressively less capable of purity as it achieves success; like any scheme, and like any man.

Part Six

Wingless Victories: War, Conscience, and Power

Is Nuremberg Still Valid?

Twenty-five years after the International Military Tribunal rose at Nuremberg—and the surviving Nazi leaders were hanged—*Shalom* asks me to dilate briefly on the question, Is Nuremberg still valid? It is one of the few questions I know of that can be dilated upon briefly. My answer to it is: It never was.

The Nuremberg Tribunal of 1946 was a classic—I think *the* classic—case of "victors' justice." During the course of its proceedings, one of the defendants marveled at it, saying, "All this trouble just to hang us." It was a blatant violation of the first principle of the common law: No man shall sit as a judge in his own cause.

It neither established nor reflected international law, because there was, and still is, no such thing as international law except by weak analogy. Law has got to be enacted by a legislature, promulgated so that all who come under it understand its terms, and its application confined to acts committed after its enactment, not before. Judgment must be impartial and as dispassionate as human beings can be. And its findings must be implemented by an executive established by law.

Nuremberg was none of these things. The crimes it prosecuted—crime against the peace, crimes against humanity, and war crimes—were not crimes in any clearly defined and universally accepted sense, nor were they clearly crimes under the only standing law which could have been applied to them: the law of Hitler Germany.

Nuremberg was not taken seriously by anybody except professors of international law. No nation prior to Nuremberg or since has accepted the "Nuremberg doctrine" for its own armed forces—requiring the soldier to disobey his superior officer when he is ordered to commit what *he* regards as an atrocity. No army has ever functioned under such conditions. No army could.

There is no international law, no court to hear it pleaded (the International Court of Justice at the Hague does not have compulsory jurisdiction), and no executive to administer such a court's decisions. If Nuremberg were still valid—or ever was—My Lai and all the other My Lai's of Vietnam would have had to be tried before an interna-

Reprinted from *Shalom*, Spring 1973. Copyright (c) Jewish Peace Fellowship, 1973.

tional tribunal. The captured American airmen, whom the North Vietnamese once called war criminals, would doubtless have been tried by a tribunal composed of North Vietnamese, Viet Cong, Chinese, and Russians—and then hanged—*if* the United States had been forced to surrender unconditionally.

The lesson of Nuremberg is marvelous in logic and in law, and even more marvelous in life. The lesson is: Be sure not to lose a war.

The Devil Is a Traveling Man

My friend the Devil was in town last week between train wrecks. He let me stand him a drink— he never buys, lest he be suspected of trying to corrupt me—and he asked me about conditions. I told him conditions were bad.

He said he hadn't noticed, and I asked him where he'd been keeping himself.

"On the move," he said. "Going like mad. Meetings, conferences, hearings, reports, investigations, speeches, editorials. On the move all night, on the go all day. Haven't been home in months. Ah, me," he sighed, "no rest for the wicked."

I asked him how conditions looked to *him*.

He blew his nose with a bandanna that covered his face. "I couldn't say," he said. "So help me, I really couldn't. I never get to read the papers any more, and as for a quiet evening's schmoos, I don't know when I've had one in how long."

I said I knew what it was like, as I am flying around all the time myself. "They're after me all the time," I said, "if it isn't one thing it's another. It's getting so that a man can't call his soul his own."

The Devil coughed violently and spilled his drink. "Must have got a little of it up my nose," he said.

"Another round?" I said.

"No thanks," said the Devil, "I haven't much use for the stuff myself. I remember an old distiller friend of mine who used to say he'd rather sell the stuff than drink it. That's the way I feel about it."

"I know," I said, "but there's another side of it. Old Gene Debs had to have his gin and when his friends tried to take it away from him he used to say, 'How can a man live sober in a world like this?' "

"You mean the Old Socialist?" said the Devil. "What ever became of him?"

"Died years ago," I said.

"You don't say," said the Devil. "Funny how you lose track of people—of *some* people. Drank himself to death, I suppose?"

"No," I said, "It took more than gin to kill Gene Debs. I don't believe he ever recovered from that stretch in Atlanta."

Reprinted from the *Progressive*, April 1947. Originally entitled "The Great Admission."

"To be sure," said the Devil. "That was for impeding the draft in the First World War, wasn't it?"

"That's right," I said. "Harding pardoned him, but it was too late. I suppose Truman will grant an amnesty to war resisters of the Second War some day, but they'll all be dead."

"A sort of second Harding, I suppose you might say," said the Devil.

"In some ways better," I said, "and in some ways worse. This Greek-Turkish aid thing of Truman's means war, of course—."

"You don't tell me," said the Devil.

"What else?" said I. "The whole Turkish grant is specified for military purposes, and how much of the Greek grant do you suppose will be used for anything else?"

"Not much, I suppose," said the Devil. "But then they tell me there's an amendment to make the aid to Greece and Turkey non-military. How is *it* coming along?"

"Buried," I said.

"You don't say so," said the Devil.

"UNRRA's ended, too," I said, "the UN Relief and Reconstruction program".

"I know," said the Devil, "but you couldn't expect the United States to carry the whole load, could you?"

"It all depends," said I. "If we're trying to stop the Spread of Communism, we've got to give people a stake in the social order. The proletariat is composed of those who have nothing to lose but their chains. It seems to me that if we want to cut down the size of the proletariat we've got to give people something to lose besides their chains. If we can afford eleven billion dollars for armaments this year, we can afford at least eleven billion to fatten up people who turn Communist when they've been turned into wolves."

"There's something to that," said the Devil, "but we Americans—*you* Americans, that is—have got to protect America from Russia. Confidentially, I think war with Russia is inevitable. You don't know the Russian hordes as I do. They're Cossacks at heart, half civilized. It's ridiculous to think of them as a Western people. You've got to be realistic, my boy."

"I know," I said, "but you sound a little like the authors of the Declaration of Independence."

"*Do* I now?" said the Devil, obviously flattered.

"They accused George III of sicking 'the merciless Indian Savages' on them, you will remember, and in the same sentence they describe these merciless Savages as 'inhabitants of our frontiers,' without of course ever saying who pushed the Savages to the frontiers."

"I'm not worth a hoot in hell," said the Devil, "on ancient history, but I think you'd do well to hold on to the atom bomb, just in case."

"Maybe that's what worries the Russians," said I. "And not our holding on to it, either, but our letting go of it. You know," I added, "that it was we who let go of it over Hiroshima."

"But that was to end the war," said the Devil.

"That's what Goering said about Rotterdam, Warsaw, and Coventry," said I.

"I know," said the Devil, "but Hitler had to be stopped."

"By the way," said I, "do you know for sure what ever became of Hitler?"

"Rumors," said the Devil, "nothing but rumors. But tell me, is universal training going to go through?"

"You mean peacetime conscription?" said I.

"As you will," said the Devil, "But President Truman said he didn't want the word 'military' used even though the Army would run it, and I don't know why we shouldn't string along with the President."

"You mean 'you,' not 'we,' " I said.

"Did I say 'we'?" said the Devil. "I'm sorry. But what are its chances?"

"Good, I'm afraid," said I. "The President is waiting for the report of his nine-man commission, seven of whom were committed to peacetime conscription when he appointed them."

"Hmm," said the Devil. "Packed, you might say. And still, it might save millions of men in case of another war."

"That's what President Truman says," said I, "and President Roosevelt before him. But General Marshall and Secretary of War Patterson admit that it would take six months or longer to mobilize the graduates of peacetime conscription, and nobody seems to think that atomic warfare will last six months."

"A short war, eh?" said the Devil.

"Well," said I, "General MacArthur was asked the other day how the Red Cross could do a better job in the event of another war, and he said, 'There won't be time for the Red Cross to do a better job in the event of another war. The next war won't last long enough for that.' "

"A funny cuss, MacArthur," said the Devil.

"Very funny," said I.

"But," said the Devil, "if everyone else has universal training, America has to have it, too. You have got to be realistic,"

"But universal training is what we went to war against in '41," said I.

"You mean Prussianism," said the Devil. "I remember."

"And," said I, "we've got the atomic bomb, we've got airborne bacteria to eliminate life over whole areas, we've got the biggest and best air force in the world, we've got a professional army of over a million volunteers, and we've got a navy bigger than all others in the world combined. Isn't that about enough?"

"I don't know," said the Devil, "I'm not a military man. But I remember George Washington saying—I remember it as if it was yesterday—that in time of peace we have to prepare for war. And Washington was the Father of Our Country."

"Where do you get that 'our' country stuff?" I said.

"I'm sorry," said the Devil.

"And this loyalty oath," said I, "is the worst thing yet."

"Loyalty oath?" said the Devil. "You mean that Hearst proposal for school teachers? I thought that was killed in 1935. I watched the fight with great interest, believe me, and I was amazed at the solidarity of the country against it."

"That," said I, "was 1935. And it isn't a Hearst proposal for school teachers now. It's a Presidential order for all Government employees. If they are found 'subversive,' and, of course, nobody says what 'subversive' means, they are fired."

"*Really*, now," said the Devil. "I think," he went on, taking a quick squint at his water-proof, shock-proof, rust-proof, split-second wrist watch, "I have time for just another drink. It's really a wonderful thing for low spirits," he said.

"Yes, sir," said I, and before I had my hand up the bartender was there. "There's a loyalty oath for every employee of the Government. And it's not a proposal, it's an order. And it's not before Congress, it's in effect."

"The devil you say," said the Devil.

"It all adds up to the great admission," said I.

"Of what?" said the Devil.

"Of the fact that we lost the war."

"Oh, get out," said the Devil. "I guess I know who won the war and who lost it. Who do you think you're kidding?"

" 'Whom,' " said I.

"I'm sorry," said the Devil. "I never went to night school, you know."

"Look, my friend," said I, "you and I don't have to kid each other. You remember the time I was planning to go to Sun Valley and that crippled kid's mother came to me and—"

"I remember," said the Devil. "You don't need to keep telling me and everyone else how intimate you and I are. I know who my friends are, and I wouldn't be sitting around with you if I didn't."

"All right," said I, "then lay off that won-the-war stuff. In Hitler Germany only Nazis could hold office. In Stalinist Russia only Stalinists can hold office. In democratic America, as of even date, only Republicans and Democrats can hold office, and I'm not even sure about Democrats."

"You mean we're—beg pardon, *you're*—moving in the direction of one-party government," said the Devil. "Dear me."

" 'Dear me' is right," I said. "Why, do you realize," I went on, warming to my subject, "that in 1917 Mr. Wilson told us we were going to war against the three apocalyptic evils of Prussianism—imperialism, treaty-breaking, and atrocities against helpless civilian populations—and that two world wars and ten million lives and five hundred billion dollars later we have embraced all three of these evils?"

"Tsk, tsk," said the Devil.

"And what's worse," said I, waving my arms around and attracting the attention of everyone in the bar, "we have not only embraced these evils; we are calling them *good.*"

"No, no," said the Devil, "not *that.*"

"Just that," said I. "I've already pointed out how Hiroshima 'ended the war.' That's good, isn't it? And our seizure of the Japanese mandated islands will protect American democracy from future Japanese aggression. That's good, isn't it? And Russia's unprovoked invasion of Japan helped end the war. Isn't *that* good? And peacetime conscription provides free dental care for the conscriptees. Isn't *that* good, too?"

The devil muttered something like, "It does beat the Devil."

"What's that?" I said. "Nothing," said the Devil, "nothing at all. I was just muttering."

"Oh, I said, "it's rum. It's really rum."

"I'll have another," said the Devil.

"Why," said I, "we are parties to the hanging of Nazis for mass deportations of civilians and the enslavement of military prisoners, and at the same time we are parties to the deportation of at least twelve million civilians in eastern and southern Europe and the enslavement of anywhere from one to three million German prisoners of war."

"This is too much," said the Devil. "This is enough to drive me to drink."

"I'll buy," said I.

"Not on your tintype," said the Devil. "I happen to own a piece of this joint. Put that Confederate money away."

There was a pause.

"Did you notice," said the Devil brightly, "the Federal Trade Commission statement the other day that the Big Four distilleries hold

75 percent of the bonded whiskies in this country? Isn't that an outrage?"

"I'm still thinking about those wars," I said, "and if I had tears to shed, and beer to shed them into, I would shed them now."

"Come, come," said the Devil, "pull yourself together. Shall I tell you what your trouble is? You're an unrealist. People are only human, and I've been contending for years that you can't change human nature. You are one of these all-or-nothing boys, that's what's wrong with you. You remind me of Henry Wallace before he came out for war against Hitler. You're a perfectionist, that's what you are."

"And conditions," said I, "are getting less perfect all the time, and it's not the perfectionists who are running the show."

"It's all a matter of the point of view," said the Devil. "The truth is relative, and we've got to make the best of what we have."

"But what we have is none too good, and it's getting worse," said I.

The Devil shrugged his shoulders. " 'Better,' 'worse,' " said he. "Those are University of Chicago terms."

"Don't forget," said I, "that the University of Chicago made the atom bomb."

"I'm willing to give the University its due," said the Devil. "But I still don't see this 'great admission' stuff."

"Look," said I, "when the war began, Hitler said, 'Even if we lose the war, we will still win, for our ideas will have penetrated the hearts of our enemies.' "

"I don't know anything about that," said the Devil, taking his hat. "I never meddle in politics."

Friend Nixon

*I warn and charge you from the Lord not to make any of the world's
jewels your God.*
                    —George Fox, *Epistle* 169 (1658)

T he Religious Society of Friends, of which Richard Nixon
is a member, was founded by Jesus freaks whose street-
corner raptures earned them the scornful sobriquet of
"quakers." Their faith and practice were alike anathema
to the buttoned-down hypocrisy of seventeenth-century
England. They were whipped and jailed and hanged and transported
on the catchall charge of conspiracy—though everything they said and
did was said and done openly. Toward the end of the century when
they achieved toleration, their reputation for openness immediately
prospered them. Within a matter of years they waxed fat—and the
salt lost its savor. The revolutionary became the bourgeois, the bourgeois the capitalist; one chronicler of the time says that by 1700 the
Gracechurch Street Friends Meeting was composed of "the Richest
trading men in London."

The "thee" and "thou" of the founding fathers abided—a memento
of their radical refusal to address the gentry in the plural—but the
peculiar credibility (which rested on their openness) gave place to
the cagey pursuit of the world's jewels. Within a century the "honest
Quaker" had become the cautious, cunning Quaker—even, here and
there, the tricky Quaker. In 1743 an English Friend advised his young
trainee in merchandising to "keep thy Business to thy self. . . . Endeavor to know what prices other people give for Goods, but Say
nothing of what thou gives thy self. . . . If thou finds out a place
where they Sell cheap, keep it to thy self . . . it will increase business."
Polonius counsels Laertes.

The second hundred years was the period of Quaker "quietism,"
in England and especially in frontier America. Orthodoxy no longer
emulated the antics of Fox and his ragtag-and-bobtail "witnessing"
for social justice. It now consisted of the standard piety of the established sectarians (about some of whose ancestors Christ had said that

Reprinted from the *Christian Century*, 10 October 1973. Originally entitled
"Disownment: The Quakers and Their President."

they devoured widows' houses and made long prayer for a pretense). The Quakers were no longer called a peculiar people.

The new orthodoxy swept the Friends from their foundations. They gave up the meetinghouse for the steeplehouse—just like the gentiles. Just like the gentiles they engaged a hireling ministry in contravention of their doctrine of a priesthood of believers. They listened to sermons, no longer sitting in silence to listen to "the Christ within." In 1878 the Ohio Yearly Meeting actually repudiated "the so-called doctrine of the inner light, or the gift of a portion of the Holy Spirit in the soul of every man, as dangerous, unsound, and unscriptural."

But the voice of Fox was still heard, calling his followers back to their original openness of speech and act, their original plainness of dress and furnishings, their original passion for the world's dispossessed. The principles of Fox were revived, and in the middle of the nineteenth century schism rent the American Quakers. Whole meetings, whole movements were disowned by the dominant "orthodox" who had taken to the camp-meeting evangel of the westering wagon trails. By the end of the century there were two Quakerisms in America—one the steeplehouse communion of the new West, the other the meetinghouse communion of Fox.

It was into the steeplehouse (or church) Quakerism of southern California that Richard Nixon was born, on his mother's side, and it is in the East Whittier Friends Church that he holds his dormant membership. He has, of course, made great political hay of his evangelical religiosity and, on deliberate occasion, of his Quaker heritage and his Quaker mother's devotion to peace. The designation—a harmless people, the Quakers—raises no political hackles. But it is the meetinghouse Quakerism of Fox which has restored the sect's reputation.

Even Nixon's steeplehouse-Quaker connection is tenuous: "I lived in Whittier for six years"—this is an elderly Quaker speaking—"and during that time he came to the Friends Church only once, and that was to have some pictures taken during a political campaign. When he was in this area over a Sunday, and went to church at all, it was usually to one of the swanky churches on Wilshire Boulevard." He has never worshiped at the Washington meetinghouse, where Herbert Hoover (himself a church Quaker) worshiped regularly.

During the first half century of their existence the Friends had no formal membership. They didn't need any; they were readily identified by their untoward behavior, and at any given time a comfortable majority of them were likely to be found in one of His

Majesty's gaols. Their *pièce de nonviolent résistance* was their refusal
to take an oath, doff a hat, or say a "Sire" except to the Lord God
Jehovah. When they became respectable, and then conformist, and
then rich, they began to be finicky about membership. As it got to
be more difficult to distinguish a Friend by his life, it became more
urgent to distinguish him by his card. Disownment flourished with
the flourishing of church Quakerism.

The very term "disownment" has now disappeared from the
Friends' Book of Discipline. A procedure more than a bit inaccurate-
ly known as "Quaker excommunication," its most recent discover-
able instance was seventy-five years ago. But the principle (under
"Discontinuance of Membership") is still accepted by both church
and meetinghouse Friends. A member who has fallen into error must
be labored with long and tenderly by his brethren, and at all times
"held in the light" of their love. Only if he remains obdurate after
prayerful labor directed at his restoration may his name be removed
from the rolls. The power of disownment is vested in the local meeting or congregation.

Thus a handful of citizens might conceivably topple Friend Nixon
from the presidency—and they would not even have to vote (Quakers
do not make decisions by voting). The Whittier Friends would have
only to reach a "sense of the meeting" that he had disunited himself
from spiritual fellowship. Rejection by his own Quaker congregation
would be a serious blow to the religious prop which holds up the
President's crumbling image in Middle America. His disownment
might prove cataclysmic where congressional or judicial action (short
of a determination of criminal guilt) might not.

It is not likely that Friend Nixon will be disowned, despite the
ever-increasing pressure on the Whittier Friends to take action. The
pressure, from church as well as meetinghouse Friends, began long
ago (almost as soon as his first appearance in public life). Vietnam
intensified it, and the Christmas bombing of 1972 brought it to an
apparent peak. The Whittier Friends resisted, many of them resent-
ing the intrusion of "outsiders." But Watergate confronted them
with a new dimension. Here was no question of great public policy
about which small-town Friends (most of whom had long since
abandoned the Quaker "peace testimony") might feel diffident. Here
was a question more fundamental by far—a question of a Quaker's
credibility. Could Friends who swallowed the camel at My Lai and
Bach Mai swallow the camel train at Watergate?

The preponderance of church Quakers everywhere undoubtedly
supported the war in Vietnam—though no tenet of the Religious
Society of Friends is as sharp as that which Fox and his followers

laid before Charles II in 1660: "We utterly deny all outward wars and strife, and fightings with outward weapons, for any end, or under any pretense whatever. This is our testimony to the whole world." These flabby days, there may be found even meetinghouse Friends who support war. One of them was then professor Paul H. Douglas, who joined the Marines at fifty to fight Hitlerism with outward weapons. He offered to withdraw from Chicago's 57th Street Meeting, but the meeting would not let him go. He continued to worship there (when he was not busy with wars and strife in the South Pacific) and in time became one of the most intrepid men ever to sit in the U.S. Senate.

But as recently as the American Civil War disownment was regularly visited upon Friends who enlisted in the northern cause—though Friends had been the first Americans to oppose slavery. Some 400 colonists—though Friends had been among the first Englishmen to oppose despotism—were read out of meeting for taking part in the American Revolution. (One was Betsy Ross, though she got into trouble initially by marrying outside the faith.)

Nearly all the Whittier Friends accept Vietnam and everything else that the government did or does. Nearly all of them stand in awe of the presidency, the President himself, and the corner policeman—though their first forebears *quaked* in the presence of the Lord alone. Nearly all of them were—and still are—proud of their great Friend's eminence, even his now tarnished eminence. Some of his relatives belong to the Whittier congregation, and in Friends' practice it takes only one "uneasy" member to defer action in any matter. (Since Watergate two entire meetings of the committee on Ministry and Counsel have been given over to consideration of Friend Nixon's membership, culminating in the conclusion that "it would be unchristian to ask for his resignation.") A few members of the congregation are known to have been sore distressed by the Christmas bombing, and a few more by Watergate—but not to the point of scandalizing themselves and their church. They are nice, quiet people in Whittier.

But they are Quakers.

In the pristine age of Quakerism, disownment was a consequence of "disorderly walking." Disorderly walking included (at various times and places) violating the peace testimony, paying war taxes, taking or administering oaths, absenting oneself from meeting, keeping slaves, marrying "out of Meeting," suing at the law, proclaiming "rationalist doctrine," dancing, and drinking. Friend Nixon might be had up on the first four counts—and the last two—and many a fine Friend with him. Further, as a freshman at a Quaker college he organized a secret society in the face of the faculty's stern reaffirmation of the Friend's testimony against such societies—but the statute of limitations has probably run out on that one. "Disgracing the Society" is likewise a traditional cause for disownment, but that count is a hard one to make stick.

There are, however, other offenses, specified in one or another of the Disciplines of the Society, that come a bit closer to the oval office. He has "spoken evil" (as long ago as his second congressional campaign, against Helen Gahagan Douglas) and "published lies" (as long ago as his first congressional campaign, against Jerry Voorhis— and as recently as his April 30, 1970, denial of the Cambodia bombing). He has violated the prohibition against "the acceptance of any office or station in civil government, the duties of which are inconsistent with our religious principles, or, in the exercise of which they may be under the necessity of exacting of their brethen any compliance of which we are conscientiously scrupulous." And as the General Accounting Office continues to up the ante on San Clemente and Key Biscayne, another Quaker stricture may prove to be applicable: "defrauding the public revenue."

Citing these delinquencies is nothing more than an attempt to particularize the faith of the first Friends, who enjoined one another to "keep out of plots and bustling and the arm of the flesh"; to "live in the virtue of that life and power that takes away the occasion of all wars"; and, above all, to "reach the witness of God in all men." Fox told his followers:

> Be patterns, be examples in all countries, places, nations, wherever you come; that your carriage and life may preach among all sorts of people, and to them. Then you will come to walk cheerfully over the world, answering that of God in every one; whereby in them ye may be a blessing, and make the witness of God in them to bless you. . . . keep yourself clear of the blood of all men, either by word, or writing, or speaking.

Closer to that faith than the sundry Disciplines are the Queries which Friends are asked to put to themselves. The Queries played a central role in early Quakerism, then gave way to the more formalistic Disciplines with the rise of the new orthodoxy. But they revived, among meetinghouse Friends, with the revival of Foxism. They direct themselves to the secret heart:

> Are you honorable and truthful in all your dealings?

Are you careful of the reputations of those who offend you?

Do you remember that all work and change must be carried out with trust in the steady operation of the Spirit to win men rather than defeat them?

Do you observe simplicity and moderation in your manner of living?

Do your counsel and example encourage young people to enter vocations which will serve society?

It is not an easy thing to hold Friend Nixon in the light. There is something antimagnetic about this "little man in a big hurry" (the characterization is the late Robert A. Taft's). He does not walk very cheerfully over the world; he seems to be a singularly cheerless man, compelled to crisis. Nor does he answer to that of God in every man, but instead evokes pride and contention and fear in many. Neither has he been an undoubted blessing among all sorts of people. There is a Quaker admonition to "keep down, keep low, that nothing may reign in you but life itself," but the reigning force in this Quaker's life seems always to have been the brightest of the world's jewels: public power. He panted, this Quaker, for a place in history—and he has it, sooner than he expected. But it is not a Quaker place. A friendlessness seems to pervade this Friend's associations. He seems to have used and been used by every one of the labyrinthine men he has had as close companions.

A hard man to hold in the light, but held in the light he must be— at least by Quakers. A lust is abroad in the land for the blood of the man who in his whole political career (and his whole career has been political) has never kept himself clear of the blood of all men by word, or writing, or speaking. But the script does not call upon Christians to devour the wounded lion. It calls upon them to labor with him tenderly. But they cannot get near him. He actually has a surrogate—appointed for the purpose—to receive those Friends who come to comfort him and to turn away his discomforters.

The *Friends Journal*, a tender laborer, which for months and years labored not only tenderly but gingerly, now suggests that the Whittier Friends consider asking Friend Nixon to resign. There would be no great difference in this case between resignation and disownment. However, Quakers must not "molest, trouble or persecute any [disowned members] in their outwards," and either disownment or resignation might do just that, pulling Friend Nixon down from the presidency.

Were he an open man—the thing above all else that a Friend wants to be—he might stand before the East Whittier Friends Church in

Ministry and Counsel and say that he had found his birthright principles inoperative (perhaps he could think of another term) in the life
of statesmanship; or that he had been carried away from the faith by
plots and bustling and the arm of the flesh; or that he was now standing before his brethren to confess himself a fool for the jewels of
this world and implore them to join their prayers to his penitence.
He might stand before his brethren (as Paul Douglas did in Chicago)
and assert his unworthiness of their fellowship. And they might say
to him (as the Chicago Friends said to Paul Douglas) that they would
neither cast him out nor let him cast himself out.

From Deliquescence to Survival—Watergate and Beyond

In the sense that our body politic is getting to know how sick it is, and what it is sick of, I submit that ours is a far healthier body politic than it was a year ago. A year ago it was in an advanced stage of deliquescence from hidden causes. It is now undergoing diagnosis and confronting the possibility of surgery—and survival. I would suggest that the indicated surgery has nothing to do with the guilt or innocence of any guileful or guileless individual. The blood-lust abroad in the land may do credit to our bull-baiting instinct. It does not do credit to the better angels of our nature.

As a primitive Christian I know that we are all sinners. As a primitive Chicagoan, I have a fair idea of which precincts cast, and recast, and cast yet again the votes that put John F. Kennedy in the White House exactly one hundred years after Abraham Lincoln paid a Missouri delegate's expenses to the Republican Convention in that same city. You see before you a native of the town in which Mr. Dooley's Mrs. O'Shaughnessy, when she wanted to awaken the drunken aldermen, was told by Mr. O'Shaughnessy, "Lave them be, while they sleep, the city's safe."

The mortal responsibility which devolves upon the Select Committee arises from the asseveration of John Locke—the Founding Father's Founding Father—that the legislative is all. All modern and most ancient tyrannies have been characterized by the emasculation of the legislative by the executive power, with the judiciary in its appointive discretion, maintaining the pernicious illusion of representation by a popular assembly.

I suspect that the reason the legislative is all is not its custody of lawmaking process but its power of investigation. The only serious mistake the Select Committee has made is its occasional defense of itself on the ground that most of the testimony it has heard would be admissible in a judicial proceeding. No judicial proceeding would have availed this body politic in its hour of need; it is only an accident that there was a man on the bench last spring who made the nonjudicial observation that he did not believe a witness.

I do not presume offhand to attempt to outdo Shakespeare's

Remarks delivered at a conference on the basic constitutional issues raised by the Watergate controversy, at the Center for the Study of Democratic Institutions. Reprinted from the *Center Report*, February 1974.

animadversions on the judicial process. Attorney Scott Stewart, whose speciality was the springing of rough-and-tumble Ciceronians in Cicero, Illinois, used to argue *seriatim*, and sometimes simultaneously, as follows: his client didn't do it; if he did do it, he was insane when he did it; if he was sane when he did it, the prejudicial outcry against him precluded a fair trial in this or any other venue; and, all else failing, that the County Commissioners had been involved in a real estate deal with Mayor Anton J. Cermak—"Bebe" Cermak to his intimates—in which the very courthouse in which the trial was docketed had been built outside the original limits of Cook County.

The only thing that could, and can avail the body politic *in extremis* is the charter of the Select Committee, committing it to the investigation of unethical—not just illegal—conduct in the 1972 campaign. The unethical is not necessarily—not even often—the illegal, as Congress attested in separating the two. It was the unethical, not the illegal, activities in 1972 that did this country down, and it would take more than sixty million dollars worth of Scott Stewarts to prevent the Select Committee—constitutionally empowered to subpoena witnesses and interrogate them under oath—from investigating those unethical activities.

In a court of law most of the corporations, cooperatives, and labor unions which have appeared or will appear before the committee can present the philanthropic spectacle of *quid* without *quo*. To fine a soulful corporation $5,000 for putting a hundred thousand or a million on the drum is nothing. To ask of that soulful entity, "What did you get for it?" is nothing. But to be empowered to ask, "What was the hope or fear that moved you to do it?" is everything. This is what the soulful entity calls invasion of privacy or, in the bright day of the soul, character assassination. Character is the domain of ethics.

The discoveries of the Select Committee have been spectacular. But it is charged with discovery for the sole purpose of recommending legislation to detoxify the American political system. I do not see how it can discharge its obligation short of the radical surgery of the Federal Constitution that will bind the states each and several and, in so far as ethics is susceptible to constitutionalization, save the Republic from the metastasis of legalized corruption.

Radical restorative surgery may save us still. Frederick the Great objected to the noise of a windmill that disturbed him at Sans Souci and ordered it demolished. The miller obtained a permanent injunction against him and when the King heard about it he said wonderingly—in French, of course—German was reserved for horses and servants—"So there is still a judge in Berlin!" We had hoped that there was still to be found a defense of freedom in Washington, and the Senate committee has gratified our hope. What we had long despaired of was a defense of freedom by a press owned and operated for private profit. One night in Prague, as I was entering a hotel, the lights went out in the area. Under the salubrious cover of darkness the Czechs vented their irritation. "It's getting so that it happens every two weeks," said one. Thinking to be a good guest I said, "It happens in New York, too." And under cover of darkness another Czech said, "The difference is that when it happens in New York it's in the newspapers. That's the way we are building socialism here."

Permit me to quarrel gently with those brethren among us who do not think much of the American press and ascribe its present valiance to the bandwagon impulse. I direct their attention not only to Prague when the lights went out, but to the queasiness of the Old Lady of Threadneedle Street. I direct their attention further to the presidential campaign of 1936. If the American press is a bandwagon climber, why didn't it climb on the bandwagon then?

My friends, I have blushed my whole life long to have to admit that I was one of those hump-backed bums and petty grifters who call themselves newspapermen. I blush no longer. I belong to an occupation whose rise from its reprehensible nadir in the thirties, forties, and fifties could not have been imagined by Bob Hutchins in his long-ago dream of professionalizing the American press. Down in darkest Orange County in California a few months ago a brash young reporter thought he smelled something funny in a residential real estate operation on the seacoast and went to his editor with it— the editor of what a few years back was the most comically reactionary paper in the country. The editor sat there shuddering a while and then said, "If you get it, we'll print it." Since one of the company here this evening is a Pulitzer Prize man in journalism, I charge Harry Ashmore, late of the Little Rock, Arkansas, *Gazette*, with the responsibility to propose the Santa Ana, California, *Register* for next year's award for its heroism in breaking the saga of San Clemente.

If the newspaper racket can be professionalized, what can't be? Why not the law? Bob Hutchins has never been able to convince himself that the law can not be a profession, and even a learned profession. All his life, and in spite of every indication to the contrary, he has clung to what Gibbon would call the pleasing prospect that the lawyer can somehow he brought to profess something more exalted than bacon and beans. Fifty years ago he undertook the reconstruction of the curriculum of the Yale Law School, introducing economics, psychology, and history on the novel ground that it would not do a lawyer any durable harm to be an educated man.

So far did he carry this mad design that when an extremely stout old gentleman said to him, "Well, young man, I suppose you teach your students that the judges are all fools," the young man was able to reply, "No, Mr. Chief Justice, we teach them to find that out for themselves."

He even introduced ethics—ethics, mind you—into the legal curriculum in case the prospective lawyer some day finds himself in a pinch in which it might be useful to be able to distinguish right from wrong. What Hutchins did at Yale, and then at Chicago, was to transform legal training into legal education, and lay down the rudiments of converting a practice into a profession.

Bob's business—his cover has been education—has always been the public law in relation to the life of the Republic. He was a relatively small boy when he joined Felix Frankfurter—a still smaller, though somewhat older boy—in attacking the Supreme Judicial Court of Massachusetts for its evidentiary atrocities in the Sacco-Vanzetti case. He and Antonio Borgese got a World Constitution written in case there should ever be a world. He committed the Fund for the Republic not merely to the defense but to the extension of the Bill of Rights when McCarthyism was trying to destroy it. From the establishment of the Center he has focused the work of the refounding fathers on the identification and exploration of the basic issues that will confront the society that means to be free. Always *basic*—this is the singular character of the Center. Always, in a word, constitutional. He has held Rex Tugwell's hand—sometimes both hands; it's hard to restrain youthful impetuosity—through thirty-eight drafts of a new U.S. Constitution that will serve the next century as well as the present version served the one before last.

To ask whether the law can be professionalized is at once to ask whether ethics can be constitutionalized. Thomas Aquinas—*a'leve shalom*—said that the law is a teacher. (He did not say that the lawyers are teachers.) But we are all teachers, whether or not we mean to be, for all men learn something and they learn at the school of example. The Select Committee is an exemplar. The press is an exemplar. The Center is an exemplar. Every human institution is an educational experience for those who are open to education. But education is not an inevitable consequence of experience. Yesterday Professor Samuel Beer articulated the pious hope that the Watergate investigation will lead us all to pull up our socks and do better. History applauds the piety, but I am afraid that it discountenances the hope. The Burton K. Wheeler investigation—*there* was a Sam Ervin for you—the Wheeler investigation of the concentration of corporate control in the nineteen thirties should have moved us to pull up our socks. It moved us instead to water our stocks.

Neither can I string lightly along with the faith expressed by Mortimer Adler and others of the brethren here that salvation cometh through the law. True, we have got to have new law. The Watergate investigation will have been a poor investment if it leads to the Oval Office. It has got to lead—perhaps *through* the Oval Office—to the Constitutional Convention. We have got to have new law. It has long been evident—and as long ago as 1937 spectacularly evident—that the buck cannot stop at the swing-man on a nine-man court. We have got to have new law—and the law is a teacher.

But what can the teacher teach and—more importantly—what can't it?

Can the teacher teach men to be, not legal, but ethical? Can common honesty and common decency be instrumentalized? Can probity be prescribed and rascality enjoined? Can candor ever be an operation? This is the basic issue on which all the other basic issues turn. The crisis of our time and of all times is not at bottom a constitutional crisis. It is a spiritual crisis. I urge this conference—and all conferences—to consider quite literally a recent observation by a British journalist—an observation that may have been intended sardonically. The journalist said: "If the American people had demanded moral leadership, Richard Nixon would have been willing to give them even that."

The Ability to Kill Christ

*Successful guerilla commanders of the past have never had to cope
with the stunning mechanical ability to kill which the Americans have
brought to Vietnam.*
—Dispatch from Saigon in the *New York Times*, October 30, 1965.

here are no battles or battlefields; no cities, territories, or
provinces taken or lost, no armies surrendered or triumphant; no victories or defeats to celebrate or lugubriate. The last pretense that war is a game to be followed on maps and charts and scoreboards, with alternate cheers and groans in the grandstand, is gone. There is only the
ability to kill.

This is America's special Christmas present this special Christmas:
The ability to kill.

The headline on the dispatch quoted above is, "Saigon: Victory
to Those Who Bear Suffering."

Now Jesus Christ was born, we are told, to bear suffering. We are
told further that he who would be a Christian—and co-heir with
Christ to the Kingdom—will take up the Cross and bear the suffering
with Christ as an earnest of the Kingdom's coming. Maybe America, if it bears enough suffering, will prove to be a Christian country
after all.

But this does not seem to be the American intention.

The American intention seems, rather, to be the infliction of
enough suffering to destroy the Communists, who, as we know, are
the godless enemies of Christ.

But who is the greater enemy—those who deny Christ and his way
or those who affirm him and deny his way? Whose is the greater
damnation than those who "make long prayer for a pretense"?

I am an American, and so are most of you. The American intention
is mine, for I rule this country as the holder of its only permanent
political office, the office of citizen. I cannot pass the buck to my
ministers of state on the ground that they know best. Or because my
refusal to pass it will comfort the enemy. When my ministers of state

Reprinted from the *Progressive*, January 1966.

—mere ministers, ministering to my needs—tell me to do as they say and not what I know is right and I ask them why and they say, "Because you may comfort the enemy," I must tell them that I must comfort myself by doing what I know is right, even at the cost of comforting the enemy. Politics ends at the waterfront. Doing right does not.

This is not the first war in Asia (thought it may be the last). Nor is the tyranny of South or North Vietnam the first Asian tyranny. There was one long ago, and it came about, says Plutarch, because "the inhabitants of Asia did not know how to pronounce one word, which is 'No.' " If I must do what is right, and not what somebody else tells me to do, and still less what somebody else is doing. I must know how to pronounce that one word.

"No" is the word of a sovereign. "Yes" is the word of a sovereign. "I'll do as you say" is the word of a slave. If I would not be a slave, if an American must be a sovereign, I must either say "Yes" and *enlist* to kill in Vietnam, or say "No" and enlist *not* to kill in Vietnam. I must not dodge the draft or let myself be hauled off by the draft board, kicking and squealing like a stuck pig, to be an involuntary hero.

And that is the politics of it. But the Asians and the rest, including the godless Communists, all have their politics. The religion of it *I* have. I have the religion that was proclaimed this midnight clear by the angels. I have the glad tidings of eternal life and of temporal life. I have the good news that the way to be saved hereafter is to love— and that the way to be saved even here is to redeem my enemy from his enmity by loving him.

This is the Christmas gift and there is no other. There are not two ways of reading Matthew 5, 6, and 7. Whosoever tries to read them a second way—let him cry "Lord! Lord!" in his steeplehouse—is blasphemous. Whosesoever country says, "In God We Trust," and inflicts suffering on the innocent and retaliation on the guilty, is godless.

Christ had to enforce the Law of Moses because the Jews, who sought righteousness by the Law, were not up to obeying the Law. Christ's enforcement order is plain: Man must live by faith if he means to be Lawful. Without faith he cannot obey the Law even if he would. The Lord, seeing man's plight, sent a Son of the House of David, one Jesus, to enforce the Law upon him, and men marveled because this Jesus spoke *as one having authority, and not as the lawyers.*

This is Christmas, the birthday of Christ the King. Even the Vatican Council has abandoned the Old Testament for the New this Christmas and declared that those Jews who betrayed him and cried out, "His blood be upon us and our children," had no power to invoke damnation upon their innocent children or their innocent fellow Jews. But the Christian knows more than that. He knows that the betrayers of Christ Crucified as King of the Jews did not even have the power to invoke damnation upon themselves; for they knew not what they did.

Do we Americans know what we have done and are doing in Vietnam? Whoever of us does not know will be forgiven. But whoever knows will not be forgiven. Christ cannot pray for these last, but only die for them on the Cross.

I remember an American sergeant who turned a German woman and her two babies out of her house at the end of the war and, when she wept, said, "Too bad, lady." I am sure that our ministers of state, whose soldiers burn up the house and the woman and her children in it, are saying, in their hearts, "Too bad, lady," for I am sure that they are humane men. It can only be that they do not know what they are doing.

If they did, they would certainly stop doing it. They would certainly stop even if the rest of the world were not begging them to stop. They would certainly stop even if it meant their country's ignominy (and their own). They would certainly stop even if it meant that godless Communism were to conquer the world, for whoever trusts in God knows that it is better to be Godly and dead than either godless or red.

My only claim to sovereign American citzenship is that I know what I am doing. I shall not be forgiven if I do what I know is wrong. I shall not be forgiven if I add my ability to the godless ability to kill. As surely as I love my country I must save its soul if I can. That is the only way to save my country. I am responsible for America. It is my subject. I am its ruler. My "No" to it in Vietnam, if it is not the only way to save it, is this Christmas Day's way and I must choose this Christmas Day.

Knowing (1) what I am doing and (2) what is good for my country, I, I alone, its dread and responsible sovereign, must say "No" to my ministers of state who, all unknowingly, betray the double trust that I have reposed in them and that they have reposed in God. My "No" is a mortal challenge to their perfection of the ultimate weapon—the recoilless man, who does not jump no matter how hard he is jolted by what he has done. Too bad, gentlemen, but I cannot be that man. I cannot be that man because I am an American.

The Russians and the Chinese, like the Americans, have the stunning mechanical ability to kill. But of the three of them only the Americans have the stunning mechanical ability to kill Christ, for the others do not know who he is. I would not be an American *and* a Christian this Christmas for all the tea in Taiwan, for I would not be good enough to be both the one and the other. I would not be able to be—as the American General Knowles said when he counted the Vietcong dead—"delighted."

Christmas is come and gone, and what Paul said is still true, that the whole creation groans in travail until now. But Christmas comes again, and yet again. For the Lord promised my people, along with punishment for their sins, that for all their sins his hand would be stretched out to them still.

Christmas is come this season to Vietnam, where my ministers of state crucify whole villages by mistake and villages by intention and stop Communism by burning the poor alive. Christmas is come this season to my own, my native land, where my ministers of state crucify the American reality along with the American image and roll the stone into place and harry those who would roll it away. And I, in my warm and worldly discomfort, must celebrate Christmas.

I must celebrate Christmas whether or not it is celebrated in Washington, Moscow, or Peking. But how celebrate it this season?

How celebrate it except to cease to do evil *and then* learn to do good? How celebrate it except only to stop killing and renounce my ability to kill? How celebrate Christmas this season? Is this the season to be jolly? Is Christ this season a jolly man? I am glad that I am an infidel, under the Law and not under Christ. I can jollify the Winter Solstice and be a good American.

The Professor's Problem

I am now engaged in grading my students prime, choice, good, commercial, or unfit for human consumption. Among them are my unmarried male students between the ages of eighteen and twenty-six, a category which, since I perform in a coeducational institution, covers about half of the lot. If they do not sustain a grade average in the top two thirds of their sophomore class they will lose their deferment, or reprieve, from military service, "service" being defined as the infliction of death upon as many of their fellow men, who have never offended them, as possible.

This recent regulation of the Defense Department (which, when this new-speak country was last at peace, was called the War Department) makes of me and every other college schoolma'rm in the country its handmaiden in the perpetration of its around-the-clock atrocity in Vietnam. I am too old and limp to be anybody's handmaiden and, besides, I am already spoken for by, among others, the Lord and the Devil.

We schoolma'rms have in fact been filling this role ever since 1940. The conscription classification 2-S—full-time student in good standing —has been the basis of deferment without distinction since the Korean "police action." The introduction of the distinction simply forces us to see our role without blinking, and Vietnam simply forces us to face the fact that the decision we make, this month, between a B and a C, or a C and a D, constitutes a life-or-death sentence.

Our role is all the more ignominious because those of us who have a little learning have done all that we could to weaken the morale, or blind submission, of the young men who are being required to save one Asian tyranny from another by killing the helpless victims of both. In season and out we have been blowing the whistle on President Johnson's (and some of us on President Kennedy's) betrayal of our national ideals and our national faith. Our efforts to rescue our country from its government have, willy-nilly, so vitiated the susceptibility of the young to believe what they read in the papers that a considerable proportion of them have abandoned honor for any and every sordid dodge, even unto the pretense of mental instability or homosexuality; and when the dodges all fail them, and their aban-

Reprinted from the *Progressive*, June 1966.

donment of honor hasn't saved them, they are dragged off to salvage freedom where no freedom has ever been.

We who have contributed to their moral degradation by opposing the American war on Vietnam have had to live unhappily with the immorality we have induced by trying ourselves to be moral. We have had to live unhappily with the craven cunning which our opposition to Vietnam has nourished in the hearts of the rising generation.

Some of us who are very old and tenacious of memory are reminded of the stampede of the "interventionists" for armchair jobs after Pearl Harbor. I do not know any of these wretches—some of my best friends were wretches—to have been ashamed of their shameful behavior then or in retrospect. What they had had in mind, it seems, was that somebody else, not they, should do the intervening; it went without saying, as it still goes, that the people who reason why should do so in comfort while the clods who are fit to do and die should stop the bullets.

The reasoners-why went to every length, just like the kids now, to find a better 'ole than a fox's. Everybody who wanted the world saved from Hitler wormed himself out of doing it personally if he could; everybody, at least, in my then acquaintance except Prof. Paul H. Douglas, who, having sedately sounded the tocsin, enlisted as a private in the Marines at the age of fifty; and I have had the impression ever since that Paul thinks that his noninterventionist friends have never forgiven him, when the fact is that there is scarcely another man that we could praise then and now for (as we say in the South) putting his money where his mouth was.

The characteristic figures of the Second World War, or Great Crusade, were no different from the Rolls-Royce-driving young gentleman whose intimate relationship with the country's leading family has proved to be no obstacle to his drawing a pass from his draft board as the sole support of his mother on her Beverly Hills estate, or from that rapidly lengthening list of high government officials who, 'mid the rockets' red glare, the bombs bursting in air, are deserting their posts to sacrifice themselves to the rigors of private enterprise. (When one of them, an Undersecretary of State, resigned last month, one of his friends explained to the *New York Times* that this fiercest anti-Communist Crusader of them all wanted "to earn some money.")

But this is the way the world wags, and always has, and always will, I suppose, until the Angels' Ministry at the end of mortal things. The professor's problem is whether to wag with it. The professor's problem is whether to present his students with their most

inspiriting example of servitude to truth. or their most dispiriting example of subservience to falsehood. The professor's problem is not
to publish or perish, but to perish here or hereafter.

I do not, myself, object especially to the American attack on Vietnam (or to the Russian attack on Hungary); I see no persuasive basis
for picking and choosing wars. However glorious the objective may
be—to liberate Boston from the sales tax in 1776 (it was restored last
month by the state legislature), or to emancipate the Negro, or to
save the world for democracy or the Jews from Hitler—every war
is just as unjust as every other because it can not be otherwise. It
can not be otherwise because it is war.

The just war will be fought when men who are perfectly good, in
a perfectly good cause, are fighting men who are perfectly bad in a
bad one, and not before; and when no man is handed a gun and, with
another gun at the back of his head, ordered to use force and violence
and other unholy means to kill another man similarly situated. The
just war will be fought when no one unoffending person, be he only
a very small Vietnamese person in swaddling clothes, is burned up
alive. In a word, the just war will not be fought, and whoever says
that you can not make an omelet without breaking eggs is making
the cannibalistic error of using men as eggs. If men may be used as
eggs, there is no just or unjust war or peace.

No civilized society can raise a volunteer, or even a mercenary,
army. The volunteer army—as witness the location of the recruiting
stations in the old days—is a skid-row mission without the faith, the
hope, or the charity. It is the end of the line, and nobody who hasn't
come to the end volunteers for it except, nowadays, in the hope of
avoiding conscript transportation to the Hot Spot. Like everybody
else in the world who has it good, the American would rather live on
his knees (or on another man's back) than die on his feet. Nobody
in the United States wants to stop Communism or anything else at
the cost of his money, let alone his life, and we all understand why,
in the very thick of the current Great Crusade, there is a rapidly
lengthening list of high government officials who are taking a powder.
They have passed their twenty-sixth birthdays. There is no gun at
their heads. And so they are doing what comes naturally to the
Twentieth Century American, to you, to me, and to the conscripts
in Vietnam who would take a powder, too, if they could do so without being court-martialed and shot.

What is wanted, now as always, here as everywhere, is the volunteer. No man conscripted to do anything will ever serve the purpose
with more than half a hand, and with no heart at all. He will work
or fight for his life, even for his buddies; but that is not the purpose,

and men will work or fight that way for good or bad purposes indifferently. Nor will short-term, hot-and-cold enlistments serve the purpose much better. What is wanted is the twenty-year man, the forty-
year man, and the sixty-year man who will still be standing up when
he has to do it from his wheelchair.

Age eighteen is not a moment too soon to start standing up, but
not with that first and last careless rapture than subsides at twenty-
eight—or at nineteen. We want men to stay the course; we do not
have the money to finance dropouts. It is men of A. J. Muste's
eighty years that justify the investment. So we are not overly concerned with the boy who resists the draft—though we like to see
him. We are still less concerned (though we know that men may
change) with the dodger.

But Vietnam is rolling, rolling all the way to China. Push-button
warfare, when it is waged against people with push and no buttons,
seems to demand as many shatterproof coconuts as the primitive
tooth-and-claw procedure of Verdun (which shattered a million
of them). So the bottom of the economic barrel has been scraped,
and the Pied Piper of Washington has to begin creaming the economic top. The economic top is in college.

Draft deferment for college students has always been deferment
for the rich and nothing else. No matter how unpromising the American high school graduate, he can always find some kind of licensed
institution to accept him under the false pretense that it communicates the higher learning—*if* his folks have the thousand to three or
four thousand dollars a year plus a surplus of hands on the farm.
Thus college attendance in the United States has always been—and
continues to be—preponderantly white. And thus conscription is
disproportionately black. One of the splendors of the desegregated
Army is the impossibility to discover how many of our killers and
diers in Vietnam are black.

Half our high school graduates go to college because nobody else—
except, of course, the Army—wants them. We store them for four
years unless flagrant delinquency compels us to throw them out to
preserve the institution's image. Many of my students, who are good
kids, and better than I was, belong, not in college but in high school.
Some hopeless few, not many, belong in trade school or in semiskilled jobs. By passing those who, on their "merits," need flunking,
I have in the past preserved them from two years of barracks-room
banality and the moral disintegration inherent in one man's voiceless
obedience to another. By flunking them now, or even by giving them
a C or a D instead of a B or a C, I consign them to the flames of Vietnam (worse yet, to the flame-throwing) and to the premature de-

lights of a life (while it lasts) which one of my young friends epito-
mized when he asked his folks to send him some powdered milk.
"We can get all the whiskey we want," he wrote, and he is eighteen,
"but there is no milk."

I am now required to decide which of these young men are to be
spared for a season and which of them are to be bound aboard the
black-sailed ship destined for the jaws of Minotaur Mac. I do not
mean to do them this disservice; or myself. Nor do some of the
troubled colleagues whose views I have heard. I doubt not that
most of my colleagues will retire sedately to the classic escape of the
technician who renounces political responsibility in the name of "simply" doing what he has been hired to do—the plea in avoidance for
which we hanged Keitel at Nuremberg.

Eighty percent of all college and university research and development is now financed by the government with its attendant infiltra-
tion and control overt and covert. Now teaching itself is to be tied to
the chariot, not by the devious means of money but by fiat. The recent Naval Academy scandal revealed that the student caliber is so
low that, with civilian instructors grading tough, the students are
passed by "administrative grading" because the Navy can't get enough
officers. Now we are invited, in the civilian institutions, to accommodate the Army by flunking in the same way.

The classic, or Keitel, escape has some validity. It always has. If
Vietnam is none of my business, and teaching alone is, I have no problem unless, like Keitel's, my country loses the war and I am put on
trial. If Vietnam is my business, and I am a teacher, I have a whole
congeries of problems. If I give my students all A's, I am letting the
Army make me make a mockery of education, apart from the fact
that I thereby condemn another instructor's students to death. If I
am a tough grader, I am already avoided by the worst students, and
now I shall be avoided by all of them. If my courses are important
(and difficult), and another man's trivial (and easy), the threat of the
Army will drive my students from the important to the trivial. If my
school has fairly high standards—as mine has—the student who might
or might not make it in such a school will hotfoot it to one with
lower standards, preferably to the worst school in the country, where
he can be sure of shining. One of the ineluctable consequences of
the Army's present assault on education is thus the debasement of
education the country over.

Grading, whatever it may be in beef, is a dicey business in men,
above all in the education of men. Jones comes from a literate home
and is both gifted and cunning, and maybe crooked besides. He frugs
away his nights and pots away his days while Smith, who comes from

an illiterate home and is not very bright anyway, sweats blood at his books. In addition, Jones has money and Smith is holding down two jobs—one of them at night—to stay in school and is electing the hardest courses because he wants to learn. Am I to send Smith to Vietnam instead of Jones, when Vietnam, if it would do anybody any good, might be the only thing that would do it for Jones?

On the record Jones gets an A or a B, and Smith a C or a D. But not on my record. Incapable as I know myself to be of knowing what another man or boy deserves, I grade according to application and earnestness, and even according to need, and so do most of the teachers I know who do not want to be had up, on the Last Day, for the sacrilege of having played God. Nor do I flunk a student unless he compels me to, and he has to be pretty canny to do that. I live in terror of being remembered as the man who handed young Ruskin an F in English composition.

The inequity (and iniquity) of grading students at all is more and more widely recognized. In every good college and university, including mine, the curriculum (if there can be said to be one) is under agonized reappraisal. Experimentation is the order of the day, and one of the commoner experiments is the nongrade course—which was all that there was when education was in its prime on an Athenian street corner. The experiment is peripheral, confined, on the whole, to electives. Even so, the die-hards are as overheated about it as the computers.

There is a sense that the massive collapse of the whole educational enterprise in America impends. Nothing was done even to prepare the plant—not to say the staff—to survive the inundation of the war babies of twenty years ago. Nothing was done to examine the program in the light of the leisure-time implications of the cybernetic revolution that began fifteen years ago. Nothing was done to acquaint the students with what happened in Russia fifty years ago, or in Flanders Fields, or at Bergen-Belsen or Hiroshima. The reason that nothing was done was explained—to an empty house—by Robert M. Hutchins thirty years ago: The fragmentation of American society, faithfully reflected in the curriculum, was producing an impentrable jungle, and premature specialization was producing a whole race of uneducated specialists without a common concern or a common language adequate to its communication.

Now we are in the thick of it. At the same time that awareness is growing acute that "more, more" is no solution, a dreadful suspicion is dawning that we do not have the liberally and generally educated men to tackle the monstrosity.

Most of our teachers are teachers because they went to graduate school, not knowing enough (as Hutchins once put it) to leave when the party was over. Most of our students are in college for no reason other—and they say so—than that they are in college. Most male students stay there for no reason other than Vietnam. (Most graduate programs are bigger for the same reason, and therefore worse every semester.) The student who ought to drop out—or who ought never to have dropped in—hangs on for all he's worth, be it ever so little. The prolongation of adolescence in the a-go-go society indicates a year or two off, before or during college, for kids to catch their breath, write poetry, sling hash, or hit the road and figure out what they are and what they want to do and be; but the possibility is foreclosed by the draft.

As the cafeteria curriculum has become more and more bewildering in its choice of tasties, the lockstep of grades, credits, and cumulative averages has become more and more rigid. What the student wants is points, and the young instructor, himself a product of the point system, spends his life splitting them as assiduously as his predecessors in the late Middle Age split hairs. The enthusiastic teacher reprobates grading and always has, and, along with grading, the passivity induced by the lecture-and-recitation routine and the examination that calls for the rote recital of feedback facts worthy of instant oblivion. The suggestion that the teacher was once the Master, or Rabbi, charged with the cure of souls, has long since been established as First Amendment heresy.

Into this electronic confusion the Army throws its dread weight— as when did it not?—on the side of stultification. The male freshman has to be in the "upper" half of his class, the sophomore in the upper third, the junior in the upper three fourths, and the senior entering graduate school in the upper fourth; or away he goes in the black-sailed ship. It matters not how good the man, the class, or the college. There is an alternative escape hatch, a Selective Service College Qualification Test. Since the Army intelligence requirements are paleolithically low—and have just been lowered still further to meet the demands of the body-snatch—it may be assumed that any high-grade moron can pass the test. But the students have learned to be afraid of *all* tests as dirty tricks.

Henry Ford thought that the way to end war was to take the profit out of it. What Henry Ford did not understand (and what Adam Smith did) is that men prefer profit to peace. What Adam Smith did not understand (and Karl Marx did) is that the profit system can not be maintained without war. And what Marx did not understand (and

Sigmund Freud did) is that the nonprofit system can no more be maintained without war than the profit system, because men prefer war to peace.

The way to end war is to take the men out of it. I have spent my life trying to take at least one man out of it—myself—and I see no countervailing advantage, in my old age, in serving as a body-snatcher for Vietnam.

I do not know precisely how I am going to work my way out of this box and still respect my solemn obligation to teach and my low inclination to eat. But I know that as a loyal American I must not be a party to the ruin of the country I love and I know that the bridal procession of Moloch and Mammon is leading it down the road to ruin. My students may not know how to read and write, but inability to read and write is not a crime punishable by death, and I am not going to pass such sentence on them.

By Power Possessed

Morris Cohen of C.C.N.Y. was lecturing at Chicago in 1941 (prior to December 7) and his old friend Irving Salmon (like Cohen a Jew) was giving a reception for him at the University. The small talk was large and loud with the European war. Salmon, a rabid interventionist, was saying, "I just want to bash in a few Nazi heads before I die." "It seems to me, Irving," said Cohen, "that bashing heads is for the 96 percent—not for the 4 percent."

Now Stokely Carmichael is not for bashing in heads—though I don't suppose it's excluded, since White Power doesn't exclude it. And I think I comprehend what he means by Black Power. What I don't apprehend is how he thinks Black Power will be come by and what he thinks it will do. His counsel of desperation is not better counsel for being a reflexive response to a condition he and I find unendurable; any more than the starving man's theft of bread is a meaningful attack on *his* condition.

Nor do Stokely Carmichael's references (outside his essay) to Irish Power enlighten me. The Kennedys could shuck their Irish skins—even their Catholic skins, which, incidentally, put them into the 25-30 percent Power bracket—and emerge as rich and beautiful young Americans with plenty of everything. Rich, young, beautiful—and White. The Negro has plenty of nothing, and when he has plenty of everything—jobs, houses, schools, votes—he will still be Black: the one discernible *other* in a society whose Know-Nothings were never able to close the door altogether against the "Irish." The discriminable Negro is the uniquely irresistible object of discrimination.

The Kennedys represent a majority amalgam of special interests. The Carmichaels represent the Negro (who is poor) and nobody else; least of all the poor White. The Negro's is a special interest in which nobody else is interested. His special interest is, to be sure, *intelligible* to a rich society which rocks along without any consuming concern for the common good, but the small special interest (like the corner grocer's) is increasingly inconsequential in the age of amalgamation.

Irish Power never mobilized the white Anglo-Saxon Protestants, except sectionally and sporadically; and they were so sharply divided

Reprinted from the *Massachusetts Review*, Spring 1967, copyright (c) 1967 The Massachusetts Review, Inc. A commentary on Stokely Carmichael's "Toward Black Liberation" in the *Massachusetts Review*, Autumn 1966.

among themselves that they could not focus their hostility on the Irish. But Black Power mobilizes the Whites in an ad hoc alliance in which (as is usual in such situations) they sink their differences and gang up. If Stokely Carmichael means to pit the 10 percent's Power against the 90 percent's, the 90 percent will be delighted to accommodate him and see what it can do against the 10 in a fair and free contest. "It is white power that makes the laws," he says, as if he were somehow arguing *for* his position, "and it is violent white power in the form of armed white cops that enforces those laws with guns and nightsticks."

Let us suppose, contrary to likelihood, that the 10 percent comes out on top in the contest. What will it be and do then? It is not beyond a reasonable doubt that coercive triumph, over the centuries, has improved the triumphant Wasps. Nor has modern triumph over the Wasps much improved the Irish beyond putting lace curtains in their windows. Whatever the Wasps did in their day, the Irish (and the Portuguese, the Poles, and the Patagonians) do in theirs; and this is not necessarily improvement. Socrates, Acton, and Fulbright all seem to be saying that Power is not an unmixed blessing, and the statesman of ancient days said of the horrors of his triumphant Rome, "All that we do, we do because Power compels us."

What makes Stokely Carmichael think that the Negroes will use Power to better advantage than the Whites have been able to use it? I know there is no great point in describing the disappointments of freedom to the untutored slave. But Stokely Carmichael is a tutored slave. He may hope that the Negro would master Power rather than be mastered by it, but his tutoring must have acquainted him with the dictum of Confucius: "He who says, 'Rich men are fools, but when I am rich I will not be a fool,' is already a fool."

I say "would," rather than "will," because I can not see how Black Power, as I understand it, will come into its own until Blacks are 30 or 40, or 51 percent of the whole society. It will elect a sheriff where it is 51 percent of the electorate; but there are not many such counties, and still fewer states. White Power will fight for its commercial control of the "inner city"—where the Negro already has 51 (or 85) percent of the overnight populace; and when it surrenders what will we have then, except the ghetto unpolluted, with the Negro completing the wall the White began?

The exploitation of the huddled "nationality" neighborhoods, Irish, Italian, Jewish, German, Polish, Swedish, and Bohemian, tore our metropolitan communities to pieces three quarters of a century ago. Their "leaders" delivered them en bloc to the boodlers and got them a statue of Kosciusko in exchange. Stokely Carmichael has to convince us that his high hope will be realized; that the Negroes will be an exception to the classic pattern and their inner city serve the welfare of its inhabitants and the general welfare on which the particular ultimately depends. It will not be radical idealists like Stokely Carmichael or Martin King who will do what has always had to be done to win American elections. It is much more likely that the present Congressman from Harlem will be the mayor of Stokely Carmichael's New New York.

Stokely Carmichael is righter than he is wrong. Integration does mean what he says it means—the assimilation of the psychologically suicidal Negro into the White man's society on the White man's intolerable and unenviable terms. And he is right in suggesting that the White's guilt is collective—I and all the other "friends of the Negro" have exploited him; and not through our grandfathers, either. We travel as effortlessly as we do because we, not our grandfathers, are riding on the Black man's back.

Stokely Carmichael is righter than he is wrong; but he is mortally wrong. He is mortally wrong because he accepts the White definition of Power and ignores the demonstrable (if mystifying) fact that there is a kind of power that a majority (be it all men but one) can not handily dispose of. I speak of nonviolent noncooperation, nonviolent resistance, and nonviolent action undertaken in a nonviolent spirit.

Even on the White man's view of power, the Negro may get some mileage out of nonviolence. American society can live easier every year without menial labor, but for a few years or decades yet it cannot live in the manner to which it is accustomed without the Negro 10 percent. They perform its filthiest jobs and return the profit on its filthiest property. At excruciating cost to themselves, but in solid self-interest, they can leave some of its filth unswept and unprofitable. They still have a small margin of muscle in noncooperation, and by muscle I mean nothing more exalted than Stokely Carmichael or the White man means.

But the margin, in a society which cannot employ its Whites, and does not need to, is shrinking. It is the powerlessness inherent in nonviolent noncooperation that the Negro can, perhaps—I say only "perhaps"—turn to account as a peculiar form of power. The Whites are guilty. And they would rather fight than switch to expiation. If the Negro can find a weapon that will take the fight out of them, the Whites' only remaining course may be justice, not only for the Negro but for every other oppressed minority.

In his *Massachusetts Review* statement, where he purports to present the essentials of the matter, Stokely Carmichael seems never to have heard of Martin King, or of Greensboro. Or of Rosa Parks—who brought Martin King and Greensboro *and Stokely Carmichael* into being. Rosa Parks had something less than 10 percent of the Power (as Stokely Carmichael reckons it) when she could not bring herself to move to the back of the bus in Montgomery. But without the strange power she exercised that day in 1955, Stokely Carmichael would not have the familiar power he has now.

Her power wasn't Black. It was human (and, for all any of us know, divine by virtue of its being human). It was the power to heap coals of fire on the heads of the Powerful until they would *want* to do differently than they were doing. It was the power of redemption, and it came out of the most impotent segment of American society, the psalm-singing Southern Negro with his childlike power to believe that he would overcome some day. Out of that power came the Movement; out of the Movement came all that came in the next decade; and out of the deliquescence of the Movement, as it went North to the unbelieving Negro, comes the present vacuum into which Stokely Carmichael would proceed with hopeless weapons instead of none. The analogy with India is colossally imperfect, but it has this much application: We do not *know* that the American White man is less susceptible of being civilized than the British were at Amritsar.

Stokely Carmichael pointedly ignores the power that gave him birth, and he divides the Negroes into the unaccepting (like himself) and the acceptable "passers." He cannot possibly be unconscious of the singular phenomenon of our time and of all time—the power of one powerless person, neither murderer nor victim, neither combatant nor suppliant, to overcome; and, what is more, to win supporters from the ranks of the enemy. Until Montgomery nothing else had ever moved the White man's church at all. And without moved and uncoerced allies the 10 percent will never make it in the halls of Congress or the streets of Selma or any other center of Stokely Carmichael's kind of power.

The Movement is failing, if it is failing, because it has gone North, where the Negro is who doesn't see why he, of all people, should have to be better than the White man. The primitive Negro of the South sees why. Washed in the blood of the Lamb, he sees why he has to be responsible, not for the Negro, not for the White man, but for Man and the salvation of Man through sorrow and suffering and endurance to the end. But moving mountains is slow going, and Stokely Carmichael sounds like Marx's London businessman who would cut off his own right arm for a short-term profit. The short-term Negro will not even get the profit; he hasn't enough to invest.

The redemptive love to which men are called—and to which the Psalm-singing Negro responded—is not assured of a profit either. Its prospect of short-term success is slight, but the slightest prospect is better than no prospect at all, and Stokely Carmichael's way has been tried (by the White man) again and again and again. It has failed.

Its very failure may be a sign that men are not bad, and that treating them (and oneself) as if they were is therefore inefficacious. "We have repeatedly seen," says Stokely Carmichael, "that political alliances based on appeals to conscience and decency are chancy things, simply because institutions and political organizations have no consciences outside their own special interests." ("Men are bad," says Machiavelli, "and if you do not break faith with them, they will break faith with you.") If Stokely Carmichael is right, his way is no worse than Martin King's, only more tiresome as a spectacle; except that Martin King's is directed to the refinement of our sensibilities and Stokely Carmichael's is not.

The issue between them is the issue of knowing. Stokely Carmichael knows, and Martin King doesn't. Martin King doesn't know what power may be within us, or working through us, or what we can and can not do. William Penn was the first White man the Indians had ever seen without a gun. He went to them, saying to his followers that they had only to love the Indians, nothing more than that, and on that occasion, and as long as Penn and his successors governed Pennsylvania, and in Pennsylvania alone, the prospect proved to have been splendidly justified. But it was so slight that it took faith above all knowing.

Stokely Carmichael does not display that faith. For all the good his having been a Southern Negro has done him, he might as well have been a White man. He appropriates the White man's racism as the Black's and adopts the White man's Power without either God *or* the big battalions. So far is he from supposing that there may be an omnipotence which empowers its votaries, that he has got to settle in the end, not for God, or even for man, but for brute. Count clubs or noses—and if men are brutes, it matters not which—coercion carries the day in the jungle. Whoever chooses the jungle had better be a lion.

Box-Office Quakers

I have a concern, which is what a Quaker has when he has a squawk. I am not a Quaker, but I have a concern.

I am concerned about a movie called *Friendly Persuasion*, to which friends persuaded me to take my children.

Especially non-Quaker friends, and it is very important for the delineation of my concern that you understand that most of my non-Quaker friends think I'm a Quaker because I hang around with the Quakers and make Quaker noises. They said I must see *Friendly Persuasion*, and take my children to it, and report my reaction. These friends, who wanted me to tell them what I thought of the movie, all thought it was wonderful.

These friends are all discriminating people. Some of them are religious people, and all of them say that they are interested in religion. Some of the latter are shopping around and they like the unpretentiousness of Quakerism—its nay-saying to the outward show of religion. They don't like churches and ministers and sermons. They identify Quakerism with no-church and no-minister and no-sermons, and that appeals to them.

What they say they don't understand—or didn't, until they saw *Friendly Persuasion*—is the Quaker position on war.

Nor do they understand it when they are told that there *is* no Quaker position on war or on anything else; no creed, no dogma, no sacrament, no liturgy. It sounds very liberal to them (and they like liberalism), but they thought, they say, that Quakers objected to war.

"Well," I say (or said before I saw *Friendly Persuasion*), "I reckon everybody objects to war. But there is very strong feeling in Quakerism that people shouldn't do what they object to doing."

"But," say my friends (or said they before they saw *Friendly Persuasion*), "don't you have to be a pacifist to be a Quaker?"

"Not," I say, or said, "as I understand it. You don't *have* to be anything. You're *liable* to be, that's for sure, but some Quakers are pacifists and some are swordsmen, and some are sword-swallowers, and some are this, that, and the other thing. It's a passing peculiar religion."

Reprinted from the *Progressive*, June 1957.

I suppose that there isn't anything that Hollywood doesn't figure it can grind in its mill. The Quakers have been on the Hollywood agenda since they said to Charles II: "The Spirit of Christ which leads us into all truth, will never move us to fight and war against any man with outward weapons, neither for the Kingdom of Christ nor for the kingdoms of this world."

That was in 1660. Hollywood couldn't find a mill to grind up Quakerism until almost three hundred years later. Then it found, as I understand it, a Quaker novel by, as I understand it, a Quaker lady named Jessamyn West. Mrs. West is a fine writer. She may have written a fine novel. (I'm ashamed to say that I haven't read it yet, but I'm even ashameder to say that I haven't yet finished Gibbon.) By the time Hollywood got through with it, it might have been anything, except for the fact that Hollywood sent for Mrs. West to consult, or advise, or supervise, and her name appears in this position on the screen, and not just as author of the book. So Mrs. West must have liked, or at least stood for, the Hollywood account of Quakerism.

Friendly Persuasion is a story about a southern Indiana farmer and his wife and their almost grown son and daughter and a smaller son, in 1862. They're Quakers, and the wife is a Quaker minister (that's historically correct; some Quaker meetings have ministers, who may be women). But Pa's full of beans; he likes to race horses, can't resist it even on First Day (the old Quakers wouldn't use the pagan names of the days). He wants to dance and to have a harmonium in the house, and his wife, an old-fashioned Quaker, is literally hell on dancing and music; deviltry and the hand of the devil. Pa's got the old Adam in him, but, with the help of his wife, he's always chopping it down (cutting it back, rather).

It's 1862, and the war is coming close to the border of the Ohio in the form of Morgan's Reb Raiders. The Quakers won't fight. They sit silent in their Meeting when a Union recruiting officer comes in to persuade them to fight and gets so mad that he accuses them of using their religion to cover their cowardice, and specifically asks Pa's oldest boy, Josh, if he's afraid to fight.

But the Quakers are brave—it takes more courage to be set upon, as they are in this scene, than to set upon somebody else. They won't kill. They won't fight with outward weapons. They will fight with redemptive love. The officer leaves, properly baffled; the audience stays, properly enthralled.

But by the time the picture ends, Morgan's Raiders are there and the Quakers are all fighting with outward weapons. The last thing

Pa's Methodist friend Sam says to him, before setting out for the fray, is, "We need a few men like you to show us that there's a better way. I'll do the killing for both of us." But when young Josh doesn't come back from the skirmish—he has prayed and been prayed for, but still he goes to kill—and his horse comes back riderless, Pa gets out his gun and goes out to kill the Rebs. Then come the two big, symbolic scenes that prove to the audience that Quakerism is a pious fraud, but a pleasant one.

Pa gets to the fray, but it's over. First he finds his best friend, Sam, dying of Rebel wounds. Then a Reb shoots at Pa from the wood, nicks him, and Pa pretends to be dead. So Quakers are pretenders, just like the rest of us, who will play dead to save their lives. The Reb comes up unsuspecting, Pa jumps him, gets his gun away from him, shoves the muzzle into the Reb's tenderloin—and then, with the Reb at his mercy, remembers his Quaker principles and lets him go.

"Gee," said our Dicken, who's eleven, and a fighter whose parents want him to want to be a Quaker, "that was good. That's the part I liked. He could have killed him, and he let him go. Didn't you like that?"

"Not very much," I said, not wanting to say it, but, because I'm in training for truth, having to want to.

"Why not?"

"Gosh," I said, breaking training, "I hardly know. I guess it's because a Quaker usually doesn't pretend to be dead and then fight a man to get his gun and threaten to kill him and then let him go. Usually the Quaker doesn't have a gun, doesn't pretend to be dead until he is, and doesn't fight a man. So usually he's not in a position to let him go."

"He sure had the drop on him," said Dicken.

"He sure did," I said.

"What's wrong with that?" said Dicken.

"I don't know," I said, breaking training again, "I just can't imagine Rufus Jones with the drop on anyone."

"Who's Rufus Jones?" said Dicken.

"A Quaker," I said.

Pa, having let the Reb go, goes on across the bloody ground and finds his boy, wounded alongside a young Reb he has killed. The boy is crying and he won't let go of the young Reb's jacket. But Pa gets him away and takes him home, where he recovers and is as good as new.

But while Pa and the boy are down at the carnage, a band of Raiders comes to the farm. They've burned down some farms roundabout, and the farmers have tried, in vain, to fight them and save their houses and barns. But not Ma, the Quaker minister. She welcomes them, overcoming her fear with God's love and their evil with God's good. The house and the barn and the smokehouse are full of goodies, which she ladles out, and the Raiders stuff themselves, "enough to eat for a week," and ride on, leaving the farm and Ma and her daughter and smaller son untouched.

The big symbol in this scene is Samantha, a vicious old goose whom Ma loves (like a good Quaker) and (like a good Quaker) never despairs of redeeming from a life of almost-human vice. One of the Rebs grabs the goose and is going to wring its neck, when Ma comes out on the porch, just in the nick, grabs a broom, and beats the daylights out of the Reb. The Reb, not too badly injured, retreats and Samantha is saved, but Ma breaks all the way down when she realizes that she has taken an outward weapon, the broom, and used it outwardly on the Reb Raider, in whom there is that of God. She makes the kids promise never to tell their Pa—proving that Quaker ladies are liars and unfaithful wives and teachers of lying to their children—but after the trouble's all over and everyone's home the little boy blurts it out and Pa smiles a big, broad smile; it's time to go to Meeting, First Day, and Pa says, "Come along, Veterans." They're all in it together—all killers, all Quakers.

"I'll bet I know what you didn't like," said Dicken as he was getting into bed. "I'll bet you didn't like the part where the father goes to war to save his son."

I didn't say anything. I didn't want to train *or* break training. And it was Dicken's bedtime. "*Did you*?" said Dicken.

"Er—no, I guess I didn't, much," I said.

"You wouldn't go to war to save your son, would you?" said my son, Dicken, with something much less than admiration in his voice.

"Well, son," I said, sweating hard, "I'm afraid I *hope* that I wouldn't. Maybe I couldn't help myself, but I *hope* that I wouldn't." He was looking hard at me. He had the drop on me. If he were a Quaker, he would have let me go then. But he's Dicken, aged eleven. "You see, son," I said, "it wouldn't help my son if I did, or maybe it would, but probably not, and I'd have to shoot somebody else's son. So then there'd be two sons dead, and I guess the other father would love his son as much as I loved mine."

"You wouldn't fight to save *anybody*, from a burglar or a Russian or *anything*?" said Dicken.

Mommy got the gun out of his hand by saying it was time for bed and for coming in to say prayers.

Rock, who's almost sixteen, and is a pacifist, but is only almost sixteen, didn't say anything. Rock, praying and prayed over, was sweating it out with the Quaker boy Josh, his own age, who was taunted and taunted and even (at a county fair, in the picture) beaten up unresisting by bullies, but who couldn't last the course and grabbed for a gun and killed a downy-cheeked boy like himself and then cried—but comes out at the end happy as can be and unreconstructed, a "veteran," a killer, loved, as a good killer should be, by his Quaker mother and father and confirmed in his ways by the fact that they, too, when the chips were down, grabbed a gun.

Friendly Persuasion is not a misrepresentation of a Quaker family or of any family. The experience is common, in and out of Quakerism, of the parents' inability to get their children to take hold of parental ideals—or to hold on to them themselves; so common, indeed, as to indicate the real misrepresentation of *Friendly Persuasion*. What is really, and criminally, misrepresented is the human condition, which is tragic. Tragedy is the choice between two unhomogenizable goods, each seen differently every time they are looked at. There is resolution—in death or in madness—but there is no solution. The reason that Hollywood movies are terrible and Italian movies great is that Hollywood has a solution: The ending is happy, and on the road to the ending principles are scuttled in every reel without penalty or pain (oh, a few tears), every obstacle scuttles itself, and the heroes emerge miraculously reprincipled and rich.

The early scene in the Meetinghouse, when the recruiting officer comes in, and the scene at the fair, when the bullies clip the Quaker lad, show how manfully the Quakers hold to their faith against glancing taunts and glancing blows. But when the Rebs approach, their faith fails them and they go violent, and when the Rebs reach the house and go for Samantha, Ma grabs for the broom.

The moral of *Friendly Persuasion* is irresistible: The Quakers are a little bit queer, but it doesn't mean a thing. They're just like the rest of us, "only human," and we can count on them to admit they're only human, and behave like brutes, when the time comes to do it. They hold out a little, kind of slow to enlist. But, brother, let those intercontinental ballistic missiles start dropping, or a burglar break into the house, and watch them fight. And what fighters they are! Big, strong, tough, unbeatable fighters with their hands and their guns. What shots! What winners!

Of course they say, "Peace," but that's all right, as long as there's peace. As long as they say, "War," when there's war, and that's what they do in *Friendly Persuasion*, they're OK. By gosh, they're *more* than OK. They're useful, saying, "Peace." Because everybody believes in peace, and Christ was the Prince of Peace, you know that. So as long as there aren't too many of them, and they say weekdays what the rest of us say Sundays, and they don't impede the war effort, and they get in there and kill in the clinches, what's wrong with them? *Migh*-ty fine people, do our worshiping for us and ready as rain to get into the killing when the killing has got to be done.

Quaint people, too. Quaint talk, with with their "theeing" and "thouing" and "thying." Good Hollywood. And their plain dress— let's have a song, says the producer, about love in a bonnet. And their prejudice against music and dancing, that's good for a rise, a wonderful rise, because everybody's worried about what Elvis Presley is doing to their kids.

The trouble is that the Quakers aren't quaint any more. Their plain talk and their plain dress and their dread of music and dancing are long since gone. These were manners; important manners, still observable in the Quaker tendency (not universal among them) to live simpler and less showily than their neighbors, and to keep away from fat living, two-dollar restaurants, and booze. But still manners—the talk and the dress and the dread of wordly passions.

What isn't a matter of manners in Quakerism is peace, and all the suffering and sacrifice that go into the making of peace, or at least the keeping of their own. Since social and economic injustice is war, and the cause of worse war, the Quakers are famous for good social works. And because some of them will not hate and kill the enemy, their religion is famous when the war is over and the enemy are starving and the half-stricken conscience of the winners produces postwar relief.

In one word, what the Quakers no longer are is preserved in *Friendly Persuasion*, while what they are they are shown to have abandoned.

This is a travesty upon Quakerism (which doesn't matter) and a travesty upon the Christianity of Christ (which does). It portrays the Son of God containing himself until the Romans close in on him— then he seizes his sword, with Peter, and mows them down. And behold! His sword is better and his arm surer than those of the Romans. And he is rich (like the Quaker farmer, in *Friendly Persuasion*, who has enough hams in the smokehouse to satisfy the hungry Rebs), and with his worldly riches he buys off the attack of the Romans. And then, in the penultimate scene, he is crucified, flailing and killing all the while, but, by gosh, he is only scratched on the Cross, and he comes down, along toward the Ninth Hour, which is suppertime in southern Indiana, and his Kingdom is established right here and right now, his granaries full again, in case the Roman Raiders raid again and have to be bought off, and he smiles lewdly at his brethren, who smile lewdly back, and says, "Come on, Veterans," and, proud, rich, successful, popular, and rosy with fighting good health, Christ leads the way to Meeting.

April 15—If You Want My Lai, Buy It

Young men are a dime a dozen.

What the Army wants is a dime to buy a dozen young men with.

Either give them the dime or don't give them the dime—but stop asking, "What can an old man do?"

April 15 is the date. April 15 is the date you turn over a quarter of your income to Behemoth, and half to three quarters of what you turn over goes to the Army to buy a dozen young men to populate (and depopulate) Perforation Paddy. "I sent them a good boy," said Private Meadlo's mother after My Lai, "and they made him a murderer."

If you want it, buy it. If you don't, don't. But stop asking, "What can an old man do?"

If, like me, you had a good year and made more than $625 in 1970, the Internal Revenue Act requires you to file an income tax return. If you refuse (rather than evade) the requirement to file, you are still a felon, but you should notify Behemoth and all its minions lest you be hanged for the wrong reason. (The Act simply punishes "failure to file" and "failure to pay.") I shouldn't refuse to file, myself, but better men than I have taken the position that filing is more than a formality; the best of them, A.J. Muste, always filed an appropriately marked Bible instead of a return.

So, too, as the antics proceed, you will be asked (unless you have a readily attachable paycheck) where you stash your money so that Behemoth's little boys in blue can go and get it. Here again I should comply, myself, lest Behemoth get the impression that I am playing a cat-and-mouse (or mouse-and-cat) game. But this decision, too, like whether or not to file a return, is probably a matter of temperament.

The purpose of taxation is to enable people collectively to buy what they want. Sometimes when some of them want a little something special and some of them don't—for instance, throughways financed by tolls—those who want them pay for them and those who don't want them don't. But My Lai is financed by the general fund of the Treasury, on the assumption that everybody wants My Lai.

Reprinted from the *Progressive*, April 1971.

Behemoth has no way of knowing that the assumption is false unless those who don't want it refuse to buy it. A *vote* for Nixon (or Humphrey) or Johnson (or Goldwater) is a vote for My Lai. (*"It was murder. We were shooting into houses and at people—running or standing, doing nothing"*—[Sergeant Charles Hutts].)

The nation-state is not merely fallible; it is, as every Judeo-Christian (or Christo-Judean) schoolboy knows, unholy because it divides the family of man into *we* and *they*. Only men are, or may be, holy in a world of nation-states, and they dare not perform an unholy act to preserve such an institution. Still the conscientious tax refuser is a conscientious citizen of the nation-state. He would gladly pay his taxes for the things all the people in it (including him) want. In Norway (in this respect the only even halfway civilized country in the world) the conscientious citizen may have his tax payment segregated for the support of the United Nations if he does not want to buy My Lai.

Bucking always for salvation, the conscientious citizen is nevertheless up against some serious objections to his refusal to send a dozen young men to the edge of the ditch in My Lai. The objections appear to be six in number:

Objection 1: The legal penalty of five years in stir and/or a ten-thousand-dollar fine. The U.S. Government has not yet pressed for the penalty in any case of tax refusal that I know of—partly, I suppose, because Behemoth does not know what to do about conscience, partly because the use of force, violence, and other lawful means of penalizing conscientious people always increases their number. (Better pretend they're not there—up to a point.)

But the number is increasing anyway, and it is not unlikely that it is approaching that point. When it is confident that it has got its Haynsworth-Carswell Court, Behemoth may feel constrained some one of these days to press for the penalty. The tax refusal movement, for twenty years amorphous, is now coordinated by War Tax Resistance, whose address, I am reliably informed, is 339 Lafayette Street, New York, NY 10017, and whose telephone number (212-477-2970) was discovered in the Manhattan telephone directory by a task force of forty FBI agents led personally by J. Edgar Hoover. Desperado Bradford Lyttle of WTR reports 181 active refusal centers across the country and estimates 15,000 refusers in 1970.

Answer To Objection 1: There are worse things than losing five years and/or ten thousand dollars, and My Lai is one of them.

Objection 2: The loss of job or reputation. Ten years ago (even five) many tax refusers lost jobs (or failed to get them) as a consequence of the invariable FBI "inquiry." That's less likely (but only less likely) now. Loss of reputation, on the other hand, has never appeared to be consequential; I have never known anybody to the left of Orange County, California, who thought that a tax refuser was anything worse than crazy, and even in Orange County they hate taxes.

Answer To Objection 2: There are worse things than losing a job (though that is easier for a light-fingered clown like me to say than it is for an honest workingman).

We proceed now from the nuts-and-bolts to the nitty-gritty, as follows:

Objection 3: Tax refusal is ineffective because "they" get the money anyway (by force, violence, or other lawful means).

Answer To Objection 3: True, true; but, then, so is everything else ineffective (including two victorious world wars to save the world for democracy). To man, all things are impossible. If whatever you do is ineffective, you might as well buck for salvation and do what is right.

Objection 4: Tax refusal is illogical: If you refuse to pay half your income tax, half of what you do pay will be used for My Lai, as will *more* than the other half (since Behemoth, when it seizes the other half by force, violence, and other lawful means will also seize 12 percent per annum interest on it).

Answer To Objection 4: This is true only if logic is a branch of effectiveness—and even then it is only half true. Behemoth will lose money on the deal because it will have to spend more to collect it than it gets. In one instance I know of, where the refuser took his case "on up," it must have cost $25,000 in salaries and travel expenses of Treasury and FBI dicks, district attorneys, assistant attorneys-general, judges, and court attachés to collect and hold on to $32.27 (and the refuser took his own expenses in the case as a tax deduction). It is true, nonetheless, that in the end Behemoth will get all the money it wants for My Lai, by raising the tax rate if necessary.

But there is another, and more significant, logic: the logic of symbolism (not to be confused with symbolic logic). The only action a man can take against the nation-state is symbolic. He can not prevent its depredations but only repudiate them persistently in the hope of (*a*) salvation and (*b*) the sympathetic infection of his fellow citizens. It is not logical symbolically (for instance) to bomb the ROTC building, because people sympathize with the victim of a bombing and, besides, Behemoth has all the ROTC buildings it wants and is always eager to build new ones and add the building costs to its Gross National Product billboard. (The Army doesn't need ROTC buildings *or* ROTC except as a symbol of militarism; no European army would dare ask a university to disgrace itself by letting its students be marched around the premises.) What is logical symbolically is for students to sit nonviolently in front of the ROTC building and be hauled violently away. Tax refusal is logical symbolically.

Objection 5: Tax refusal is a disavowal of representative government.

Answer To Objection 5: It is, if, and only if, by representative government is meant majoritarianism and not representation at all. If you are an American citizen and you do not want My Lai and won't buy it, you are not represented. The Congressmen (including the Senators) who deplore My Lai all buy it, without exception. The last one who wouldn't was Representative Jeannette Rankin of Montana, who voted all alone against the second go-around of the War to Make the World Safe for Democracy. The conscientious citizen who does not want My Lai, and will not buy it is driven to self-government by the failure of representative government to represent him.

Objection 6: Tax refusal is anarchy, and anarchy is the worst thing that can befall society.

Answer To Objection 6: Anarchy is not the worst thing that can befall society; it is the second worst. The worst is tyranny, and the worst tyranny is self-evidently that which requires the innocent to kill the innocent. ("*I love women. I love children, too. I love people.*" —Lt. William L. Calley.) He who does not want and will not buy tyranny must, like George Washington, take his chances on anarchy.

So hopelessly unholy is the nation-state that it drives the conscientious citizen to anarchy and then accuses him of driving *it* to anarchy when he tries to disengage himself from its tyranny. In the interesting case of the $32.27 cited above, Attorney Francis Heisler was arguing for the refuser before the U.S. Circuit Court of Appeals, and one of the judges said to him: "Counsel, is your client aware that if this Court holds in his behalf the Court itself will be laying the ax to the root of all established government?" "I think he is, your honor," Attorney Heisler replied.

The objections considered, we proceed to the obstacles. There is only one that appears to be insuperable: withholding, the worst crime ever committed against liberty by a good man. When Beardsley Ruml thought up "pay-as-you-go," everybody cheered except the company bosses who had to do the detestable New Deal's detestable bookkeeping for it. (Anybody remember when the Connecticut manufacturer, Vivian Kellems, led the Old Guard attack on Social Security by refusing to make the employee deductions?) Under withholding, most of the people who don't want to buy My Lai have already had it bought for them by April 15. They can sue to recover—some have—but nobody has made it to the Supreme Court yet. Others reduce or eliminate the withholding by claiming excess dependents (the whole population of Vietnam, for instance) in calculating their estimated tax. Again, I suppose, a matter of temperament, and mine doesn't happen to run that cat-and-mouse way—though their cause it is just, and we have indeed made the whole population of Vietnam our dependents.

A few religious organizations—not the churches, of course—have refused to withhold the tax from the pay of their employees who do not want to buy My Lai. The most respectable of them is the American Friends Service Committee, with which I confess to being associated. (Personally leading a task force of eighty FBI agents, J. Edgar Hoover discovered the association by looking in the Philadelphia telephone directory, so there is no point in my denying it.) But the AFSC has a task force of eighty Philadelphia lawyers, and one of these years a test case will go to Washington. Meanwhile, however, the conscientious citizen who waits for a test case will go on buying My Lai until the whole of Vietnam is a ditch.

A few years ago a new form of refusal got rolling, available to people trapped by withholding. This was nonpayment of the telephone tax (which goes into the general Treasury), on the ground that Chairman Mills of the House Ways and Means Committee had argued its necessity for continuance of the war against My Lai. I'm uneasy about the telephone tax refusal myself; again, I suppose, a matter of temperament. There seem to me to be two visible arguments, and one invisible, against it.

First, I can not bring myself either to do or not to do anything on the basis that what a Congressman says is true. And second, it seems to me that if you are going to fight City Hall you should go for the jugular. The income tax is the jugular. The telephone tax is one of those petty excises, no more significant fiscally, and no more to be singled out, Congressman Mills to the contrary notwithstanding, than the whiskey, movie, or airplane tax.

But the invisible, base-of-the-iceberg, stem-of-the-martini-cherry argument for paying the phone tax is, I'm afraid, one of craven convenience. If Behemoth were to put me in jail for five years for income tax refusal, I'd refuse to pay my telephone tax instantly. But living where and how I do, running a little back-bedroom sweatshop out in the country, I can't make it very well (still worse, very sick) without a telephone. Discussing telephone tax refusal with some of my anarchist friends, I have discovered that some of them were for it because they didn't feel quite up to going to the mat on the income tax, and still others because they understood that the telephone company, like Vivian Kellems, was no more enthusiastic about collecting the My Lai tax than they were about paying it and would not jerk the phone out for nonpayment of the tax.

This last seemed to me to be a misreading of history. Unlike Vivian Kellems and the American Friends Service Committee—Right and Left united across the years by the mounting terror of the Middle— the telephone company has no principle except money; and Behemoth's agent, the Federal Communications Commission, is where the money is. In the Communist countries like Spain and Greece and, come to think of it, every other country in the world, the post office operates the telephone and telegraph systems, whose profits subsidize the carrying of the mails; in the only truly free country in the free world the money-losing branch of the communications system is communized and the money-making branches are Government-protected private monoplies.

But telephone tax refusal caught on until, according to the calculation of War Tax Resistance, there are now more than 100,000 practitioners of it. For a couple of years nobody did anything about them. But reports have begun to filter in of Government agents swarming over refusers and, more ominously, of the jerking of telephones by the company on behalf of its protector, the Government. As the reports spread it may be anticipated that there will be a falling-away of telephone tax anarchists, as, I suppose, there will be of income tax anarchists when Behemoth decides that they are getting to be too much of a nuisance and starts throwing them into the pokey.

Until that time the only obstacle (not objection) to income tax refusal, other than withholding, is the harassment it entails. The smart way to live alongside Behemoth is not to attract his attention, and whoever attracts his attention is in for it. Twenty years ago Behemoth was paying his hireling harassers $40 a day. It must be $80 now, or $100; there is nothing niggardly about Behemoth.

He sends two kinds of harassers around. The first is a ritualistic cut-out character whom it's a positive pleasure to be harassed by. He

is the warm handclasp type, around thirty-five and running to pudge
from running around in his down-payment Impala. He wants to have
a little talk with you.

"Homyonum's the name, Mr. Murgatroid, from the Internal Revenue Service."

(Warm handclasp.)

"Sit down, Homyonum, sit down, and tell me what I can do for
you."

"To be perfectly frank, Mr. Murgatroid, I think that *I* may be able
to do something for *you.*"

"Well, now, Homyonum, that is nice—I never expected the Internal
Revenue Service to do something for me. Do sit down and have a nice
glass tea."

(He will, and he does.)

"Mr. Murgatroid, we of the Treasury Department are actually your
agents. We are here to help you."

"How sweet of you, Homyonum. One lump or two?" *(Two.)*

"Mr. Murgatroid, I want you to know that I respect your position,
but I think you are ill-advised to refuse to pay your income tax."

"Homyonum, my boy, your advice is ill. Milk? Lemon?" *(Milk.)*

"I beg your pardon, Mr. Murgatroid?"

"Not at all, and do let me tell you why your advice is ill. If my position is, as you say, respectable, then yours is not, since the two positions are contradictory. Do you follow me?"

"I . . ."

"What I am trying to tell you, Homyonum, since you respect my
position, is that you are trying to tell me that I ought not pay my
income tax and neither ought you. You do want to be respectable,
don't you?"

A little more of this standoff, a warm handclasp, and Homyonum
is gone wherever such people go nights and is seen no more. He makes
his report, the report spends two or three months going through chan-
nels, and then Behemoth hands one of his judges a distraint warrant
to sign and sends one of his blue-boys around to attach your unattached property (money in the bank, wages coming in, shoes off your
feet) in the amount in which you are delinquent in buying My Lai.

The other kind of harasser is another glass tea entirely. He is tall,
sallow, dour, ulcerated: a certified public accountant who doesn't
know anything about your income tax refusal (*he* says) but has been
sent to audit your return. "I suppose," he says, "that your name
came up on a spot check. Of course you have all your records and a
receipt for each expenditure— if I may just look at them." At the end
of two weeks, at $40, $80, or $100 a day, reducing the Gross Na-

tional Product by that much, he has discovered that you owe Behemoth $1.14 (or Behemoth owes you $1.14; that's not the point of it at all) and you and your back bedroom are a shambles.

He turns up the next year, on the dot, to do it all over again, and then you know he is lying about the spot check (and even he begins to suspect he is). Meanwhile, he has converted you into a fox. You spend half your life (at $40, $20, or $10 a day) keeping records of your expenditures. You spend the other half of your life like the mouse you were not going to play in the cat-and-mouse game, scurrying for loopholes down which you can hurry. You end up beating your wife, cursing your children, and, of course, kicking the cat. And that, not the $1.14, is the point of it. If Behemoth can make your life unbearable, you will buy My Lai.

It is the very devil to be harassed, but what did you expect—a valentine from Mrs. Mitchell? It's like (or even as) Give-'em-Hell-Harry used to say: If you can't stand the heat, stay out of the kitchen. You harass them, and they harass you back, and they've got the big battalions on their side. (You know Whom you've got on yours.)

And you harass them back and they harass you back. Who said *ineffective?* Behemoth has the whole country, the whole world, computerized to take care of everything—everything but one man who says No, sir, instead of Yes, sir. It takes one (count 'em, one) man to obstruct the machine by introducing the human element into it. The grind-organ monkey is suddenly a monkey wrench. I put it to you: What more can an old man do? The machine has not been built yet, and won't be, that does not come down with the gripes while it digests a human being.

Mind you, I am not advocating income tax refusal; not I. For all I know the advocacy itself constitutes a felony, especially if it creates a clear and present danger that the Army won't be able to buy a dozen young men with machine guns at the edge of the ditch in My Lai. Operating on a very low and cautious level, I say unto you only, Give them the dime or don't give them the dime—but don't ask, "What can an old man do?" If you want My Lai, buy it; if you don't want it, don't. *That's* the free enterprise system, and do you believe in the free enterprise system or are you some kind of a Communist?

Operating on the highest level of all, under a law that even the Supreme Court (*Girouard,* etc.) admits is higher than the Internal Revenue Act, Jesus Christ was asked by the Pharisees whose the tribute money was, and you know what he said and you know that he said it *perceiving their wickedness.* (Matt. 22:18.) If you have to choose between Christ and the Pharisee who, like the Pharisee of old, occupies the highest seat in the Temple, you are in a tight spot. I'd play it safe myself: Better to do time than eternity.

No Holier Than Thou

It is time to blow the whistle on His Holiness and have another go at breaking his stranglehold on Christ. It was the high priest who turned the Pacifist over to the secular arm for trial. He is still doing it, "fornicating" (you should pardon the expression, but it's Dante's) "with kings."

Of course he no longer fornicates with actual kings, his claim to temporal power ("the gift of Constantine") having been exposed as forgery's finest hour. What he does nowadays, Catholic, Protestant, Muslim, or Jew, is confer with Presidents and deliver Messages (with a capital *M*) on Peace (with a capital *P*). And the Presidents sing the Amen chorus, for the Presidents are Men of Peace, too.

And the war goes on.

They are wise to do evil, but to do good they have no knowledge. All the wars go on, and the watchword in Rome, Geneva, Mecca, and Tel Aviv is still *Pax*, the *Pax Romana* of which the ancient historian said, "They make a desert and they call it peace."

His Holiness is no holier than thou—and thou knowest in thy secret heart how holy *that* is. He may be even less holy than thou, not because he is supposed to be more holy but because he still has some power or (as they say these days) muscle. Muscle corrupts, and when he had absolute power he was absolutely corrupt. The Black Popes of Protestantism are porkchoppers, too; their kingdoms, too, of this world, though theirs are a mule and forty acres compared with the White Pope's and they cannot call themselves, as he does, the Universal Pastor.

Would they be different, Geneva from Rome, if they had Rome? Were their World Council a world council like his, would they, when they say, "War is contrary to the will of God," themselves undertake then and there to do the will of God and say, "Hell, no, we won't go"? *They say and do not.*

Like him, they won't level with war: *Not by might, nor by power . . .*

Or with peace: *. . . but by my spirit.*

Or with racism (*There shall be neither Greek nor Jew*) or with capitalism (*What mean ye that ye grind the faces of the poor*) or with

Reprinted from the *Progressive*, February 1968.

nationalism (*One body, one Spirit, one Lord, one faith, one Shepherd, one flock*) or with disobedience of unholy law: *We should obey God rather than men.*

Or with themselves: *And I, if I be lifted up, will draw all men after me.*

Or with Jesus Christ: *He that believeth on me, the things that I do he will do likewise.*

This is the Flesh made Word, and there are no two ways of reading it, and the White and Black Popes are Sunday humbugs like the rest of us. Maybe even a little worse, because we deceive only ourselves, while they come *in my name, saying, "I am Christ," and deceive many.*

The wars go on and on, because the porkchoppers of Rome and Geneva will lift a hand, two hands, in prayer but never a finger to stop them. *Yea, when ye raise your hands in prayer, I will not hear; for your hands are full of blood.*

Out in the nonuniversal boondocks, far from Rome and Geneva, there are Nonuniversal Pastors, priests, and monks, and nuns, and rabbis, and ministers, and seminarians who lift a finger. And for their sake the city may be spared, *the careless city, that saith, There is none like me.* They put their presence—Christ's Presence—on the line where the heads are split and split no more hairs about the Nature of the Presence.

They don't talk about Peace with a capital *P*, or War with a capital *W*. They talk about this war now and this peace now. The Episcopalian rector of Williamsburg got it in the neck for talking about this war now and this peace now when Lyndon Johnson went to church in (for the first time in his life) the misplaced confidence that he'd hear about War and Peace in general.

They are tut-tutted and hooted and transferred and rebuked for *their* little Encyclicals. Or buried in the *Catholic Worker*, where Father Philip Berrigan, S.J., of Baltimore, has an audience of hundreds, instead of hundreds of millions, for his:

> We [Americans] cannot ravage the ecology of Vietnam and kill ten civilians for every soldier and expect to have anything but do or die opposition. We cannot bomb North Vietnam and support U Thant's program for peace. . . . We cannot manipulate encephalitis and yellow fever into person-to-person transmission and have other men trust us. We cannot have the Pentagon owning fifty-three percent of all Federal property and have civilian control of government and diplomacy. We cannot fight the abstraction of Communism by killing the men who believe in it. We cannot propagandize for peace while our deeds give the lie to our words. We can't have it both ways.

The President would not have to fly around the world to exchange Pius platitudes with a high priest. There's a low one close by, in Baltimore. But Father Berrigan would let him have it, while Papa Sancto, or Papa Diplomatico, the Universal Pastor who has to keep his Universal Fences mended, will deliver another Message. The rest of the aspirants for the kingdom of this world in 1968 will all pile into Rome behind the President, for the Vatican, like the Legion Convention, is one of the bases the 1968 aspirants can touch without being tagged out.

In his Christmas Message his Holiness called upon the faithful (and the faithless; that's a base His Holiness has to touch these days) to celebrate a "Day of Peace." As long as the Day of Peace was to be confined to celebration, commemoration, inspiration, exhortation, exaltation, and prayer, and as long as we were to "beseech Christ who was immolated for us to 'grant us peace!' "—the aspirants of 1968 could all touch base.

But His Holiness had a little something special for them in the Christmas bag this year. This was the anathematization of Christ the Pacifist. "Peace," His Holiness explained, "is not pacifism; it does not mask a base and slothful way of life, but it proclaims"—here we go again—"the highest and most universal values of life: truth, justice, freedom, and love."

Base and slothful and worse: "It is to be hoped that the exaltation of the ideal of peace may not favor the cowardice of those who fear it may be their duty to give their life for the service of their own country and of their own brothers, when these are engaged in the defense of justice and liberty, and who seek only a flight from their responsibility, from the risks that are necessarily involved in the accomplishment of great duties and generous exploits."

Could the President ask for anything more?

Could Christ the Pacifist ask for anything less—the Pacifist who repudiated "his own country and his own brothers," yes, and his brother? Christ the Pacifist, who rejected the "defense" (by human slaughter) "of justice and liberty," who "fled from his responsibility" to kill, from the "great duties" to the Roman Proconsul, from the "generous exploit" of passing the cup of death to another and drinking it himself instead? So the base and slothful Pacifist—who called upon men to emulate the ravens who sow not and reap not—is anathematized.

Monsignor Poupard, the Vatican Secretary of State, had to explain that His Holiness did not include in his anathema those who "for reasons of conscience refuse to bear arms." The distinction, said the Monsignor, had to be drawn between conscientious objection " and mere pacifism and cowardly evasion of military service." (But what is and what isn't conscience is, of course, determined by the President, with whose determination the Pope does not presume to interfere.)

Christ was not a conscientious objector. He was never asked to bear arms, and he never refused to. He was never called upon to perform what the Monsignor calls military service—the service of killing a man on pain of being killed by your commanding officer. Christ was, and is, the Commanding Officer of Pacifism. He ordered his Christians not to fight and told them that whoever drew the sword would perish by it. He contented himself with words.

"Pacifism is a negative quality that contents itself with words and makes no contribution to the construction of the world that is essential to true peace," Maurice Cardinal Roy, President of the Pontifical Commission for Justice and Peace, said by way of helping Monsignor Poupard explain what His Holiness *really* meant. (*Violence has always achieved only destruction, not construction; the kindling of passions, not their pacification; the accumulation of hate and ruin, not the reconciliation of the contending parties.*—Pope Pius XII, *Allocution* on the Feast of the Pentecost, June 13, 1943.)

Cardinal Roy and Monsignor Poupard had *their* little helpers, too, in explaining what His Holiness really meant. The Rome correspondent of the *New York Times* explained that "the Pontiff's references to the need for"—here we go again—"justice, balance, and independence as ingredients for true peace, once again, as in many previous declarations, marked his distance from those who argue that the path to peace in Vietnam, for example, is by way of a unconditional United States withdrawal." I.e., the path to peace is war. *Ye shall walk in His path, and He will show you His way.*

Could the President ask for anything more than war as the path to peace? He could. But he didn't have to. He got it from His Holiness without asking. He got an incitement to riot against the pacifists: "The world," said His Holiness, "must be educated to . . . defend [peace] . . . against the snares of tactical pacifism, intended to drug the enemy [*Give way to wrath*] one must overcome [*Overcome evil with good*], to smother in men's minds the meaning of justice, of duty and of sacrifice." *Crucify him! Crucify him!*

The *New York Times* had *its* little helpers in the press generally. With the usual honorable exception of the *St. Louis Post-Dispatch*, the newspapers spread the attack on pacifism across the page and (so far as I have been able to discover) spake not a mumbling word of editorial protest. The *Post-Dispatch* spake alone:

Pope Paul VI has suggested that pacifists are cowards, and the most charitable thing that can be said of his remark is that it is egregiously uncharitable. . . . His gratuitous comment implies that there is some litmus paper test by which a man can determine when his country is defending justice and liberty, and if his country passes the test he is a coward if he is not willing to wage war. . . . Would the Pope venture to say which side is defending liberty and justice in Vietnam?

Pacifism may be unrealistic, but it is not cowardice. In fact it comes a good deal closer to the virtue of Christian love than the kind of military nationalism the pontiff's remark tends to endorse.

The phrase *tends to endorse* is accurate. The artful dodgers of Rome, Geneva, Washington, and Moscow never come right out with it. They weave their webs of loopholes and then slip their Secretaries of State and Presidents of Commissions into the appropriate loophole as the occasion requires, to explain that His Holiness or His Excellence or His Majesty is a Man of Peace. We are all Men of Peace, who would not make war except as a last resort.

This mealy-mouthing of Peace isn't meal at all, but meat. It is the poisoned meat—it, not atheism—on which apostasy battens. The business of His Holiness is to defend and disseminate the faith. He has failed to defend it; the Holy hogwash that cascades from the balcony, and thence from the pulpit, at Christmas is the despair of the faithful. As to dissemination, he who runs may read the record of total failure in the success of a contrary faith, capitalist and Communist materialism, in overcoming the world.

But Christ overcame the world by being born, and went with the Devil to the mountain top to be offered the kingdoms of this world so that those who came after him would know what to do and never abandon Christ for the crusaders and the Baptist for the bomber and the Kingdom for the kingdoms. The infallible Popes, Catholic, Protestant, Jewish, and Druid, have fornicated and failed, and their failure is a sign that no man can serve two masters or, as Father Berrigan says, "We can't have it both ways."

But what (you say) of John XXIII? See (you say) how even the agnostics and the atheists love him. My friends, have you read *Pacem in Terris*, or just "read in it," or just celebrated it? It is as nice, "in its time," as Leo's *Rerum Novarum* was in its. The only thing wrong with it is that its time is past before it is signed and sealed. On social justice the secular reformers have already said it and said it straight and scandalized the world. Marx the bloody atheist said it straight before Leo (described by the encyclopedia as "opponent of socialism and Communism"), and Lenin the still bloodier atheist before John. And Christ the Pacifist said it straight before all of them.

Pacem in Terris? Not a word on miscegenation, the only answer to unchristian racism. Not a word on universal conscription, the most blasphemous of all sins against the doctrinal person of man. Not a word on civil disobedience, except St. Thomas's homily that an unjust law does not bind in conscience. ("And who, Your Holiness, decides whether conscription is an unjust law?" "Ah, my child . . .") Not a word about the Honorable Profession of Arms, of which the word of God says:[4]

> We wrestle not against flesh and blood. Wherefore take unto you the whole armor of the Lord, your loins girt about with truth, and having on the breastplate of righteousness; and your feet shod with the preparation of the gospel of peace . . . the shield of faith . . . the helmet of salvation . . . and the sword of the Spirit.

Not a mumbling word. But the United Nations is praised and prayed for and "the public authority of the world community" invoked. ("And the admission of China, Your Holiness?" "Ah, my child . . .") The phony public authority that has no authority against unilateral sovereign aggression and despotism: "The public authority of the world community is not intended to limit the sphere of action of the public authority of the individual political community, much less take its place. On the contrary . . ." *But* the UN Declaration of Human Rights is praised and prayed for. ("And America's and Russia's refusal to sign it, Your Holiness?" "Ah, my child . . .")

War? War is dreadful, simply dreadful, and "it is hardly possible to imagine that in the atomic era war could be used as an instrument of justice." ("So you repudiate the Church tradition of the just war, Your Holiness—or does 'hardly possible' mean a little tiny bit possible? And does 'atomic era' mean that a total war fought like World War II in Europe, or like Korea, the Congo, Algeria, Vietnam, may still be a just one?" "Ah, my child . . .")

War is simply dreadful, and men and governments should "give serious thought to the problem of peaceful adjustment . . . founded on mutual trust, on sincerity of negotiations, on faithful fulfillment of obligations assumed." *Faithful fulfillment of obligations assumed:* Is it His Holiness John or His Unholiness Rusk who is saying it?

A good man, John XXIII. One of the best to have jingled the Keys of Peter. As Popes go—as Boniface goes, as Luther goes—a most excellent, a most noble man. But *Holiness?* My child, if the servants of

God are sinful, how should the servant of the servants of God be holy?

You see, by the time you get to be a Prince—of the Church, or the State, or the Elks Club—you are fit to be a Prince. You have been measured, and measured, and measured again on the way up and never found wanting That's the Establishment, and do you know what happened to the hippie who called himself Jeremiah and said, "In righteousness shalt thou be established"? They told him, "Prophesy smooth things. Prophesy sweet deceits," and when he didn't they put the cuffs on him.

A persecuted Prince, stripped of his Principality, a Niemöller or a Faulhaber, has been known to be established in righteousness; but never yet as long as Presidents kept coming to him for his blessing. Such princes are we all, some of us two-spots in Pocatello and some of us face cards in Geneva or Rome. You don't see us upsetting the tables in the temple. We *are* the temple, and we don't want things upset. So they're upset by the bloody Communist atheist, the "Assyrian" of old: *And the staff in his hand is the rod of mine indignation.*

And so, no *Pax.*

And one of these days, no *Terra:*

Thou shalt be visited with thunder, and with earthquake, and great noise, with storm and tempest, and the flame of devouring fire. And the shepherds shall have no way to flee, nor the principal of the flock to escape.

Operation Bootstraps

When I was first informed of the theme of this Conference I thought I understood it. But I am not so sure now. My perplexity arises from what appears to me to be a series of buried axioms in its three terms, "present society," "alternatives" and "peaceful"—axioms which in turn appear to rest upon the grand axiom of human progress. It is an axiom which no longer commands much enchantment.

Progress is, as we know, not a universal concept. It is not Oriental —and neither is it universally Western. As the tide of their empire rolled westward, the Romans (some of them, certainly not the Stoics nor the Lucretians) thought they discerned the possibility—at least the possibility—of bringing progress to such savages as the Britons. But the Greeks all saw the world (and, indeed, the cosmos) as an eternal cycle in which cities and civilizations rose and fell as the world rolled on unchanged. Neither is progress a Christian notion in the Gospel dispensation, and such inklings of it as appeared in Hebrew thought subsided with the rise of the prophets.

The Enlightenment gave it a nebulous currency, and Gibbon found it "a pleasing prospect," but it took hold of the generality of men only with the advent of the factory, the revolutions in France and America, and the social Darwinism of the nineteenth century. It is a modern vision, and a secular one: Operation Bootstraps.

The expression "present society" then, in the last quarter of the twentieth century, suggests that, as there has been a rising curve, or staircase, of human association, so will there continue to be. But it wasn't a contemporary observer, rather an ancient Athenian, who said that every city is two cities—a city of the rich and a city of the poor, and that these two cities are always at war.

The present world is a political and economic anarchy—as it always has been. And a moral anarchy, too. The low comedy of the United Nations is nowhere more entertainingly staged than in that provision of the UN Declaration of Human Rights which exempts the solemn signatories, each and several, from any of its provisions which

The Swanwick Lecture, British Friends Peace and International Relations Conference (Quakers), Swanwick, Derbyshire, 23 March 1974; delivered under the conference title, "Peaceful Alternatives to Present Society."

violate their domestic statutes. After two world wars fought and won in the name of liberty, it would take a bold man to argue that there is more liberty today than there was before those wars were fought and won. I can testify that there is considerably less in the United States.

Having lost every other claim to their admiration, Friend Nixon can still commend himself to the cheerful acquiesence that he has saved his countrymen from one particularly spectacular form of destruction. So transfixed have we been by the melodramatic terror of Hiroshima—and the relaxation of that terror—that it does not readily occur to us that the world may actually be ending with a whimper instead of a bang.

For two hundred years there has been an inexorable motion in the direction of the centralization of power of all kinds—the aggregation of communities, the division and depersonalisation of labor, the packaging of rest and recreation, the isolation of the individual, and the homogenization of tastes and sensibilities. I can discern no countervailing motion. I can imagine no way in which this condition will not inexorably worsen. The villains of the piece have escaped our clutches: Euclid, Pythagoras, Archimedes, and the unsung Mesopotamian who discovered that the family car rode more comfortably on round wheels than on square ones. I submit on hypothesis that our social progress (if what we mean is socialization) has been marvellous, our human progress illusory.

Any alternative to the present society would, on its face, be an alternative to capitalist parliamentarian nationalism maintained by violence against its offenders domestic and foreign—and similarly maintained in the despotic nationalist socialisms of the East. We Americans, we Englishmen, we Westerners, live in and on and for an economic order that is so innately, and so palpably, unjust and inhuman that it is ideologically, not to say religiously, indefensible against the most elementary of its critics. Its only case against the hostile social organization that overspreads the earth is that most desperate and unpersuasive of pleas in avoidance: *tu quoque*.

We are at once confronted, then, with the axiom buried in the term "alternatives." To say that we seek an alternative to the present society is to proclaim ourselves revolutionaries root and branch. Do we mean to be? Do we want to be? By and large we Quakers are the servitors and stewards of the present society. More or less boldly, more or less guiltily, we batten on its evils and perpetuate them, accepting from it an occasional privilege (a privilege, mind you) such as our exemption from bearing arms as long as our number is inconsequential. We are not bad men and women—only good Englishmen and Americans, good middle-class, grumbling, dues-paying Englishmen and Americans. How badly do we want to change the present society root and branch? How wholeheartedly could we want to change if we would? Our habituation disheartens our intentions. Each of us is the omnibus upon which our ancestors ride.

Our Quaker forebears were revolutionaries. Being Quakers they had no choice. They were not bad Englishmen. They were not good Americans. It would have been ridiculous to suggest that one of them might ever be his country's chief executive. It is ridiculous no longer. We are comfortable Quakers, *relevant* Quakers, and we have been for a long time inextricably involved in the institutions of the present society. I address myself here not to our dreams nor to our honest intentions or our honest professions. I address myself, rather, to the naked condition of our social relationship. How badly can people like us—people like me—want a root and branch alternative?

The alternative we seek here as revolutionaries, is, we say, a peaceful alternative. And here, I suggest, is the last and, for us Quakers, the most cataclysmic of the buried axioms in the theme of this Conference.

Agreed: if the present society rests upon war, an alternative to it would be peaceful. Georges Clemenceau's dictum that war is not the worst of evils but the cause of all others, requires modification now. War was once an inexpensive sport with relatively insignificant consequences to the human lot in general. It consumed a few thousand—or a few hundred thousand—men and a few hundred thousand barrels of gunpowder and a few hundred thousand tons of iron. It was fought, like all respectable sports, on a field of limited dimensions. Today it consumes almost all of our substance. It may not be the worst of evils or the cause of all the others, but it has long since become the single obstacle to the relief of mass starvation. These are platitudes, commonplace platitudes. Just as commonplace and platitudinous is the recognition that the prevention of war is the precondition of any real effectiveness whatever in any other area of social concern. We Quakers are not moved in the first instance by the consideration of effectiveness, as if we should lay down a program that was right but ineffective or embrace one that was effective and wrong; but neither do we exercise our energies without the wish that others, more influential, will join their energies to ours.

So the peaceful alternative (and its unremitting evangelism) is the only alternative. Nothing in Quakerism comes closer to being a social gospel than the abjuration of violence. Who has a more relentless commitment to the peaceable kingdom than we? But who among us would say that our commitment is as clear, not just to the world, but among ourselves, as it once was? The whole world is a mission. But who shall be the missionaries?

George Gorman, in his forthright booklet, *Introducing Quakers*, informs the reader that "Friends are not always able to agree on the ways in which their concern for peace can be implemented. Some Friends would accept the idea of an international 'police force' while others would reject this as a denial of their witness for peace." It is hard for an American Quaker to forget that his government designated Korea as a "UN police action." It may be equally hard for a British Quaker to forget the words of Chesterton: "I am a walking civil war."

If the voice of 1660 is the voice of Quakerism, denying all wars and strife and fightings with outward weapons, are we not a backslidden Society? Until our eye is single, turned not today to the Cross, tomorrow to the powers of this world, how shall we see, much less show, the peaceable alternative to the present society? How much less can we do in behalf of that alternative than constitute ourselves, first of all, a mission to the Religious Society of Friends—a mission, in a word, to our own hearts?

The peaceable alternative has never been further from probability than it is now. I am told that your speaker last year said that the only way to educate people for peace was to bring them up in a peaceful society. The circularity of this proposition is as plain to us as it was, I am sure, to the speaker. The circle has got to be broken into, the irresistible logic resisted. There is no other way, for it is still true, as was said long ago, that states are not made of oak and rock but of men, and as the men are so will the states be. Nothing less than an act of faith is wanted to resist the irrestible logic—the faith that says, "And I, if I be lifted up, will draw all men after me."

Erasmus insists that man learns at the school of example and will attend no other. We are all—*nolens volens*—exemplars. I am an exemplar. How shall I be lifted up? What can a man do, whose faith discountenances the bootstrap operation? The princes of this world have shown themselves powerless. They have not been able to disarm the world by so much as one man; but I, if I be lifted up, can disarm the world by so much as one man.

Operation Bootstraps has come to a dead end, a dead and, withal a deadly, end. We may repair, at its end, to the nature of the fallen angel, neither beast nor god but in potentiality both. Paul's New Man in Christ was still a man, a man whose unbelief was healed. Now we hear the challenge of old: "Where are thy gods that thou hast made thee? Let them arise if they can save thee." Now we hear the olden explosion of all our wisdom:

"And the vision of all is become unto you as the words of a book that is sealed, which men deliver to one that is learned, saying, Read this, I pray thee: and he saith, I can not; for it is sealed: and the book is delivered to him that is not learned, saying, Read this, I pray thee: and he saith, I am not learned."

Our faith is not blind. It is illuminated at every step by an inward light and marked again and again in all of history. If there was, not one Christ, but one Socrates, one Woolman, one Gandhi, then it is within the nature of man, neither beast nor god, to become a Socrates, a Woolman, a Gandhi. So we go about our work, knowing that our work is ourselves; knowing that the social revolution will be a moral revolution or it will not be at all; knowing that it is not necessary to hope in order to undertake, nor to succeed in order to persevere; knowing that His hand is stretched out to us still.

I think that this is my burden, imposed upon me by the buried axioms of the theme of this Conference. I know, at sixty-five, that my little life has flown willfully away while I hung on to its tail feathers. I am not a good Quaker, and I never have been. I am a chipped and crumbling pillar of the present society, and for all my fine talk my Quakerism is not my life but an ornament of it. I exert myself sporadically in behalf of the witness that joins us, and, as the years pile their corruption on me and increase my meanness and my peevishness and my timidity and my conformity and my infirmity, I exert myself ever more painfully.

For all my fine talk, and for all my few deeds, I shall leave the world a worse place than I found it. I can not now help pondering that I may have been sent not to change the world but to try to keep the world from changing me. I can not help pondering the centrality of the Scripture that the peaceful alternative is not as the world giveth. I can not help pondering the three strangest words ever addressed to the sons and daughters of Adam: "Be ye perfect."

I am surely no better a man today than I was ten years ago or twenty, but a worse; not a more cheerful man but a less. A settled wistfulness at once informs and disqualifies my standing here. But I once heard a man (a mere man; neither a god nor a beast) say, "If I can not love Hitler, I can not love at all." And hearing him, I knew what it was to be a Friend. And knowing what it is to be a Friend, I do not despair, even now, of myself or of all men. Knowing what it is to be a Friend, I do not despair, even now, of a peaceful alternative to the present society.

Acknowledgements

I have had more periodicals (of all kinds) shot out from under me than General Albert Sydney Johnston had horses at Shiloh. Unlike General Johnston, I have survived this deadly cannonade. I have survived it because so many good (and, what is more important, kind) men and women have done so much to get me started and keep me going and get me going again that I can no more than acknowledge my categorical indebtedness to some of them:

The late Henry Goddard Leach (of the late *Forum*); John Fischer, Catherine Meyer, and the late Lee. F. Hartman and Frederick Lewis Allen (all of *Harper's*); Studs Terkel and the late Carl Sandburg (both of them of Chicago and everywhere else); Harold Fey (of the *Christian Century*); James O'Gara (of the *Commonweal*); Henry Geiger (of *Manas*); Clare Boothe Luce (when she was Clare Boothe Brokaw of the late *Vanity Fair*—and ever since); the late Adam Kulakowski (of *Opportunity*); the late Charles Angoff (of Mencken's *American Mercury*); the late William Weaver, Donald Plant, and Robert Pollak (of the long ago late *Chicagoan*); Sydney Justin Harris (of the *Chicago Daily News*); Esther Schultz Wohl and the late Hazel MacDonald Casey (of the late *Chicago Evening American*); Michael W. Straus and Kenneth D. Fry (of the late *Chicago Evening Post*); Maurice English, Alec Morin, and Nancy Romoser (late of the University of Chicago Press); William O'Meara, Edward H. Levi, Robert M. Hutchins, Joseph J. Schwab, William V. Morgenstern, George Probst, Frances Stutzman, Howard W. Mort, Don Morris, and the late G.A. Borgese, Percy Holmes Boynton, Robert Morss Lovett, Philip Schuyler Allen, Charlton Beck, and William Benton (all of them at various times of the University of Chicago); Leon M. Despres; Francis Heisler; Bertha Tepper Mayer; Catherine Carver; Kimi Nagatani; William Brandon; C. J. Van Peski; Robert C. McNamara, Jr.; Harlan Watkins, Ruth Hammen (of Hampshire College); Peter Viereck; Thornton Wilder; John H. Hicks, David R. Clark, Andrew Fetler, Jules Chametzky, Richard Haven, Malcolm Call, Robert Tucker, Howard O. Brogan, and Leone Stein (all of them of the University of Massachusetts at Amherst); the late and lovely George T. Bye, who peddled my worst stuff to the slicks; Ivan von Auw, Jr., lately of Harold Ober Associates, who wanted books out of me and kept telling me (and kept telling me) that my articles and essays were draining my creative power, which I didn't know I had; Clifton Fadiman—Kip, taking it apart and putting it together without a seam; Stringfellow Barr and the late Scott Buchanan, whose St. John's College really meant (and still means) what the rest of them call the liberal arts; Henry Regnery (of Henry Regnery Publishers in Chicago); the late Samuel Sloan and Charles A. Pearce (of the late publishing house of Duell, Sloan & Pearce); down the years and decades, John McGrath and Erwin Knoll and, especially and uniquely, Morris and Mary Rubin (all of the *Progressive*); Eric Gustafson (of course); and down the decades and the ages Ms. Baby ("My Name Is Jane") Mayer, who at all hours in every wind and weather and on and between continents and worlds has had to listen to me read my enchanted prose aloud and tell me how to make it less enchanted if no more enchanting.

It has been a long life, and goes on being one. It has been a sheltered life, too, sheltered by these friends (and others) to whom I have gone and gone and gone and said, as the angel said to Augustine, "Take up and read." They knew (and that's why I went to them) that their flattery would get me nowhere.

Milton Mayer
Paris 1974-Hadley 1975